Responding to Critical Cases Counseling

MW00997447

This book helps school counselors and other school personnel navigate the complexities of the most common critical cases that are urgent and difficult in schools in the 21st century.

Counselor educators who use this text will help trainees learn to take a methodical approach to critical cases and to be prepared for the difficult situations they will encounter including cases involving violence, cases of an existential nature, cases involving inappropriate adult behavior, and cases impacting the school community. After a description of the case, the reader is provided with the theories, standards, and experiences that are relevant to the case to formulate a response that is based on foundational principles of the school counseling profession.

Contributing counselors from around the country explain what they do when critical cases present themselves, and this text provides their tools, wisdom, and professional judgments and offers training that embraces the reality of the school counselor profession to all counselors, educators, and trainees.

Judy A. Nelson, retired associate professor, resides in Tucson, Arizona. She enjoys travelling and hiking with her husband as well as reading for pleasure.

Lisa A. Wines is an associate professor who enjoys being credentialed as a certified school counselor and licensed professional counselor in the state of Texas.

"This book is a gem. School counselors inevitably encounter crises and challenging cases, and although there are resources on crisis counseling in general, more focused and specific information is often needed to respond in a professional and ethical manner. This collection of true-to-life incidents presents each case along with background information, theoretical perspectives, practical considerations, and a discussion of relevant ethical standards. Multicultural factors are addressed as well. The wide range of types of issues is current and comprehensive. Students and professional school counselors have an opportunity to examine these cases and the issues each one exemplifies to increase their own confidence and efficacy for responding in their own setting. I look forward to having my students read this book as part of their training."

Dr. Sheri Bauman, Professor, College of Education,
University of Arizona, Tucson, USA

"This book needs to be in the hands of all school counselors who in today's world deal with a multitude of crisis situations. It is written by well-trained and experienced counselors for responding to tragedies, and it provides a wealth of information and is a tour de force about how to help students after a myriad of crises. School counselors are first responders in helping traumatized students, and this book provides a wealth of practical knowledge and guidance. It is an essential, invaluable resource for all school counselors regarding crisis events. This must-have book provides a comprehensive examination of the many crises that school counselors face and provides them with hands-on strategies that have been successfully implemented in schools."

Dr. Scott Poland, Professor at Nova Southeastern University and
the Director of the Suicide and Violence Prevention Office, Florida, USA

Responding to Critical Cases in School Counseling

Building on Theory, Standards, and Experience for Optimal Interventions

Edited by Judy A. Nelson and Lisa A. Wines

Routledge
Taylor & Francis Group

NEW YORK AND LONDON

First published 2021
by Routledge
2 Park Square, Milton Park, Abingdon, Oxon OX14 4RN

and by Routledge
52 Vanderbilt Avenue, New York, NY 10017

Routledge is an imprint of the Taylor & Francis Group, an informa business

© 2021 selection and editorial matter, Judy A. Nelson and Lisa A. Wines; individual chapters, the contributors

The right of Judy A. Nelson and Lisa A. Wines to be identified as the authors of the editorial material, and of the authors for their individual chapters, has been asserted in accordance with sections 77 and 78 of the Copyright, Designs and Patents Act 1988.

All rights reserved. No part of this book may be reprinted or reproduced or utilised in any form or by any electronic, mechanical, or other means, now known or hereafter invented, including photocopying and recording, or in any information storage or retrieval system, without permission in writing from the publishers.

Trademark notice: Product or corporate names may be trademarks or registered trademarks, and are used only for identification and explanation without intent to infringe.

British Library Cataloguing-in-Publication Data
A catalogue record for this book is available from the British Library

Library of Congress Cataloging-in-Publication Data
A catalog record for this book has been requested

ISBN: 978-0-367-34281-4 (hbk)
ISBN: 978-0-367-27675-1 (pbk)
ISBN: 978-0-429-32483-3 (ebk)

Typeset in Times New Roman
by Apex CoVantage, LLC

We humbly dedicate this book to the school counselors across the globe, who respond to a myriad of crises providing solace to children, families, and school staff. We cannot give them enough credit for the contributions they make to our youth and the communities in which they live. Through their programming, interventions, and counseling skills, they inspire students to achieve success and live more satisfying lives.

Our Personal Dedications

I dedicate this book to my sons, Nicholas Carey Nelson and Lucas Anthony Nelson. They have provided more joy and excitement to my life than I could ever have imagined. How could this mother have been so fortunate to have these two wonderful humans in her life? I learned so much from their joy of discovery, their creativity, integrity, and vitality! When they were young, every day was an adventure in child-rearing, and when they became young men, I am proud to be their mother and their friend.

Dr. Judy A. Nelson

I would like to dedicate this book to my mother, Helen M. Lamar. You are always there—never missing a beat. You stand, inevitably somewhere close, and cheer me on. Besides GOD who loves us all, you are not far behind. Similar to the Almighty, I can share my life and expect an unwavering type of love. To Austin, I love you and will always only ever, want the best for you. To my father, you are full of charisma. You are never boring and tell the kind of stories that will last me a lifetime. To my family members who have endured great difficulty in life, whenever opportunity for goodness comes, take it, and know I am proud of you for doing so! To Dr. Judy A. Nelson, you are my friend! Thank you for your creative ideas, hand of mentorship, over a decade of talks, and our collaborative experiences . . .

Dr. Lisa A. Wines

Contents

Contributors

Editors

Judy A. Nelson is a retired associate professor from Sam Houston State University and coeditor of this book. She worked in the field of counseling for more than 30 years, and her research and subsequent publications have won numerous awards. She was a licensed professional counselor, marriage and family therapist, and certified school counselor in Texas and is now a licensed professional counselor in Arizona. Dr. Nelson was the president of the Texas Counseling Association from 2009 to 2010. Her research interests continue to be professional school counseling, at-risk students, families with school-aged children, and organizational cultural competence. Dr. Nelson currently conducts program evaluations, presents workshops, offers trainings on a variety of topics, and served as an adjunct at the University of Arizona.

Lisa A. Wines is a tenured associate professor at Lamar University and coeditor of this book. She holds credentials as a licensed professional counselor and a certified school counselor for the state of Texas. Dr. Wines is the founder and chief executive officer for L & A Professional Services, LLC.—*The Center for Healing, Therapy, and Wellness* in the Houston/Cypress area. Dr. Wines is passionate about diversifying treatment options with expressive alternative methods such as meditation, massage therapy, progressive muscle relaxation, and use of essential oils (aromatherapy). Research exploring the use of virtual reality and neurofeedback are her next endeavors, if proven effective in working with clients. Dr. Wines has had the privilege of working, multifacetedly, in the area of school, clinical mental health, and marriage, family, and couples' counseling. She consults with school districts and truly is committed to the field of counselor education, where she can teach, innovate, triangulate data and infuse research, mentor, publish, and supervise graduate students.

Contributors

Jasmine S. Akrie is a recent graduate of the master of education in counseling program at the University of Houston. She holds an undergraduate degree in psychology from Sam Houston State University and has been working in the field of education for six years. Her counseling and research interests include children, adolescents, and families. She plans to obtain her certification as a school counselor and, in the future, wishes to pursue licensure as a professional counselor.

Natalie Fikac has been an educator for 24 years, serving in this capacity as a teacher, interventionist, school counselor, campus and district level administrator, and adjunct professor and most recently joined the Texas Education Agency. She is passionate about finding ways to address mental and behavioral health needs of students, growing aspiring school counselors and leaders, and promoting self-care and self-compassion in those she serves. She believes that building positive relationships is at the core of leading and learning for both children and adults.

Kayla P. Gaddy has a master of education degree in counseling from the University of Houston while also continuing her education to obtain licensure as a professional counselor in the state of Texas. She received her bachelor of arts degree in psychology, with a minor in sociology from Texas A&M University. Kayla has a passion for working with children and adolescents and clients who experience difficulty in their lives through individual and/or group therapy. Her aim is to help clients achieve a healthy quality of life through a mindful and supportive therapeutic relationship.

Linda M. Hart served students in a Title I school district as a school counselor for ten years. Her research interests include homeless students and crisis response. Her professional counseling presentations are well received around the United States and Europe. She is currently serving aspiring counselors as an assistant professor at North American University while maintaining a small private practice.

Ronda L. Henry is a first grade teacher for the Garland Independent School District and coauthor of a chapter in this book. She currently holds eight years of experience in education working with various grade levels and districts. She holds a master of education degree in educational leadership and a master of education degree in counseling and development from Lamar University. She authored her first publication in 2013 and is pursuing her license as a professional counselor and certification in school counseling within the state of Texas.

Danny Holland (Ph.D., LPC, NCC, ACS) is a licensed professional counselor and assistant professor at Regent University's School of Psychology and Counseling. He is a former law enforcement officer who has specialized in creating safer environments in public schools. He is the author of two books and has conducted training on the topic of school safety internationally. He has studied active threat response since 1995 and has written guides and plans utilized by thousands of schools. Dr. Holland has worked with victims of mass shootings across the nation, as well as first responders and other stakeholders.

Jamie Holland (DNP, AGCNS-BC, RN) is an advanced practice nurse with a doctorate degree in nursing practice. Her passion for research and training surrounding holistic care and the body/mind connection have fueled her to consult with schools and professionals and to provide care to victims of mass shootings. Her work has brought her recognition for her leadership in her field, and her passion to provide care has been noticed by families, government officials, and members of Congress.

Leigh Falls Holman has been a mental health professional for 25 years and a counselor educator for over ten years. She has worked and supervised school counselors in elementary, middle, and high school settings in rural, suburban, and urban schools that are socioeconomically and culturally diverse. She has also worked extensively with children involved with child protective services and juvenile justice.

Eunice Lerma is an associate professor in the Department of Counseling at The University of Texas Rio Grande Valley. She is a certified school counselor and a licensed professional counselor (LPC) and board-approved counselor supervisor (LPC-S). Her research interests include Latinos in counselor education, counseling at-risk and adjudicated youth, and effective school counseling with Latino students.

Benny Malone is an author, speaker, and mental-health advocate and holds a master of social work from the University of Houston. She has completed more than a hundred hours of postgraduate training in professional counseling, special education, and educational leadership.

Benny has served on the board of directors and various committees of the Texas Counseling Association and coauthored several articles on school counseling best practices and mental health. She also wrote a book titled *Psychotic Rage! A True Story of Mental Illness, Murder, and Reconciliation*, which details her son's long journey with serious mental illness. In her professional career of over 30 years, Benny has worked as an educational administrator, school counselor, special education teacher, state agency social worker, and consultant. Benny is a trained volunteer educator for the National Alliance on Mental Illness (NAMI).

Shannon McFarlin is a licensed professional counselor, board-approved counselor supervisor (LPC-S), and certified school counselor (CSC) in the state of Texas. For the past 22 years, Dr. McFarlin has worked as an educator, a counselor, and a counselor educator with students and clients in educational and clinical settings. Her primary area of expertise is LGBTQQIA issues in counseling. Currently, she is employed as an assistant professor for the Department of Counseling at Lamar University in Beaumont, Texas.

Amberleah Mercado is a Navy veteran working toward the completion of her doctorate of philosophy degree in counselor education and supervision from Walden University. She received her master of science degree in professional counseling from Texas A&M University-Corpus Christi. She is a licensed chemical dependency counselor-intern and currently works with trauma clients and has a passion for promoting awareness among female military veterans.

Frannie E. Neal is a professional school counselor at two elementary schools in the Tucson Unified School District. Ms. Neal's research interests include crisis counseling, adverse childhood experiences faced by at-risk students, influences of social media and technology on student success, and social justice issues in counseling, specifically on systematic oppression and issues faced by immigrants and refugees. Ms. Neal previously worked in college counseling at Palo Verde High Magnet School and Salpointe Catholic High School in Tucson, Arizona. Recently graduated from the University of Arizona Counseling Program, Ms. Neal serves as the communications officer and conference chair with the Counselors for Social Justice National Division.

Kristi L. Nobbman is a mental health counselor in Memphis, Tennessee. She holds her master's degree in school counseling and doctorate degree in counselor education and supervision from the University of Memphis. She has experience working in schools and in the community with children, adolescents, and adults. Kristi is the developer of Nobbman's SAFETY Model of Crisis Intervention. Additionally, she is a trained, independent facilitator of the Love and Logic® curricula.

Clarissa Salinas is an assistant professor in the department of counseling at The University of Texas Rio Grande Valley. She also works as a licensed professional counselor and is a registered play therapist. She enjoys using play therapy techniques in counseling with children and adolescents impacted by trauma and preparing students to counsel this population. She has published research on the topic of play therapy and presented at both local and national conferences on topics of childhood traumatic grief.

Cheryl Sawyer is a retired professor of counseling, formerly at the University of Houston, Clear Lake. Specializing in trauma and crisis response, she has extensive experience in working with children and teens involved in the public schools. Cheryl has supported school counselors in both supervisory and consultant roles for more than three decades.

Cheryl Schindler (MA, LPC, RPT) recently retired from Texas public schools after 18 years teaching elementary special education (mostly emotionally disturbed children) and 16 years counseling in elementary schools. Her counseling experience included extremely high at-risk/

low-income schools, high to mixed SES schools, diverse populations, and a disciplinary alternative education program. In her school experiences, previous years as a music therapist, and 17 years as a therapist in part-time private practice, she served many children and adults who were victims of varied traumatic or potentially traumatic experiences.

Tiffany Simon is a child/adolescent specialist with a license in professional counseling and certified school counselor. She earned her doctorate of philosophy degree in counselor education from Sam Houston State University, along with a master of education degree in counseling and bachelor of science degree in biology from Prairie View A&M University. She served as a 2018–2020 board member for the Texas Association of Counselor Educators and Supervisors. In addition to her work as a counseling practitioner, she was a university faculty member, hired as the director for the School Counseling Program, counselor-intern supervisor, and counseling professor. Dr. Simon has provided training to counselors and other professionals through local, state, and national conferences and is a published author, and curriculum developer for university coursework.

Le'Ann Solmonson is a licensed professional counselor supervisor and certified school counselor in Texas with over 14 years of experience as a school counselor. She is a retired professor and currently owns a private practice and online professional development company. She is one of the authors of the Texas Model for Comprehensive School Counseling Programs.

Helena Stevens holds a doctorate of philosophy in counselor education and is an assistant professor of counseling at Minnesota State University-Mankato and a school counselor in a parochial school. She is passionate about providing evidence-based services and training future school counselors to be culturally responsive and transformative in their professional work. Her research focuses on infusing mindfulness in school-based services and wellness interventions for holistic student growth.

Deborah Webb Johnson has worked in the field of education for more than 35 years. She has been a school counselor for the past ten years and recently, within the last year, has been employed as a field supervisor for counselors-in-training enrolled in the Department of Counseling at Lamar University. After receiving a master of education degree in clinical mental health counseling from Lamar University in May 2018, she has been pursuing clinical hours as a licensed professional counselor-intern to become fully licensed as a professional counselor in Texas. Mrs. Webb-Johnson's professional interests include teaching students, through guidance lessons, to serve as peer mentors within the school setting.

Natalie Alfonso Welsch has a master's of education in counseling degree from the University of Houston. In the near future, she will work toward licensure as a licensed professional counselor (LPC). She received her bachelor of science in psychology degree with a minor in sociology from Texas A&M University. Her theoretical orientation is cognitive behavioral therapy, and her immediate goals include protecting the welfare of the client and maintaining a supportive, therapeutic alliance. She is passionate about working with individuals' experiencing trauma-related disorders.

Rachael Ammons Whitaker is currently the program director and clinical assistant professor for the master of education counseling program at the University of Houston. She has helped develop the counseling program and works in the area of school and family counseling, along with implementing specifically designed behavioral interventions for school districts. She has served in leadership roles, such as coordinator of field experience and field supervisors, and designed residency programs. She is nationally involved in many professional organizations and holds offices in Association for Assessment and Research Conference (AARC) and International Association of Marriage and Family Counseling (IAMFC).

Austin Ellis Wines is a high school student, soon to graduate from a school in Cypress-Fairbanks ISD. He is a co-founder of L & A Professional Services, LLC.—*The Center for Healing, Therapy, and Wellness* in the Houston/Cypress area. Austin's endorsement for his graduation plan is in science, technology, engineering, and mathematics (STEM), with interests in pediatric anesthesiology, law, and commercial real-estate development. While there is time to develop his postsecondary and graduate school interests, he has had involvement in the athletics program for both basketball and track and field.

Graduate Student Contributions

Oluwatosin O. Akintan is a master-level graduate student in counseling at the University of Houston graduating in May 2020. She led the following team of graduate students in completing the PowerPoints for this textbook. She currently works as a graduate research assistant for the Office of Institutional Research at her university.

Amy Barton is a graduate research assistant at the University of Houston, and a doctoral candidate in the School Psychology Ph.D. program. She served as a graduate student in completing the PowerPoints for this textbook.

Shanell Bradley is a graduate teaching assistant at the University of Houston and a graduate student in the master of education counseling program. She served as a graduate student in completing the PowerPoints for this textbook.

Carey Galliher is a graduate student in the University of Houston Master of Education Counseling Program. She served as a graduate student completing the PowerPoints and online companion for this textbook.

Li Jen Huang is a master's level, graduate student in counseling at the University of Houston. He became a Buddhist monk at the age of 11 in Puli, Taiwan, and has lived in a monastery with more than a hundred monks practicing with him. He served as a graduate student in completing the PowerPoints for this textbook.

Sarah Agar Michener is a graduate student at the University of Houston pursuing her master's of education in counseling. She served as a graduate student in completing the PowerPoints for this textbook. Current research interests include undocumented immigrant children and students involved in criminal activity within school systems.

Kathryn Molsberry is a graduate student intern for Dr. Lisa A. Wines at L & A Professional Services, LLC and is currently pursuing her Master of Education in Counseling at the University of Houston. She served as a graduate student in completing the PowerPoints for this textbook.

Ramsha Patel is a graduate student at the University of Houston in the Master of Education Counseling Program. She served as a graduate student for completing the PowerPoints for this textbook.

Foreword

Introduction

When the editors of this text put a call out for school counselors to tell us to what types of critical cases do they respond, we found ourselves wondering *how on earth do they cope?* Regardless of state, city, school district, or grade level, school counselors mitigate critical cases that have become more serious, require good judgment, and remarkable skill to navigate. Whether or not school districts and professional organizations want school counselors to respond to these serious cases is unknown; instead, they are doing it out of immediacy, necessity, care, and expertise. Often, the school counselor is the only person on a campus with mental health training and, therefore, must be prepared and willing to respond in these instances, which are becoming increasingly prevalent and more severe.

Status on Children and Adolescents

Combined and in isolation, a person's cognition, behavior, affect, and physiological conditions affect the status of their mental health. For one reason or another, it seems that school leaders and stakeholders have forgotten that students' mental health conditions always accompany them. Prioritized academic success, high stakes testing, and the quality of delivering curriculum have taken precedence. The truth is that our bodies and brains are interwoven, conditioned uniquely by individual choice, judgment, ecological influences, and biological and genetic factors. Essentially, they help promote a self-reliant management of the multitude of core issues regarding the human life experience.

According to the Centers for Disease Control and Prevention Youth Risk Behavior Survey from 2007 to 2017, health behaviors and experiences related to sexual behavior, high-risk substance use, violence victimization, suicide, and mental health instability contribute to substantial morbidity for adolescents. Although some adolescent sexual behaviors have improved, it continues to be a concern that 39.5% of students surveyed reported that they "ever had sex," 9.7% "had four or more lifetime partners," 28.7% "were currently sexually active," and only 53.8% had "used a condom during last sexual intercourse" (CDC, 2017, p. 9). As for high-risk substance abuse, 14% "had ever used select illicit drugs," and 14% "had ever misused prescription opioids" (CDC, 2017, p. 23). Violence and victimization continue to plague students while they are at school and online. For example, 6% of respondents "were threatened or injured with a weapon at school," 6.7% "did not go to school because of safety concerns," 14.9% "were electronically bullied," 19% "were bullied at school," 7.4% "were forced to have sex," 8% "experienced physical dating violence," and 6.9% "experienced sexual dating violence" (CDC, 2017, p. 31).

Perhaps the area of the utmost concern is that of mental health and suicide, because over a 10-year period, there have been increases in high-risk behaviors regarding depression and self-harm. For example, 31.5% of those surveyed "experienced persistent feelings of hopelessness and sadness," 17.2% "seriously considered attempting suicide," 13.6% "made a suicide plan," 7.4% "attempted suicide," and 2.4% "were injured in a suicide attempt" (CDC, 2017, p. 47). When school counselors learn that students are at-risk for self-harming behaviors, they understand the need to assess this potential, and respond to the urge for stabilization until the student's parents are contacted and/or a hospital or agency becomes involved.

In addition to these problems that adolescents are experiencing in alarming numbers, we know that many children attend school after being abused themselves or witnessing the abuse of a parent or sibling. Estimates are that in the United States, more than 15 million children witness domestic abuse annually (https://ctccfv.org/evidence-of-need/), and a report of child abuse is made every 10 seconds, involving 6.6 million children each year (www.childhelp.org/). In addition, in 2019, by May 1, there were already 17,255 gun violence incidents reported in the United States, which included 4,538 deaths, 188 children killed or injured, and 578 home invasions (Gun Violence Archive, 2019). These incidents affect children—regardless whether they were direct victims of the violence. In fact, active shooter drills in schools, which impact thousands of students, have become commonplace, with 95% of schools in 2015–2016 participating in these drills according, to the National Center for Education Statistics (2018–036). Additionally, nearly half of all schools (45%) employ police as school resource officers (SROs) due to increases in violence in schools. This is a dramatic increase from just 10 years ago when only 31% of schools employed SROs.

What Are School Counselors Doing?

These alarming statistics impact the role of the school counselor as that role continues to magnify and evolve in this dynamic, ever-changing society. Providing mental health services in schools has been a growing expectation among some political leaders, the public, and school personnel. However, districts are also hiring licensed professional counselors and licensed marriage and family therapists with no school experience and no certification in school counseling, to serve as mental health intervention counselors. These professionals must collaborate and coordinate services with the school counselor, who holds the knowledge and skills required specifically for working in school environments. For example, key components of adequate training for school counselors are crisis counseling, resource referrals, skill building, grief and loss, and disaster education and awareness. School counselors have the training and expertise to respond to crises and should be the lead interventionist when these occur. After the assessment period and the immediate responses are made, the school counselor can hand off much of the responsibilities to other individuals or create a team to help with the responding.

Some state legislators and school administrators alarmed at the numbers of students with mental health issues have called for increases in numbers of school counselors to assist students with social/emotional problems to be able to be successful academically. For example, in one large suburban district near Houston, Texas, with over 200 school counselors, 29 more counselors were hired to address the needs of students, including academic, career, and social/emotional areas. However, often school counselors have multiple roles with varied expectations from state legislators, campus administrators, and other stakeholders that may impede their ability to respond to crises appropriately.

Generally, the adequately trained person responsible for the mental health of students in schools is the school counselor, sometimes with the support of other stakeholders, who may also provide mental health services such as the school psychologist, social workers, or behavioral specialists. However, on many campuses, a lone school counselor works to ease the pain and suffering of many students who come to school emotionally spent due to their family or community situations. This phenomenon is becoming more and more of a reality, and school counselors are equipped to assess the mental health status of students, provide short-term interventions to those in need, develop safety plans or self-care agreements (see Appendix A), and work with community mental health providers and community agencies for increases in favorable outcomes in extremely urgent critical cases.

While there is a societal push for school counselors to address students' mental-health challenges, they must also create conditions and environments conducive to privacy and confidentiality. The need to foster continuity of care processes with outside mental-health specialists, agencies, and hospitals is critical. These responsibilities make the demand for a comprehensive school counseling program (CSCP) more essential and relevant. Equally important is the need for school counselors to know and have a role in the development of the campus crisis plan (see Appendix B). With impactful and intentional delivery of counseling services, the results of a CSCP benefit the whole child. By eliminating non-counseling-related duties and using their credentials and training appropriately, school counselors are in a perfect position to perform their jobs by design and positively affect student outcomes, stakeholders' expectations, school climate, and the needs of the community at large. Optimally, school counselors' use of time becomes more efficient, and the needs of students are comprehensively addressed.

Some states have their own specific school counseling model programs or use the American School Counselor Association National Model (2019), which outlines the important and necessary tasks that school counselors must perform and those that are not appropriate. One example of how state legislation supports school counselors is found in the online Texas Administrative Code §239.15, which lists the Texas Model for Comprehensive School Counseling program multiple times, requiring university counseling departments to have trained their graduates on the Texas model, along with statements made that establish a call for a balanced school counseling program. Districts across the state of Texas are seeking training on this model because it is developmental, with adaptable curriculum and guidance on how to use data to evaluate their program, make decisions, and improve the delivery of services. Ultimately, the Texas Model for Comprehensive School Counseling Program transforms low-performing school counseling programs into high-quality plans, thereby positively affecting all students and the campus community.

Unfortunately, expectations for the role of the school counselor are not consistent across district, state, and national lines. In some states, school counselors are licensed and in others they are certified. However, school counselors who are trained in gold standard programs take courses in the school counselor's role in the management of emergency plans for crises, disasters, and trauma; knowledge of the characteristics, risk factors, and warning signs of severe mental health issues; knowledge of medications that impact student learning, behavior, and mood; signs and symptoms of substance use by the student and/or in the home; knowledge of community resources and referrals; and leadership and advocacy knowledge and skills (www.cacrep.org/for-programs/2016-cacrep-standards/). With the exception of a few job specific graduate courses, school counselors take the same courses that clinical mental health counselors take, and many school counseling programs are arranged in such a way that graduates can become licensed professional counselors as well as school counselors.

Conclusion: What Should School Counselors Be Doing?

Our textbook is a testament to the true occurrences in our nation that school counselors do indeed respond to critical cases and will continue to do so because of the serious need for such services. We have asked school counselors around the country to tell us what they do when these critical cases present themselves, and they have provided our profession in this text their tools, wisdom, and excellent professional judgment. That being said, we believe it is time to offer training that embraces the reality of the school counselor's job to all counselors before they are faced with the unthinkable. That is, school counselors must respond to difficult, serious cases throughout the school year. It is time for the argument of the school counselor's role as educator versus mental health professional to stop. School counselors are both and always will be. In the light of the most basic tenet of our profession to "do no harm," we are called to respond when the need arises. No self-respecting school counselor will throw up his or her hands and claim "That's not my job" in the midst of a crisis.

In addition to excellent training, school counselors are bound to advocate for their appropriate roles at the local, state, and national levels. Unfortunately, many administrators and legislators do not understand the role of school counselors nor the extent of the training that they have received. In one state, a legislator argued that school counselors are not qualified to recognize when students are struggling with mental illness. Nothing could be farther from the truth, and it is a dangerous precedent to allow this type of thinking to go unchallenged. Misinformation like this is dangerous for the role of the school counselor and the clients they serve.

Our text is divided into four sections: critical cases involving violence, critical cases of an existential nature, critical cases involving inappropriate adult behavior, and critical cases affecting the whole school community. As stated previously, these are similar to cases that school counselors reported to us they are currently responding to. Some of them involve individual students, others affect groups of students, and some even affect the entire school community. We invite our readers to learn from the experts, those who have been in the field and responded to critical cases with their school counseling and mental health knowledge base as their guide.

Respectfully submitted,

Judy A. Nelson and Lisa A. Wines

Acknowledgments

The editors wish to acknowledge the American School Counselor Association for providing permission to use the exact wording of the *ASCA Code of Ethical Standards for School Counselors* (2016) in each chapter. Readers will find the relevant standards to each chapter under the section titled "Ethical Considerations."

We would like to acknowledge all students who might experience any of the situations described in this book. We know that these crises do not only affect the immediate person or persons but also extend to the larger peer group, the grade level, the entire school setting, and ultimately to the community in which these situations occur. What is it like to be a student in grades K–12 in the 21st century? Adults can only imagine. We think the answer is best understood from the actual words of one of these students. Austin helps us wrap our heads around the complexities of being in a school system in the present day.

My Journey Through a School System Is Like . . .

My journey through a school system is like, well my name—just another one—like many others added to a list known as the total school enrollment. My road traveled when it comes to ethnicity—well, just another form of identification—which does not seem to have enough options available to truly describe each of us anyway. My excursion, huh, thus far my gender is just another demographic—apparently not limited to male and female only.

My journey through a school system is like, I am one, among everyone indeed, who is charged to receive an education, perform well, follow rules, and obey direction from our parents, law enforcement, teachers, and school administrators. I am with it, I guess, but have not in any way ignored the truth that is before me. The reality is that my classmates and I go through a lot. Emotionally, we say we are happy, but many are *stressed the hell out* because we know pressure bursts pipes. Not the urban dictionary version of course, but just that we are challenged and trying to excel and compete in various ways. Mentally, we are developing and we *bob and weave* in and out of our own thoughts, more often than not, adopting the consciousness of our peers. We are confusing in that way. Socially, it is true, birds of a feather always flock together. Do not test it. We congregate with those we are most like and tend to separate from those who are too different from us. It is uncomfortable hanging around people who just do not get us.

Through my journey in a school system, I have known a student who was raped by her stepdad and a student who made a threat on Snapchat, warning us not come to school because they are going to blow it up. This happened twice in one school year, and boy was there low attendance. Gosh, and not to mention, the kids vaping and smoking marijuana seems all too high in number (no pun intended). I wonder when we actually come to realize that every decision made has a future with us—kind of a unknown longevity—would that influence our choices? These critical incidents happened in my K–12th grade experience.

So, in closing, I suppose *my journey through a school system IS* what it is . . . .

Austin Ellis Wines

Section I

Critical Cases Involving Violence

"Violence colors our worldview. Is this world a safe place? Can I trust people? How do I protect myself? Children should not have to answer these questions, but violence requires that they do that very thing."

Dr. Judy A. Nelson

"When a precipitating factor occurs that ignites negative emotions, such as rage, it causes an invisible swelling inside the chest cavity, making one feel out of control. Violence takes place, in that split second, where hostility meets faulty thinking- both inviting uncontrolled behavior to come along for the ride."

Dr. Lisa A. Wines

Violence plagues us directly and vicariously. Cases that involve violence include the use of weapons, verbal assaults, intimidation, physical violations, technological badgering, harassment, and fear. Violent acts can be best explained by premeditated motives, circumstantial loss of control, efforts to attain power and respect, dysregulated conditions of the mind (mental-health instability), emotional turmoil, or learned and modeled behavior. These violent acts are not limited to the adult person but can also be experienced and caused by our youth. This section introduces critical cases involving violence that school counselors have actually experienced. The authors maintain confidentiality by describing cases that are similar to cases they actually experienced. The details do not represent a specific case but rather a composite of cases they have encountered. Names, places, and details are fictitious.

1   Gun Violence in the Neighborhood

Cheryl Schindler

Background

After the 1968 assassination of Robert Kennedy, Mister Rogers, also known as Fred McFeely Rogers, in a special national broadcast urged parents and caregivers to do all they can to keep children safe, to help children express their feelings, and, when children express fear about publicized events, to tell them, "[l]ook for the helpers. You will always find people who are helping" (Hodgman, 2018, para. 4). Sixty-one years later, children all too often hear news of gun violence in schools and neighborhoods. Unfortunately, too many children directly witness or experience gun violence themselves. By May 1, 2019, there were 17,255-gun violence incidents reported in the United States, which included 4,538 deaths, 188 children killed or injured, and 578 home invasions (Gun Violence Archive, 2019).

After a traumatic incident, adults are frequently unaware of children's mental health needs partly because childhood stress symptoms often look different from adult stress. In addition, adult victims are usually preoccupied with providing physical safety for the family and community while coping with their own stress (NOVA, 2009). Lack of early intervention with those traumatized children, whose brains are developing, can result in detrimental brain restructuring (NOVA, 2009). For the aforementioned reasons, schools are often the first place for mental health intervention, and in neighborhoods of poverty, sometimes the only place. The campus professional best trained to lead the staff in being *the helpers* promised by Mister Rogers is typically the school counselor. The following case study describes a school counselor's interventions with students and their families who were victims of a neighborhood drive-by shooting incident.

Description of Case

At the time of this incident, fifth-graders Alexandra and Claudia were neighbors and classmates in a large suburban school district, which is adjacent to a large city in the southwestern United States. It was the fall semester of the school year. Alexandra's brother Julio, age 5, was a kindergartener at their elementary school, and her brother Mateo, age 15, was a tenth-grader at the neighborhood high school. Their elementary school was identified as an at-risk campus, with 85% of the students being on free or reduced meal plans. On numerous occasions, Alexandra's parents had warned them about staying safe while playing outside. In fact, they were not really allowed to go outside without their father's supervision.

One Sunday afternoon, Julio was playing with toy cars in front of the garage while Alexandra and Claudia were playing basketball in the driveway, which is in the front yard of Alexandra's home. An automobile with young males drove by their house and fired multiple gunshots into the front of their house through windows and into walls. Alexandra quickly directed Julio and Claudia to run into the garage and hunch down out of sight. Alexandra's uncle, who lived with them, came out of the house during the shooting and told the perpetrators to leave. Her father called the police, who arrived quickly. He also called Claudia's parents, who came to take her home. Fortunately, no one was hurt physically in the incident. Alexandra heard her brother, Mateo, state that he knew the boys in the car.

When Alexandra and Claudia arrived at school Monday morning, they immediately asked to see the counselor. Initially, the girls relayed the incident by speaking quickly, interrupting each other, and jumping around the sequence of events. The counselor responded empathically, validated their anxious feelings and their choice to talk to the counselor, and normalized the fact that they could not focus on school after such a frightening experience. The counselor used clarification, summary, and a simple timeline to help the students develop a chronological narrative including incident details and their own roles, as well as those of family members who helped achieve safety for the families and neighborhood.

The counselor specifically affirmed Alexandra's leadership in bringing the others with her into the garage. The counselor asked about siblings at the elementary school and elsewhere. The girls calmed down and went to class but returned in agitation five minutes later before the counselor could get Julio, the kindergartener, from his class. Listening and establishing details were continued, but the girls remained very anxious. The counselor explained, "Sometimes it helps to draw or create a sand tray to take some of the scary feelings out of your head and onto the paper or sand tray. Would you like to try something like that?" Drawing was chosen. The first of the several drawings were intensely and rapidly created with bold, dark red and black designs. Their bodies and verbalizations gradually relaxed as their drawings progressed to calmer colors and designs. They asked to go back to the classroom and to return at lunchtime.

The counselor talked to the girls about calling their parents in order to report how they were doing and so that she could assure parents of confidentiality regarding all the sessions and content. The girls asked the counselor to make the calls. The counselor made the calls as explained to the girls and discussed plans to check on Julio, also. The counselor also suggested to Alexandra's father that the high school counselor be informed and asked to check on Mateo. The father agreed to the plans for Julio and asked the counselor to call the high school counselor. During Julio's play, he talked some about guns shot at the house, that it was loud, that he was scared, and that his sister and her friend were crying. At the lunch meeting, the girls were much calmer, retold the story again, this time with more chronology and a few added details. After drawing peaceful pictures and describing love for family members, they returned to class for the remainder of the day.

The counselor called the parents to report on the three elementary children's most recent meetings, explain plans to check on them the next day and regularly throughout the year, and to discuss possible referrals for outside therapy and other resources if signs of stress persisted. The parents indicated they did not have insurance or funds to support a referral to outside mental health professionals. Church-based counseling, local community assistance programs that use interns and charity funding, and private therapists who offer a sliding scale were all discussed.

The next day, the girls expressed relief as they reported the perpetrators as having been arrested. All three children were placed in the Junior Counselor Program at school, in which fifth-graders were assigned a kindergarten or first-grade student who needed encouragement and support from an older friend. This allowed the counselor to monitor the three students' progress with weekly contact in group meetings in addition to less frequent individual meetings. Also, Junior Counselors are taught feeling vocabulary and empathy skills, which helped the students to better express their feelings when discussing the trauma with the counselor. Julio, previously a calm, cooperative child at school, showed increased signs of continued stress at school and home with regression to tantrums, increased irritability, crying and aggression, and increased off-task behavior. His parents agreed to place him in play therapy with a counselor in a community service program. The parents also found a counselor at that program for Mateo. The district task force assigned to monitor and address gang behavior was notified about the incident by the high school counselor.

Strategies for Consideration

School counselors are encouraged to have a theoretical orientation that helps address this form of crisis. As such, person-centered theory and cognitive-behavioral theory both are appropriate frameworks for understanding and processing traumatic events. The professional experiences of school counselors, with an emphasis on receiving training on the NOVA model, enhance their ability to effectively respond. This section also addresses the impact had on school counselors and the mental health implications for the students involved.

Theoretical Frameworks

Person-centered counseling (Rogers, 2003) in a safe, supportive environment helps a victim of trauma ventilate by repeatedly telling the story of a traumatic event in order to experience gradual relief from the intense stress. Cognitive behavior therapy (CBT) [Beck, 2011], an evidence-based practice for counseling persons with anxiety, partially includes teaching self-regulation, with such skills as thought-stopping, naming feelings, deep breathing, muscle relaxation, and positive imagery. Affirmations (positive reinforcement) regarding decisions made during the event and afterward help victims reinstate positive self-identity and autonomy.

While person-centered counseling and CBT are effective theories for trauma victims, they must be adapted to the developmental level of each individual. Young children primarily communicate through play, making play therapy or counseling with toys most effective. Older children, including adolescents, still largely communicate with physical action, so ventilation occurs primarily through forms of play (NOVA, 2009). Therefore, with children and youth, expressive therapies (such as play, art, music, sand tray, drama, dance) and games are important modes to use within those theories (NOVA, 2009; Strickler, n.d.). Play and art are helpful with very young and elementary-aged children, as used in this case study, because they usually create narratives along with the play or art. Beginning with early adolescence (e.g., girls ages 10–13, boys ages 12–15), students start to think more abstractly, and therefore including altruistic activities, such as the junior counselor groups offered in this case, may assist in their healing from traumatic stress (NOVA, 2009).

Professional Experiences

The author of this chapter served as a school counselor at five different elementary campuses, with the numbers of at-risk students varying from approximately 85% to 100% of the total school population. While the frequency of crises was greater in at-risk schools, skills and knowledge from the crisis intervention training developed by the National Organization for Victim Assistance (NOVA) were used often in each school. Without some comprehensive crisis intervention training such as NOVA, responding to these crises would have been difficult and less effective. The NOVA training and manual (NOVA, 2009) provide skills, practice, and important information, such as (a) the effect of trauma on the brain and on overall development; (b) strategies, procedures, and prompts to assist trauma victims; and (c) modifications for victims of varied ages (preschool through senior citizens), for specific cultures and backgrounds, and for different types of trauma.

The NOVA training and manual also describe symptoms of post-trauma stress in order to know when to recommend community support. This is especially important for school counselors because anxiety usually presents differently in children than in adults, resulting in traumatized children being underserved. For example, due to the shorter attention spans, traumatized children normally cycle between showing grief or trauma symptoms. However, they play normally, which can cause stressed parents to believe their children are adjusting. Julio's significantly regressed behavior, a symptom of childhood anxiety, prompted the counselor to meet with the parents and refer him for counseling. School counselors need crisis intervention training to help them adequately address the needs of crisis victims within the school setting.

The high school counselor in this case study notified the district's gang task force because drive-by shootings are typically associated with gang behavior. The counselor or the task force would have also probed to determine whether Mateo was being bullied by gang members, seeking gang membership, or actively involved in a gang. The gang task force, in a large suburban school district in southwestern United States, consists of trained district employees and local police. That task force does such things as monitoring local gang behavior, educating campus staff including counselors about signs and incidents of possible gang behavior, trying to prevent violent gang activity when alerted to such plans, attempting to persuade youth to avoid gang membership, and helping youth desiring to leave a gang.

School counselors' days can become overwhelmingly busy due to many roles, responsibilities, and tasks to meet the needs of their large caseloads. A crisis usually prevents the continuation of the day's commitments for a significant amount of time. Enlisting the assistance of clerical staff, counselor partners, and other administrators to assist with schedule changes and to step into some of the commitments requires an effective working relationship with staff. Some commitments, such as leading the school in several hours of high stakes testing or trainings, can be nearly impossible to reassign. Proactively planning for such possibilities with the administrative team early in the year and again before the dates of those tasks is advisable.

In this case study, only the three elementary students and the one high school student were in crisis. Suppose, however, that other children living in the neighborhood heard of the incident and told additional students, causing fear to spread among many students, who then requested counselor assistance. In that case, the assistance of district personnel and their crisis counseling team should be requested because a well-organized team can assist with large numbers of students. When the team arrives at the school, they follow the directions of the campus counselor, meeting with individual students, staff, and groups as needed. This is a highly coordinated and documented effort (e.g., which students were seen and determining, of those, who will require follow-up). Accessing district assistance allows the campus counselor to focus on the needs of the direct victims. On the other hand, if the campus counselor is also a trauma victim, only the crisis team works with the traumatized individuals, while the campus counselor coordinates their services. The campus counselor, in that case, may also receive psychological support from the team.

Counselor Impact

The ASCA Ethical Standards for School Counselors (2016) expect school counselors to "monitor their emotional and physical health and practice wellness to ensure optimal professional effectiveness. School counselors seek physical or mental health support when needed to ensure professional competence" (ASCA B.3.f). Self-care is critical for the health of the counselor and for their effectiveness with their clients (students). School counselor self-care should be implemented in two main areas, proactive wellness habits and professional relationships for support:

Proactive Wellness Habits

Health and wellness activities such as exercise, play, hobbies, rest, meals, meditation or prayer, family, and private time help to (a) prevent burnout with the job, (b) maintain mental and physical health, and (c) preserve personal relationships. A counselor can then work more effectively and efficiently, even when a crisis occurs. Due to the magnitude of the school counselor's job—the large student caseloads and the number of roles and activities required—wellness self-care must be planned and scheduled. It can be tempting to skip lunch, work late, and not address other glaring self-care needs for just a few days to catch up. As a result, temporarily working long hours to catch up can extend to a daily practice. Some educators schedule one regular night per week to stay late in order to leave much earlier other days for family and personal needs. During the workday, counselors need short breaks such as meals, a walk outside around the school, deep breathing, or stretching. Finally, effective time management at work helps allow for self-care. Some helpful scheduling strategies for school counselors follow: (1) Prioritize tasks. (2) Create a realistic weekly calendar using group, guidance, and meeting schedules and district, campus, and personal calendars and scheduling self-care. (3) Review and tweak calendar daily. (4) Create reminders for the next day rather than staying unnecessarily late.

Professional Relationships for Support, Supervision, and Consultation

Counseling and empathizing several hours in a day with children traumatized by gun violence can result in counselors' vicarious trauma, burnout, or a reexperiencing their own past traumas. If, unlike in this case study, the incident resulted in the injury or death of a student, the counselor may experience traumatic grief. Sometimes personal situations can affect school counselor effectiveness. In instances such as these, counselors need mental health support or debriefing and possibly professional counseling.

Regardless of experience, school counselors encounter new and sensitive situations for which they need consultation. Inexperienced counselors need regular supervision and training to assist their learning curve. Counselors must develop supportive relationships with campus partner counselors and with colleagues in the district and in community professional organizations. Districts should also provide a structure to facilitate these supportive relationships, such as mentors for new or struggling counselors, availability of administrators in the counseling department, crisis response teams (as previously discussed), and regular trainings for all counselors, with additional professional development for new counselors. One district divides counselors into small groups that meet regularly at district meetings, giving each counselor approximately six colleagues to contact for support when needed. That district also provides a program similar to an employee assistance plan, in which district mental health professionals provide a few free counseling sessions to district employees by their request, which can lead to referrals to community professionals, if needed.

Mental Health Implications

In this case study, three factors potentially protect the students from developing lasting mental health disorders in response to the trauma (NOVA, 2009): (a) the short duration of the traumatic event in this case study gives some hope that lasting anxiety might not develop; (b) the counselors intervened with the students and family the day after the shooting; when the first intervention occurs within the first week of the trauma, before defenses have built up, the victims are more receptive to assistance than if the first intervention occurs later; (c) the students received follow-up and group counseling most of the school year due to the incident being in the fall; and (d) those with symptoms of continued anxiety received therapy with community professionals.

However, other factors are less hopeful (Strickler, n.d.). Research indicates that gun violence exposure is significantly associated with traumatic stress among youths (Slovak, 2002). Trauma can be especially detrimental to children because it can affect brain growth and the development of responses in a child's brain, the sense of safety and security, the formation of identity, their affect, and the formation of attachments and empathy (NOVA, 2009). Crises can often co-occur (Keller-Dupree, 2013). This is especially true in low-income areas. If Alexandra's or Claudia's family had experienced other recent crises, such as a car accident, sudden relocation, or death of loved one, before or right after the shooting, the compounding crises could increase the intensity of the traumatic stress. In at-risk schools like the one in this scenario, various students experience crises on campus, in their neighborhood, or at home throughout the year. The students in this case study might reexperience their own trauma when hearing of others' traumatic experiences. Healing from anxiety is difficult in situations of multiple traumatic experiences.

Several additional factors in this case study further indicate a risk of lasting cognitive symptoms: (1) Since Mateo knew the perpetrators, the children may fear the family remains in danger, causing the anxiety to continue even though the incident duration was short. (2) Alexandra's family and Claudia were in the center of the danger, which significantly increases the chances of long-term anxiety. (3) Compared to victims of natural disaster, persons victimized by other people are angrier, which can lead to further distress and can negatively affect trust and relationships. (4) Early adolescents (girls ages 10–13, boys ages 12–15) respond to trauma with high emotionality and become more at risk of suicide or depression than nontraumatized youth (NOVA, 2009). The many risk factors for mental health symptoms after the trauma supported the early and continued interventions at school, follow-ups over time, and referrals to community mental health professionals in this case study.

Ethical Considerations

Other than the ASCA (2016) standards mentioned in the multicultural and counselor impact sections, the primary ethical considerations for this case study are confidentiality, parent rights, and referrals to community mental health professionals.

Confidentiality and Parents' Rights

> A.2.f. Recognize their primary ethical obligation for confidentiality is to the students but balance that obligation with an understanding of parents'/guardians' legal and inherent rights to be the guiding voice in their children's lives. School counselors understand the need to balance students' ethical rights to make choices, their capacity to give consent or assent, and parental or familial legal rights and responsibilities to make decisions on their child's behalf.
> A.12.d. Recognize the sole-possession records and case notes can be subpoenaed.
>
> B.1.g. Respect the confidentiality of parents/guardians as appropriate and in accordance with the student's best interest.

Some school counselors post a sign explaining confidentiality, including the limits to help with confidentiality disclosure, at the beginning of each meeting with students or with parents. This was particularly relevant to this case since the incident was a legal one, making a future subpoena of counselor notes possible. The students (and later their parents) were assured that their counselor visits, names, and discussions would not be disclosed to other students, staff, or other persons, even if those persons talked to the counselor about the incident.

Usually, elementary students want their parents to know about their distress. However, sometimes students do not want their parents to know they talked with the school counselor. The counselor should inquire about the reason, ascertaining, for example, if there is history or fear of abuse or whether they were directed not to talk about the incident at school. Because these students were experiencing high anxiety, it was important for the parents to be informed so they could support the students at home. It is a good practice to discuss with the students how parent involvement can help them and to get their permission to call parents. The students can choose whether to be present when the counselor calls. In this case, the students wanted the counselor to call their parents while they were in class. Furthermore, counselor records were not subpoenaed in this case study.

Referrals to Community Mental Health Professionals

A.7.a. Facilitate short-term groups to address students' academic, career and/or social/emotional issues.

A.6.a. Collaborate with all relevant stakeholders, including students, educators and parents/guardians when student assistance is needed, including the identification of early warning signs of student distress.

A.1.b. Aim to provide counseling to students in a brief context and support students and families/guardians in obtaining outside services if the student needs long-term clinical counseling.

Because the counselor monitored the students' behavior and stress by consulting with parents and teachers and by following up with the children both in the junior counselors (small group counseling) program and individually, all with parent permissions, Julio's symptoms of continued stress were identified, and he was referred for community counseling. Julio's family was willing to see Spanish-speaking therapists who worked in a community center that provided services on a sliding scale or at no cost. Otherwise, they might have followed the practices of some traditional Hispanic families who prefer to see their religious leaders or their *curanderos* (faith healers), primarily because of the lack of communication barriers (shared language, beliefs, values, cultural background) and no fee requirement (Gillette, 2011). School counselors must maintain a list of counseling referrals that include professionals with specialties and services for various cultures, languages, financial situations, and disabilities or other needs. District-prepared community services and referral guides, when available, are particularly helpful in preparing campus referral lists.

Multicultural Considerations

When counseling families of a different culture from oneself, a significant challenge is to maintain an awareness and respect for both the beliefs, attitudes, and values within their culture (ASCA A.1.f), and the individuality of the student and the family. This is especially true of Hispanic families, who can originate from a variety of countries, each of which have their unique cultural traditions and beliefs. As explained by Fortuna (2019) other factors, which can affect mental health beliefs and values, are socioeconomics, education, acculturation, and English proficiency. Specific examples follow: (1) Some traditional Latinos consider mental illness or counseling services to be stigmatizing; fortunately, this was not a factor with the families in this case. (2) Many have poor access to mental health care due to lack of insurance or money (as in this case study), immigration status, and cultural and/or language barriers. (3) Hispanic individuals with higher levels of acculturation can be more susceptible to developing mental disorders. (4) However, remaining bilingual and bicultural, while assimilating into U.S. Western culture, can be a protective factor against developing mental health disorders in response to stress. (5) A strong religious faith can also be a protective factor, reducing suicide attempts and/or risk of substance abuse disorders.

Despite cultural variations, understanding the following traditional Hispanic cultural concepts explained by Carteret (2011) can be helpful when working with Hispanic families. The traditional Hispanic family is hierarchical, the oldest male (usually the father) being the member who makes decisions and maintains the honor and integrity of the family (*machismo*). Therefore, it may be helpful to call the father first, as the counselor did in this case study. In the meeting with the family, counselors should direct most of the conversation and questions to him first. On the other hand, *familismo* (a strong emphasis on the importance of family and close friends) suggests the counselor should then seek opinions from other family members present at a meeting and allow time for the extended family to discuss decisions about interventions. Due to *respecto* (deference to persons in authority), Hispanics may respect the counselor by neither asking questions nor expressing disagreement; nods are intended to communicate attentiveness, not necessarily agreement. This can be confusing to counselors of a different culture. Directly asking such questions as, "How can I help you?" or "What are your thoughts about seeing a counselor?" helps the counselor clarify the family's view and respects them by being collaborative. Hispanics expect professionals to show *simpatico* (polite kindness), *personalismo* (formal friendliness), and confidence. Warm handshakes, use of Mr./Mrs. or *Señor/Señora*, attentiveness, respect, and taking time with them are expected of professionals. Awareness of Hispanic culture and variations among subgroups is important. Investigating school records, consulting with the teacher and students about the family's language, providing and attaining permission for a Spanish interpreter if needed, and using a respectful, curious attitude toward acquiring social/cultural/immigration background from the family can lead to more effective, culturally respective collaboration with the family in order to meet students' needs.

Discussion Questions

1. Consider a non-Hispanic cultural group in your school that is different from yours. What cultural considerations would help you work with those students and families?
2. The counselor is in the process of leading the school in state testing on the day students come to school traumatized after gun violence in their neighborhood. How can roles be modified that day so the school can meet both the needs of the school in testing and of the students in crisis? If the counselor must lead the testing, who would meet with the children and how can that person be prepared or notified to do so?
3. If the district has no crisis response team, how can the counselor get assistance, if needed, to respond to a large number of traumatized students (and staff)?
4. Who can you contact for consultation? For emotional/mental health support?

Resources

Duncan, D. (1996). Growing up under the gun: Children and adolescents coping with violent neighborhoods. Journal of Primary Prevention, 16, 343–356. https://link.springer.com/article/10.1007/BF02411740

Kottman, T. (2001) Play therapy: Basics and Beyond. Alexandria, VA: American Counseling Association.

The National Child Traumatic Stress Network, www.nctsn.org

National Organization for Victim Assistance (NOVA), www.trynova.org

Reinbergs, E., & Fefer, S. (2018). Addressing trauma in schools: Multitiered service delivery options for practitioners. *Psychology in the Schools, 55*, 250–263. doi:10.1002/pits.22105

References

American School Counselor Association. (2016). *Ethical standards for school counselors*. Alexandria, VA: American School Counselor Association.

Beck, J. (2011). *Cognitive behavioral therapy: Basics and beyond* (2nd ed.). New York, NY: Guilford Press.

Carteret, M. (Ed.). (2011). *Cultural values of Latino patients and families*. Retrieved from www.dimension sofculture.com/2011/03/cultural-values-of-latino-patients-and-families/

Fortuna, L. (2019). Best practice highlights for working with Latino/as and Hispanic patients. *American Psychiatric Association*. Retrieved from www.psychiatry.org/psychiatrists/cultural-competency/treating-diverse-patient-populations/working-with-latino-patients

Gillette, H. (2011). *What are curanderos in Hispanic cultures?* (first published in the Spanish website Saludify). Retrieved from https://newstaco.com/2013/09/26/what-are-curanderos-in-hispanic-cultures/

Gun Violence Archive. (2019). Retrieved from www.gunviolencearchive.org/

Hodgman, A. (June 2018). Mister Rogers talks to kids about gun violence: We need the children's television icon now more than ever. *Smithsonian Magazine*. Retrieved from www.smithsonianmag.com/arts-culture/mister-rogers-pioneered-speaking-kids-about-gun-violence-180969002/

Keller-Dupree, E. A. (2013). Understanding childhood trauma: Ten reminders for preventing retraumatization. *The Practitioner Scholar: Journal of Counseling and Professional Psychology*, 2, 1–11.

National Organization for Victim Assistance. (2009). *The community crisis response team training manual* (4th ed.). Alexandria, VA: National Organization for Victim Assistance (NOVA).

Rogers, C. R. (2003). *Person-centered therapy: Its current practice, implications, and theory*. London, England: Constable & Robinson Ltd.

Slovak, K. (2002). Gun violence and children: Factors related to exposure and trauma. *Health and Social Work*, 27, 104–112.

Strickler, H. (n.d.). *Fundamentals of working with children who have experienced trauma and loss*. Audio course accessed from Association for Play Therapy website on May 23, 2019. Retrieved from https://apt.digitellinc.com/apt/conferences/29/view

Reflections: In the space provided, write your notes and reflections regarding this case study.

2 Dating Violence

Tiffany Simon

Background

Violent and abusive behavior in adolescent relationships may mirror similar abusive behaviors, which counselors see in adult domestic violence cases, including physical, sexual, emotional, and financial abuse. Although many studies focus on the occurrences of physical and sexual abuse, psychological abuse also has a lasting impact on victims of adolescent dating abuse and has been found to occur at a higher rate than other forms of dating abuse (Burton, Halpern-Felsher, Rehm, Rankin, & Humphreys, 2016; Hébert, Lavoie, Vitaro, McDuff, & Tremblay, 2008). It is critical for adults to understand that although teen relationships may not be viewed at the same level of seriousness as adult relationships, teens are susceptible to involvement in abusive relationships due to their lack of knowledge about healthy dating behaviors and are more likely to confuse control and jealousy for affection (Gallopin & Leigh, 2009). In response to the alarming rates of violence in dating relationships, the Centers for Disease Control and Prevention (CDC) has deemed dating violence a public health problem (CDC, 2019).

Additionally, at least 23 U.S. states have created and passed legislative mandates that address the development and implementation of dating violence initiatives (National Conference of State Legislatures [NCSL], 2018). During the 2019 legislative session, states including Wisconsin, South Carolina, Oregon, and North Carolina had legislative bills in review that address dating violence (NCSL, 2019). In addition to state mandates, the American School Counselor Association (ASCA) has also tasked school counselors with an ethical responsibility to provide support to victims and perpetrators of dating violence (ASCA, 2016). In the following case study, the escalation of unhealthy behaviors in an adolescent relationship is examined. What may be missing from the discussion of dating violence is the fact that through modeling or direct communication, parents and families often only teach their teens about relationships based on their personal experiences. Hence, measures may need to be in place so that counseling or coaching on dating is made available to teens (Wines & Nelson, 2017a; Wines & Nelson, 2017b).

Description of Case

Tommy and Holly are students in a large suburban high school and are involved in a dating relationship. Tommy is a 16-year-old Caucasian male, junior class officer, active member of the debate team, and honor student. Holly is a 15-year-old Caucasian female, varsity cheerleader, and honor student. Tommy and Holly each live in a two-parent, middle-class household, regularly attend church services, and have healthy relationships with friends and family. Neither student has a history of mental illness or behavior issues at home or school.

During the beginning phases of Tommy and Holly's courtship, both were courteous and respectful, and Tommy and Holly's parents approved of their relationship. However, a month after the two began dating, Holly had the lead role in the school's play. Holly divided her time between her academics, cheer practice, and practice for the play—leaving little time for Tommy. In addition to the decreased amount of time Holly was spending with Tommy, Holly was also gaining additional attention from others due to her popularity as the leading lady in the school's play. Tommy's behavior began to change, and he started to show signs of jealousy. Holly initially shrugged off Tommy's behavior as harmless jealousy and thought it was cute and his way of showing how much he liked her.

A few weeks passed and Tommy's jealous phase continued, and unfortunately, his behavior escalated. The frequency of his text messages increased, and the messages became more accusatory in nature. He repeatedly accused Holly of ignoring him and choosing her friends over him. His grades declined, and he blamed Holly. Tommy played the victim and told Holly if she would spend more time with him or answer his calls, he would not spend so much time worrying about her or trying to find her. His inability to concentrate was because of Holly, and he needed her with him in order for him to get back on track academically. If she really cared, she would be there for him because he loves her, and no one else will love her as he does. Holly hated seeing him so down, so she began to cancel plans with friends and miss play and cheer practice. During their time together, Tommy told Holly how no one understands him as she does, and he does not know what he would do without her. He asked her to promise she will never leave him, and she did promise him that.

As Holly spent more time with Tommy, her friends noticed changes in Holly's behavior. More often they heard Holly say things like "Tommy doesn't like it when I wear skirts to school" or "Tommy says I should stop eating carbs because I am getting fat." Her best friend was worried and told Holly she did not think Tommy was a positive influence. When Holly told Tommy about her friend's feelings, he made her choose between her best friend and him, but he reminded her that she made a promise never to leave him. Holly felt torn but believed she had to keep her promise to Tommy, so she pulled away from her friends. Holly became isolated, spent her time with Tommy, and was fearful that if she gave attention to anyone else, Tommy would see this as her being disloyal to him.

Holly's parents also noticed a change in Holly. She no longer spent time with family and friends. She constantly responded to text messages from Tommy when she was not with him, and when she was asked to break plans with him to spend time with the family, she responded, "But he needs me." Holly's mom decided to read the text messages between the two teens and was concerned with the way Tommy was treating Holly. Holly's parents had a talk with her and explained that Tommy's behavior was controlling and was not healthy for her. After they talked with her, Holly admitted that she was afraid to break it off because Tommy had threatened to hurt himself if she ever left him.

Holly's parents decided to schedule an appointment with school officials to make them aware of what was occurring and the threat to the safety of Holly and Tommy. School staff scheduled a meeting with the school administration, the school counselor, Holly, and her parents. The school's administrators and school counselor worked together to put a plan in place to support both Holly and Tommy. They then held a meeting with Tommy and his parents to discuss school policy and to explain support and resources that were available. A safety plan was created and included input from school administration, campus law enforcement, the school counselor, the social worker, the victim and perpetrator, and their parents.

Strategies for Consideration

The case study provides an awareness of how school personnel, including the school counselor, formed a team to assist two students who were at-risk of escalating unhealthy behaviors. Creating a safety plan and including the students and their parents in the planning process guaranteed that all parties understood the problem and agreed to the interventions. The following sections detail specific strategies used by school counselors and their support teams to assist students dealing with dating violence.

Theoretical Frameworks

School counselors need to determine the risk level of the involved students to determine if student safety is a concern and if they are experiencing a mental health crisis. Students may need more directive and action-oriented support during the initial phase of awareness of involvement in dating violence (Schmidt, 2014). In this case, Tommy's threat of hurting himself may be an indication of self-harming behaviors or ideations, and school staff should be prepared in the event that his behavior becomes a safety concern.

After students' mental well-being and safety have stabilized, school counselors may begin to explore brief counseling techniques. School counselors are trained to use cognitive behavioral therapy (Beck, 2011) and solution-focused brief therapy (Corey & Corey, 2016) techniques in school counseling to help students meet academic and career goals. When emotional and social issues overwhelm students and inhibit their ability to achieve these goals, school counselors can assist using counseling theories and techniques that are evidence-based.

The school counselor can work with the students individually in a safe environment to help identify the problem, identify what actions already occurred, and identify other possible options that may have been more healthy and appropriate ways to communicate those needs. Srikala and Kumar (2010) recommended the incorporation of critical thinking lessons that are solution focused and work on communication skills, coping skills, and self-esteem. Providing lessons and activities targeting mental health and self-esteem may have a positive impact on student problem solving skills and conflict resolution abilities.

Professional Experiences

The author of this chapter surveyed secondary school counselors in a large county in the US state of Texas regarding their experiences in working with students who had been involved in dating violence (Simon, 2014). Of the 104 respondents, 67 (64%) responded that they had counseled students who had been involved in teen dating violence (TDV). Only 27% expressed that they had no experience in adolescent dating violence. The results of the survey are indicative of the need for school counselors to be prepared in how to support students. Sixty-three percent of respondents have participated in at least one TDV activity within the past five years; however, only 25% stated that they receive annual training on TDV, compared to 91% receiving annual training on academic/college readiness.

The author of this chapter, Dr. Simon, has worked with multiple students over her career as a secondary school counselor who either have been involved in or have a friend who was currently involved in an unhealthy adolescent dating relationship. Students are apprehensive to talk to adults about what they are experiencing because adults tend to brush off their concerns. In trainings with school counselors, Simon often starts sessions by asking, "Raise your hand if you are married to your high school boyfriend/girlfriend. Keep your hands raised. Now raise your hand if you know someone who is married to their high school boyfriend/girlfriend." In each session, there are a number of hands that go up. This often helps break the misunderstanding that the dating relationships adolescents are in are not serious and have no future. When students see that their concerns are taken seriously and they feel that the counseling office is a safe place to share what may be occurring in their dating relationships, they are more likely to seek help.

Strategies for creating an environment where students may feel safe to seek help from the school counselor include:

1. Recognize National Teen Dating Violence Awareness and Prevention Week. This awareness week occurs in the first week in February. School counselors can play an active role in the coordination of the week's events. However, it is a team effort! Spread the work and include campus student organizations, local law enforcement officers, community agencies, and other outreach organizations.

2. Attend trainings and professional development on dating abuse and trends in adolescent dating behaviors. As social media and technological devices become more available to adolescents, the result has been new and different means in which abusive behaviors might be displayed. Invite colleagues and administrators to help create a campus of knowledgeable adults.

3. Educate students, parents, and staff members on healthy and unhealthy dating behaviors. Community agencies or women's shelters often have educational curriculum on healthy relationships and will come and speak to students or groups for no charge.

4. Become familiar with campus, district, and state policy and mandates on how to work with victims and perpetrators. Determine if there is an established protocol on your campus and what the school counselor's role is in the plan. Who are the other required staff members included in the plan, and what are their roles?

5. Avoid punishing the victim. If changes need to be made in schedules or daily routines, consider whether having the victim change his or her routine is in his or her best interest. For example, if both students share their first period class, and the decision has been made to remove one of the students from first period, discuss the impact of this change with the victim. The victim may volunteer to be the one moved because he or she is uncomfortable remaining in the same environment in which the abuse occurred. However, the victim may want to be the one who remains in the class because there has already been so much disruption to his or her routine. The victim might prefer to stay in that first period class because it is where he or she feels more comfortable and would prefer that the aggressor be moved.

6. Have resources available for all parties involved: victims, aggressors, and parents. Provide information explaining what dating violence is and how it looks in adolescent relationships, referrals to counseling services, an explanation of the role the school plays when working with students involved in dating violence, and descriptions of the follow-up activities that will be carried out.

7. Develop relationships with law enforcement officials and community agencies. In the event that the situation involves police, school officials may have to determine how to follow protective orders. Law enforcement officials may also help provide support by spreading the awareness of the potential for legal action to occur due to behaviors associated with dating violence.

8. Recognize that dating violence does not discriminate based on gender, socioeconomic status, student popularity, or sexual orientation. In this scenario, both students were actively involved in school, well liked, and were not displaying any risk factors when they started dating. Tommy and Holly did not begin to have concerning behaviors until after they entered into a dating relationship and experienced feelings they had not experienced before.

Counselor Impact

Awareness and prevention methods for dating violence can be addressed through a teamwork approach in which students' physical and mental well-being is considered. School counselors are a critical part of this team, as dating violence may have a negative impact on the students' academic success and mental health. School counselors can coordinate activities to foster relationships between school professionals, health care providers, and law enforcement officials. The outcomes of these relationships can lead to a greater awareness of dating violence in the community and connect victims to resources, which can provide guidance on legal remedies, counseling assistance, and other supports available to individuals involved in violent relationships.

School counselors can also serve as advocates for effective prevention programs that are implemented by staff members who are sensitive, competent, and have appropriate training. In a 2014 research study, school counselors who had more dating violence training and had a greater self-efficacy in understanding current trends in dating self-reported being more involved in prevention and awareness campaigns on their campus (Simon, 2014). In addition, adolescent students involved in dating relationships are more receptive to awareness programs that are current and relevant to today's changing society. Current trends in adolescent dating relationships include factors affected by social media and easy access to technology.

As school counselors consider the impact of dating violence on adolescent students, they also must be careful to recognize if any of these factors of dating violence may have a negative impact on their own mental well-being. School counselors are ethically responsible for their own self-awareness of topics that may trigger stressors in their own lives. In the event that the counselor is a survivor of domestic abuse or has emotional ties to a loved one who has experienced interpersonal violence, a plan should be created to help address any mental stress that may occur. School counselors can create safety plans for themselves that include positive support systems (including friends, family, or their own counselor), self-help measures, and self-affirmation strategies.

Mental Health Implications

Students who have experienced abusive behaviors in dating relationships may also be at risk for other mental health issues. Dating violence might impact the mental health of both the victim and aggressor. Students exposed to dating violence may be at risk for feelings of depression, low self-esteem, anxiety, suicide ideations, risky sexual behaviors, drug abuse, and school-related concerns. In this case, Tommy mentions self-harming if the relationship ends. Although his threat could be his way of trying to control or manipulate Holly, it may also be an indication of Tommy's plans if the relationship ends.

In addition to the mental health concerns that may be present during adolescent years, dating violence may have a lasting impact that persists into adulthood. It is also not uncommon to see victims become isolated, develop eating disorders, or change their sleeping and daily activity patterns. Another aspect of adolescent behavior that might be influenced by students' involvement in abusive dating relationships is their potential to be involved in abusive relationships as an adult (CDC, 2019). In addition, a failure to address the needs of dating violence victims' and perpetrators' future mental health, such as depression, may be present during adulthood (Burton et al., 2016).

Ethical Considerations

A.1.g. Are knowledgeable of laws, regulations, and policies affecting students and families and strive to protect and inform students and families regarding their rights.

The school counselor does not investigate situations to determine if a violation of law has been committed. A school counselor is aware of the laws and policies that may aid in supporting students and their well-being. In addition, the school counselor assists in educating students and parents of potential consequences of risky behaviors. School counselors provide referrals to students and families to local law enforcement in the event that a criminal offense is suspected.

A.1.i. Consider the involvement of support networks, wrap around services and educational teams needed to best serve students.

School counselors consider the importance of helping students identify and access support systems and other networks that may aid in the successful student outcomes and assist in the implementation of safety plans. Students in distress may need access to psychological services, special education, or section 504 services. Section 504 is a civil rights statute guaranteeing students with certain disabilities the necessary accommodations for optimal learning. Conducting meetings that involve all of the possible services that may aid the student(s) can be an essential role of the school counselor.

> A.6.a. Collaborates with all relevant stakeholders, including students, educators and parents/guardians when student assistance is needed, including the identification of early warning signs of student distress.

The school counselor includes the appropriate campus, district, and community members to provide input that may positively affect the students' physical and mental safety. In this case study, the school counselor included input from administration, campus law enforcement, school counselor, social worker, victim/perpetrator, and parents. Teachers and campus nurses are also staff members that should be involved in early warning signs of student distress due to teen dating violence.

> A.6.b. Provide a list of resources for outside agencies and resources in their community to student(s) and parents/guardians when students need or request additional support. School counselors provide multiple referral options for the district's vetted list and are careful not to indicate an endorsement or preference for one counselor or practice. School counselors encourage parents to interview outside professionals to make personal decisions regarding the best source of assistance for their student.

School counselors understand that dating violence may affect a student's mental health and physical safety. Referrals to law enforcement, shelters (if appropriate), and outside counseling may be necessary to provide students with the proper assistance. Providing a resource book to students and parents allows them to choose the resources that are within their means, close to their homes, and culturally relevant.

> A.9.d. Report to parents/guardians and/or appropriate authorities when students disclose a perpetrated or a perceived threat to their physical or mental well-being. This threat may include, but is not limited to, physical abuse, sexual abuse, neglect, dating violence, bullying or sexual harassment. The school counselor follows applicable federal, state and local laws and school district policy.

In the event that the perceived threat is reported to the school counselor, the school counselor will notify appropriate campus staff, law enforcement agency, or child protective services. In the case scenario with Holly, the parents were already aware of the situation. However, if they were not aware of the dating violence, the counselor would work with campus administration to inform the parents.

> A.11.a. Report to administration all incidents of bullying, dating violence and sexual harassments as most fall under Title IX of the Education Amendments of 1972 or other federal and state laws as being illegal and require administrator interventions. School counselors provide services to victims and perpetrators as appropriate, which may include a safety plan and reasonable accommodations such as schedule change, but school counselors defer to administration for all discipline issues for this or any other federal, state or school board violations.

School counselors are required to work with both the victim and perpetrators of dating violence. However, the school counselor does not provide disciplinary consequences for the perpetrator. Instead, the school counselor will work with the perpetrator to help provide resources such as counseling services, information on healthy relationships, and information on the types of consequences they may face if involved in dating violence.

Multicultural Considerations

In Holly's case, her parents were active in her life and noticed the changes and unhealthy relationship behaviors Holly exhibited. However, this is not always the case. Schools and counselors still have a vital role in helping students, school personnel, and families understand risky dating behaviors and healthy relationship behaviors in order to assist in identification of students in need. As school counselors are working to increase awareness of healthy and unhealthy dating relationship behaviors, along with encouraging appropriate dating relationship dissolution (Wines & Nelson, 2017a), it is critical to remove the stigma that victims and perpetrators belong to a certain ethnic group, socioeconomic class, age group, or even social status. When providing scenarios, awareness videos, or posters, school counselors should ensure that awareness materials include a diverse representation for both victims and perpetrators. Consideration of both male students as victims and students involved in LGBTQ relationships are important, as these cases are often underreported. Other considerations for awareness and prevention activities include access to materials in languages that reflect the student and community population and inclusive forms of accessibility for students or parents with visual or hearing impairments. School counselors should also take into account the diversity of the student population when compiling referrals to outside resources.

Case Discussion Questions

1. In this case, Holly's parents were able to identify the unhealthy dating behaviors based on Holly's behavior at home and the text messages between her and Tommy. Who else may have been able to help identify that there was a problem? What could be possible indicators of concern displayed by Holly and/or Tommy?
2. Holly's parents were able to identify signs of unhealthy behaviors; however, all parents are not as aware and may dismiss the signs. What are some ways you can educate parents and the community on healthy and unhealthy adolescent dating practices?
3. Safety plans were created for Holly and Tommy. In small groups, discuss what components should be included within the plan, who the responsible parties are for implementing/monitoring each activity within the plan, and how to inform students/families of the policy.
4. Social media and technology play a role in the dating environment. What are some trends or habits that may be factors that contribute to unhealthy dating behaviors? What technological features may be useful for victims of dating abuse?
5. What components of the safety plan would you change or modify if one or both of the students were a different ethnicity? If the students involved were in a same-sex relationship, how would you respond? Are there other cultural factors that need to be considered when working with students involved in dating violence?

Resources

American Bar Association: www.americanbar.org/content/dam/aba/migrated/unmet/teena
    buseguide.authcheckdam.pdf
Centers for Disease Control: www.cdc.gov/violenceprevention/pdf/ipv-technicalpackages.pdf
Love is Respect: www.loveisrespect.org/
SAFE: www.safeaustin.org/our-services/prevention-and-education/expect-respect/

References

American School Counselor Association. (2016). *Ethical standards for school counselors*. Alexandria, VA: American School Counselor Association.

Beck, J. (2011). *Cognitive behavioral therapy: Basics and beyond* (2nd ed.). New York, NY: Guilford Press.

Burton, C. W., Halpern-Felsher, B., Rehm, R. S., Rankin, S. H., & Humphreys, J. C. (2016). Depression and self-rated health among rural women who experienced adolescent dating abuse: A mixed methods study. *Journal of Interpersonal Violence*, *31*(5), 920–941. https://doi.org/10.1177/0886260514556766

Centers for Disease Control. (2019). *Preventing teen dating violence*. Retrieved from www.cdc.gov/violenceprevention/intimatepartnerviolence/teendatingviolence/fastfact.html

Corey, M. S., & Corey, G. (2016). *Becoming a helper*. Boston, MA: Cengage Learning.

Gallopin, C., & Leigh, L. (2009). Teen perceptions of dating violence, help-seeking, and the role of schools. *The Prevention Researcher*, *16*, 17–20.

Hébert, M., Lavoie, F., Vitaro, F., McDuff, P., & Tremblay, R. E. (2008). Association of child sexual abuse and dating victimization with mental health disorder in a sample of adolescent girls. *Journal of Traumatic Stress*, *21*, 181–189.

National Conference of State Legislatures. (2018). *Teen dating violence*. Retrieved from www.ncsl.org/research/health/teen-dating-violence.aspx

National Conference of State Legislatures. (2019). *Injury prevention legislation database*. Retrieved from www.ncsl.org/research/health/injury-prevention-legislation-database.aspx

Schmidt, J. J. (2014). *Counseling in schools: Comprehensive programs of responsive services for all students* (6th ed.). Boston, MA: Pearson.

Simon, T. T. (2014). *Professional development of secondary school counselors: Counselors' self-efficacy on teen dating violence* (Order No. 3581912). Available from Dissertations & Theses @ Sam Houston State University. (1635277089). Retrieved from https://ezproxy.shsu.edu/login?url=https://search-proquest-com.ezproxy.shsu.edu/docview/1635277089?accountid=7065

Srikala, B., & Kumar, K. (2010). Empowering adolescents with life skills education in schools-school mental health program: Does it work? *Indian Journal of Psychiatry*, *52*, 344–349.

Wines, L. A., & Nelson, J. A. (2017a). Dating coaching. In J. Carlson & S. B. Dermer (Eds.), *The SAGE encyclopedia of marriage, family, and couples counseling* (Vol. 1, pp. 411–414). Thousand Oaks, CA: SAGE.

Wines, L. A., & Nelson, J. A. (2017b). Dating relationship dissolution. In J. Carlson & S. B. Dermer (Eds.), *The SAGE encyclopedia of marriage, family, and couples counseling* (Vol. 1, pp. 414–417). Thousand Oaks, CA: SAGE.

Reflections: In the space provided, write your notes and reflections regarding this case study.

3   Terroristic Threats to School Personnel and Students

Rachael Ammons Whitaker

Background

Terroristic threats have become somewhat common surrounding counselors in school settings, but what specifically does this language entail? Before we can begin to conceptualize such a case scenario, we must first have a clear understanding of the meaning. Additionally, it is necessary to take into account what terroristic threats and violence mean specifically within the parameters of individual state laws. US Legal defines a terroristic threat as

> a crime generally involving a threat to commit violence communicated with the intent to ter-rorize another, to cause evacuation of a building, or to cause serious public inconvenience, in reckless disregard of the risk of causing such terror or inconvenience. It may mean an offense against property or involving danger to another person that may include but is not limited to recklessly endangering another person, harassment, stalking, ethnic intimidation, and criminal mischief.

> (https://definitions.uslegal.com/t/terroristic-threat/)

While this definition may seem clear, try to examine all the ways this could present confusion sur-rounding the term *threat* or *violence*. Each individual may have different perceptions, emotions, or cultural biases surrounding an act of a threat or violence, which makes the interpretation of events very personal. Threat means communicated intent to inflict harm or loss to another person or prop-erty, and violence can be interpreted as the behavior or action of following through on a threat as defined previously. Clearly, withstanding one's choice to select a definition, violence in the schools is a major concern as indicated by the data collected by the National Center for Education Statistics.

In the 2018 *Indicators of Crime and School Safety* (Musu, Zhang, Wang, Zhang, & Oudekerk, 2019), it was reported that among students ages 12–18 in 2017 there were approximately 827,000 total victimizations at school and 503,800 victimizations away from school. These victimizations included theft, violent and heinous crimes, and even simple assault. In that same year, about 20% of students from ages 12–18 reported being bullied at school. Additionally, about 16% of students in grades 9–12 reported that they had carried a weapon at least one day during the previ-ous 30 days, and 4% reported carrying a weapon on school property at least one day during the previous 30 days. Finally, about 6% of students ages 12–18 reported avoiding school activities, classes, or one or more places in school during the previous school year because they feared someone attacking or harming them.

Many school districts are not required to report violence to districts or campus authorities within schools unless police charges are filed (Melvin, 2011). So, if a failure to report exists, then this tends to ignite questions regarding exactly how other cases are being handled within the school setting. Melvin (2011) explored schools that have adopted zero-tolerance policies regarding violence and terroristic threats in schools, but some of these policies appear unclear, confusing, and harsh in questionable circumstances. These observations begin a necessary conversation that would help answer the following questions: (1) What policies are currently in place in any school district regarding threats and violence? (2) What are the questionable circumstances or situations surrounding reports? (3) Are faculty and staff trained to recognize and report threats and violent acts to administrators? (4) What is explained to students about violence and school safety? (5) When should individuals report threats? (6) When does outside law enforcement become involved in such cases that begin in the schools? These questions should be examined among district professionals and clearly stated within the school district's emergency policy for preventing, preparing, and responding should any problematic event arise. Terroristic threats may not be completely preventable; however, protocol, preparation, and precaution can certainly reduce the impact and fear related to such threats. The following case poses some of these difficult questions regarding how schools should proceed when a terroristic threat is issued.

Description of Case

Jon is a middle school student who entered a new suburban school last year. Many students were rezoned after a new middle school was built in the area. Several of Jon's friends were also zoned to this same school, including Jose and Dwain, Jon's best friends. Jon enjoys school and is showing real talent in art class with his ability to draw and use watercolor. Jon's mom is very active in the school and is a member of the Parent Teacher Organization (PTO), while Jon's father is a volunteer during many of the middle school athletic events. Jon does fairly well in school but really enjoys the arts. Jon's math instructor, at his old school, once described Jon as a freethinking, kind, and observant kid who tolerated math. Jon can sometimes be quiet and introverted but loves many activities with his dad including hunting, fly-fishing, and skeet shooting.

Jon's Dad recently bought Jon a new hunting rifle. Jon was so excited that he brought a picture to school to show his friends. Jose and Dwain, friends since elementary school, thought it was cool and knew Jon had a love of guns for hunting. Jon's new friends seemed shocked, asking what he needed a gun for and questioning his reasons for hunting and his disregard toward animal life. Jon shrugged it off and was excited to go target practicing with his father that weekend.

Several weeks later, a group of older boys started to pick on Jon, Dwain, and Jose. One day after school, the older boys hit Dwain with a paintball from a paintball gun walking home from school. Jon was furious and concerned that these boys would continue their antics toward his friend. Jon was right! The bullying continued for weeks. A few months later at school, the older boys were picking on the three best friends in the boys' bathroom. Without much consideration, Jon pulled out the picture of his new riffle and said to the older boys, "If you don't leave us alone, I will bring my real gun to school, shoot you, and all of your friends in seventh grade." One of the older boys was visibly shocked and ran out of the bathroom. The others were stunned, seemingly frozen. The rumor quickly spread around the school and on social media outlets.

A few days later, a teacher caught word of the story from a concerned classmate. The older boy, visibly upset, confirmed that Jon had threatened them in the bathroom and that they had, in fact, been teasing the younger boys for weeks. The school counselor was informed, and Jon was pulled from class to discuss his threats to the older boys. Jon confirmed what he said, but explained how it was out of anger because the older boys had been bullying them for weeks. Jon said he did not want to hurt the boys but only wanted to scare them so they would leave him and his friends alone. The school counselor later called Jon's parents, who were very upset with the whole ordeal. Later, Jon was suspended for making terroristic threats to another student, as listed in the handbook, but Jon's parents were furious that the other boys were not punished for bullying. The parents also explained that they were uninformed about this threat and violence policy.

The following year, the school policy was edited to include punishment for bullying. Additionally, the school counselor did mandatory training on the school's terroristic threat and violence policy for all students, parents, and staff. Many parents and staff were polarized from mixed feelings surrounding this event. Some felt the punishment was too harsh, others felt it was not harsh enough, and some felt that there should be no punishment to Jon because it was an antecedent action in line with self-defense. In this case, how might you respond as the school counselor?

Strategies for Consideration

Terroristic threats and acts of violence concern all students, school personnel, parents, and community members. Parents want to believe that they send their children to schools each day that are safe from harmful incidents. School counselors often have a pulse on students' behaviors that teachers and administrators may not have. The following sections provide helpful information regarding policy making, interventions, and the challenges of managing threats and violence.

Theoretical Framework

Cognitive behavioral therapy (CBT) (Beck, 2011) would be an effective theoretical framework for assisting all students involved in terroristic threats. Cognitive behavioral therapy is designed to help individuals understand thoughts and feelings and how these might influence behaviors. The CBT model is widely known for treatment of anxiety, addiction, depression, phobias, and an array of other disorders. Extensive research supports these treatments, so it would be fitting to tailor such an intervention for terroristic threats because such a scenario will include many of the symptoms listed here. Using targeted techniques, this model could be extremely beneficial for the student body impacted by threats of violence and the person(s) that inflicted the threats of violence, as well as teachers and staff. The following therapeutic techniques would be helpful: journaling, ABC functional analysis, script playing, relaxed breathing, and cognitive reconstruction. These are all techniques that can aid anxiety or fear-based concerns for the entire school community that school counselors learned to use in their training.

Professional Experience

School counselors must ask for support when needed. Although this seems to be a standard topic in school counseling preparation, especially regarding response to intervention (RTI) and prevention programs, many counselors may feel ill equipped to handle such topics. Stop and think about the imagined scenario and the support and consultation needed to support both victim and perpetrator. In this case, counselors should especially reach out for collaboration and guidance from counselors who specialize in terroristic threats, community law enforcement members, and school counselors across the country who may have experience. Using social media platforms and group sites are easy ways to gain resources and not feel alone in establishing policies to protect the entire school community. Additionally, there are workshops and trainings at conferences that can add to the knowledge base relevant to school violence, assessing students who may be prone to violence, and classroom lessons that help students understand the importance of alerting school personnel if they hear or see situations that could lead to violence. Serving the entire school body is not only ethical; it is a moral expectation as a helping professional.

The following are ideas to engage and begin protocol around system wide support:

1. The school counseling staff must be a part of the RTI, prevention, and emergency response teams.
2. If the district or school does not have terroristic threat and violence policies in place, the school counselor(s) should begin the conversation immediately and help write relevant procedures that address such campus-wide events.

3. School counselors can assist in implementing a threat and risk assessment plan for when a threat arises.
4. The school counselor(s) should engage other school counselors and personnel on what school district polices worked or failed. Do research to gain information on polices that could be adapted and best support the specific school community. Consult with other school districts regarding their policies.
5. School counselors can reach out to community stakeholders for information and school-wide training. For example, schools can collaborate with the local police and fire department to conduct training for teachers, staff, and students (with possible bystander emphasis). In addition, the counselor can make sure the school community understands threats, policies, and procedures by conducting staff development for school personnel and classroom lessons for students.
6. School counselors can work with community partners, stakeholders, and teachers to develop and revise policies yearly.
7. School counselors should advocate for training and continuing education to stay on top of emergency school protocol and procedures.
8. Once policies are implemented, amended, or changed, school personnel need policy training and awareness. For example, if the policy states that any statement of harm or violence to a student, staff, or teacher will result in a review and police report, all parties need to know this specific language and consequence.
9. School counselors and emergency response teams should always review policies annually and hold information sessions for the school community.

Counselor Impact

It is very important to consider how taking on a challenge such as writing, preparing, and training on policies surrounding terroristic threats and violence might be overwhelming. With school counselors' ever-growing caseloads, they cannot complete all of these tasks alone, especially when dealing with such emotional topics and concerns. School counselors should take extra precautions to be self-aware on how managing such difficult emergency protocol could have emotional impacts. Conducting policy changes, assessments for violent behavior, or the aftermath of a violent incident could trigger past events, cause anxiety, or even fear for the school counselor. In the event that emergency protocol is needed, the school counselor must take the time to debrief and practice self-care. It is perhaps priority that school counselors seek consultation. Consultation is not only the ethical choice but also an important avenue of self-care.

   Remember that such topics within the school district could be very difficult discussions. Mental preparation and doing research on what is needed for a specific school district is essential. Being mentally prepared for resistance and understanding personal and outside biases might help the counselor address the main goal of school safety. Let us be honest: such topics will trigger bias through others' life experiences. School counselors know this happens, but being mentally prepared for such scenarios can aid in discussion and conversation balance in such a weighted topic of conversation. Self-reflection, self-talk, and conversation rehearsal can help in the mental preparation. Counselors may encounter many teachers or parents that feel such a protocol is unwarranted or excessive. Approaching conversations with confidence and understanding that language around terroristic threats and violence triggers fear responses is key. The school community needs to understand that this is about prevention and keeping all students safe. While these conversations might seem tough and even scary, the safety of schools depends on the tough conversations.

Mental Health Implications

In this particular case study, there are several mental health implications to consider. Often writing out a flow chart of events can help map out an understanding of the case, events, and follow-up procedures. Keeping records of dates ensures ethical responsibility for all those involved in the scenario. The following are mental health implications to consider in detail.

1. Jon appears to be a typical, well-adjusted middle school student, but given the scenario, what needs to occur to ensure safely for all in the school?
2. How can the counselor follow up on Jon's anger toward the bullies? What protocol should be followed to aid Jon? Jon may have been suffering from extreme anxiety due to the length of time the bullying from older students occurred. Now that he has been named the perpetrator, he may feel depressed as well as anxious. The school counselor must assess Jon's mental health status in order to recommend outside therapy.
3. Jon should see the school counselor not only to handle the events outlined in the case study but also to outline his return to school. It is important to assess Jon's mental health and make certain he is progressing with coping skills and resilience as he manages the consequences surrounding his verbal threats. Jon could potentially lose friends or have lasting impacts from the school intervention and fellow student awareness. Helping Jon integrate success-fully back into the school environment is critical.
4. Jon also needs support in managing anger toward the bullies and processing how words have consequences. How will school personnel address these issues within the school for awareness?
5. Dwain and Jose need to receive adequate support for opportunities to communicate concerns and fears. They, too, may suffer from anxiety or depression due to the chain of events. The school counselor can assess for their mental health and make referrals as needed.
6. The three older boys involved in the bullying need support in working through changes in behaviors or concerns.
7. Best practice would also be implementing a debriefing policy for students that may have received incorrect information through social media or hallway talk.

Ethical Considerations

The following ASCA (2016) code of ethical behavior must be taken into account when dealing with student issues.

A.9. Serious and Foreseeable Harm to Self and Others

a. Inform parents/guardians and/or appropriate authorities when a student poses a serious and foreseeable risk of harm to self or others. When feasible, this is to be done after care-ful deliberation and consultation with other appropriate professionals. School counselors inform students of the school counselor's legal and ethical obligations to report the con-cern to the appropriate authorities unless it is appropriate to withhold this information to protect the student (e.g., student might run away if he/she knows parents are being called). The consequence of the risk of not giving parents/guardians a chance to intervene on behalf of their child is too great. Even if the danger appears relatively remote, parents should be noticed.

Administrators did not perceive Jon as a foreseeable risk, but was there a formal assessment to document this? The school counselor did her diligence in changes made to the terroristic threats and violence policy and educating the parents, staff, and faculty the following year, but clearly all policy must be available to everyone before such an event occurs.

    c. Do not release a student who is a danger to self or others until the student has proper and necessary support. If parents will not provide proper support, the school counselor takes necessary steps to underscore to parents/guardians the necessity to seek help and at times may include a report to child protective services.

The school counselor should always follow up with parents to discuss ongoing support. The school counselor should always follow up in cases such as these to make sure students are getting the proper emotional support and parents have the tools needed to support their children. A resource book with community support can be very helpful to parents who need specific kinds of assistance.

    d. Report to parents/guardians and/or appropriate authorities when students disclose a perpetrated or a perceived threat to their physical or mental well-being. This threat may include, but is not limited to, physical abuse, sexual abuse, neglect, dating violence, bullying or sexual harassment. The school counselor follows applicable federal, state and local laws and school district policy.

School counselors must be knowledgeable regarding all applicable laws, regulations, and policies that can affect students and school personnel. When students are at risk of harm, school counselors must inform parents or guardians of the threats and relay to them what school personnel are doing to insure the safety of their students as well as all others.

Multicultural Considerations

It is important to step back and truly examine the multicultural considerations present when reading this specific case scenario. The author left out specific details intentionally as a discussion for multicultural bias and assumptions. What if the student's demographics had been revealed initially? Would you have immediately jumped to a different conclusion if the student's name or skin color were different? When you read the student's name as Jon, did you already make assumptions? Does simply hearing or seeing the words *terroristic threats* bring a specific image to your head, and how might this image be social/environmental conditioning? Would you feel differently if Jon's parents were not active in the school? All of these are questions that directly affect how school personnel might handles threats. Making assumptions based on all of these questions can become the biggest roadblock in the prevention of terroristic threats and violence. Protocol and policy are not biased when written correctly. Additionally, when protocols are properly followed with accuracy, that adherence streamlines a difficult process. It is important always to include multicultural implications when reviewing emergency protocols annually.

Case Discussion Questions

1. In this case study, what was considered an appropriate response from the school counselor?
2. What could the school counselor have done differently?
3. What information could school personnel provide to the students after this threat and after disciplinary actions were taken?
4. There were many mistakes made in handling this terroristic threat. List these out and provide prevention strategies that could have eliminated concerns.
5. How could the school district personnel better prepare for such terroristic threats or violence?

6.   How would school counselors address this situation to the student body, teachers, staff, parents, and community?
7.   What prevention and intervention strategy does your current school implement on reinforcing and preventing terroristic threats?

Resources

CDC Understanding School Violence 2016 Worksheet. www.cdc.gov/violenceprevention/pdf/School_Violence_Fact_Sheet-a.pdf

Engemann, K., & Henderson, Douglas M. (2013). *Business continuity and risk management essentials of organizational resilience*. Brookfield, CN: Rothstein Associates.

Philpott, D., & Serluco, P. (2010). *Public School Emergency Preparedness and Crisis Management Plan*.

Strang, S., & Delicath, T. (2012). *A Comprehensive School Safety Plan for a Rural High School: Enhancing Safety & Security*. ProQuest Dissertations and Theses. Web.

School Safety and Security Training Modules: www.winwardacademy.com/school-safety/?utm_campaign=schoolsafety&utm_source=google&utm_medium=cpc&gclid=Cj0KCQjwxMjnBRCtARIsAGwWnBNKILcjohFlYlC-jpr5zuBctlhY5-O_Ejcfp6s9-K_zaFsmiJ7kSZ8aAlj8EALw_wcB

References

American School Counselor Association. (2016). *Ethical standards for school counselors*. Alexandria, VA: American School Counselor Association.

Beck, J. (2011). *Cognitive behavioral therapy: Basics and beyond* (2nd ed.). New York, NY: Guilford Press.

Melvin, B. (2011). Zero tolerance policies and terroristic threatening in schools. *Journal of Law & Education, 40*, 719–724.

Musu, L., Zhang, A., Wang, K., Zhang, J., & Oudekerk, B. A. (2019). *Indicators of school crime and safety: 2018* (NCES 2019–047/NCJ 252571). Washington, DC: National Center for Education Statistics, U.S. Department of Education, and Bureau of Justice Statistics, Office of Justice Programs, U.S. Department of Justice.

Reflection: In the space provided, write your notes and reflections regarding this case study.

4 Sex on Campus With Multiple Partners

Tiffany Simon

Background

Adolescent students engage in a variety of risky behaviors, including sexual behavior. Risky behaviors include activities such as sex without the use of a condom, participating in sexual activity while under the influence of drugs or alcohol, and multiple partners within a short time period. These behaviors may contribute to unplanned pregnancies, HIV, and sexually transmitted infections. In a 2017 survey conducted by the Centers for Disease Control and Prevention (CDC), 1,257 students in grades 9–12 were asked to self-identify their participation in risky behaviors, including sexual activity. According to the Youth Risk Behavior Survey, 39.5% of high school students self-reported having experience in sexual activity. Male students had a slightly higher reporting of sexual activity at 41.4%, compared to females at 37.7% (CDC, 2019). The CDC has deemed the risky sexual behavior of adolescents as a public health concern, due to adolescents contributing to over 50% of the newly diagnosed cases of sexually transmitted diseases in the United States (CDC, 2019).

The literature defines risky sexual behaviors based on different criteria including but not limited to use of condoms, number of sexual partners, substance use, use of oral contraceptives, and age of initial sexual experience. Due to the different definitions and some of the behaviors being lumped into one category, data demonstrating evidence on how specific behaviors may be predictive of risky behaviors actually may be inconsistent and noncorrelational. For this case study, a focus on concurrent partners as a risky sexual behavior is a priority. A concurrent sexual relationship is defined as having more than one sexual partner at the same time or having overlapping sexual partners. This is in contrast to sequential sexual partners, which are partners that do not overlap but occur close together in time (Vasilenko & Lanza, 2014). Although research is available on the relationship between concurrent partners and the effects on the physical and mental health of adolescents, the literature is inconsistent on the use of concurrent.

In a 2012 research study examining the factors that influence concurrent sexual relationships, female adolescent respondents provided qualitative responses stating they engaged in multiple partner sexual relationships when their boyfriend was unavailable, and one respondent explained that she and her friend both had engaged in sexual intercourse with a male peer at the same time (Reed et al., 2012). Dir, Coskunpinar, and Cyders (2014) included hazardous sexual activity as a domain in their investigation and defined the domain as "sexual encounters with added risky situational factors (i.e., sex with a stranger, sex while intoxicated, and sex with multiple partners simultaneously)" (p. 533).

Description of Case

Elena is a 16-year-old Hispanic female who, as a sophomore, attended a large urban high school that opened in the current school year. The students are still trying to establish connections to the school and staff while building new traditions and school norms. All sophomore students attended one of three other high schools during their freshman year, so many are adjusting to now being part of the new school. This transition had been especially hard for Elena, as she has trouble making friends, particularly with other girls in her class. Elena has previously had struggles with depression and was seeing a therapist outside of school when she was in the eighth grade; however, she had not returned to see her therapist for more than a year.

Elena made a promise to herself, her mom, and her older brother that this year she will do better socially and emotionally as well as academically in school. During her ninth-grade year, she often had issues with truancy, which caused her to attend summer school to make up courses she previously failed. While in summer school, she met Jaime, a 15-year-old sophomore male. Jaime and Elena often talked during summer school; however, when the new school year began and the rest of the students returned to school, Jaime spent less time with Elena and focused on other friends. Elena missed the attention she received from Jaime because it helped distract her from the issues she was having at home. Elena's brother was involved in criminal activity and was in trouble with the law. The related stress became even more unbearable when Elena's brother was arrested for aggravated robbery.

Elena's text messages to Jaime became desperate, and she would tell him how much she needed to see him and how she would do anything to have their relationship remain as it was in the summer. Even though Jaime now had a steady girlfriend, he continued to text with Elena but did not want his friends at school to see him with Elena. Other girls and students said that Elena was strange because she was so quiet and plain looking. One day during lunch, Elena sent Jaime a text and told him she really needed a friend. He agreed to come meet her, but he said that she had better make it worth his time because he was hanging with his friends.

Jaime met Elena by one of the girl's bathrooms that was usually vacant. She hugged him and told him how glad she was that he came. Not wanting to be seen with Elena, he convinced her to go into the bathroom so they could talk. While in the bathroom, Jaime reminded Elena that she said she would make it worth his time. Jaime was already aware that Elena was not a virgin because she had told him about her previous sexual experiences. While in the bathroom, Elena performed oral sex on Jaime. A few days later, Elena asked Jaime to come and spend lunchtime with her again. Jaime turned her down because he was with his best friend, and his friend needed him, too. Elena told Jaime both he and his friend should come because she could use the company. Jaime said he wanted to, but he really liked what they did last time, and they could not do that with his friend there because that would not be fair to his friend, unless Elena would do it to both of them. Elena asked if he would think she was a bad person if she performed oral sex on him and his friend. Jaime says "Heck no! That makes you one of the coolest chicks I've ever met." So Elena agreed. Jaime, his friend, and Elena were caught in the bathroom by one of the teachers as the three students were engaged in sexual intercourse. Each student went to see his or her respective discipline administrator. All agreed that the sex was consensual, and Elena was not forced at any point during the course of events.

Elena's school counselor received information about the incident and set aside time to meet with Elena prior to speaking with Elena's mother. The school counselor created an environment where Elena would not feel judged and reminded her that administrators work with students and consequences of code of conduct violations, but as her school counselor, she was there to help Elena worked on good decision-making skills to help in her success on and off campus. The two focused on life events that led Elena to the place she was now, how she made the decision to participate in sexual intercourse on campus, and other options available to Elena that were less risky. Elena explained that she and her mom have not really talked about what happened because her mom is ashamed of Elena's behavior. The school counselor suggested the two of them role-play ways to communicate with Elena's mom and agreed to be present when Elena's mother came to pick her up from school. The school counselor's presence in the meeting helped Elena to feel more confident in talking to her mother and to explain the stressors she had been experiencing. The school counselor also provided Elena and her mother with information on how to find an outside therapist who would accept clients on a sliding scale fee.

Strategies for Consideration

Adolescent sexuality elicits a great deal of negativity from parents, teachers, and community members. While it is understood that sexual feelings are normal during adolescence, adults prefer that teens would refrain from sexual activity due to the physical and mental health issues surrounding teen sex including pregnancy and sexually transmitted infections, as well as the anxiety and depression that may accompany early sexual encounters. The following strategies for consideration provide common sense approaches to help school counselors cope with this trying time in the development of young people.

Theoretical Frameworks

Adolescent behavior can be impulsive, with little regard to consequences or future outcomes. Solution-focused brief therapy uses a strengths-based approach to help clients recognize strategies and behaviors that support their desired outcome by focusing on the future Solution-focused techniques can help students learn to think critically and problem solve by focusing on solutions. Murphy (2015) explained solution-focused techniques as those that focus on student-driven goals that separate the behavior from the student. For example, students can help find alternate solutions to situations by examining how they would help another student faced with certain situations. This removes the student from being directly associated with the behaviors so they can think through a solution. Understanding that alternate solutions exist can help the student realize that when they are faced with certain dilemmas, there is usually more than one way to react, and if they think through to find the best solution, they may experience positive outcomes.

Solution-focused techniques also help to encourage and support positive self-image of students. Providing students with compliments when they have made positive decisions, even if small, helps to promote positive self-images. In instances where negative behaviors occur, counselors can focus back on how students have the ability to make good decisions by reviewing the times when they were successful and determine what was different between the events. For example, in the scenario with Elena, the school counselor determines that last school year Elena had issues with truancy. This school year, those behaviors have improved. After the bathroom incident, Elena and her counselor can process what strategies she is using to help improve her decision making when it comes to truancy and see if any of those strategies are applicable to her decision making regarding the bathroom incident. If Elena states that she makes better decisions regarding truancy because she does not want to get into trouble at home or at school, the counselor can ask her how that same thinking could have applied to the bathroom incident.

Professional Experiences

In the experience of the author of this chapter, Dr. Simon, students often engage in risky behaviors that consist of multi-risk components. For example, in this case Elena experienced multiple partners, sex in a public place, violation of the student code of conduct, and unprotected sex. As is often the case, Elena experienced other stress-related incidents in her life that led to risky behaviors. In the case study mentioned, Elena was struggling with stressors from home related to her brother's arrest and lack of parental support because her single mother was working multiple jobs to support the family financially. Additionally, the added pressures of a son who was involved in criminal activity and lack of a peer circle to help provide social support added to the stress and anxiety that Elena's mother felt. All of those stressors prohibited Elena's mother from providing the guidance and support that Elena needed during her teen years.

Reed et al. (2012) stated that having concurrent partners is more common among heterosexual males; however, females tend to engage in concurrent partners as a way to seek love or attention due to low self-esteem and peer pressure from boys. In Elena's case, her engagement in risky sexual behaviors met each one of these patterns. Elena's involvement in the sexual activity in the bathroom was a way for her to try to seek the affection, attention, and acceptance of Jaime. In the moment, her feelings of not being pretty or popular were disregarded because the boys were giving her attention and made her feel wanted. In Elena's mind, the male partners could have chosen any girl, but they chose her. If she did what the boys wanted, Jaime would be happy, he would keep talking to her, and their summer relationship would be renewed.

During a Girls' Empowerment Summit in one school district, group members consisting of ninth-grade females discussed how conflict within the cliques of other girls could be a factor that pushed girls to find acceptance from boys, even if this acceptance were negative in nature. The group members participated in a great dialog on how being more accepting of the differences of their female classmates and creating a more inclusive environment for everyone could help decrease the exploitation of girls. Additionally, group members worked on strategies to increase their use of self-affirmations to help increase their self-esteem instead of relying upon extrinsic affirmations from others. The girls also stated they would be more conscious of using negative terms to describe other girls who may be engaging in risky sexual behaviors because "we don't know what they have been through, and we have to do a better job of supporting one another."

Areas that school counselors can play active roles in addressing factors that affect risky sexual behaviors in adolescents include (but are not limited to):

1. Healthy relationships curriculum and presentations are available for use on school campuses. School counselors can work with community agencies and administrators to gain access to curriculum and host student and parent presentations to help increase awareness of traits present in healthy and unhealthy relationships. A healthy relationship curriculum typically includes information on various types of relationships including romantic relationships and peer relationships. By strengthening student awareness of how to identify healthy and unhealthy patterns in relationships, students may increase their positive social supports.
2. The ASCA ethical standards require school counselors to serve as advocates for appropriate services for students. One area of advocacy in which school counselors may participate is in the advocacy for sex education, which will help address risky behavior trends in your student/community population. Not all states and districts have sex education curriculum that provide students with the information needed to make healthy decisions related to sexual concerns.
3. Educate administrators on the need to inform school counselors when students are involved in risky sexual behaviors. Although discipline consequences often are warranted, students engaging in risky sexual behaviors might be experiencing mental health concerns as well. Work closely with administrators to determine how and when the school counselor will be notified.
4. Work with students on decision-making skills that help decrease their impulsive behaviors.
5. Be aware that students involved in consensual and nonconsensual risky sexual behaviors are at-risk for experiencing negative mental and physical effects.
6. Dispel myths related to gender-based stereotypes. Both female and male students might face mental health concerns after involvement in risky sexual behaviors, and both male and female students might initiate involvement in risky sexual behaviors.
7. Stay current on trends that influence risky sexual behaviors, including (but not limited to) social media, sexting, and how drugs and alcohol are used to impact sexual behaviors.

8.   Collaborate with other medical community helpers (including the campus nurse) to help spread awareness of the dangers of contracting sexually transmitted diseases due to risky sexual behavior.

Counselor Impact

School counselors may have different views on sexual behavior based on their religious views, cultural background, and generational views on sexuality. This internal conflict may cause additional stressors on school counselors as they try to practice within the ethical scope of serving students. In addition to the internal conflict, talking to students about sex is still a controversial topic for schools. Depending on the school district and region, some school districts refrain from teaching safe sex practices and rely on teaching abstinence (Center for American Progress, 2018). This political tug of war versus the actual needs of students can also be the cause of additional stressors for school counselors. It is crucial for school counselors to have a network of colleagues who are available to help navigate district and state policy while adhering to ethical responsibilities and student welfare. Having access to best practices used within the counseling field and colleagues who may have successfully implemented programs or interventions with students can help decrease the negative stressors school counselors may face.

Mental Health Implications

Depression, substance use, anxiety, and sexually transmitted diseases have all been associated with adolescent risky sexual behaviors (Dir et al., 2014; Ghobadzadeh, McMorris, Sieving, Porta, & Brady, 2018; Reed et al., 2012; Vasilenko & Lanza, 2014). Ghobadzadeh et al. (2018) stated that depressive symptoms do not have to be present in order for adolescents to engage in risky sexual behaviors and that stressful life events may lead to risky behavior, as sex may serve as a coping mechanism to high stress. However, adolescent depression is a strong indicator of participation in risky sexual behavior in adolescence through young adulthood. School counselors can educate students and parents on the importance of seeking mental health assistance for depressive symptoms and learning and applying coping mechanisms for stressful life events to help impact the risk of involvement in unsafe sexual behaviors during adolescence and through young adulthood.

In addition to the mental health of students, participation in risky sexual behaviors also has a direct relationship with health concerns such as exposure to sexually transmitted disease and unplanned pregnancy. Vasilenko and Lanza (2014) found that having concurrent sexual partners is a better predictor of contracting sexually transmitted diseases compared to the total number of non-overlapping sexual partners over a span of time. Risky sexual behaviors also put adolescents at risk of pregnancy due to inconsistency of condom and other contraceptive use (Vasilenko & Lanza, 2014). Unplanned pregnancy and the diagnosis of a sexually transmitted disease can lead to financial struggles, anxiety, depression, and other adjustment disorders.

Ethical Considerations

It is important for school counselors to take into consideration the ASCA (2016) ethical codes when working with students.

A.1.b. Aim to provide counseling to students in a brief context and support students and families/guardians in obtaining outside services if the student needs long-term clinical counseling.

In Elena's scenario, the school counselor is able to meet with Elena and use solution-focused counseling strategies to help work through decision-making skills and explore possible stressors

Elena may be experiencing. Referrals also can be provided to Elena and her mom in the event that the stressors and depressive symptoms warrant more long-term routine counseling.

> A.1.f. Respect students' and families' values, beliefs, sexual orientation, gender identification/expression and cultural background and exercise great care to avoid imposing personal beliefs or values rooted in one's religion, culture or ethnicity.

School counselors are self-aware of their own value systems and beliefs and are deliberate about not applying those values when working with students. School counselors will bracket their personal opinions and work with students toward goals and the use of appropriate behaviors that might help to maintain the student's mental and physical well-being.

> A.6.a. Collaborate with all relevant stakeholders, including students, educators and parents/guardians when student assistance is needed, including the identification of early warning signs of student distress.

The school counselor includes the appropriate campus, district, and community members to provide input that may positively affect the student's physical and mental safety. In this case study, the school counselor included input from administration and provided referrals to outside counseling. In addition, including campus nursing staff and outside medical professionals also can help to increase knowledge of possible health risks students place themselves in when participating in risky sexual behavior. Also, campus and local law enforcement officers can help spread awareness about possible legal consequences due to age of consent and pictures or videos that might have been taken that could be spread via social media or other devices.

Multicultural Considerations

When working with students and families concerning sexual behaviors, there are several cultural aspects that must be considered: religious views, societal norms (will differ based on location), views of the school's influence on topics related to sexuality, socioeconomic status, access to outside resources, views on sexual orientation, and differences in double standards based on gender. School counselors must be considerate of how cultural implications will affect how they work with students and the types of resources that should be provided. In addition, school counselors will also want to be knowledgeable that certain cultures may be at a higher risk for negative outcomes of risky behaviors. For example, African American females are 11 times more likely to engage in risky sexual behaviors that lead to sexually transmitted diseases compared to Caucasian females, and four times more likely than Latinas.

Case Discussion Questions

1. In the case scenario, Elena was described as a student with a history of depressive symptoms; however, she did not display any other mental health concerns. What other mental health issues should be considered when creating a plan of action for a student identified as engaging in risky sexual behaviors? In your response, include what considerations should be made and who should be involved in the plan for the student.
2. In the Reed et al. (2012) research study, generational views on concurrent sexual partners shaped the views and behaviors of adolescent respondents. Read the Reed et al. study and in groups discuss ways to address the factors contributing to adolescent participation in concurrent sexual relationships. Discuss how cultural norms may influence views on risky sexual behaviors.
3. The ASCA (2016) Ethical Standards for School Counselors requires that school counselors avoid imparting their values and beliefs on students. What ethical dilemmas do you face, if

any, when working with students engaged in risky sexual behaviors? How do you avoid biased language and ensure you are being considerate of the student's background and experiences?

4. Sex education laws vary from state to state. In 2018, the Center for American Progress examined sex education in a state by state analysis. What is your home state's policy on sex education? Do you agree that the policy meets the needs of students within your community? Why or why not?

5. In the provided case study, the female was a Latina female. In groups, create different cultural dynamics for the female in this case study and discuss what changes should be made, if any, to the resources and services provided or the behavior of the school counselor and/or other campus staff members. For example, groups might discuss the case study from the lens of a female African American student who is caught in the bathroom with other female students.

6. In groups of two, role-play how the school counselor could help Elena discuss what to say to her mom or role-play the ways the school counselor can work with Elena on how to make different decisions the next time she is in a difficult situation.

Resources

A K-12 Sexuality Curriculum: https://3rs.org/3rs-curriculum/

Science and Success: Sex Education and Other Programs that Work to Prevent Teen Pregnancy, HIV, and Sexually Transmitted Infections: www.advocatesforyouth.org/wp-content/uploads/storage// advfy/documents/thirdeditionexecutivesummary.pdf

Love Notes 3.0—Classic: www.dibbleinstitute.org/love-notes-3-0/

References

American School Counselor Association. (2016). *Ethical standards for school counselors*. Alexandria, VA: Author.

Center for American Progress. (2018). *Sex education standards across states*. Retrieved from www.american progress.org/issues/education-k-12/reports/2018/05/09/450158/sexeducation-standards-across-states/

Centers for Disease Control and Prevention. (2019). *Sexual risk behaviors can lead to HIV, STDs, & teen pregnancy*. Retrieved from www.cdc.gov/healthyyouth/sexualbehaviors/index.htm

Dir, A. L., Coskunpinar, A., & Cyders, M. A. (2014). A meta-analytic review of the relationship between adolescent risky sexual behavior and impulsivity across gender, age, and race. *Clinical Psychology Review, 34*(7), 551–562. https://doi-org.ezproxy.shsu.edu/10.1016/j.cpr.2014.08.004

Ghobadzadeh, M., McMorris, B. J., Sieving, R. E., Porta, C. M., & Brady, S. S. (2018). Relationship between adolescent stress, depressive symptoms, and sexual risk behavior in young adulthood: A structural equation modeling analysis. *Journal of Pediatric Health Care, 33*(4), 394–403. doi:10.1016/j.pedhc.2018.11.006

Murphy, J. J. (2015). *Solution focused counseling in schools* (3rd ed.). Alexandria, VA: American School Counseling Association.

Reed, S. J., Bangi, A., Sheon, N., Harper, G. W., Catania, J. A., Richards, K. A., . . . & Boyer, C. B. (2012). Influences on sexual partnering among African American adolescents with concurrent sexual relationships. *Research in Human Development, 9*(1), 78–101. doi:10.1080/15427609.2012.654435

Vasilenko, S. A., & Lanza, S. T. (2014). Predictors of multiple sexual partners from adolescence through young adulthood. *The Journal of Adolescent Health: Official Publication of the Society for Adolescent Medicine, 55*(4), 491–497. doi:10.1016/j.jadohealth.2013.12.025

Reflections (for students or counselors to write)

5 Cyberbullying Precipitates a Suicide Attempt

Rachael Ammons Whitaker

Background

In this author's experience, cyberbullying has been a strongly debated topic in school settings over the last several years. While bullying problems and prevention programs have received a lot of attention, school officials seem to shy away from the connection between bullying and suicide. Suicide is a frightening topic and difficult for even the trained professional to explain to school-aged kids. However, what is even harder is children who believe ending their lives is the only way to escape the pain. In order to dive into this case scenario surrounding cyberbullying and suicide, we must first understand the research and how researchers define these terms.

Olweus and Limber (2018) examined how the last several years of research conducted on cyberbullying has vast implications and lack of replication due to varying definitions and concepts of cyberbullying. This lack of replication can impede prevention and intervention and offset the necessary course of action one should take in remediation. However, the U.S. Department of Education (DOE) released a report in January 2019 that universally defined cyberbullying as willful or repeated harm using computers, cell phones, or other electronic devices. The Centers for Disease Control and Prevention (CDC) and the U.S. DOE are currently putting more funds into studying, understanding, and supporting bullying interventions. The DOE report revealed that principals believed that daily and weekly cyberbullying had increased from 7.9% in 2010 to 12% in 2016 (School Survey on Crime and Safety, 2016). Additionally, school districts that implemented rules that prohibit cell phone use during school days resulted in higher cases of cyberbullying (Mayer & Jimerson, 2019).

In looking toward the connection between cyberbullying and suicide, researchers (Gini & Espelage, 2014) found that cybervictimization was more strongly associated with suicidal ideation. Mitchell et al. (2018) found students who are cyberbullied over a 12-month period were four times more likely to have suicidal ideation over peers who did not experience cyberbullying. With today's technology and access to multiple forms of social media, school counselors need to lead the conversation in schools about prevention and intervention.

Description of Case

Lydia is a high school student at Groves High School in a suburban area near a large metropolitan city. She is currently involved in her school's choir group and dance team. Several months ago, Lydia's mother (Dianne) reported to the school counselor that Lydia was being bullied by other students. Dianne received this information about her daughter from another mother in Lydia's class. When Dianne asked Lydia about the bullying, her daughter confirmed she was indeed being bullied and began to cry. The bullying had been going on for months, but Lydia's mom had no idea about it. The school counselor met with Lydia the day after Dianne confronted

Lydia and discovered several students had created a social media page targeting many students at the high school. The social media site was created by an anonymous user, and Lydia was not sure who the original creator was; however, many of her peers had posted hurtful comments. The school counselor was able to locate this page, but the setting was *private*; therefore, the counselor was not able to access the social media page that included the bullying comments. Lydia produced screenshots of a post on the page to show the school counselor proof of the cyberbullying.

Lydia began to cry as she showed the school counselor the screenshot, claiming if anyone found out she told the counselor about the site, the comments would get even worse. The school counselor saw photographs of girls, including Lydia, in which her peers had rated her on her looks and figure. Under Lydia's picture were many cruel comments about her complexion, hair, breast size, and body type. The school counselor later called to follow up with Dianne, who had no idea that Lydia even had a social media account. The school counselor explained to Dianne how this was indeed cyberbullying and was concerned about Lydia and the other peers targeted.

The school counselor arranged an emergency meeting with school personnel two days later and discovered many teachers had heard about this website but had not reported it to the administration. The administrators seemed perplexed as to how they would handle this issue because they could not actually view the social media site, and in most instances, the district's jurisdiction had no policies on cyberbullying and social media. The day after the meeting, the school counselor sent home information to all the parents informing them of this social media page, the cyberbullying, and tips for how to talk to your child.

The next day Lydia informed the school counselor that the page was deleted. The school counselor noticed that Lydia seemed visually distraught, with very large dark circles under her eyes. The school counselor asked how Lydia was doing, and the student replied that she had not slept well the last a few nights in fear of her peers finding out that she had revealed the page to the school counselor. Several days later, just when things seemed to calm down, Lydia began receiving text messages from an anonymous number claiming the sender knew she had told the school counselor. Several of these messages included comments like, "You are so ugly you should just kill yourself." The school counselor spent the next hour meeting with Lydia about the texts, and every day over the next several days she met briefly with Lydia. The school counselor checked in on Lydia two weeks later, but Lydia did not divulge concerning information. The school counselor asked Lydia how she was doing and if she had received additional messages. Lydia claimed she was much better and had received no more messages.

Several weeks later, the school counselor conducted a school-wide assembly on cyberbullying. Two days after this assembly, the school counselor received a phone call from the school's principal informing the school counselor that Lydia was in the hospital and had attempted suicide. Lydia was currently unconscious but expected to make a full recovery. Several days later, Lydia's mother, Dianne, brought her phone to the school counselor and showed her the text messages that had been ongoing for weeks, including a new site that was created. Dianne was furious at herself for not knowing more about social media pressures and the school for not doing more to protect her daughter. Lydia's mother threatened to involve the police. What would you do?

Strategies for Consideration

One way school counselors can advocate for all students is to implement strategies and interventions to wipe out any kind of bullying. Bullying can wreak havoc with students' self-esteem, academic progress, and social interactions. Both victims and bullies need help. The following sections provide information relevant to creating safe schools where all children feel welcome and valued.

Theoretical Framework

Cognitive behavioral therapy for suicide prevention (CBT-SP) (Stanley et al., 2009) would be one theoretical framework to use when conceptualizing this case and addressing the needs of individual students and the entire student population. This theoretical framework aligns with cognitive behavioral therapy, but it also includes interventions for risk reduction, relapse, and bullying prevention. The CBT-SP model focuses on developing increased interactional skills to increase open communication for help, coping, and triggers. The following are strategies to consider with CBT-SP.

1. Can be implemented school-wide for better mental health awareness and prevention.
2. Teaches kids positive communication skills to communicate with peers or teachers/staff if they have concerns about themselves or a friend.
3. Allows and prepares professionals (school counselors) to address and identify risk.
4. Treatment/techniques focus on prevention and small goals. Can be used to support class-room guidance, school-wide programs, and individual counseling.
5. CBT-SP supports safety and emergency plans.
6. Supports the development of skills to deal with immediate situations and coping to address vulnerable students.

Professional Experience

Many school counselors report feeling unequipped to handle suicide or preventative strate-gies on their campuses. School counseling preparation programs should provide future school counselors with essential tools for handling such protocol and prevention, and school dis-tricts must have appropriate protocol in place for dealing with emergencies regarding suicide ideation, attempts, and completions. School counselors must be a part of the leadership or the leader in the school-wide emergency plans that include bullying and self-harm. Suicide, harmful behavior, and cyberbullying should be a part of the school-wide school counsel-ing curriculum that counselors present to all students. Based on professional experience and research, the following are suggestions for including school counselors in the school-wide suicide prevention plan:

1. School counselors need to be leaders in developing and/or revising a suicide protocol that aligns with the school-wide emergency and violence policies and protocol.
2. School counselors need to lead the conversation surrounding all bullying and fears/concerns of self-harm and suicide and document these quantitatively and qualitatively.
3. Policies must be very clear that ALL form of bullying must be reported immediately by students, staff, parents, and teachers. District policies must contain information that spe-cifically instructs how and when police/local authorities will become involved in cases of cyberbullying. District/school policies must clearly lay out consequences for bullying of any form.
4. School counselors should implement yearly mental health and suicide prevention programs for students.
5. School counselors might consider collaborating with community members to bring informa-tion to schools about mental health and suicide prevention programs.
6. When a student returns to school after cyberbullying or a suicide attempt, clear guidelines need to be established for providing the student with appropriate support.
7. When a suicide or suicide attempt occurs at your school, there must be debriefing procedures for protecting the school body.

Counselor Impact

Counselor impact and reach can be broad when school counselors advocate for awareness and prevention strategies. If the school counselor feels a need for more education in such topics, advocating for training and seeking consultation is best practice. School counselors might also decide when to reach out to other school counselors nationwide via social media groups such as ASCA SCENE (https://scene.schoolcounselor.org/home). While self-care at all times is imperative as a counselor, it is crucial when working with such emotional concerns like suicide. School counselors should take extra precautions seeking additional supervision or therapy when needed. School counselors who continue their own self-work through a therapeutic environment will enable themselves to make better judgments on behalf of their students and school.

Mental Health Implications

Mental health implications are extremely important for school counselors to consider when dealing with cyberbullying and suicide. It is important for the school counselor to think about the multiple layers of individuals impacted by such trauma. Often school counselors forget that when tragic events such as these occur, not only are individual students impacted, but also the entire student body, staff, teachers, parents, and community can have reactions and emotions that need to be addressed. It is essential for the school counselor to be a part of the team that debriefs all these multiple layers of the school system and community. It would be highly beneficial for the school counselor to implement or develop an impact assessment framework when dealing with such broad mental health implications. This framework would be specific to the district but include the following: school district policy, school impact/students impacted, social/community impact, training, and follow-up monitoring. This specific framework would help a school counselor identify urgency and create a structural process for identifying vulnerable impacted populations as well as follow-up protocol for all those impacted.

For a student who has experienced cyberbullying and has resulting suicidal thoughts, the school counselor must consider the safety of the student above all else. Cyberbullying can result in severe depression and/or anxiety. School counselors are knowledgeable regarding the signs and symptoms of these serious mental health disorders and must be aware of students who show these at school and at home. In large school populations, school counselors count on students, staff, and teachers to inform counselors if they know of a student who is struggling. Additionally, parents have the right to know all pertinent information about their children, according to the Family Educational Rights and Privacy Act (FERPA) (20 U.S.C. § 1232g; 34 CFR Part 99), which is a federal law that protects the privacy of student education records. The law applies to all schools that receive funds under an applicable program of the U.S. Department of Education regarding negative experiences and signs of self-harm their children might have. Alerting parents or guardians regarding the health and safety of students is necessary.

Ethical Considerations

School counselors must adhere to the ethical standards of their profession. The following standards from the ASCA (2016) ethical code are relevant to this case.

A.11. Bullying, Harassment and Child Abuse

a. Report to the administration all incidents of bullying, dating violence and sexual harassment as most fall under Title IX of the Education Amendments of 1972 or other federal and state laws as being illegal and require administrator interventions. School counselors provide services to victims and perpetrator as appropriate, which may include a safety plan and reasonable accommodations such as schedule change, but school counselors defer to administration for all discipline issues for this or any other federal, state or school board violation.

School counselors, teachers, students, and administrators should all know how to report any form of bullying or suicide concerns. In this specific case study, the teachers failed to inform the school counselor about the social media site. Additionally, appropriate protocol was not in place to protect all parties involved.

> b. Report suspected cases of child abuse and neglect to the proper authorities and take reasonable precautions to protect the privacy of the student for whom abuse or neglect is suspected when alerting the proper authorities.

School counselors must take extreme caution in making sure that students' privacy is protected while protecting others that might be in danger. Providing teachers and school staff information about confidentiality might create a school-wide respect for students' private matters. Periodic faculty meetings are excellent venues for reminding teachers about confidentiality, parents' rights, school district policy, and legal ramifications of student issues.

> c. Are knowledgeable about current state laws and their school system's procedures for reporting child abuse and neglect and methods to advocate for students' physical and emotional safety following abuse/neglect reports.

The school counselor is required to understand the state laws and methods of advocacy and prevention involved regarding student safety. Individual states have laws and regulations that define how and when abuse or neglect should be reported. Counselors should conduct training for their staff on these laws as well as how to identify students who might be experiencing abuse or neglect.

> e. Guide and assist students who have experienced abuse and neglect by providing appropriate services.

School counselors should always conduct follow-ups and check-ins with all students impacted by cyberbullying and suicide. Standing appointments with affected students, checking in with teachers, and communicating with parents are ideal ways to assess the mental health and safety of impacted students.

Multicultural Considerations

While this case might seem all too familiar, there could possibly be some multicultural biases or unconscious biases that could have affected the outcome of this case scenario. A student's culture, environment, or beliefs might directly affect the actions of the school counselor or administration. Counselor self-awareness and reflection on policy implementation will improve the process of responding appropriately. School counselors should not shy away from collecting data to support multicultural considerations when implementing prevention and intervention strategies. Some multicultural considerations with students, faculty, and staff might be perception and religious thoughts around death/suicide, individual experiences, school demographics, parents' concerns/support, school culture, and so forth. It should be considered how the school counselor might have assumed Lydia was OK because she "looked OK" and said she "was OK." How might multicultural considerations have played into this incorrect assumption? Additionally, it is important to remember that the school counselor and designated emergency team meet the needs of the entire school and not just those immediately and directly affected.

Case Discussion Questions

1. In this case study, what did the school counselor do well as part of a safety plan for students?
2. What did the school counselor do poorly as a part of prevention and advocacy strategies?
3. Consider the ethical considerations listed here and designate how an emergency team could have handled these more efficiently in the case study provided.
4. How can the school counselor advocate for prevention protocol in the school district for the following year?
5. What other social media websites could school counselors use to support development and implementation of bullying and suicide prevention programs?

Resources

Mayer, M., & Jimerson, S. (2019). *The importance of school safety and violence prevention.* (pp. 3–16). American Psychological Association.

Reio, T. G., Ledesma O., & Cyntianna C. (2016). Cyberbullying and its emotional consequences: What we know and what we can do. In *Emotions, Technology, and Behaviors* (pp. 145–158).

References

American School Counselor Association. (2016). *Ethical standards for school counselors*. Alexandria, VA: American School Counselor Association.

Gini, G., & Espelage, D. (2014). Peer victimization, cyberbullying, and suicide risk in children and adolescents. *JAMA, 312*(5), 545–546.

Mayer, M. J., & Jimerson, S. R. (Eds.). (2019). The importance of school safety and violence prevention. In M. J. Mayer & S. R. Jimerson (Eds.), *School safety and violence prevention: Science, practice, policy* (pp. 3–16). Washington, DC: American Psychological Association.

Mitchell, S., Seegan, P., Roush, J., Brown, S., Sustaíta, M., & Cukrowicz, K. (2018). Retrospective cyberbullying and suicide ideation: The mediating roles of depressive symptoms, perceived burdensomeness, and thwarted belongingness. *Journal of Interpersonal Violence, 33*(16), 2602–2620.

Olweus, D., & Limber, S. (2018). Some problems with cyberbullying research. *Current Opinion in Psychology, 19*, 139–143.

School Survey on Crime and Safety. (2016). U.S. Department of Education, National Center for Education Statistics, 2015–16 School Survey on Crime and Safety (SSOCS), 2016. Retrieved from https://nces.ed.gov/pubs2019/2019053.pdf

Stanley, B., Brown, G., Brent, D. A., Wells, K., Poling, K., Curry, J., . . . & Hughes, J. (2009). Cognitive-behavioral therapy for suicide prevention (CBT-SP): Treatment model, feasibility, and acceptability. *Journal of the American Academy of Child and Adolescent Psychiatry, 48*(10), 1005–1013. doi:10.1097/CHI.0b013e3181b5dbfe

Reflections: In the space provided, write your notes and reflections regarding this case study.

6 Coaching Staff Allows Students to Fight

Lisa A. Wines, Natalie Fikac, and Amberleah Mercado

Background

Athletics is a way of life for many young men in junior high and high school. Many believe that athletics is a *way out* of a difficult circumstance. The cards some young men have been dealt seem unfair and create a consciousness that something must be changed (Heinrich, 2013). Athletics provide opportunities for students to develop character, to forge positive relationships, to build leadership and resiliency skills, and to be accountable for behavior and academics all while in school. The public glamorizes the lifestyles of professional athletes, and many high school young men dream one day of making it big (Heinrich, 2013).

Young men are often not taught how to appropriately express themselves emotionally or verbally (Atkinson, 2017). As a result, this places them in positions of possibly becoming inept and falling short of having emotional intelligence. Men, at a young age, are socialized to believe they are providers, protectors, and establishers of family units. Young men are also taught not to be afraid and to maintain a stone or poker face in the face of fearful events (Atkinson, 2017). In fact, boys can feel emotionally strained because our society, their homes, and school culture convey boys as tough, not sensitive, and ones who can seemingly handle anything—just do not cry about it (Heinrich, 2013). They simply tend to be nonverbal in their interactions. Thus, when emotions get heated and there is a confrontation or disagreement, it may be easier to throw a fist than to talk it out.

Both social media and television glorify the lives of athletes, making anyone wish they were in the shoes of these ball-handlers (Atkinson, 2017). Media is just one way to obtain information but often gives the impressionable mind aspirations that are not likely for all. This false sense of reality often becomes difficult to combat, and without maturity, versions of individuals' narratives are not likely challenged (Heinrich, 2013).

Forging the cultural rearing of young men and athleticism together can have positive results. Coaches have a dynamic, yet powerful, influence on our youth, their mindsets and interpretations on the way life should be passed onto our youth, whether positive or negative (Pleasant, 2017). The cultural aspects of coaching are, at times, negative and inundated with hostile patterns of communication (e.g., overuse of profanity and vulgarity), intimidation, and unfair promotion and practices of their student athletes. Sometimes when the athletes have conflict among themselves, coaches keep it internal and promote a hash-it-out spirit (Heinrich, 2013).

Male students have difficulty understanding that fighting in a school can have a negative effect on admission into college. Students might record the fight and post it on social media to feel good about themselves. According to Pleasant (2017), 41% of high school students threatened to hurt one another over social media, and 29.5% reported that students fight a significant amount in school. Students do not realize that college admissions personnel check out social media pages of college applicants.

Learning to be male, and sticking to a certain code, must be asserted, repeatedly, for young men to prove their masculinity to themselves, their peers, and society. This stems from young boys being told at a young age to not have fear or be afraid of things they cannot control. Boys grow up to be men still holding onto that ideology (Heinrich, 2013). Boys are told at an early age that it is OK to fight friends to work out their problems and is seen as *play fighting* and does not infringe on their friendships (Dixon, 1996). Boys and men find it difficult to back down from a fight because they might seem weak, whereas strength is often more desirable to the opposite sex. Males also feel shame if they back down from a fight but a sense of pride when they do fight because their reputation is on the line (Atkinson, 2017).

Description of Case

During a school year, there are many times when students' excitement, anxiousness, and levels of aggravation rise, particularly with the anticipation of an upcoming break. These breaks in the school year are usually during holiday seasons and at the end of a year for the summer break. Student behavior tends to ramp up or change so drastically that school counselors and administrators realize how important it is to monitor hallway behavior and to heighten all adult visibility and security in order to reduce potential safety concerns.

At Harlem High School, the athletics program was largely reflective of African American male athletes, with a predominantly white (Caucasian) coaching staff. The physical aesthetics of these students was a look of true fitness, confidence, and strength. Some white educators in the building felt fearful of these strong, headstrong boys. During a particular week that lead up to Thanksgiving break, there were several cases of physical altercations that the school administration was attempting to manage. Educators, as a whole, were growing tired and frustrated, particularly with the black-on-black violence that was evident, and the male coaching staff was no exception. They, too, were feeling frustrated and apathetic.

It was football season, and the team had just lost their first playoff game. With goals of being undefeated, Marlon, an 11th-grade star player and team captain, took this loss quite personally. It was the end of 7th period, and students were released to go home for the day. Preparing for after-school practice, the players were on the field and spread out across the bleachers doing various calisthenics. Music was playing loudly, as the school counselor, Ms. Johnson, proceeded outside to talk with the coaches about students needing schedule changes for the spring term. Within a moment, Ms. Johnson, an African American, was shocked to discover students were hanging over the bleachers and running toward an altercation. The students recorded the incident on their cell phones, posted it to various social media sites, and chanted obscene and profane comments while Marlon and DeShawn, a respected 12th-grade athlete, mutilated each other. Both boys, over 160 pounds of muscle, were physically wreaking havoc on each other. The coaches appeared to remain in position, laughing, pointing, and talking with each other, seemingly too calm and not moved by the hostility and lack of safety present among all students.

Ms. Johnson began to run quickly toward the two students, shouting for them to stop. The coaches noticed Ms. Johnson running toward the boys, and only then did they too run toward the mass chaos. What felt like an eternity was only five minutes of a real crisis. The coaches broke up the fight and told the boys to separate and sit down somewhere. Out of breath, Ms. Johnson went over to the coaches, who immediately stated they would take care of the situation. Referring to these boys as asshole-idiots, they tried to reassure Ms. Johnson not to worry, and they would soon notify the principal when time permitted. In a state of uncertainty (not knowing if the boys were OK, unable to gauge the nonresponsive approach of the coaches, and worried about the vicarious trauma experienced by other students), Ms. Johnson walked the hallways, in tears and shaking, to the principal's office. Her tears were a result of adrenaline and realizing that what had just occurred felt confusing and emotionally taxing. Knocking on the door, Ms. Johnson entered the principal's office when she was invited to enter. Ms. Johnson, clearly distressed, walked in and reported the entire incident to the principal.

Strategies for Consideration

In this section, the strategies for understanding how growing boys are socialized into becoming young men allows counselors to work more effectively with students. Various theoretical frameworks, professional experiences, counselor impact, and mental health implications are presented.

Theoretical Frameworks

Social role theory suggests that men and women change according to the societal expectations placed upon them. This includes gender stereotyping. Young men learn to behave according to ways in which they are *supposed* to act. This theory postulates that the differences related to gender begins in the division of labor that characterizes a society. For example, men are in higher-paid positions as opposed to the designation women carry to be nurturant.

Gender role conflict theory (GRCT) is a model that suggests emotional states are socialized gender positions that have an adverse significance for individuals (O'Neil, Wester, Heesacker, & Snowden, 2017). This model's premise happens when inflexible, sexist, or obstructive gender roles end in personal constraints, aberrations, or harm of others or themselves (O'Neil et al., 2017). The definitive result of this conflict is a hindrance of the individual's potential, either for the people practicing it or for those around the individual (O'Neil et al., 2017).

Feminist theory is another framework to interpret the process of male socialization. This model focuses on the ways men and women fit into societal structures. Growing young men must be masculine, and therefore, as seen in the case, must demonstrate their masculinity in times of conflict. In an article written almost three decades ago, Good, Gilbert, and Scher (1990) stated:

> Men are prohibited from "giving voice" to that which is perceived as "unmasculine," such as fears, vulnerabilities, and insecurities. Thus for many men, normal life reactions are denied expression and perhaps eventually even blocked from self-awareness.
>
> (p. 379)

Professional Experiences

Situations such as the one described here reflect the challenges many school counselors might face in their roles on a campus. School counselors often find themselves in the middle of a situation that has ethical implications. In many cases and on many campuses, school counselors are considered a part of the administrative team. This team usually consists of the principal, associate principal, assistant principals, school counselors, and sometimes department heads, including the head coaches and/or athletic coordinator. Depending on how the school counselor fits into the dynamics of the campus administrator vs. non-administrator role determines how a situation such as this one is or should be handled.

As cited earlier, Ms. Johnson has done the right thing. She headed to the office of the leader on her campus. Once she begins to tell the principal about the incident, this leader will take the necessary steps to address the situation from an administrative standpoint. These steps could include ensuring that the students in the altercation are safe and well, identifying witnesses, receiving statements from those involved, interviewing the two coaches involved, taking necessary disciplinary action on the students and coaches, discussing with the athletic director or athletic coordinator the outcomes or next steps, and ensuring extra supervision is available for the football team. There are also some vital steps for either Ms. Johnson or the school counselor of these two students to take. The appropriate counselor must assess the well-being of these students. This could include individual counseling, group counseling, or mediation between the two athletes.

The ethical dilemma involved with the two coaches makes this a difficult situation. It is pertinent that additional yet personal mentorship and professional development are required by campus and district leadership in the areas of implicit bias, cultural sensitivity, and/or equitable practices. Based on the experiences of these counselors from around the United States, the following suggestions and interventions emerged:

1. School counselors must be a part of the administrative team with a direct connection to their campus leadership and are in a position to help make decisions based on what is best for students.
2. School counselors should advocate for the students that they serve.
3. School counselors should be a part of department level meetings or professional learning communities (PLC) as often as necessary to establish relationships with all stakeholders and gain insight into departmental dynamics.
4. School counselors should have immediate forms of communication (i.e., radio, cell phone, etc.) in order to directly contact leadership when there is a crisis.
5. School counselors should be a voice at the table when professional development plans are made for staff members. School counselors hold a unique lens to the needs on the campus, based on feedback from the students, parents, and staff members with whom they have close relationships.

Counselor Impact

Serving a campus population of both students and staff members can be overwhelming. There are many instances where a school counselor may feel that they are *playing both sides of the fence*. It is not unheard of that some campuses have a *them versus us culture*. Essentially, school counselors must remain neutral and supportive to all involved including their colleagues, the students and their families, and the administration. For example, the school counselor described here may be close friends with these two coaches outside of school, yet the incident necessitated going to her campus leader with an alarming concern, one that will need to be addressed.

Supervision, consultation, and self-care are essential for the success of a school counselor, and knowing when to exercise these options becomes vital. There must be someone that supervises the school counselor who can act as a consultant and/or liaison in a situation like this. In an ideal world, this would be a fellow school counselor, a district level director of guidance and counseling, a lead counselor, or a mentor counselor. Knowing when and where a school counselor needs debriefing is essential. The campus leader, in this case the campus principal, must know who to direct the school counselor to. A situation such as the one described in this case study could easily be described as an incident with forms of vicarious trauma that could require time to debrief, a time for reflection, and a time for self-care.

Mental Health Implications

In this particular case, there are no known signs of mental health concerns directly stated. There are still some concerns with the two athletes. They are obviously in a state of rage at the height of this incident. After the incident, it might be beneficial for the school counselor to go to teachers and coaches of these two athletes to learn if there are any other mental or behavioral health concerns. This incident could also cause forms of vicarious trauma for those who are observing as well as those who view the incident on social media. Concerns of anger, anxiety-induced, or stress-related disorders are quite possible for all involved. All of this campus's school counselors should be ready to support any students who may be affected.

Ethical Considerations

The standards of behavior for school counselors are set forth by ASCA (2016). The following standards should be considered when working with cases that are complex, involve adult behavior, and may put student safety at risk.

> A.1.a. School Counselors have a primary obligation to the students, who are to be treated with dignity and respect as unique individuals.

The school counselor in this situation must keep the needs of the students as her first priority. Because she went directly to her campus leader, it is evident that she was aware of this. Students and their dignity were compromised. Additionally, the school counselor can counsel these students later by increasing their knowledge and understanding of effective communication, self-respect (i.e., which includes not giving people ammunition to make a mockery out of self and culture) and discipline, and conflict resolution.

> A.3.a. Collaborate with administration, teachers, staff, and decision makers around school-improvement goals.

Following this incident, it would be imperative for district leadership to listen and appropriately respond to the thoughts and concerns that this school counselor highlights related to this scenario. Professional development that focuses on inclusivity versus the coaching department operating in a silo would be one avenue to grow their skill set so that instances like this are not repeated.

> A.7.a School counselors facilitate short-term groups to address students' academic, career and/or social/emotional issues.

It would be important to create an appropriate group counseling session for those affected by and who were witness to such an act, including the two athletes involved. Considerations to wait until the mood is less tense or to address the circumstance in the moment should be weighed.

> A.10.a. School counselors strive to contribute to a safe, respectful, nondiscriminatory school environment in which all members of the school community demonstrate respect and civility.

This school counselor obviously strives for a safe, respectful, and nondiscriminatory school environment, as she immediately brought this concern to her leader's attention.

> A.10.b. School counselors advocate for and collaborate with students to ensure students remain safe at home and at school.

When this school counselor immediately alerted her campus leader of this incident, her intent was to ensure that all students were safe on campus.

> B.2.m. School counselors promote cultural competence to help create a safer more inclusive school environment.

When this school counselor immediately alerted her campus leader of this incident, her intent was to ensure that all students were safe on campus. A recommendation made to campus leadership for professional development around equity, implicit bias, and inclusivity echo her promotion of cultural competence.

> B.2.s. School counselors work responsibly through the correct channels to try *and remedy work conditions that do not reflect the ethics of the profession.*

It is evident that this school counselor understands the correct channels to remedy a crisis, as she immediately reported to her campus leader.

> B.3.f. School counselors monitor their emotional and physical health and practice wellness to ensure optimal professional effectiveness. School counselors seek physical or mental health support when needed to ensure professional competence.

As stated earlier, it is very important for school counselors to understand their own physical and mental health needs and practice wellness, including time for debriefing, consultation, and self-care.

> B.3.h. School counselors seek consultation and supervision from school counselors and other professionals who are knowledgeable of school counselors' ethical practices when ethical and professional questions arise.

It is very important for a school counselor to seek consultation and supervision in situations such as the one described here. Consulting with a fellow school counselor lends a different conversation, lens, and problem-solving approach to instances such as this one.

Multicultural Considerations

Generally, African Americans males are raised to be strong, fearless, competitive, and to appear anything other than weak. They learn this in their social circles, from mentors, through the church, via their family structure, and within their community. Another contributing factor is that their mothers, due to lack of male presence or a fatherly figure in the home, often teach them. The appearance of an African American male sometimes creates intimidation and fear in others. *Looking hard* or seeming invincible can be the characterization of these young men. When educators reference back to the underlying theoretical frameworks of this critical case, they immediately come to the realization that African American males are absolutely socialized in these ways.

Additionally, African American males are sometimes reared with patterns of thinking that are not true and maladaptive. Because their group membership with one another takes precedence over establishing affiliations with others, this sometimes causes *recycled thinking and behaviors*, making exposure to new things or people more challenging. When you reference back to the underlying theoretical frameworks of this critical case, you immediately come to the realization that African American males are absolutely socialized in these ways.

Case Discussion Questions

1. There are clear methods for reporting, such as for abuse and neglect of our youth. What about when it includes a colleague? What approach or reporting methods would you take?
2. How might you make an effort to change the societal trajectory of male socialization and gender roles in your school?
3. Consider the idea of emotional intelligence. How could you increase awareness among coaching staff and athletes?

Resources

> *ASCA Ethical Standards for School Counselors:* www.schoolcounselor.org/asca/media/asca/
> Ethics/EthicalStandards2016.pdf

References

American School Counselor Association. (2016). *Ethical standards for school counselors.* Alexandria, VA: Author.

Atkinson, S. (2017). *Why men fight-and what it says about masculinity.* Retrieved from www.theguardian.com/world/2017/sep/12/modern-masculinity-men-fighting-scott-atkinson

Dixon, C. (1996). Having a laugh, having a fight: Maculinity and the conflicting needs of the self in design and technology. *International Studies in Sociology, 6*(2), 147–166.

Good, G. E., Gilbert, L. A. & Scher, M. (1990). Gender aware therapy: A synthesis of feminist therapy and knowledge about gender. *The Journal of Counseling and Development, 68*, 376–380.

Heinrich, J. (2013). The making of masculinities: Fighting the forces of hierarchy and hegemony in the high school setting. *The High School Journal, 96*(2), 101–115. http://dx.doi.org/10.1353/hsj.2013.0001

Pleasant, J. (2017). *School fights posted to social media can be a barrier to college admission.* Retrieved from www.wkrn.com/news/local-news/school-fights-posted-to-social-media-can-be-barrier-to-college-admission/

O'Neil, J. M., Wester, S. R., Heesacker, M., & Snowden, S. J. (2017). Masculinity as a heuristic: Gender role conflict theory, superorganisms, and system-level thinking. In R. F. Levant & Y. J. Wong (Eds.), *The psychology of men and masculinities* (pp. 75–103). Washington, DC: American Psychological Association. https://doi.org/10.1037/0000023-004

Reflections: In the space provided, write your notes and reflections regarding this case study.

Section II

Critical Cases of an Existential Nature

"We must allow children to play their games and learn about life from them. This is how children begin to confront their existential questions. Children can work through angst and fear through play."

Dr. Judy A. Nelson

"There comes a time in our lives where we question our existence, and if consciously aware, we are at rest knowing we gave it our all. However for some, when that time comes, there is a great chance they are left with an unfathomable and insurmountable amount of regret and guilt, because they believe their life was without purpose, with no real meaning."

Dr. Lisa A. Wines

An existential crisis can occur at any point throughout the life span. It is the moment in which a person questions the meaning, worth, value, authenticity, and the integrity of their life. Will I leave a legacy? Do I matter? Why was I born? Why did I pretend to be someone I was not? Who am I in spirit and in action? Placing great effort into the process of *making meaning* of our lives can significantly affect our mental health. It could be that your personality, mood, and/or emotions are off-kilter, which causes existence-related questions to arise. Our youth go through these same internal processes in an attempt to better understand themselves. This section introduces critical cases of an existential nature and how school counselors help children believe in their worth amidst sometimes overwhelming odds.

7 A Serious Mental Health Issue

Benny Malone and Judy A. Nelson

Background

Schools now endeavor to teach the whole child, recognizing the necessity to meet children's developmental needs and address differences in learning styles. Today's educational approach is student centered and real-world focused. The new teacher graduate most likely has taken courses in child development, psychology, critical thinking, problem solving, technology, professional communication skills, special needs learners, multiculturalism, and courses pertaining to subject matter and teaching strategies. However, they more than likely did not take courses that trained them how to:

- recognize early symptoms of serious mental illness;
- respond in crisis situations involving students;
- interact with a student who reports or shows evidence of child abuse; or
- understand what to say to a student who expresses suicidal ideation.

What a teacher sees in a student who is at risk is a young person who is struggling academically, behaviorally, socially, and/or emotionally in the school environment. The school counselor is the on-site professional consultant for teachers and administrators precisely because school counselors are uniquely trained to *recognize*, *respond*, *interact with*, and *understand* the four critical incidents listed that a student may experience while at school. In fact, all four situations combined may exacerbate the symptoms of mental illness experienced by a child or adolescent. Professional school counselors engage with students who suffer with severe mental illness every day, but they may not know these startling facts about this group of students. Research (NCBI, www.ncbi.nlm.nih.gov) has shown that 50% of all lifelong cases of mental illness begin by the age of 14 and 75% begin by the age of 24. What we can garner from these statistics is that mental illness appears to attack our youth first.

Mental illness is a medical condition that often is invisible in the young child or teen until the condition is very advanced, largely because symptoms emerge intermittently and often look like a more intense version of *normal* development. A December 2018 report by the Centers for Disease Control and Prevention (CDC, www.cdc.gov) revealed 1 in 6 U.S. children aged 2–8 years (17.4%) had a diagnosed mental, behavioral, or developmental disorder. Additional statistics from the National Institute of Mental Health (NIMH, www.nimh.nih.gov) and the National Alliance on Mental Illness (NAMI, www.nami.org) report that 20% of youth ages 13 to 18 experience severe mental disorders in a given year. For ages 8 to 15, the estimate is 13%.

Approximately 50% of students age 14 and older with a mental illness drop out of high school, and 70% of youth in state and local juvenile justice systems have a mental illness. Almost one-half of youth ages 8 to 15 with a mental illness received NO mental health services in the previous year. The average delay between onset of symptoms and intervention is 8–10 years for youth (NIMH, www.nimh.nih.gov).

Because mental illness is considered an *invisible* illness, both difficult to identify and late to receive treatment, the negative impact is often very great. Of students 14 and older who have a mental health condition AND are served by special education, 50% drop out of school. This is the highest dropout rate of any disability group. Suicide is also more prevalent for young people than for adults. For the population as a whole, suicide is the tenth leading cause of death in the U.S., but it is the third leading cause of death among ages 15 to 24 years. More than 90% of those who die by suicide had one or more mental disorders (NIMH, www.nimh.nih.gov).

Mental illness, in general, occurs on a continuum of severity from mild to serious. Serious mental illness (SMI) is defined as a mental, behavioral, or emotional disorder resulting in serious functional impairment that substantially interferes with or limits one or more major life activities (NIMH, www.nimh.nih.gov). For children and teens, the life activities affected are academics and school activities, relationships with peers, and family and community relationships and involvement (McFarlane et al., 2010). The most commonly diagnosed mental disorders in children are behavioral disorders; attention deficit hyperactivity disorder (ADHD); major depressive disorder (MDD); and anxiety disorders (AD), including generalized anxiety disorder (GAD), obsessive-compulsive disorder (OCD), panic disorder (PD), and post-traumatic stress disorder (PTSD). Bipolar disorder tends to appear in adolescence but may also occur in younger children. Schizophrenia spectrum disorders may occur as early as the mid-teen years and have a typical onset during the late teens to the late twenties.

Mental illness has a kinship with many of the chapter topics covered in this book, including trauma, child abuse, physical and emotional neglect, substance abuse, suicide, brain injury, family violence, gun violence, incarceration of a parent, and loss. Critical incidents like these potentially are damaging to children and are referred to in the literature as adverse childhood experiences (ACEs). Studies show that child abuse and family violence in particular have a major impact on the future mental health of victims (DeVenter, Demyttenaere, & Bruffaerts, 2013).

Description of Case

This case study of a student with a serious mental illness follows a fifth-grade student, Marcus, through elementary, middle, and high school. The case study depicts an accurate example of the roller coaster ride that characterizes serious mental illness—onset, crisis, treatment, recovery, relapse, escalation, crisis. Marcus represents a composite of actual stories of many students who were seen by the authors of this chapter when working as school counselors. The names and details are fictional.

Marcus, Age 11, Elementary School

Marcus is 11 years old and is in the fifth grade. He was born six weeks premature with a late summer birthday and repeated kindergarten. He has been on track, academically, since the retention year, making average grades. He is small in stature but otherwise seems to have normal development. Marcus is an only child and lives with his mother. She currently is working two jobs. He has no contact with his father. His grandparents are elderly and live in another state. Marcus stays by himself after school until his mother gets home around 9:00 in the evening. His teacher has never met his mother.

Bullying, a potential trigger for mental illness onset in vulnerable youth: In fourth grade, other students started to tease Marcus. They nicknamed him *Little Marcus* and called him "gay," "fag," "pansy," and "sissy" on the playground, in the restroom, and at the bus stop. Marcus soon became a full-fledged target of bullying. A very regrettable incident occurred in the fall semester of fifth grade. Because Marcus tried to avoid the restroom when other boys were present, one time he urinated on himself in class. This was a hugely embarrassing experience for him that quickly made Marcus an even greater target of derision by the bullies. His mother knew about his accident in the classroom because he had changed clothes in the clinic and had to bring his own clothes home in a plastic bag in his backpack. Because he felt ashamed, he did not tell her about the bullying that had been going on for almost two years.

Negative coping increases negative symptoms: By mid-fifth grade, Marcus's entire day was spent trying to avoid the bullies. He went to the library instead of going to recess. He offered to help his teacher in the classroom while the other students were outside playing. He sat up front close to the teacher during instruction. He started walking to and from school instead of riding the bus. There was one girl, Susan, in fifth grade who befriended Marcus. She had asthma and often stayed in from recess. She and Marcus crossed paths in the library or when both stayed inside to help their teachers while other students were outside playing after lunch.

Marcus's teacher noticed that he did not seem to have many friends, nor did he try to join in with other students in any activities. He rarely smiled and did not seem happy. He had worked with a reading mentor for more than two years. Previously in elementary grades, he consistently had made B's and a few C's, but now in fifth grade, his grades were mostly D's and one F.

A crisis finally brings adult attention: Two weeks before the end of the school year, Marcus wrote a letter to Susan telling her about the bullying. He was very angry in the letter and told her how much he hated the bullies and how he wished he could hurt them. When Susan saw him after lunch, she asked him about the situation. He told her he did not think he could take it much longer. He never got to talk to his mother about anything, because she worked so hard and was always exhausted when she got home.

He told Susan that it would be better for his mother if she did not have him to care for. Then she would only need to work one job. He ended the conversation by saying, "Poor Bullies! Who will they pick on next if *Little Marcus* isn't around anymore?" Susan was scared after talking to Marcus and went to the librarian to tell her what he had said and showed her the letter. The librarian met with the school counselor that afternoon and showed her Marcus's letter.

How Should a School Counselor Respond in a Situation Like This?

Obtain school-related background information: The counselor's conversation with the librarian filled in much of the educational history about Marcus. The librarian had known him since his first kindergarten year. From first through third grade, Marcus had participated in a library reading mentor program. The extra support was exactly what he needed, and his academic progress improved and was consistently on level. He was a dedicated student, well behaved, and loved pleasing his teachers with his hard work. He was not particularly athletically inclined and steered away from the groups of boys who played active sports during recess.

Considering the Seriousness of the Statements of Self-Harm Made by Marcus and the End-of-Year Timing, What Steps Should Marcus's School Counselor Take?

Little time, big problem: In this case study, the school counselor only had nine days to respond to this student's needs. Marcus would be transferring to middle school in the fall. The first thing the counselor did was make a copy of Marcus's letter for her records and made personal notes of the meeting with the librarian about Marcus' school background.

- The counselor requested an emergency at-risk meeting involving the counselor, principal, assistant principal, two teachers, and, at a minimum, a parent-teacher conference via phone, if Marcus's mother was unable to come to a conference at school.

- The counselor quickly scheduled a one-on-one meeting with Marcus and shared a specific plan for helping him.
- The counselor reached out to a Community Youth Services (CYS) social worker who was assigned as a liaison for Marcus to receive private therapy for depression, anxiety, and social skills strategies. The CYS social worker had access to all treatment resources that were recommended for Marcus while in therapy over the summer. He began to see a psychiatrist mid-summer, and his mother attended a weekly family support group.
- The CYS social worker also obtained the services of a job specialist for Marcus's mother to help her find employment that was more suited to her providing the home supervision and support Marcus needed.
- Marcus's elementary counselor scheduled this case for an at-risk transition meeting with the middle school counselor responsible for Marcus the following school year. All of the information available to the elementary counselor was shared verbally and in writing with the middle school counselor.

Marcus, Age 12, Middle School

A good plan in place and followed for both home and school: During the summer, Marcus was diagnosed with a serious illness, childhood depression, and was in an ongoing treatment program. Throughout middle school, Marcus kept all of his treatment appointments and made steady progress toward recovery. His mother had signed a two-way authorization form that allowed the counselor and the treatment team to communicate regarding Marcus's progress. Marcus's mother also continued to attend the family support group. She was now working only one job, and the home situation was less stressful.

As Marcus entered middle school, his schedule was hand-picked because of his history with being bullied and suicidal ideation. All of his teachers had been cautioned to watch out for the bullying of Marcus and were quick to intervene with an adult presence and disciplinary referral if necessary. Marcus eventually let go of his expectation of being bullied. The school counselor connected with Marcus early in the semester, and he began to hope and trust that this year might be better. Preceding the beginning of each school year, the counselor met with Marcus's new teachers to update them on his needs and progress. The counselor had a standing appointment to have lunch with Marcus at least once each grading period. He knew the counselor was his go-to person on campus if he needed help. Marcus was placed on the official at-risk list and was identified as eligible for 504 services.

Positive changes yield positive results: With the positive changes resulting from the services provided by CYS, Marcus bloomed with confidence, and his strengths reappeared. He liked school and still wanted to please his teachers. He worked hard at school and could now tell his mother about his day when he got home from school. Early in the fall semester, an alert sixth-grade physical education (P.E.) teacher discovered that Marcus was a fast runner and encouraged him to try out for the track team. This was the first time Marcus had ever thought or been told he might have some athletic ability. The P.E. teacher continued to encourage Marcus and remained his coach throughout the three years of middle school. By the end of middle school, Marcus had friends, won races for the track team, and passed all of his classes. He also grew a little taller but remained the smallest kid in his class.

Marcus, Age 15, High School

Poor transition to high school: The successful progress for Marcus in middle school did not continue into ninth grade. By mid-school year, Marcus's entire day was again spent trying to avoid the bullies. He thought he should be able to handle this on his own because things had changed for the better during middle school. In fact, things had gotten so much better that he and his mother decided to stop the therapy and psychiatric treatment. Unfortunately, the middle school counselor did not schedule a transition meeting to inform the high school counseling team about Marcus, primarily because he had not really needed any counselor or academic support during the last year of middle school. Middle school staff removed Marcus's name from the official at-risk list.

Now Marcus's life felt just like fifth grade again. Marcus's grades fell to C's and D's instead of A's and B's, and he had to stay off the track team for one grading period. When he got home from school now, he was home alone. Just like fifth grade! He felt angry about his situation and began to think about taking revenge on his tormentors.

Emotional stress triggers strange behaviors: Marcus began to experience hallucinations, paranoid delusions, and unsettling sensations, all key symptoms of first episode psychosis. If he saw two or three students standing in the hallway, he thought they were talking about and laughing at him. He felt he could sense them sneaking up on him, but before he could turn around, they had disappeared. He began watching out for them between classes. He sometimes heard a voice in his head that said, "Get 'em!" followed by a jeering laugh. This would happen three or four times in a row. Then the voice was quiet. When he was tardy for one class, the teacher asked where he had been. Marcus told her it was not any of her business and then stormed out of the classroom cursing.

The next day the assistant principal (AP) summoned Marcus to the office. Since this was the first discipline referral Marcus had ever received, the AP asked what was going on. Marcus was very polite. He had felt surprised and confused when he was told to come to the AP's office. Marcus told the AP that he did not remember the incident with the teacher. Nevertheless, he offered to apologize. The AP sent Marcus to a disciplinary class for one hour and told him to write a letter of apology to the teacher and return to the office for the AP's review. Marcus complied, and the teacher allowed him to return to class.

Escalation of symptoms: Marcus did not like being in trouble any more than he liked being bullied. After the disciplinary action, he began to take various hallways to his classes and made no eye contact with anyone. The voice in his head became more of a tormentor, frequently saying, "Get 'em!" faster and faster until it turned into one long, jeering laugh. Sometimes, he would hear, "You win!" as he entered the classroom along with loud laughing and clapping sounds. The sounds make him feel dizzy and sick at his stomach. Marcus made no eye contact and slipped into a back-row desk with his head down. He could feel everyone's eyes looking at him, all with sly, mean grins on their faces.

Marcus also stopped eating lunch in the cafeteria to avoid the taunting. He would hide out in a storage room. That is when he started drawing pictures of guns, knives dripping with blood, and bombs exploding. Sometimes he would hear the voice say, "Get 'em!" repeatedly. The voice motivated Marcus to draw faster, and he filled page after page in his notebook with the same images. For 25 minutes every day, Marcus would hide and draw. When the lunch bell rang, he would leave and go to class.

High-risk alert: One day, the custodian came into the storage room during his lunch period. He ran Marcus out and told him to get to class. The next day, the custodian found the notebook of Marcus's drawings. He turned the notebook in to the office. There was no name on it and the custodian did not know the student. The school's security team called an emergency meeting.

Strategies for Consideration

This section highlights a plethora of frameworks recommended by a national organization and the authors of this text. It is important to remember that the theoretical framework selected should fit the intricacies of the case. The professional experiences of school counselors are vital and highlighted in this sections. Counselor impact and mental health implications are also addressed in detail as well.

Theoretical Frameworks

The following is an abbreviated list of different theoretical approaches for working with children and adolescents that is available online from the American Academy of Child and Adolescent Psychiatry (AACAP, www.aacap.org). The school counselor should have knowledge of all of these approaches in order to give appropriate information to parents about the counseling process. Some of the approaches clearly are appropriate solely in the office of a psychotherapist or psychiatrist. Others are equally useful and appropriate for the school counselor to implement. The following therapies are listed on the AACAP (www.aacap.org) website in the Facts for Families section.

- Cognitive Behavior Therapy (CBT) helps improve a child's moods, anxiety, and behavior by examining confused or distorted patterns of thinking.
- Trauma-Focused Cognitive Behavioral Therapy (TF-CBT) is effective for children 3–17 years old with PTSD, depression, anxiety, behavior problems or other difficulties related to sexual abuse, intimate partner violence, multiple traumas, traumatic grief or disasters.
- Group Therapy is a form of psychotherapy where there are multiple patients led by one or more therapists. It uses the power of group dynamics and peer interactions to increase understanding of mental illness and/or improve social skills.
- Play Therapy involves the use of toys, blocks, dolls, puppets, drawings, and games to help the child recognize, identify, and verbalize feelings.
- Supportive Therapy gives children and teens support in their lives to cope with stress, identify helpful and unhelpful behaviors, and improve self-esteem.

(AACAP, 2019)

The authors of this chapter have also found the additional theoretical approaches here to be helpful.

- Behavioral Therapy is commonly used in school settings. The counselor helps the student identify goals he or she wants to meet but has difficulty because of intervening variables, such as the inability to stay focused in class or impulsively speaking out in class inappropriately. Positive reinforcement is usually a strategy the counselor uses to support and encourage meeting the goal.
- Crisis Intervention Therapy is useful in helping a student return to a safe, pre-crisis state following a critical incident. When the school counselor is dealing with a student who has a serious mental disorder, the crisis may be a sudden anxiety attack, auditory or visual hallucinations that cause a student to lose touch with reality, or a loud sound or other stimulus that triggers a post-traumatic stress episode. At times, crisis intervention is much more directive and closed ended than traditional counseling methods.

(Allen et al. 2002)

An important side note on crisis intervention training for school counselors deserves mentioning. A 2002 research study showed that school counselors wanted more training in how to deal with school crises involving students. The first need cited was to be better prepared for dealing with suicides of students and school staff, and second, safe intervention strategies for situations involving aggression and violence (Allen et al., 2002). Results of a more recent study in 2013 showed that 11 years later, the same need still exists. The authors of the later study suggested that counselor educators consider ways to infuse knowledge and skills regarding crises throughout the curriculum (Solmonson & Killam, 2013). The authors of this chapter were very fortunate to be provided annual, school district-funded training opportunities in crisis intervention as well as other important continuing education topics.

Professional Experiences

Importance of data: Most school counselors understand the value of data in developing programs and assessing an individual student's needs. The authors of this chapter had ready access to the following data sources that were helpful in assessing the needs of a particular student:

- disciplinary actions and reports;
- attendance and tardiness records;
- school clinic records on frequency of visits; and
- grade reports for both current and previous school years.

Assessing a student's social relationships and emotional demeanor requires observed data that are subjective in nature. Obtaining this data presents challenges in documenting changes in a student's social or emotional interactions. Other school personnel who know the student will be a resource to the counselor in assessing the following behavior-based social and emotional indicators:

- self-isolation from friends during noninstructional times including before the start of school, in the lunchroom, on the playground, riding the bus;
- less classroom participation, lack of interest shown in topics of study, avoiding study group and team assignments;
- looking distracted for long periods of time;
- showing little or no emotional affect; and
- hiding of strong emotions like crying or anger by spending lengthy periods of time in locations that are unsupervised like bathrooms, stairwells, empty classrooms, or offices.

Explore the bullying problem with the student: No one seemed to be aware of the bullying Marcus was experiencing. While the librarian was an excellent support person for Marcus, she did not observe him in the classroom, at lunch, or on the playground and did not have an opportunity to observe negative interactions with peers. Best practices in this kind of situation call for the school counselor to take the following steps.

- Step 1—If a parent, teacher, or Marcus himself had revealed what was happening much earlier, the counselor would have met with Marcus individually and let him experience the counselor's office as the safe place where he could come to ask for help.
- Step 2—The counselor would have conferenced with Marcus's mother and help him tell his narrative about the bullying. If this step had happened early in fourth grade, perhaps Marcus would not have written his letter to Susan at the end of fifth grade.
- Step 3—The counselor would invite Marcus to join a small group on social skills.
- Step 4—Marcus would be allowed to participate in the social skills group in consecutive school years to help him gain self-confidence and learn additional coping.

Small group counseling tips: Including a student who is socially or emotionally at risk in a small counselor-facilitated social skills group with his or her peers helps children see that they are not alone and that others understand how bullying makes a person feel. The counselor should choose group members and the activities for the group with an overall goal of fostering camaraderie, friendship building, and mutual respect as well as teaching developmentally appropriate social skills. Both authors of this chapter have found that small groups are a very successful and encouraging way to enhance students' social and emotional development.

Counselor Impact

Many school counselors feel like the job is never finished. Always moving on to the next task is the usual mindset for school staff during a busy school day. The basic system underlying a school's operational structure is a schedule—for classes, start and ending of the school day, bus runs, lunches, athletic activities, clubs, and more. However, critical incidents never occur on *schedule*, and they always are stressful for everyone involved, especially the school counselor, who is looked to as the one with crisis training. For the school counselor, a critical incident or crisis occurs with the same suddenness, high risk potential, and demand for on-the-spot decision making and action, just as it is for professional first responders like fire fighters and law enforcement officers.

What may differ for the school counselor is that he or she will likely return to the counseling office and engage with the next student, teacher, administrator, or parent who is waiting patiently—or not—for the counselor's return. A final step to resolving the immediacy of a critical event must always include an opportunity for debriefing with a professional colleague or supervisor. Not only does debriefing provide the counselor with a needed psychological relief valve, it is a valuable learning opportunity than can actually enhance the counselor's skills when called on again to intervene to help a student in crisis.

The fifth-grade counselor must have had some mixed feelings when she first learned of the seriousness of Marcus' emotional state. *How did I miss this? Why didn't someone let me know sooner? It is so late. School is almost out.* The counselor's concern for this student was genuine and sincere, but all of the pressing end-of-year responsibilities piled on the counselor's desk must have also come to mind. The good part about this counselor's critical incident is that the knowledge of resources and available options quickly came to mind, too. A strong plan involving a team of critical incident responders was implemented successfully. A piece of the plan that may have been left out was help with the responsibilities waiting on the desk. When a counselor is called on to perform at a high level on a critical task, the administration must provide a back-up plan for support with the customary tasks.

The eighth-grade counselor must have had her first moment of shock when the high school principal called for help in identifying the student whose notebook revealed a potentially dangerous situation. The second shock undoubtedly came when she saw the television report of the lockdown at the high school. She, too, must have questioned herself. *How did I miss this? Why didn't someone let me know sooner?* Perhaps she could have questioned Marcus' mother about the psychiatrist's agreement with stopping medication and treatment abruptly. A wise NAMI mantra when dealing with severe mental illness guilt-busting is, *You can't know what you don't know.* The counselor did not cause this new critical incident in Marcus's mental illness roller coaster journey.

Finally, what is the impact for the ninth-grade counselor? There are so many new students at the beginning of the school year, an entire class of faces and names that are basically all strangers to the counseling team. Which one is the neediest? What does he or she need the most:

- academic support?
- social and peer support?
- behavior management support?
- support for trauma or recently experienced loss?

A quick review of Marcus' incoming records showed no red flags. On paper, he did not look like the *neediest one*. This counselor probably asked the same questions. *How did I miss this?*

Why didn't someone let me know sooner? The wise NAMI mantra comes to mind again, *You can't know what you don't know.* The counselor did not cause this new critical incident in Marcus's mental illness, which was very much a roller coaster journey.

What does this point to? The four points listed here represent the big picture of school counseling best practices:

- the need for a counseling staff at all levels that meets the American School Counselor Association recommended ratio of one counselor to 250 students;
- resources for the development and implementation of a comprehensive school counseling program (CSCP) for all students;
- elimination of non-counseling duties for school counselors;
- opportunity and funding to stay abreast of new developments in best practices in responding to critical incidents and support for students with mental disorders; and
- an employment contract that allows sufficient planning time to create the program through a collegial team process.

Mental Health Considerations

***Onset and course of mental illness*:** There are no typical circumstances for onset, nor is there a typical mental illness journey. The primary clue for the school counselor is the presence of significant changes that have occurred in a student's social relationships, emotional demeanor, behavior, and academic performance. It is common for changes to occur in all four areas.

First episode psychosis (FEP) is a serious condition in which the early onset of a serious mental illness such as depression, bipolar disorder, or schizophrenia is complicated by co-occurring psychotic symptoms. Psychosis is characterized by loss of contact with reality and may involve severe disturbances of the brain in perception, cognition, behavior, and feelings. A student experiencing psychosis may have hallucination, delusions, disordered thoughts, and/or bizarre sensory perceptions. Psychosis does not occur in all cases of mental illness and it may be present in other brain illnesses or disorders. The presence of psychotic symptoms is a serious complication of mental illness. It is important that school counselors understand how to recognize signs of psychosis. The terrifying symptoms—hallucinations, delusions, disordered thinking, and distorted sensory perceptions—may be the first indication a child or adolescent has that something is not right. If psychosis is suspected, prompt medical attention is necessary (Mental Health Evaluation & Community Consultation Unit [MHECC], Ministry of Health, Province of British Columbia [MHECC], www.health.gov.bc.ca).

***Transforming individual student interventions into a school-wide program*:** Systemic changes are sometimes necessary to improve the school culture and bring commitment to creating a preventive mental health focus in a school. Protocols for incidents that represent high risk for either one student or the student body as a whole should be in place prior to the occurrence of a critical incident. The counselor, through the consultation and leadership role, is the key school professional skilled in developing the school's CSCP. Protocols, like those listed here, should be part of the school's guidance and counseling program. Written procedures that are consistently applied help ensure that counseling best practices will benefit all students. Even under huge time constraints at the end of the school year, the counselor in this case study pulled together a very successful intervention before Marcus entered middle school. Suggested protocols associated with responding to mental illness in students include:

- At-Risk Protocol for Early Warning Signs in Students (see Online Resources for Chapter 7)
- steps to follow when reporting suspected child abuse;
- procedures for obtaining authorization for release of information;

- collaborative agreements (i.e., with outside student support and mental health organizations);
- procedures for school staff completion of physician-requested rating scales; and
- informing parent/guardian of student's mental health crisis (i.e., to be used with incidents of suicidal ideation; self-harm; extreme anxiety/panic reaction; unexplained extreme sadness or elation not appropriate to circumstances; running away from campus when extremely distraught; unexplained bizarre behavior).

Teachers are the frontline intervention for the student who is at risk academically. Counselors are the frontline intervention for the student who is at risk socially, emotionally, and behaviorally. For the student who is experiencing early onset of mental illness, all four areas of development are impacted. Counselors and teachers form a powerful team when working together for the support of just one student or the whole school student body.

Ethical Considerations

While it is not the role of the school counselor to diagnose mental health disorders in students, they must be able to recognize and have training and practice in these disorders to assist students, families, and school personnel as they navigate the challenges of mental health issues. School counseling graduate programs that are accredited by the Council for Accreditation of Counseling and Related Educational Programs (2016) include training in mental health disorders, and school counselors have the knowledge and tools to assist students who are struggling with serious mental health issues. While school counselors approach all students with ethical behavior, the following ethical standards hold special meaning for counselors who work with students diagnosed with or presenting symptoms of serious mental health disorders.

A.1.c. Do not diagnose but remain acutely aware of how a student's diagnosis can potentially affect the student's academic success.

A.1.d. Acknowledge the vital role of parents/guardians and families.

A.1.g. Are knowledgeable of laws, regulations and policies affecting students and families and strive to protect and inform students and families regarding their rights.

A.1.i. Consider the involvement of support networks, wraparound services and educational teams needed to best serve students.

A.2.a Promote awareness of school counselors' ethical standards and legal mandates regarding confidentiality and the appropriate rationale and procedures for disclosure of student data and information to school staff.

A.2.f. Recognize their primary ethical obligation for confidentiality is to the students but balance that obligation with an understanding of parents'/guardians' legal and inherent rights to be the guiding voice in their children's lives. School counselors understand the need to balance students' ethical rights to make choices, their capacity to give consent or assent, and parental or familial legal rights and responsibilities to make decisions on their child's behalf.

A.3.b. Provide students with a comprehensive school counseling program that ensures equitable academic, career and social/emotional development opportunities for all students.

A.6.a. Collaborate with all relevant stakeholders, including students, educators and parents/guardians when student assistance is needed, including the identification of early warning signs of student distress.

A.6.c. Connect students with services provided through the local school district and community agencies and remain aware of state laws and local district policies related to students with special needs, including limits to confidentiality and notification to authorities as appropriate.

A.9.a. Inform parents/guardians and/or appropriate authorities when a student poses a serious and foreseeable risk of harm to self or others. When feasible, this is to be done after careful deliberation and consultation with other appropriate professionals. School counselors inform students of the school counselor's legal and ethical obligations to report the concern to the appropriate authorities unless it is appropriate to withhold this information to protect the student (e.g., student might run away if he/she knows parents are being called). The consequence of the risk of not giving parents/guardians a chance to intervene on behalf of their child is too great. Even if the danger appears relatively remote, parents should be notified.

A.9.b. Use risk assessments with caution. If risk assessments are used by the school counselor, an intervention plan should be developed and in place prior to this practice. When reporting risk-assessment results to parents, school counselors do not negate the risk of harm even if the assessment reveals a low risk as students may minimize risk to avoid further scrutiny and/or parental notification. School counselors report risk assessment results to parents to underscore the need to act on behalf of a child at risk; this is not intended to assure parents their child isn't at risk, which is something a school counselor cannot know with certainty.

A.10.g. Recognize the strengths of students with disabilities as well as their challenges and provide best practices and current research in supporting their academic, career and social/emotional needs.

Multicultural Considerations

Severe mental illness is no respecter of persons. It can affect anyone regardless of culture, race, ethnicity, faith, gender, or sexual orientation. The National Institute of Mental Health reports the same prevalence statistics for diverse populations as it does for the general population of adults in the United States. Studies regarding mental illness in diverse populations of children and adolescents are not readily available. However, since 50% of all cases of mental illness are diagnosed by the age of 14 and the illness will continue in most cases throughout one's lifetime, it is likely that the prevalence statistics are the same for diverse populations of children and teens as they are with diverse populations of adults compared to the general population of adults. One NIMH (www.nimh.nih.gov) study on youth depression found that highest percentage among 12- to 17-year-olds were youth who listed two or more races for their racial identity, 16.9%, compared to all 12- to 17-year-olds at 13.3%. However, the most troubling statistic for youth depression is 20% of females are diagnosed with depression compared to 6.8% of males.

The National Institute of Mental Health also reports that health utilization varies across racial/ ethnic groups. Among white, black, Hispanic, and other youth, Hispanics are the least likely of all groups to access specialty care. Approximately 7% of the families with a child with need claimed financial barriers as the reason for not getting any mental health care. One research study reviewed the literature to determine if there is an association between race or ethnicity and wait time in seeking treatment for mental illness with psychotic symptoms. The results found no difference in delay time for initial treatment by race or ethnicity (Myers, Sood, Fox, Wright, & Compton, 2019). Perhaps this points to stigma, shame, and lack of public awareness of the symptoms of mental illness as the critical factors that influence a family's decision to seek early treatment for their child or teen.

Case Discussion Questions

1. What early indicators were present that Marcus likely would need extra support in school? Did his school recognize his probable need for extra support? What did they offer? When did the support begin and when did it stop? Why do you think the school support stopped?

2. Do you think Marcus's story is an isolated situation? What do you think the demographic circumstances might be at Marcus's school?
3. Rate the implementation of the middle school plan to support Marcus. What would you change if you were his school counselor?
4. What do you foresee as the outcome for Marcus following the discovery of his notebook? Describe your prognosis for Marcus's mental health over the next six months, and explain your reasoning. What would you recommend for Marcus moving forward, since he had no treatment plan in place at the time of the critical incident?

Resources

Centers for Disease Control and Prevention: www.cdc.gov
National Alliance on Mental Illness: www.nami.org
National Center for Biotechnology Information: www.ncbi.nlm.nih.gov
National Institute of Mental Health: www.nimh.nih.gov

Anderson, K. K., Flora, N., Archie, S., Morgan, C., & McKenzie, K. (2014). Race, ethnicity, and the duration of untreated psychosis: A systematic review. *Social Psychiatry and Psychiatric Epidemiology, 49,* 1161–1174. doi:10.1007/s00127-013-0786-8
Basu, S., & Isaacs, A. N. (2019). Profile of transcultural patients in a regional child and adolescent mental health service in Gippsland, Australia: The need for a multidimensional understanding of the complexities. *The International Journal of Social Psychiatry, 65,* 217–224. doi:10.1177/0020764019835264

References

Allen, M., Burt, K., Bryan, E., Carter, D., Orsi, R., & Durkan, L. (2002). School counselors' preparation for and participation in crisis intervention. *Professional School Counseling, 6,* 96–102.
American Academy of Child and Adolescent Psychiatry. Psychotherapy for Children and Adolescents: Different Types. (2019). {See Facts for Families, No. 86}. Retrieved from www.aacap.org/AACAP/Families_and_Youth/Facts_for_Families/FFF-Guide/Psychotherapies-For-Children-And-Adolescents-086.aspx
American School Counselor Association. (2016). *Ethical standards for school counselors.* Alexandria, VA: American School Counselor Association.
DeVenter, M., Demyttenaere, K., & Bruffaerts, R. (2013). The relationship between adverse childhood experiences and mental health in adulthood, a systemic literature review. [Article in Dutch]. *Tijdschr Psychiatry, 55*(4), 259–268.
McFarlane, W., Cook, W., Downing, D., Verdi, M., Woodberry, K., & Ruff, A. (2010). Portland identification and early referral: A community-based system for identifying and treating youths at high risk of psychosis. *Psychiatric Services, 61,* 512–515. doi:10.1176/appi.ps.61.5.512
Mental Health Evaluation & Community Consultation Unit (MHECC). Early Identification of Psychosis, A Primer. (2000). *Ministry of Health, Province of British Columbia.* Retrieved from www.health.gov.bc.ca/library/publications/year/misc/Psychosis_Identification.pdf
Myers, N., Sood, A., Fox, K. E., Wright, G., & Compton, M. T. (2019). Decision making about pathways through care for racially and ethnically diverse young adults with early psychosis. *Psychiatric Services, 70,* 184–190. doi.org/10.1176/appi.ps.201700459
Solmonson, L. L., & Killam, W. (2013). A national study on crisis intervention: Are school counselors prepares to respond? Article 68. *VISTAS Online.* ACA Professional Information/Library. Retrieved from www.counseling.org/library

Reflections on Serious Mental Illness in Students

Write down your reflections about:

- the onset of childhood depression;
- the secretiveness about bullying and the student's powerful emotions of shame, hate and revenge;
- the apparent unawareness of a crisis brewing in elementary and high school; and
- emergence of symptoms as they relate to the developmental stages of children and adolescents.

8   Suicidal Ideations

Le'Ann Solmonson

Background

The mental health of teens has shown a dramatic and concerning decline since the late 2000s. During that period, there has been more than a 60% increase in the rates of reported depression among students between 14 and 17 years of age. There have also been significant increases of depression in youth ages 12–13 and young adults 18–21 (Twenge, Cooper, Joiner, Duffy, & Binau, 2019). During the same period, there was a significant increase in the number of adolescents and young adults reporting serious psychological distress, with rates doubling in some age groups. Serious psychological distress would include suicidal ideation, suicide plan, suicide attempt, and death by suicide. Between 2009 and 2017, the suicide rates for adolescents increased from 12.8 per 100,000 to 17.53 (Centers for Disease Control and Prevention, 2017). Suicide is the second leading cause of death for youth ages 12–18. These statistics are alarming and point to the need for a school counselor to have a clearly articulated plan of action to respond to a student who expresses suicidal ideation.

Students often spend more time at school than they do with their family. The daily interactions with peers, teachers, and school staff provide the opportunity to observe changes in mood and behavior. When all individuals in the school are aware of how to respond appropriately to statements or behaviors that may be indicative of psychological distress, early intervention is more likely to occur. Suicide prevention activities are often included in a comprehensive school counseling program (CSCP). Those activities should provide students, teachers, and staff members with the basic knowledge to assist the troubled student in getting the necessary professional assistance to ensure their safety. Students should be trained to understand this is not a problem that is kept confidential, and adults must be involved. Adults should be trained to involve the school counselor and not take any statement or indications of self-harm behaviors lightly. All comments, written communication, or concerning behavior should be thoroughly assessed in order to determine the level of risk. The steps for responding to a potential suicidal student should be detailed as a part of the campus crisis plan to provide for a consistent response to all students who may be suicidal. The following case study details the steps taken by a school counselor when a student expressed suicidal ideation.

Description of Case

Lori West was a third-year counselor serving in a rural school district with a student enrollment of about 1,000 students. Ms. West was assigned to the middle and high school campuses. The elementary campus counselor had worked for the district for over 20 years and had previously served all campuses. When Ms. West was hired, the older counselor chose to move to the elementary campus. Ms. West had been well trained in her graduate program and was immediately aware of some major changes that needed to occur to bring the school counselor program up to current standards. One of her major concerns was the absence of a crisis response plan. Ms. West made the development of the plan a priority during her second year in the district. Included in the plan was a suicide assessment protocol that provided quantitative data used to assess the level of risk, a well-articulated response based upon the level of risk, referral information for further evaluation, and paperwork to document the counseling response. The plan was very useful in the fall of the following year when she dealt with her first student expressing suicidal ideation.

Sara was a quiet 10th-grader who was an average student. The group of students that she socialized with were well known for engaging in at-risk behaviors. It was common knowledge that they regularly drank alcohol and smoked marijuana. However, they never brought these behaviors into the school setting, and they were all demonstrating acceptable levels of academic achievement. Sara's parents had divorced when she was in eighth grade after her mother had an extramarital affair. Being a part of a small community, the information about the affair and divorce was widely spread. The family had been active in a local church, and Sara had been involved in youth activities. Her mother was shunned by the church. Sara was embarrassed by her mother's behavior and no longer felt comfortable attending the church. She also quit playing volleyball and basketball because the games were often community events. It was at that time that her friendships changed, and she started hanging around the at-risk group of students. Her father had been very angry in the beginning of the couple's problems but had become depressed and withdrawn after the divorce was finalized. Sara felt distant from both of her parents, and her older siblings were no longer living in the home. She lived with her mother, and they became more like roommates than mother and daughter.

Sara's English teacher had given the class an assignment to write a poem. The students were to work in peer groups to provide feedback on each other's poems. After the class, the student Sara had paired with approached the teacher and expressed concern for the content of Sara's poem. She said Sara's writing was very dark and suggested she wanted to die. The teacher praised the student for alerting her and went to find Sara in her next class. She asked to see the poem and understood why the other student had been concerned. She told Sara she was concerned about her. She asked Sara if the poem was expressing how she was currently feeling. Sara was hesitant to respond initially, but the tears quickly began to flow as Sara told the teacher she was "in a bad place."

The teacher accompanied Sara to Ms. West's office, where she explained the situation and had Ms. West read the poem. Ms. West asked Sara to explain what she meant by being in a bad place. Sara talked about being sad and depressed, but did not specifically state any suicidal ideation. Ms. West asked Sara if she was having thoughts about not wanting to be here anymore. Sara looked at her lap and nodded her head. Ms. West asked her if she had thought about how she might end her life. Sara again nodded. Ms. West was able to get Sara to share that she had thought about taking a "bunch of pills." She said her mother had been prescribed anxiety medication and sleeping pills after the divorce. Sara knew where her mother kept them and planned to take them over the weekend when her mother was at work.

Ms. West had enough information to know that she needed to enact the crisis plan. She completed the suicide assessment that indicated Sara was at a high risk of self-harm. She explained to Sara she would need to contact her mother and get her involved. Her mom did not initially take the concerns seriously enough. She indicated she would talk to Sara when she got home from work. Ms. West explained to her again that Sara was in the high-risk category, and she asked the mom to come to the school to discuss options for getting Sara some help. Mom was again reluctant and stated she had concerns about leaving work. Ms. West told the mother that she was not comfortable with Sara going home alone. She explained that she had a legal and ethical obligation to ensure Sara's safety. If the mother was unable to come to the school, she would contact the local mental health authority to come to the school to do a more comprehensive assessment of Sara. The mother agreed to come to the school.

When the mother arrived, she could see how upset Sara was, and she became more concerned for her. Ms. West shared the assessment results with her and went over a list of referral options that were available in the community including the local mental health authority and a private hospital that offered free assessments. Ms. West had completed the paperwork that provided the contact information for each of the options that were available. The mother selected the local mental health authority and called from the counseling office to arrange to bring Sara in immediately. Sara indicated she was cooperative with the plan and agreed she would be open and honest about how she was feeling. Ms. West added the mother's plan to her paperwork and had the mother sign it. She also provided the mother with a copy of her assessment and the plan to take with her to the appointment. She asked the mother to call her after the assessment and update her.

The mother called later that day to tell Ms. West that Sara was going to be admitted to the hospital and to thank her for her help. Ms. West asked the mother to keep her up to date on Sara's progress. She explained the school protocol was for the student and parent to meet with her when Sara was discharged and ready to return to school so they could discuss how the school could support Sara while she was at school. Ms. West asked for permission to share a minimal amount of information with Sara's teachers so they could also be supportive on her return. The mother agreed that the teachers should know so they could assist in monitoring Sara for any concerning behavior.

Sara returned to school two weeks later and reported she was feeling better. She no longer had thoughts of harming herself and was no longer feeling hopeless. While in the hospital, Sara's parents had both participated in family therapy sessions to address ways they could be more engaged with Sara and support her. Ms. West asked Sara if she was interested in participating in group counseling with other students who had experienced similar issues. Sara agreed that would be helpful. They also agreed to daily check-ins with Ms. West for the next week to ensure Sara was maintaining the progress she had made. Sara assured Ms. West she would self-report any negative or distressing thoughts she was having. Sara's mother signed a release of information for Ms. West and the outside counselor Sara was working with to talk with one another about Sara's progress in counseling and at school.

Strategies for Consideration

The following sections provide school counselors with tools they can use to respond to serious threats that students might make regarding suicide ideation or intent. These critical and common sense strategies should mark the foundation of every school counselor's protocol for dealing with suicidal students.

Theoretical Frameworks

While school counselors usually operate through approaches based on theory, suicidal crisis requires a strategic and immediate response to ensure the student's safety. A suicide crisis intervention model consists of a multi-step plan to assess the level of risk and determine the appropriate level of intervention. The model should include specific, actionable steps that guide the school counselor's response. The model should include communication with the parents and providing appropriate resources to assist the family through the crisis. A clearly articulated plan of response assists the counselor through a difficult process and ensures nothing is overlooked. A link to The American Foundation for Suicide Prevention model policy and plan is provided in the online component of Chapter 8.

Professional Experiences

The author has 14 years of school counseling experience and has dealt with suicidal ideation in students as young as 8 years old through seniors in high school. While suicidal students are becoming more common in schools, it is not a regular part of the school counselor's routine. Because assessments like this are not conducted on a regular basis, it is necessary to have a protocol to follow to ensure a thorough response is provided. The first few times a counselor has to enact a suicide response can be anxiety provoking. It brings about an awareness of the awesome responsibility a school counselor has for ensuring a student's safety. This is not an area in which you want to make a mistake. The best approach is to err on the side of caution when determining how to intervene. The following are suggestions to remember when dealing with a suicidal student.

1. Educate yourself on signs and symptoms of suicidal ideation and appropriate interventions.
2. Be aware of your school's policies and procedures related to suicide response. If there is not a well-developed plan, develop your own and advocate for a consistent district response. The plan should include an assessment instrument and consistent paperwork to be completed with sections for signature indicating being informed and offered resources.
3. Develop a list of resources and outside referrals to provide to parents.
4. Be proactive by educating staff and students on what to do if they are concerned a student may be suicidal.
5. Always take reports of suicidal ideation seriously. Do not minimize or downplay comments, behaviors, or student writings that may indicate thoughts of suicide. You never have to make a decision about the validity of the threat; you only should address it regardless.
6. Any time you have a discussion with a student about suicide, contact the parents. This is necessary even if the student denies what has been reported. Explain the report you received to the parent and the results of your conversation with the parents. If you do not believe there is a risk, encourage the parent to be observant for any behavioral changes that may occur. Individuals who are suicidal do not always admit it when asked. Several years ago, there was a news report about a counselor who talked to a middle school student who reported being suicidal. The counselor did not contact the parent, and the student died by suicide a few days later. Needless to say, there were liability issues that resulted from the neglect, as well as the emotional impact that the incident would have on a school counselor.
7. Don't be afraid to speak frankly and ask direct questions during the assessment. If a student is not suicidal, asking questions does not give the student the idea of harming himself or herself.
8. If you have not had training on conducting a suicide assessment, attend a continuing education session or training to assist in developing the necessary knowledge and skills.
9. Never leave a student who has expressed thoughts of suicide alone. If you need to leave the room to make a phone call or consult with someone, have another adult sit with the student while you are gone.
10. There are times in which a student uses suicidal comments as a way to manipulate the situation or to express intense emotions. An angry or upset student may say, "I want to kill myself" as a way to avoid doing work, having a consequence, or communicating strong feelings. This author worked on a campus with a behavior unit. If a certain student was in a situation of having to do something he didn't want to do, he would say "I want to die" or "I am going to kill myself." The first few times it happened, I was summoned to assess him. I went through the full assessment on three separate occasions including contacting his parent. I quickly saw the pattern of using the words as an avoidance or delay tactic. He even said to me on one occasion that he did not mean it. He was just mad and did not want to have to do his time out. In consultation with the teachers in the room and his parents, we agreed I would no longer intervene immediately. He would get the consequence or have to complete whatever he was avoiding. When the consequence was over or he was done, the teacher would ask if he still felt like hurting himself. He always said he no longer wanted to hurt himself. During the consequence, he was being monitored closely for safety. The

teacher and I also worked with him on how to express his feelings in a more appropriate manner. Be very careful in using this approach. You want to be assured it is appropriate for the situation.

Counselor Impact

Dealing with a suicidal student can be an intensely stressful situation, and it never happens at a convenient time. A school counselor must learn to be flexible and respond appropriately despite what is on your schedule. It is common to have concerns about whether you are overreacting or making a mistake. If a mistake is made, it is better to overreact than to underreact. In this case study, the student was cooperative, and the intervention was successful. Schools are not always aware of suicidal thoughts or behaviors on the part of students. This author has known two students who died by suicide. In both cases, peers were aware of troubling behavior but did not report them to an adult. In reviewing both cases, we found we had done all of the prevention activities and training for teachers. None of the adults who worked with the students saw any signs of risk. While we mentally recognized we had not overlooked anything, there were still emotional responses and questions about what we could have done differently.

Mental Health Implications

As stated at the beginning of the chapter, the rates of depression and psychological distress are increasing at a dramatic rate for adolescents. A school counselor must be knowledgeable about the signs and symptoms of distress and train school staff also to recognize them. Preventative activities that promote coping skills and resilience can serve as protective factors for students. The current trends suggest adolescents and young adults are at the greatest risk of developing mood disorders and suicide-related distress. The school counselor must be equipped to respond to these trends. Excellent training standards in school counseling programs ensures that graduates are prepared to recognize signs of mental health issues and respond appropriately.

Ethical Considerations

School counselors make many decisions each day that involve student success, safety, and well-being. The ASCA (2016) standards of behavior for school counselors provide guidance to assist them in making decisions that are ethical and appropriate for all students.

> A.1.b. Aim to provide counseling to students in brief context and support students and families/guardians in obtaining outside services if the student needs long-term clinical counseling.
>
> A.1.h. Provide effective, responsive interventions to address student needs.

In this case, the counselor provided an appropriate crisis response and made referrals to outside services to assist in managing the crisis.

A.9. Serious and Foreseeable Harm to Self and Others

School Counselors

> a. Inform parents/guardians and/or appropriate authorities when a student poses a serious and foreseeable risk of harm to self or others. When feasible, this is to be done after careful deliberation and consultation with other appropriate professionals. School counselors

inform students of the school counselor's legal and ethical obligations to report the concern to the appropriate authorities unless it is appropriate to withhold this information to protect the student (e.g. student might run away if he/she knows parents are being called). The consequence of the risk of not giving parents/guardians a chance to intervene on behalf of their child is too great. Even if the danger appears relatively remote, parents should be notified.

b. Use risk assessments with caution. If risk assessments are used by the school counselor, an intervention plan should be developed and in place prior to this practice. When reporting risk-assessment results to parents, school counselors do not negate the risk of harm even if the assessment reveals a low risk as students may minimize risk to avoid further scrutiny and/or parental notification. School counselors report risk assessment results to parents to underscore the need to act on behalf of a child at risk; this is not intended to assure parents their child isn't at risk, which is something a school counselor cannot know with certainty.

c. Do not release a student who is a danger to self or others until the student has proper and necessary support. If parents will not provide proper support, the school counselor takes necessary steps to underscore to parents/guardians the necessity to seek help and at times may include a report to child protective services.

This section of the code of ethics addresses informing parents and/or appropriate authorities when a student poses a risk of harm to self or others. It also addresses using risk assessments and having an intervention plan in place. Ms. West completed the risk assessment and utilized the intervention plan. She informed the parent of the results of the assessment and the needed interventions. This section also states a student who is at risk of harm to self or others is not released until proper and necessary support is in place. Ms. West was insistent that the parent come to the school and informed her she would involve the authorities if the mother did not make herself available.

Multicultural Considerations

Suicidal behaviors, beliefs, and attitudes vary across cultures. For adolescents, white students have higher suicide rates than other racial or ethnic groups. Suicide rates are relatively low for children ages 5–12, but new research (Bridge et al., 2018) suggests the suicide rates are double for black children in this age range. Typically, males are at higher risk than females. Native American males are at the highest risk, and African American females are the lowest risk population. There are also differences in help seeking based upon cultural beliefs. The literature on culturally sensitive approaches to suicide intervention is minimal, with little to no published studies of effective suicide prevention programs based on race or ethnicity.

Discussion Questions

1. What type of training have you received related to suicide prevention or intervention?
2. Do you have any experience in dealing with a suicidal individual?
3. There is ongoing dialogue around whether or not to use direct language such as, "Do you have plans to kill yourself"? What is the debate around use of direct language as opposed to how it was addressed in the case study? What approach would you take?
4. What would be your greatest fear related to suicide intervention?
5. From the case study, what evidence is there of a well-planned approach to suicide prevention and intervention?
6. Do you think there would have been significant differences to this case if Sara had attended a large urban or suburban high school? Why or why not?

Resources

American Foundation for Suicide Prevention. A Model Policy on Suicide Prevention:

https://afsp.donordrive.com/index.cfm?fuseaction=cms.page&id=1200&eventID=1

Confident Counselors. Suicide Prevention Best Practices:

https://confidentcounselors.com/2017/04/03/suicide-prevention-best-practices/

National Suicide Prevention Lifeline:

https://suicidepreventionlifeline.org/

References

American School Counselor Association. (2016). *Ethical standards for school counselors*. Alexandria, VA: Author.

Bridge, J. A., Horowitz, L. M., Fontella, C. A., Sheftall, A. H., Greenhouse, J., Kelleher, K. J., & Campo, J. V. (2018). Age-related racial disparity in suicide rates among US youths from 2001 through 2017. *JAMA Pediatrics, 172*(7), 697–699. doi:10.1001/jamapediatrics.2018.0399

Centers for Disease Control and Prevention. (2017). *Data and statistics fatal injury report for 2017*. Retrieved from www.cdc.gov/injury/wisqars/fatal.html

Twenge, J. M., Cooper, A. B., Joiner, T. E., Duffy, M. E., & Binau, S. G. (2019). Age, period, and cohort trends in mood disorder indicator and suicide-related outcomes in a nationally representative database, 2005–2017. *Journal of Abnormal Psychology, 128*(3), 185–199. doi:10.1037/abm0000410

Reflections: In the space provided, write your notes and reflections regarding this case study.

9   Under the Influence of an Illegal Substance

Leigh Falls Holman and Kristi L. Nobbman

Background

Experimenting with risky behaviors is part of development through adolescence. However, when experimentation is with drugs and alcohol, there is a possibility of lifelong habits or addiction. Historically, marijuana was considered the *gateway drug* for youth. The reality is that early alcohol consumption is the greatest predictor of drug and alcohol use in college and beyond. Alcohol use prior to age 15 is linked to binge drinking, consuming four or more drinks in two hours, and positive perceptions of alcohol for both males and females (LaBrie et al., 2008). Likewise, alcohol use prior to age 15 is linked to early use of other drugs as well (LaBrie et al., 2008). According to the Substance Abuse and Mental Health Services Administration (SAMHSA), by age 15 roughly 33% of youth have had at least one drink. This percentage rises to 60% of youth who have had at least one drink by the age of 18.

According to Monitoring the Future (2015), alcohol and cigarette use has declined in students over the past ten years, while illicit drug use has slightly increased. In 2015, 35.3% of 12th-graders, 21.5% of tenth-graders, and 9.7% of eighth-graders reported alcohol use in the past month. The percentages are shockingly similar for illicit drug use. Nearly 24% of 12th-graders, 16.5% of tenth-graders, and 8.1% of eighth-graders reported using illicit drugs in the past month. Even if students are not consuming alcohol or drugs, they report that it is available. Thirty-seven percent of eighth-graders think it is fairly or very easy to have access to marijuana, and 53.6% think it is fairly or very easy to have access to alcohol.

School and district policies are typically in place regarding alcohol, tobacco, and other drugs and their use, manufacture, possession, and distribution, including the possession of paraphernalia. However, for new schools and for revisions on existing policies, given that substance abuse is a mental health issue, school counselors should be involved in creating school and district policies on use of illegal substances at school. The most important part of any school substance abuse policy is that it should communicate a clear *no use* (abstinence) message, and this message needs to be shared with parents as well. Prevention literature indicates that students who have more lenient attitudes toward substance use or have received the message that experimentation is normal are more likely to use substances. If other risk factors are present, these students might be at higher risk for abusing substances. Another consideration is that policies should focus on prevention and are developmentally appropriate for the students in each school level. Prevention programs can include training for teachers and administrators, parent workshops, and student interventions (United Educators Insurance, 2014).

Policies should consider self-referral procedures and legal constraints in the state in which the school operates (Gaustad, 1993). It should be clear exactly the times and places the policy and procedures will be in effect. In other words, is an off-campus school dance at night or a football game at an opposing team's school covered by the policy? School counselors can be particularly helpful in identifying resources and procedures for helping students reflect on and change destructive behaviors rather than solely focusing the policies on punishment as a way to shape behavior. School counselors are in a unique position in which they are often involved with prevention and intervention for drug and alcohol use in school. It is important to be able to identify emotional, behavioral, and academic signs of alcohol and/or drug use in students. While these risk factors may be signs of other issues, the NIH (National Institute of Health) (2016) noted the following risk factors for drug and alcohol use in youth:

- Acting withdrawn
- Frequently tired or depressed, or hostile
- Change in peer group
- Carelessness with grooming
- Decline in academic performance
- Missing classes or skipping school
- Loss of interest in favorite activities
- Trouble in school or with the law
- Changes in eating or sleeping habits
- Deteriorating relationships with family members and friends

Description of the Case

Ms. Hamilton is a middle school counselor at an urban school *zoned to be private*. There are a number of prominent families whose children go to the school, and the pressures for their children to succeed is very high. Many students on campus struggle with anxiety, depression, and substance use issues. In Ms. Hamilton's experience, it is very difficult for her students' parents to accept that their children are less than perfect, and they often deny there are mental health issues if any at all are brought to their attention. For this reason, dealing with a student who comes to school under the influence is a challenging experience.

During the spring semester, shortly after spring break, one of Ms. Hamilton's female students, Kirsten, arrives at school visibly intoxicated. She is slurring her words, cannot walk in a straight line, and is literally tripping over her own feet. A teacher calls the counselor from the hall as she observes Kirsten entering the school and immediately goes to intervene. Kirsten is walking with two longtime friends, Sammy and Jane, who both look visibly upset and seem to be nonverbally asking the counselor for help. Ms. Hamilton begins by approaching in a casual manner, greeting Kirsten as she would greet any student she sees in the morning. She answered back, "Hey Miss H, what's poppin'?" This is unusual for Kirsten, as she is generally very proper in the way she speaks to adults. The school counselor is quite concerned and asks Kirsten if she can help her out with something in the counseling office. Ms. Hamilton knows that Kirsten is great at art, so the counselor tells her that she needs help with a bulletin board. Kirsten agrees and follows the counselor to her office. Ms. Hamilton stays close to Kirsten in case she stumbles and begins to fall.

Historically, Kirsten has been a good student, easily making A's in honors level classes. She has even begun going to the high school to take a freshman biology class during her eighth-grade year. While there she met a boy, Mark, and rumor has it that they have been dating. Ms. Hamilton remembers Mark when he was at the middle school. He is 17 now and has been in trouble a great deal. His dad runs an oil company, and his parents often leave him and his brother at home for as much as a week at a time, alone. Rumors around school are that they often throw big parties with alcohol and drugs. A few years ago when Mark was in eighth-grade, he got into a physical fight with another boy. When the counselor called to speak with the students' parents, his mother told the counselor to handle it because she was busy, and added, "What do we pay you for anyway?" The counselor's experience of Mark's family was quite different from Kirsten's. The counselor knows that Kirsten's father is a prominent psychiatrist and addictionologist at a high-end inpatient facility that treats many celebrities. Kirsten's mom does not work, but she is very involved in the charity events that are part of high society in the city. To look at them, the family appears as though they have walked off the pages of *Town and Country* magazine. Ms. Hamilton has seen pictures in the society magazine of Kirsten's and Mark's parents at charity events together, so she assumes they are friends.

As the counselor and Kirsten arrive at the counselor's office, the school's resource officer shows up at the door because he has been alerted to Kirsten's behavior. He wants to conduct a breathalyzer on her to see if she has been drinking. Kirsten is a minor, and her parents are not present, so Ms. Hamilton reminds the resource officer that he needs to contact her parents if he wants to conduct such a test. The conversation with the officer is quick, and Kirsten uncharacteristically becomes very loud and verbally abusive to the officer. The counselor wants to de-escalate the situation before trying to assess and deal with the apparent substance use. She knows that the principal has asked the resource officer to intervene only if the counselor is unable to de-escalate a situation and requests help. Ms. Hamilton suggests to the officer that he consult with Dr. Smith, the building principal, about proper protocol. Additionally, Ms. Hamilton tells the officer she will stay with Kirsten in the office until he returns. He agrees and leaves. Kirsten, however, remains agitated, pacing about the office and cussing about the officer, stating that her parents "pay his salary" so "we will see who ends up in handcuffs." This language does not sound like Kirsten's parents as much as Mark's, and the counselor suspected that his influence has something to do with this situation.

Strategies for Consideration

Most school counselors in middle and high schools will deal with students who experiment with drugs or alcohol. Some students will already have a substance use disorder. The following sections provide tools and strategies for working with students who have these types of problems.

Theoretical Frameworks

Kirsten's academic functioning and social support systems are strengths, and historically she has not had these issues, so Ms. Hamilton utilizes the equilibrium model and conceptualizes the situation as Kirsten using substances because she is in a state of psychological disequilibrium. Therefore, the school counselor's focus is on stabilizing the situation and getting help for her as soon as possible. She utilizes the seven tasks of the hybrid model of crisis de-escalation to structure her interaction with Kirsten (James & Gilliland, 2017). These include:

Task 1: Engaging the student by initiating contact
Task 2: Problem exploration: defining the crisis
Task 3: Providing support and safety
Task 4: Examining alternatives
Task 5: Planning in order to reestablish control
Task 6: Obtaining commitment
Task 7: Follow-up

During this time, the counselor continually assesses Kirsten's affect, behavior, and cognition (ABCs) using the Triage Assessment Form (TAF) to inform the counselor's interactions with the student. The TAF provides guidance for counselors on how to evaluate the student's affect (A), behavior (B), and cognition (C). The seven tasks of the hybrid model are: to engage the client; to explore the situation; to provide support; to examine alternatives; to plan in order to establish control; to obtain a commitment; and to follow up.

Once the situation is stable, motivational interviewing (MI) (Rollnick & Miller, 1995), a trans-theoretical model, can be used in the counselor's future work with Kirsten. Motivational interviewing was developed by analyzing effective interventions with people struggling with addictive behaviors. Therefore, it is an ideal set of skills to incorporate when working with someone who appears to be abusing substances. There are four principles of MI. The first is to use open-ended questions (O), reflections (R), affirmations (A), and summarization (S) to express empathy. The second principle is developing discrepancy between goals (for Kirsten probably to avoid expulsion and not have a negative incident on her record moving forward) or values (love and respect for parents) and her current behavior (getting in a verbal altercation with the resource officer while intoxicated). Third is to roll with the resistance and avoid arguing with Kirsten about what she should do or how she should act. Finally, it is important for the counselor to build on Kirsten's strengths and support her self-efficacy around her ability to handle this situation and move forward in a positive manner.

Professional Experiences

The counselor used the seven tasks of the hybrid model of crisis de-escalation to structure her interaction with Kirsten. The first task in the model is to engage the student, which the counselor did initially by approaching Kirsten in a nonthreatening manner. The counselor further engaged Kirsten by having the officer, whom she perceived as threatening, leave the counseling office, which immediately de-escalated Kirsten's visible agitation. Task two is to explore the situation at hand and, as the conversation unfolds, the counselor engaged in tasks three (providing support) and four (examining alternatives). As these tasks unfold, the counselor utilizes continuous assessment guided by the TAF to evaluate Kirsten's ABCs.

Kirsten's affect is labile. She is giggly and friendly when she interacts with someone she perceives to be nonthreatening (her friends, the counselor); however, she quickly becomes agitated when she perceives a threat (officer) in her environment. This indicates a moderate to marked level of impairment. Kirsten's previous behavior, academic performance, and ability to sustain healthy relationships with family and friends is evident from the counselor's three years knowing the student. However, she recently developed a romantic relationship with a much older boy (four years older) whom she is at risk of having a sexual relationship with, a student who is known to throw wild parties at his house involving alcohol, drugs, and sex and who has poor parental supervision. Kirsten appears to be visibly intoxicated, slurs her words, and cannot walk without bumping into walls and tripping over her own feet. Based on her friends' reactions, the counselor drew the conclusion that this was unusual and concerning behavior for Kirsten. Kirsten also became verbally abusive with the school resource officer, which could result in legal charges against her. Therefore, her behavior indicates noticeable impairment, bordering on severe impairment, according to the TAF.

In this situation, the counselor utilized MI techniques to facilitate her use of the hybrid model of crisis de-escalation, which appeared to be successful. Kirsten was able to calm down and interact with the counselor. The counselor's primary aim was to de-escalate Kirsten's behavior and keep her in a safe, supervised environment until her father could pick her up. Given his profession, he was the most appropriate person to contact in this situation. Due to the nature of the parents' socioeconomic status (SES) and associated expectations of the school personnel regarding confidentiality of sensitive situations, it was most appropriate to have the school's principal contact Kirsten's father. By sending the school resource officer to the principal to inquire about intervening with the breathalyzer, the principal was notified of the situation and called the counselor to her office. The counselor answered and stated that she had Kirsten out of class working on a bulletin board. By doing this, Kirsten was not alerted to the principal's knowledge of her intoxication, so she did not perceive a threat and did not escalate at that time. After being notified,

Kirsten's father came to the counselor's office to retrieve Kirsten and get the help she needed. Given his work with addictions, he was able to handle the situation in a manner that did not escalate Kirsten, although he appeared visibly saddened by seeing his daughter in such a state.

Later in the week, the counselor called Kirsten's father to check up on the family. Her dad reported that Kirsten had apparently begun drinking and using cocaine with her new boyfriend and that they had begun a sexual relationship. The morning of the incident at school, Mark had broken up with her, which led her to binge drink alcohol she found in the house. She was at a residential treatment center (RTC) for teens. The counselor talked to her father about options for continuing her education, particularly her advanced coursework while she was at the RTC. He agreed to allow the counselor to send information about correspondence coursework in biology that was available through a state college's accredited online high school. She also reminded Kirsten's father that they had additional supports at the high school that could be arranged for her when she was ready to return.

Counselor Impact

In this situation, the counselor may experience additional stress for several reasons. The school environment of wealthy high-achieving families placed a great deal of importance on the appearance of perfection. The counselor in this situation had previous experiences in which she was targeted/blamed by parents when she notified them of problematic behavior or academic challenges their children exhibited. In this case, it would be normal to experience additional worry about how the student's parents would react to being notified about her behavior. Negative parent interactions in this school commonly resulted in threats against the school personnel's (teacher, counselor, and principal) job security or threats of filing a lawsuit, and these families had the connections and resources to follow through on such threats. It was important that the teacher, counselor, and principal all worked together to handle a situation that, although uncommon for Kirsten, was not uncommon at the school. They had planned how to handle such situations, and each followed through with her part in the plan.

Another concern for the counselor in this situation was her awareness of her potential for countertransference in her reaction to Kirsten's situation. Because of Kirsten's relationship with Mark and the manner in which Mark's mother treated the counselor years before, Ms. Hamilton had to monitor carefully her feelings and reactions in this situation. All counselors need to be aware of potential countertransference and seek counseling or supervision when necessary. She also had great concern for the student. Kirsten had been a strong student and had many strengths to build on. The counselor wanted to ensure that her parents understood the options for continuing her advanced placement in biology, even while in the RTC, if they wanted to pursue that option. This would result in her being on track academically with her original plans.

Although not a concern for this situation, if a counselor has her own addiction issues, this is another potential challenge in a scenario like this one. Counselors in recovery may have dual relationships with an addiction specialist, like Kirsten's father. Additionally, being in recovery may affect the counselor's assessment and/or suggested interventions. If this were the case, the counselor would need a plan to get more support when working with a case like this one. It is foreseeable that a middle or high school counselor will deal with students who have substance use issues, which the counselor needs to address. So maintaining clear boundaries between the counselor's recovery and the student's is crucial for ethical practice.

Mental Health Implications Symptoms

The primary mental health concern is a potential substance use disorder (SUDs). Although it is most likely that Kirsten is intoxicated, she first needs a medical exam to determine if she has substances in her system and what they are. There are other medical issues that can mimic intoxication, and only a medical facility can determine if there are other issues affecting Kirsten's presentation. If she is intoxicated, then it is important to remember that experimentation with substance use is developmentally normal for a teenager, so this could be an isolated incident of substance use, which needs early intervention to prevent escalation into a SUD. However, Kirsten has significant exposure to information about the risks of substance use, due to her father's profession, so the counselor might expect that her parents have actively engaged her in conversation about substance use and its risks.

Secondarily, counselors should be aware that underlying anxiety, depression, or trauma can be motivating factors for substance use. The school where this counselor works is populated with very successful students who live with high profile, often wealthy, parents. Their parents often have very high, maybe even unreasonably high, expectations of their children's academic or athletic abilities. When children feel the pressure to be the best or cannot meet this expectation, then it is normal that they may demonstrate signs of anxiety or depression.

Ethical Considerations

In addition to the following ASCA (2016) standards, school counselors also need to consult their school/district policies on drug and alcohol use at school.

> A.1.c Do not diagnose but remain acutely aware of how a student's diagnosis can potentially affect the student's academic success.

School counselors do not diagnose mental health problems; however, mental health challenges, such as substance use and potentially underlying depression or anxiety, can negatively impact the student's academic success. School counselors need to be aware of how these mental health issues manifest in school settings and the prevalence of mental health disorders and have resources to provide students and parents so they can get mental health treatment in the community.

> A.9. a. Inform parents/guardians and/or appropriate authorities when a student poses a serious and foreseeable risk of harm to self or others. When feasible, this is to be done after careful deliberation and consultation with other appropriate professionals. School counselors inform students of the school counselor's legal and ethical obligations to report the concern to the appropriate authorities unless it is appropriate to withhold this information to protect the student (e.g. student might run away if he/she knows parents are being called). The consequence of the risk of not giving parents/guardians a chance to intervene on behalf of their child is too great. Even if the danger appears relatively remote, parents should be notified.

Kirsten came to school clearly unable to function, and it was apparent that this was the result of ingesting a drug or alcohol. These substances are potentially dangerous physically and often signal underlying psychological issues that the student is using alcohol or drugs to hide. A student who appears to be intoxicated should be examined by a medical professional. It is crucial that parents are given information about the risks associated with alcohol and drug use. In this situation, the counselor and the principal worked together to stabilize Kirsten until a parent could bring her to be evaluated.

Multicultural Considerations

For many school counselors, working in an environment with students from high socioeconomic status (SES) or prominent families in the community can be intimidating. Additionally, some people have biases that individuals from higher SES or well-respected members of society do not have problems with addictive behaviors. We know that this is factually incorrect; however, a bias such as this may negatively impact a counselor's ability to appropriately target prevention efforts and screen for early issues with addiction among their students and decrease the probability that the counselor will effectively handle a situation like the one in this scenario.

Additionally, it can be helpful in screening students to understand statistics related to gender and ethnicity; however, it is crucial that counselors understand the uniqueness of each individual and situation so that they refrain from stereotyping students based on these characteristics. For instance, research indicates that male students and those of Caucasian or Hispanic ethnicity report more drug use than female, Asian, or African-American students (McCabe et al., 2008). However, although there are differences in gender and ethnicity regarding using drugs, there are no differences in gender nor ethnicity regarding the likelihood of abusing drugs. Therefore, universal prevention and screening for addiction issues is preferred in order to minimize issues related to counselor bias.

Discussion Questions

1. Identify your social locations regarding social and economic status. How does this affect your perception of working with students and families from higher SES? What about impoverished students and families? What about middle-class students and families?
2. Other than alcohol and drugs, what other behaviors could potentially lead to addictive disorders of which a school counselor should be aware?
3. Reflect on your own experiences with addiction or people with addictions. How do you think these experiences affect your perception of students with addictive disorders or students whose family members struggle with addictions?
4. Role-play notifying Kirsten's parent about the situation described in the case study. What did you find challenging? What did you do well? How will this inform your future practice?

Resources

National Helpline: https://www.samhsa.gov/find-help/national-helpline
National Institute on Drug Abuse: https://www.drugabuse.gov/publications/principles-adolescent-substance-use-disorder-treatment-research-based-guide/introduction
Teens Substance Use and Risks: https://www.cdc.gov/ncbddd/fasd/features/teen-substance-use.html

References

American School Counselor Association. (2016). *Ethical standards for school counselors*. Alexandria, VA: Author.

Center for Behavioral Health Statistics and Quality, National Survey on Drug Use and Health. (2016 and 2017). Table 1.2B—Types of Illicit Drug Use in Lifetime, Past Year, and Past Month among Persons Aged 12 to 17: Percentages, 2016 and 2017. Substance Abuse and Mental Health Services Administration. Retrieved from www.samhsa.gov/data/sites/default/files/cbhsq-reports/NSDUHDetailedTabs2017/NSDUHDetailedTabs2017.htm#tab1-2B

Gaustad, J. (1993). Substance abuse policy. *ERIC Digest*, 80. Retrieved from www.ericdigests.org/1993/abuse.htm

James, R. K., & Gilliland, B. E. (2017). *Crisis intervention strategies* (8th ed.). Boston, MA: Cengage.

LaBrie, J. W., Rodrigues, A., Schiffman, J., & Tawalbeh, S. (2008). Early alcohol initiation increases risk related to drinking among college students. *Journal of Child & Adolescent Substance Abuse, 17*(2), 125–141. https://doi.org/10.1300/J029v17n02_08

McCabe, S. E., Morales, M., Cranford, J. A., Delva, J., McPherson, M. D., & Boyd, C. J. (2008). Race/ethnicity and gender differences in drug use and abuse among college students. *Journal of Ethnicity in Substance Abuse, 6*(2), 75–95.

The Monitoring the Future study, the University of Michigan. TABLE 11 Trends in Availability of Drugs as Perceived by 8th Graders. Retrieved from http://monitoringthefuture.org/data/15data/15drtbl11.pdf

National Institute on Drug Abuse. (2016). What to do if your teen or young adult has a problem with drugs. *National Institute of Health.* Retrieved from www.drugabuse.gov/related-topics/treatment/what-to-do-if-your-teen-or-young-adult-has-problem-drugs

Rollnick, S., & Miller, W. R. (1995). What is motivational interviewing? *Behavioural and Cognitive Psychotherapy, 23,* 325–334.

Substance Abuse and Mental Health Services Administration (SAMHSA). *2015 National Survey on Drug Use and Health (NSDUH).* Table 2.19B: Alcohol Use in Lifetime, Past Year, and Past Month, by Detailed Age Category: Percentages, 2014 and 2015. Rockville, MD: SAMHSA, 2016. Retrieved from www.samhsa.gov/data/sites/default/files/NSDUH-DetTabs-2015/NSDUH-DetTabs-2015/NSDUH-DetTabs-2015.htm#tab2-19b

United Educators Insurance. (2014). *Public school policies: Keeping students' drug and alcohol free.* Retrieved from www.ue.org/uploadedFiles/Keeping%20Students%20Alcohol%20and%20Drug%20Free%20PS.pdf

Reflections: In the space provided, write your notes and reflections regarding this case study.

10 Gender Identity Issues

Shannon McFarlin

Background

The term *transgender* is used as an umbrella term to describe individuals whose internal gender identity does not align with their assigned sex at birth. The term encompasses those whose gender identity aligns with characteristics that normally are associated with individuals of the opposite sex (e.g., a person who was born anatomically female but who identifies as a boy) as well as those who do not identify as exclusively male or female (a.k.a., genderqueer, gender fluid, gender non-binary). Although transgenderism commonly is thought to relate to sexual orientation, it does not. Unlike with sexual orientation, "The issue [with a transgender identity] is not whom [the person] wish[es] to be *with*, but whom [the person] wish[es] to *be*" (Solomon, 2012, p. 596). Additionally, though it commonly does occur, having a transgender identity does not necessarily mean that an individual will experience gender dysphoria, defined as distress resulting from a "marked incongruence between one's experienced/expressed gender and assigned gender" (APA, 2013, p. 452).

Because many people who identity as transgender are reluctant to reveal their gender identity, it is difficult to pinpoint the prevalence of transgender individuals among the general population. However, researchers have indicated that the overall prevalence of trans (i.e., a commonly used shortened term for transgender) adults in the United States is roughly .58% (Herman, Flores, Brown, Wilson, & Conron, 2017). Among youth ages 13 to 17, approximately .73% ($n \sim 150,000$) identify as transgender (Herman et al., 2017).

Adolescents who identify as transgender tend to experience greater stigmatization within the school community than do their cisgender (i.e., non-transgender) and gay peers (Youth Chances, 2014). Name calling and physical harassment are much more common for these youths (James et al., 2016; Toomey, Ryan, Diaz, Card, & Russell, 2010; Youth Chances, 2014) and often result in poor grades, school avoidance, dropping out of school, and behavioral problems (Bowskill, 2017; James et al., 2016). Unfortunately, despite trans students' need for greater support within the school community (Stieglitz, 2010), educators generally lack the knowledge, skills, and attitude that they need to advocate for these young people and to moderate the effects of discrimination for them (Bowskill, 2017).

Regarding resilience factors among transgender youth, researchers have identified the following: (a) the ability to self-define one's gender, (b) proactive and supportive educational systems, (c) connection to a trans-affirming community, and (d) trans-affirming language, among others (Levitt & Ippolito, 2014; Singh, Meng, & Hansen, 2014). Important threats to resilience that researchers have identified include emotional and social isolation, gender policing (e.g., being prohibited from using the restroom that matches one's gender identity), and adultism (i.e., adults ignoring a youth's trans identity and/or believing that it is only a phase) [Pollock & Eyre, 2012; Singh et al., 2014]. With these resilience factors in mind, consider the following case, which depicts a dilemma that transgender youth commonly face in schools and that school counselors are encountering more and more often.

Description of Case

Elise, a 15-year-old Caucasian whose assigned sex at birth was female, is a sophomore in a large suburban high school in the southern United States. Elise, or *Ellis* as she insists, came out to her peers and teachers as a transgender male at the beginning of her sophomore year. Ellis prefers that others use masculine pronouns (i.e., he, him, his) to reference him, and his gender expression is, and historically has been, masculine. He wears clothing designed for the male gender, keeps his hair in a short cut, and speaks with an intentionally low, guttural voice.

Since coming out as transgender, Ellis has stopped by his school counselor's office regularly, usually to report difficulties with teachers who continue to reference him with feminine pronouns, problems with peers, or general feelings of disgust with his physical appearance and development. In conversations with Ms. Jackson, his school counselor, Ellis explained that he always has been different from his same-sex female peers. Beginning at the age of 4, Ellis began to loathe *girl toys* and dresses, choosing instead to play with traditionally masculine toys, to participate in traditionally masculine games, and to wear traditionally masculine clothing. Ellis's parents, who divorced when he was 9, have tolerated his gender nonconforming behaviors, dubbing Elise a *tomboy* who *will grow out of it*. He confessed to Ms. Jackson that, even though he has come out as transgender to his peers and his teachers, he has not yet explicitly disclosed his transgender identity to his parents.

Ellis told Ms. Jackson that he realized he was romantically attracted to girls at the age of 10. At the time of his self-realization, he had no understanding of transgenderism, so he had decided that he must be gay. Therefore, throughout his junior high school years, Ellis had identified as a lesbian, which had never felt quite right to him. He explained that he first realized that he was transgender, not gay, when he saw a documentary about a transgender celebrity on television during his freshman year of high school. He said that, after that, he knew he had been born into the wrong body and that he was supposed to be a guy, a *straight* guy.

It now is November of Ellis's sophomore year, and he has been struggling to transition socially at school. On the day of this incident, one of Ellis's female classmates goes to Ms. Jackson's office and reports: "There's a boy in the girls' bathroom, and I think he needs help." Ms. Jackson follows the adolescent to the girls' restroom, where she finds Ellis lying on the floor inside of a stall, sobbing and hitting the wall with his fists. The stall door is open, and Ms. Jackson gently approaches, saying softly, "Tell me what's happening." With tears streaming down his cheeks and mucous rolling from his nose, Ellis wails, "I don't belong in here! I don't belong in here! Why can't they see that I don't belong in here? I hate this school! *I hate it!!*"

After Ellis calms down, Ms. Jackson asks Ellis to accompany her to her office so that they can talk privately. Ellis acquiesces and follows Ms. Jackson out of the restroom. In the school counselor's office, Ellis explains that he needed to use the restroom, so he had gone into the boys' lavatory, where he had entered a private stall. However, one of his male peers saw him in the restroom and reported Ellis to an assistant principal, Mr. Falls, who ordered Ellis to leave. As Ellis explains, Mr. Falls told him, "Go to the girls' bathroom where you belong, or go to the bathroom in the nurse's office. When you're done, go directly to ISS, because I'm writing you up for this." At these words, Ellis begins to cry again. Between sobs, he tells the school counselor dogmatically, "I'm a *boy*. I need to go to the *boys'* bathroom. But when I go in there, they look at me like I'm a freak and tell me to leave. I *can't* go to the girls' bathroom, because *I don't belong there*. I feel like some kind of creepy pervert in there, like I'm seeing things I'm not supposed to be seeing. *Because I'm a boy!!* And I can't go to the nurse's office. It's on the other side of campus from most of my classes, and I'll be tardy if I try to go there between classes. Plus, *I'm not sick! I don't need to go there because I'm not sick!* I hate that principal! He's not Mr. Falls to me anymore; he's Mr. Fails." Ellis becomes quiet and pauses for a long moment before he states with quiet resignation, "I just want to go to the bathroom. Why can't I just go to the bathroom where I belong, like everyone else?"

Ultimately, Ms. Jackson realizes that she cannot supersede the assistant principal's decision in the immediate moment. Therefore, she stays with Ellis until he calms down, conveying empathy for his struggles and showing unconditional positive regard for him. After Ellis returns to class, Ms. Jackson walks to Mr. Falls's office and requests to speak with him. In conversation, Ms. Jackson implores him to reconsider his position that Ellis must use either the girls' restroom or the restroom in the nurse's office. However, Mr. Falls resolves to maintain his position, saying, "If we let her go into the boys' restroom, then we have to let all of them do it. And that can't happen."

Strategies for Consideration

This section includes information about Devor's (2004) transsexual/transgender identity formation model and other strategies that school counselors should know when working with gender identity development. Devor's model can be used to help school counselors understand common experiences among transgender students as they progress through the stages of gender identity development.

Theoretical Frameworks

Transgender Identity Development. Devor's (2004) transsexual/transgender identity formation model, which includes 14 stages through which trans individuals commonly progress in their processes of developing a trans identity, can be used to conceptualize Ellis's developmental struggles related to gender identity. Per Devor's model, the first three stages of development focus on gender-related anxiety (Stage 1), identity confusion (Stage 2), and identity comparisons (Stage 3) that typically occur during the early years of identity formation. With a growing sense of discomfort with one's social roles and body, individuals in these early stages often begin to question their assigned gender while simultaneously hiding their feelings of confusion from others. Although they might succumb to social expectations and attempt to abide by societally defined gender norms, many experiment with alternative self-expressions that feel more congruent with their internal experiences of gender. They compare their experimental behaviors with behaviors of their same-sex peers, seeking mirrors of themselves that might validate their nonconforming gender expressions.

The next three stages outline a process of discovering one's trans identity (Stage 4), followed by subsequent stages of identity confusion (Stage 5) and identity comparison (Stage 6). For some, the realization that one is trans entails a sense of relief, as it means that they have identified a label for their existential experience and can determine a course of action for the future. Others might not readily embrace the new self-discovery and, instead, will carry the internal conflict within them for many years. Regardless of their level of self-acceptance, most begin to seek out further information about trans phenomena, commonly turning to the internet for informational resources. They do not compare themselves only to their same-sex peers; they also make comparisons between themselves and individuals of the trans population. It is in this phase of development that questioning individuals might consider a sexual minority identity (e.g., gay male, lesbian female) in lieu of a trans identity before moving on to subsequent stages of trans identity development.

Stage 7 describes identity tolerance, which involves an initial acceptance of a trans identity. Yet before individuals move to a state of full acceptance, there commonly is a period of delay (Stage 8) in which they seek out affirmation of their trans identity via reality testing. Important questions to be answered at this stage include: Will others see me for what I really am? Will the people who love me accept my new identity? Am I really like other trans people?

After the initial period of delay, full acceptance of a trans identity can be realized (Stage 9), and one can say confidently to self and others, "I am transgender." Notwithstanding the new self-acceptance characterized by this stage, many delay the initiation of physical and social transitioning (Stage 10) while they ready themselves and others for the pending changes. At this stage, individuals typically seek out information about transitioning options, deciding the extent to which they would like to transition both socially and physically. Important tasks to accomplish at this stage commonly include (a) coming out as trans to important stakeholders in their lives (e.g., family members, friends, employers, school officials), (b) bolstering financial resources, (c) seeking counseling services to prepare for medical transitioning procedures, and the like.

Stage 11 marks the onset of transition, when an individual initiates perceivable changes that foster a sense of congruity between gender identity and gender presentation. Transitioning processes are individualized, and no two people's processes are the same. Social transitioning strategies might include changing one's name, asking others to use pronouns that align with one's gender identity, altering one's style of dress or fashion, or using public amenities that are designated for the gender with which one identifies, among others. Medical transitioning strategies might involve cross-hormone treatments, surgeries that aid in physical transformation, or no medical procedures at all. Although this stage of the identity development process can be invigorating for many, is also can be experienced as exceptionally challenging. Hostility from others is common, and safety fears are high. It is during this period that routine tasks (e.g., using public restrooms, eating in restaurants, taking public transportation) can evoke strong feelings of anxiety. Yet hope tends to run high during this period, also, as the individual begins to realize a more authentic and fulfilling existence in the world.

The last three stages of Devor's (2004) model pertain to trans individuals' post-transition experiences. Stage 12 describes self-acceptance processes, post-transition, focusing on the extent to which individuals begin to feel as though they belong as a member of another gender. Typically, after a number of years of experiencing life as the new gender, the sense of belonging becomes more salient, and individuals can achieve identity integration (i.e., relinquishment of the trans identity as one's master status, and understanding that the trans identity is only one aspect of one's overall personhood- Stage 13). The hallmark of Stage 14, the final stage, is identity pride, which includes pride in both oneself and the collective plight of the transgender population.

Professional Experiences

This author consulted with several school counselors in the state of Texas to compile a report of their experiences with cases like Ellis's. The school counselors reported that their primary obstacle in assisting students like Ellis was a lack of knowledge about transgender issues. Some reported that, because they lacked knowledge, they did not know whether or not to view a young trans person's transgender identity as an attention-seeking gimmick, a phase, or a fad or as a truly salient, stable trait within the individual. Additionally, some of the school counselors indicated that, although they wanted to be advocates for transgender students, they battled with their own values and beliefs about transgenderism, which sometimes were not affirming. The latter is especially important to consider due to counselors' duty to refrain from imposing personal values onto clients and students. It calls for the need of school counselors to engage in self-reflection and to bracket, or set aside, their own values-driven agendas when working with students.

The author of this chapter encountered a predicament that was similar to Ms. Jackson's in the case study when a young trans man who was experiencing distress in school reported to her that, although he had come out as trans to his school community, he had not come out as trans to his parents. As Dr. Williams explained, the school counselor walks a fine line when navigating this type of terrain with parents and students. She did advocate for parental involvement in the process, as parents have the potential to be strong allies and advocates for their students. Yet she also encouraged developmentally appropriate collaboration with the student when devising a plan to involve parents. Advocacy at many levels can be helpful when navigating the complexities of transgenderism. The following discussion of advocacy competencies should be helpful.

Advocacy Competencies

The American Counseling Association's Advocacy Competencies (Lewis, Arnold, House, & Toporek, 2003; Toporek & Daniels, 2018) provide counselors with a framework for addressing systemic barriers that students and clients face in their environments. The Advocacy Competencies are broken down into six categories: three that describe ways that counselors advocate *with* clients/students, and three that describe ways that counselors advocate *on behalf of* clients/students.

Working *with* clients and students, counselors advocate at the following levels:

- Individual student level (termed the *Client/Student Empowerment* level)—At this level, counselors assist individual clients and students in identifying systemic barriers, teach clients and students ways of addressing the barriers, and aid them in assessing their approaches.
- Community/school/organization level (termed the *Community Collaboration* level)—The primary role of the counselor at this level is that of an ally who works with a group or community at the local level to address and overcome systemic barriers. The counselor views the group as the expert and leader in advocacy strategies and supports the group's efforts to address the barriers. At this level, the counselor might facilitate group discussions, provide training and resources to the group, and the like.
- Public arena (termed the *Collective Action* level)—Within this level, the counselor partners with groups to inform both the public and policy makers about barriers that impede the development of the group's members. The counselor's primary role at this level is that of a collaborator who contributes professional knowledge and skills in advocacy processes.

Working *on behalf of* clients and students, counselors advocate at the following levels:

- Individual student level (termed the *Client/Student Advocacy* level)—For this level, counselors act on behalf of individual clients and students when they either are unable to address systemic barriers themselves or do not have access to key stakeholders in the system. Working at this level, counselors might speak to others on behalf of the client or student, taking care to involve the student in all aspects of the advocacy plan.
- Community/school/organization level (termed the *Systems Advocacy* level)—Within this domain, counselors act on behalf of groups of clients or students within an organization or community. Commonly, advocacy efforts take place within the counselor's work setting and might involve activities like presenting research and data to a committee group, training coworkers about the group's issues, and the like.
- Public arena level (termed the *Social/Political Advocacy* level)—At this level, counselors advocate on behalf of groups of clients or students in the larger public arena. Typically, issues related to a specific client group are not what fuel the counselors' advocacy efforts at this level; rather, the counselors' own observations of systemic barriers that affect large numbers of constituents compel them to advocate for the removal of the barriers.

Counselor Impact

School counselors who affirm trans students have reported that their efforts to advocate for them sometimes are met with resistance from teachers and administrators, as was the case when Ms. Jackson spoke to the assistant principal on Ellis's behalf. Moreover, because state laws vary in their positions for the protection of transgender students, school counselors from states that do not offer protection for these students sometimes encounter legal road blocks that impede their advocacy efforts. The school counselors reported that, when these things happen, it fosters feelings of powerlessness and outrage for them. Other school counselors have reported that, despite their desire to advocate for the needs of trans students on their campuses, they are fearful of *rocking the boat* with administrators, who evaluate them yearly. Some have indicated that their own need to self-protect within the school system has prohibited them from acting on behalf of students at times.

Mental Health Implications

Transgender students in K–12 schools experience adverse events regularly in their scholastic lives. A report of the National Transgender Discrimination Survey (Grant et al., 2011) indicated that among K–12 students in the U.S. who identified as transgender, 78% had experienced harassment from peers, 35% had been physically assaulted at school, 12% had been the victim of sexual violence, 31% had been harassed by teachers and staff, and 6% had been expelled for their gender identity/expression. Among those who had been harassed, assaulted, or expelled, 51% had attempted suicide. Among those who had been assaulted by teachers or staff, the percentage of respondents who had attempted suicide was even larger: 76%.

Considering these statistics, it is no wonder that transgender youth are at risk for mental health conditions that affect their functioning. In addition to high rates of suicidality among them, transgender youth also experience increased rates of depression (Chen, Fuqua, & Eugster, 2016), anxiety (Kaltiala-Heino, Bergman, Työläjärvi, & Frisén, 2018) substance abuse (Olson, Schrager, Belzer, Simons, & Clark, 2015), and eating disorders (Kaltiala-Heino et al., 2018). Although gender dysphoria does tend to occur comorbidly with these other conditions and often is the impetus for them (Katchadourian, Amed, & Metzger, 2014; de Vries & Cohenn-Kettenis, 2012), gender dysphoria can occur in isolation without any additional diagnoses.

Although school counselors do not diagnose mental health disorders among students, they must remain knowledgeable of diagnostic criteria and of the ways that diagnoses can impact students. In this case study, the school counselor did not have any mental health diagnoses for Ellis from an outside provider, nor did she have a record of Ellis's mental health history. During the counselor's conversations with Ellis in her office, Ellis did hint at symptoms of gender dysphoria. Also, although Ellis did not express that he was having suicidal ideation, his level of distress was high, signposting the counselor's need to assess for suicidality and self-harming behaviors.

Ethical Considerations

School counselors may face ethical dilemmas when facing complex student issues such as working with a transgender student. The ASCA (2016) provides standards designed to assist school counselors make the best decisions for all students. The following ethical standards are relevant to this case.

> A.1.f Respect students' and families' values, beliefs, sexual orientation, gender identification/ expression and cultural background and exercise great care to avoid imposing personal beliefs or values rooted in one's religion, culture or ethnicity.

Personal values and beliefs are not to guide the school counselor's practice with students. In this case study, the school counselor conveyed empathy and unconditional positive regard for Ellis, demonstrating respect for his gender identity and expression.

A.2.f Recognize their primary ethical obligation for confidentiality is to the students but balance that obligation with an understanding of parents'/guardians' legal and inherent rights to be the guiding voice in their children's lives. School counselors understand the need to balance students' ethical rights to make choices, their capacity to give consent or assent, and parental or familial legal rights and responsibilities to make decisions on their child's behalf.

The school counselor understands the student's need for autonomy while also respecting the parents' right to provide guidance for their student. In this case study, Ellis had not yet informed his parents of his transgender identity. Because Ellis was experiencing distress related to his gender identity at school, the school counselor might have worked with Ellis to devise a plan to solicit his parents' support and involvement with the problems that he was having at school.

A.6.a Collaborate with all relevant stakeholders, including students, educators and parents/ guardians when student assistance is needed, including the identification of early warning signs of student distress.

The school counselor teams with other stakeholders to assist students with issues that cause the student distress. Ellis was experiencing distress at school, and the school counselor took the initial step to collaborate with Mr. Falls, the assistant principal, to devise an equitable plan for Ellis's restroom needs. Although the case study ended with the conversation between the school counselor and Mr. Falls, the school counselor could have moved forward to engage other stakeholders for problem-solving strategies.

A.10.e Understand students have the right to be treated in a manner consistent with their gender identity and to be free from any form of discipline, harassment or discrimination based on their gender identity or gender expression.

The school counselor in this case study recognized that Ellis was being disciplined for his gender expression via a sentence to ISS and advocated for Ellis to be treated in accordance with his gender identity.

Multicultural Considerations

In this case study, Ellis has been forthright about his transgender identity with peers and stakeholders within the school community, but he has not divulged his trans identity to his parents. As Burnes and Chen (2012) and de Vries (2015) argued, some of the aspects of a person's overall identity (e.g., race/ethnicity, age, education, socioeconomic status, immigration status, sexual orientation, religious affiliation) intersect with gender identity and expression to a large extent. Some of the personal aspects might afford an individual privilege, while other aspects might generate stigma for them and cripple the individual's sense of empowerment. In transitioning processes, trans individuals might not be prepared to come out to stakeholders who can withhold privileges to which they have been accustomed, or they might not be prepared for changes in societal or familial treatment of them. Individuals with fewer privileges might also have less access to resources and experience greater stress overall (Burnes & Chen, 2012; de Vries, 2015).

When working with Ellis, it is important for the school counselor to assist him in exploring the many facets of his identity that intertwine with his transgender identity. By gaining information about his family's culture and beliefs system, the school counselor can better understand the obstacles that Ellis faces and the strengths that he possesses. The personal and familial history also can inform the counselor of appropriate ways to assist Ellis with coming out processes and self-advocacy strategies for use within the family system, the school system, and society at large.

Case Discussion Questions

1. Considering Ellis's characteristics in light of Devor's (2004) transsexual/transgender identity formation model, where would you say that Ellis is in terms of his gender identity development? What stage(s) does he exhibit? What are his strengths and challenges at his current stage(s) of development?
2. Referring to the ACA Advocacy Competencies, at what level(s) might you advocate for Ellis? Create an outline of specific advocacy strategies that you might initiate for at least three of the advocacy levels.
3. To what extent would you involve Ellis's parents in the solution for the problem that Ellis is having at school? Write a short script of what you would say to Ellis in a conversation with him about his parents' involvement.
4. What is your state's position on protections for transgender students in public schools? Do some research, and document your findings.
5. What personal values or beliefs do you have that might impede your ability to work objectively with Ellis and to advocate with/for him?

Resources

Parent of A Transgender Child? Resources & Support for You:

www.strongfamilyalliance.org/transgender/child

Resources for Transgender People:

www.glaad.org/transgender/resources

Transgender Resources:

https://pflag.org/search?keys=transgender&type=resource

References

American Psychiatric Association. (2013). *Diagnostic and statistical manual of mental disorders* (5th ed.). Washington, DC: Author.

American School Counselor Association. (2016). *Ethical standards for school counselors*. Alexandria, VA: Author.

Bowskill, T. (2017). How educational professionals can improve the outcomes for transgender children and young people. *Educational & Child Psychology, 34*(3), 96–108. Retrieved from https://static1.square space.com/static/559bd124e4b03133aaad9e03/t/5c07be9d4d7a9c7cf5349f7e/1544011422853/trans7.pdf

Burnes, T. R., & Chen, M. M. (2012). The multiple identities of trans-gender individuals: Incorporating a framework of intersectionality to gender crossing. In R. Josselson & M. Harway (Eds.), *Navigating multiple identities: Race, gender, culture, nationality, and roles* (pp. 113–128). New York, NY: Oxford University Press. Retrieved from http://dx.doi.org/10.1093/acprof:oso/9780199732074.003.0007

Chen, M., Fuqua, J., & Eugster, E. A. (2016). Characteristics of referrals for gender dysphoria over a 13-year period. *Journal of Adolescent Health, 58*, 369–371. doi:10.1016/j.jadohealth.2015.11.010

Devor, A. H. (2004). Witnessing and mirroring: A fourteen stage model of transsexual identity formation. *Journal of Gay and Lesbian Psychotherapy, 8*(3–4), 41–67. doi:10.1300/J236v08n01_05

de Vries, A., & Cohenn-Kettenis, P. (2012). Clinical management of gender dysphoria in children and adolescents: The Dutch approach. *Journal of Homosexuality, 59*, 301–320. doi:10.1080/00918369.201 2.653300 de Vries, K. M. (2015). Transgender people of color at the center: Conceptualizing a new intersectional model. *Ethnicities, 15*, 3–27. Retrieved from http://dx.doi.org/10.1177/1468796814547058

Grant, J. M., Mottet, L. A., Tanis, J., Harrison, J., Herman, J. L., & Keisling, M. (2011). *Injustice at every turn: A report of the national transgender discrimination survey.* Washington, DC: National Center for Transgender Equality and National Gay and Lesbian Task Force.

Herman, J. L., Flores, A. R., Brown, T. N. T., Wilson, B. D. M., & Conron, K. J. (2017). *Age of individuals who identify as transgender in the United States.* Los Angeles, CA: The Williams Institute.

James, S. E., Herman, J. L., Rankin, S., Keisling, M., Mottet, L., & Anafi, M. (2016). *The report of the 2015 U.S. transgender survey.* Washington, DC: National Center for Transgender Equality.

Kaltiala-Heino, R., Bergman H., Työläjärvi, M., & Frisén, L. (2018). Gender dysphoria in adolescence: Current perspectives. *Adolescent Health, Medicine, & Therapeutics, 9*, 31–41. doi: 10.2147/AHMT.S135432

Katchadourian, K., Amed, S., & Metzger, D. L. (2014). Clinical management of youth with gender dysphoria in Vancouver. *Journal of Pediatrics, 164*, 906–911. doi:10.1016/j.jpeds.2013.10.068

Levitt, H. M., & Ippolito, M. R. (2014). Being transgender: The experience of transgender identity development. *Journal of Homosexuality, 61*, 1727–1758. doi:10.1080/00918369.2014.951262

Lewis, J., Arnold, M. S., House, R., & Toporek, R. (2003). *ACA advocacy competencies* [Electronic version]. Retrieved May 19, 2019, from www.counseling.org/Publications

Olson, J., Schrager, S. M., Belzer, M., Simons, L. K., & Clark, L. F. (2015). Baseline physiologic and psychosocial characteristics of transgender youth seeking care for gender dysphoria. *Journal of Adolescent Health, 57*, 374–380. doi:10.1016/j.jadohealth.2015.04.027

Pollock, L., & Eyre, S. L. (2012). Growth into manhood: Identity development among female-to-male transgender youth. *Culture, Health, & Sexuality, 14*(2), 209–222. doi:10.1080/13691058.2011.636072

Singh, A. A., Meng, S. E., & Hansen, A. W. (2014). "I am my own gender": Resilience strategies of trans youth. *Journal of Counseling & Development, 92*, 208–218. doi:10.1002/j.1556-6676.2014.00150.x

Solomon, A. (2012). *Far from the tree: Parents, children and the search for identity.* New York, NY: Scribner.

Stieglitz, K. A. (2010). Development, risk and resilience of transgender youth. *Journal of the Association of Nurses in AIDS Care, 21*(3), 192–206. doi: 10.1016/j.jana.2009.08.004

Toomey, R. B., Ryan, C., Diaz, R. M., Card, N. A., & Russell, S. T. (2010). Gender-nonconforming lesbian, gay, bisexual, and transgender youth: School victimization and young adult psychosocial adjustment. *Developmental Psychology, 46*, 1580–1589. doi:10.1037/a0020705

Toporek, R. L., & Daniels, J. (2018). *2018 update and expansion of the 2003 ACA Advocacy Competencies: Honoring the work of the past and contextualizing the present.* Retrieved from www.counseling.org

Youth Chances. (2014). *Youth chances summary of first findings: The experiences of LGBTQ young people in England.* London, England: METRO.

Reflections: In the space provided, write your notes and reflections on this case study.

11 An Emotionally Unstable Teacher

Helena Stevens

Background

School counselors are a vital resource for teachers. They serve as partners, collaborators, and consultants with teachers. In the work done with teachers, school counselors are able to aid teachers in understanding students from a holistic perspective, provide classroom support, consult on ethical and legal matters, and be a constant support for teachers because they can help guide students' comprehensive development (academic, career, social, and emotional). While school counselors primarily consult with teachers regarding students' behaviors and academic work, a school counselor can also consult with a teacher regarding the teacher's growth and development.

School counselors strive to create school campuses that reflect positive climates in order to ensure that students are in places that are conducive to high levels of learning, positive growth, and healthy development. The *ASCA School Counselor Professional Standards and Competencies* (2019, B-PF 3.d) specify that school counselors "fulfill legal and ethical obligations to families, teachers, administrators, and other school staff." Given that teachers play a pivotal role in students' achievement motivation, emotional development, and self-efficacy building, school counselors' work should be inclusive of supporting teachers from a holistic perspective, in the same regard that students are supported, as situations warrant.

School counselors understand that students function best when areas of need—such as basic needs, mental health, emotional well-being, safety, and more—are met. School counselors also recognize that maintaining wellness and self-care is a vital protective behavior to prevent burnout and increase optimal work-place performance. In situations where teachers are struggling with work-place performance, be it due to personal issues, physical health ailments, or mental health issues, to name a few, a school counselor is equipped with the knowledge and resources to provide resources and referrals for teachers. While individual counseling is not ethically or legally a choice for supporting teachers, consulting on options for care and support is within the scope of practice and competencies of a school counselor. The following case reflects a situation in which a teacher was not operating at an optimal and, sometimes, functional level.

Description of Case

The parent of an 11th-grade student emailed the counselor because her son was struggling in his Algebra II class. The student, who normally received As or Bs in his math studies, has recently earned D's and F's on tests and assignments. The parent has tried contacting the teacher but expressed in her email that the teacher is infrequent with communication and responses. Additionally, the teacher has not followed through with providing (the parent) with the math content/ material to help the student get caught up and to help the parent with supporting the student. This is not the first time the counselor has heard about issues with the math teacher from other parents and students.

The counselor has heard from students in the past about how many of the class periods are spent listening to the teacher talk about her failed marriage or sick parents. The teacher spends little time instructing and instead sits at her desk and has students ask her questions about the assignments. The teacher assigns an abundance of homework; the students spend upwards of two hours a night completing these without the benefit of much instruction during the daytime.

In the three years that the counselor has worked at Woodrow Wilson High School, she has interacted with the math teacher at all-staff school meetings and has worked together during staff advisory council meetings, and on a curriculum advisory committee. The teacher is often friendly and outgoing and has also brought up in meetings some of her life situations. When the school counselor has participated in team meetings with the teacher, the teacher often gets off-track quickly, with slow, stagnated speech, often leading to crying during her speeches. She sometimes lays on the floor during the meetings because the teacher blames her back pain from sitting in the car for long hours as the reason for needing to recline on the floor.

The teacher currently drives four hours one way to her hometown on the weekends to care for ailing parents. She has also brought up on several occasions that because of her time away from her own home to take care of her parents, her husband has initiated divorce proceedings. The teacher sometimes sleeps in her car or her office due to driving long distances and because her home location is an hour in an opposite direction from the school.

The teacher, who has worked at the school for 10 years, was once a thriving and highly effi-cient teacher. In the last five years, she has declined in her work, and her personal life situations have highly impacted her abilities to teach effectively. She has also called off work more fre-quently because of doctor appointments and because of illness. The counselor decides to talk to the teacher to strategize how she can help the teacher and/or the students. The counselor meets one-on-one with her.

Because the teacher has tenure and because there are not many faculties who can teach Algebra II, school personnel have a great deal invested in her success. In the counselor's meeting with the teacher, she learns more about her routine needs for physical therapy, personal therapy, and com-muting. The teacher expresses that she is invested in her job and enjoys coming to work and the people with whom she works. The interaction is short and pleasant but does not generate ideas for how to fully support the teacher or students. Options the counselor considers are speaking to the principal or the teacher's department chair, without revealing confidences, to see if either of them can shed more light on providing the support the teacher might need.

Strategies for Consideration

School counselors frequently respond to the problems that teachers experience both in the class-room and in their personal lives. While counselors who work in schools cannot provide long-term personal counseling to teachers, they can provide support and resources in a variety of ways. The following sections offer considerations for working with teachers and students in a collaborative way to augment successful classroom experiences.

Theoretical Frameworks

Solution-focused brief therapy (SFBT) is a theoretical framework that focuses on the strengths and motivations of individuals (clients) to generate solutions for resolving a problem (Berg & De Jong, 1996). The focus is not on exploring and processing the problem. Attention is paid to times in which the individual successfully navigated similar situations in order to build self-efficacy and motivation to utilize those same strengths to navigate a current issue. The communication skills and methods used in this framework carefully guide the individual through co-constructive dialogues that collaboratively (client and counselor) identify goals and work toward client change

(Berg & De Jong, 1996). The counselor is not the expert in the therapeutic relationship and works to keep the focus on the present and observable parts of the issue, not the past or underlying elements.

Kim and Franklin (2008, p. 464) identify three essential components in SFBT: (1) use of conversations centered on clients' concerns; (2) conversations focused on co-constructing new meanings around client concerns; and (3) use of specific techniques to help clients co-construct a vision of a preferred future and drawing upon past success and strengths to help resolve issues. When first meeting with the client, the therapist will ask a miracle question: If you woke up tomorrow, and a miracle happened to solve this problem, what would you notice that is different? A series of follow-up questions proceed after the answer and explore what would look different, be different, and how would the client know.

Scaling questions, assessing severity, value, and perception, are used to determine the current baseline and to then decide what the ideal and realistic number change would be. For example: the counselor might ask what the current satisfaction with a work situation is. The client may answer 2 and describe what a 2 means. The therapist will then ask what the ideal number would be, which might be a 6. The 6 is described for what it would look like. From there, the counselor and client work collaboratively to identify goals, decide on homework while focusing on strengths and solutions. A key component in the SFBT is to have the client look for exceptions to the problem, which helps the client recognize that even when they do not have past successes to pull strengths from, there were times in which the current problem did not exist.

Solution-focused therapy is utilized by school counselors in schools to support students' growth in academic, social, and emotional areas (Carlson, 2017). The theoretical framework can be utilized with any school stakeholder. This approach puts the school counselor in a collaborative position with whoever is identified as the client and helps maintain an appropriate boundary to keep the school counselor in the liaison/collaborator role and not a therapist's role. School counselors can assist in helping the school stake holder in identifying the current problem and identifying desired changes and goals and can guide the individual toward *home-work* that increase proximity to achieving their goals.

Professional Experiences

Experience A. School counselors may work with special education resource classes. Classes are usually small, but school counselors have a great deal of responsibility to help these students keep up with their grade-level work. School counselors can visit several times during one week to provide some guidance lessons. In one particular situation, a school counselor was certain that she smelled alcohol on the teacher's breath. When a person drinks to the point of the odor seeping through skin pores, it can be deemed as excessive. Alcohol abuse is a serious mental health problem in our society, and the disease does not care what your race is, what profession you hold, or what your socioeconomic situation is.

The school counselor decided to approach the teacher before reporting it to the administration. The counselor met with the teacher after school and told her gently what she had experienced being around her and suggested that she find some professional help. The counselor provided referrals and community resources. The teacher was embarrassed at first, but the school counselor tried to be as understanding and yet as firm as possible. She asked the teacher to think of the students and how her drinking might impact them and their learning. In other words, was she able to do the best job possible while she was still most likely under the influence from drinking the night before? Unfortunately, the teacher became angry and denied that she had a drinking problem. The school counselor told her that her next step could be to talk to the principal. The teacher reacted aggressively and said that this was none of the school counselor's business.

The school counselor did go to the principal. The principal did not act immediately but instead set up a number of impromptu observations of this teacher, and she experienced an undeniable odor of alcohol on the woman. In addition, she reported to the school counselor that the lessons she observed were disorganized and not engaging. The principal worked with the district administrators to resolve the issue, and the case was no longer the school counselor's responsibility. Ultimately, the teacher was removed from the campus. While it is possible the teacher did not ever receive the help she needed, the main concern was the children in her classes, and their need and their right to an excellent education.

Experience B. A school counselor worked with a principal who had a dual relationship with the grandparent of a student. The student struggled both academically and socially. The student was often transported to school by the principal, and there was a great deal of uncertainty about when and how often the student was with his biological mother. It was unclear who had primary responsibility for the student, with the knowledge that the father was not involved in the family's life. The mother was very difficult to contact when school officials needed to talk to her about the student's academic needs, social situations, or medical issues, and she refused to come to parent/teacher/student meetings.

The student's English teacher approached the school counselor one day to discuss some information she had about the mother. The information was concerning and reflected a level of neglect in the mother's caretaking of the student. The school counselor consulted with the teacher and determined a child protective services (CPS) report should be made. The following day the school counselor checked in with the teacher to see if the report had been made. The teacher informed the counselor that she had talked to the principal about it first, and the principal requested that she not make the report, saying that she would intervene with the mother and student on her own.

The school counselor felt this was not only an ethical issue involving the dual relationship but also a legal issue of misconduct, which was the failure to make a CPS report when it was warranted. The school counselor decided to follow through with the CPS report for due diligence and to approach the principal about the situation. The intention was to advocate for the needs of the student and to address how the dual relationship was affecting ethical behavior and best practice in administration and leadership. The principal refused to discuss the situation with the school counselor and suggested she allow her to do her job.

The school counselor consulted with another counselor and a district supervisor, and from those consultations, the group felt that a report to the superintendent was warranted. The school counselor followed through with the report, and the superintendent's office decided to launch an investigation. The investigation uncovered a variety of situations, in addition to the student issue, that the administration felt were not handled properly. The principal was fired immediately following the close of the investigation. This situation was tricky because the principal is the leader of the school, and having a supportive relationship with the principal is important. While the report was the only cause of the firing, the right step was made in reporting the inappropriate behavior and reporting that the principal was not in an emotionally healthy place to be leading the school and was disserving the students.

Counselor Impact

This dilemma puts the counselor in several delicate positions based on her relationship and work with the student and parents, the teacher, and administrator. The school counselor has a responsibility and duty to advocate for the student's academic success. Not doing so would be a disservice. Failing to address the issue with the teacher and administrator would mean the school counselor is neglecting to remediate an issue that not only impacts the individual student but also has the potential to impact many students who are in the teacher's other math classes. Deciding against intervening could have had a detrimental impact, including the confidence that parents and other faculty members have regarding the value system held by the school leadership. Additionally, careful consideration has to be taken when informing the parent about what is happening in the classroom. Depending upon the extent to which the student's report of the teacher's behavior was truthful, the school counselor may need to advocate to the parents that the student is diligent and not deficient in learning capacity or work ethic, all while not disclosing information about the teacher that could compromise the integrity of the teacher and spread to other parents and school staff.

Intervening can also place the school counselor in a vulnerable position with the teacher. Approaching the teacher may anger her and cause her to treat the counselor poorly and damage the working relationship. The Code of Ethics is specific on the role for the school counselor in addressing colleagues who behave unethically and for supporting students and maintaining confidentiality. These dual delineations put the school counselor in a position to make a decision, and that decision can affect the working relationships that the school counselor has with other staff and students.

Lastly, the relationship the school counselor has with the administrator will be influential to the outcome of this situation. As described in the professional experiences, administrator support, or lack thereof, provides either a protective factor or a significant barrier. If the administrator at the campus provides the support and guidance needed, the school counselor is able to follow through with due diligence and return to counseling duties while the administration completes the actions that are decided upon. If the administrator is not supportive or is dismissive of the severity of the problem, the school counselor is faced with an additional dilemma to go beyond the administrator to the superintendent level. This could cause serious damage to the working relationship with the administrator, which certainly is a detriment to a school counseling program. When considering what to do, the school counselor must consider all of the ethical and relational elements that will be impacted in order to decide upon the best course of action.

Mental Health Implications

Mental health and wellness is a critical element for school counselors to be concerned with when working in K–12 schools. As stated in the example cases, mental illness does not discriminate and is a serious issue in our society. School-wide, staff work in demanding jobs that impact overall health and wellness. One study found teachers to have a higher than average level of stress when compared to other academic or client-related professions (Akca & Yaman, 2010). Teachers experience high levels of exhaustion and criticism, leading to persistent amounts of burnout among those in the profession (Wright & Hobfoll, 2004). Job-related stressors, coupled with personal life stressors and crises, are a combination for influencing poor performance, unethical behaviors, and poor health and longevity (Pietarinen, Pyhalto, Soini, & Salmela-Aro, 2013). Burnout and its subsequent performance effects also impact students' motivation and academic success in a negative manner (Shen et al., 2015).

School counselors, as well, consider their mental health and wellness along with factors that increase their burnout. In a study conducted by Bardoshi, Schweinle, and Duncan (2014), results indicated that school counselors who engaged in higher amounts of non-counseling duties (management tasks, testing administration, crisis intervention, etc.) had higher rates of burnout. Additionally, high student caseloads and low principal support were likely to increase further those rates of burnout. Burnout resulted in emotional exhaustion, decreased performance abilities, and dissatisfaction with their jobs. School counselors consider the mental and emotional well-being not only of their students but of themselves and colleagues as well. Students' mental health and wellness is understood as being a significant influence on their academic, career, and personal-social functioning and success. Therefore, school counseling programs are designed to be comprehensive in scope and to support students holistically because of this understanding.

Additionally, school counselors have an important role to advocate for their own and teachers' mental health and wellness. This can be done by providing resources to assist in preventing burn-out and to support those who are in need of restorative services due to burnout.

There are several strategies for decreasing agents of burnout in schools. Classroom-based interventions to support remediation of students' academic and social behaviors can aid teachers by decreasing the amount of time teachers spend engaging in behavior management interventions and academic remediation practices. Both of these can significantly lead to burnout. School counselors can also advocate for teachers by providing resources and referrals for personal variables that influence mental wellness and burnout prevention. These personal variables include proactive and reactive coping resources, social support networks, and mental health treatment (Bermejo-Toro, Prieto-Ursua, & Hernandez, 2015). School counselors can work closely with principals to advocate for their use of time. Collecting data on use of time and having critical conversations about emotional well-being can support dialogues with administrators that lead toward refining job duties and functions (Bardoshi et al., 2014). This will result in an increase in job satisfaction and a decrease in feelings of exhaustion.

Ethical Considerations

The *American School Counselor Association (ASCA) Code of Ethics* (2016, A.1.a) specifies that school counselors, "have a primary obligation to the students, who are to be treated with dignity and respect as unique individuals." School counselors are proactive in supporting students and provide effective, responsive interventions to support students wholly, addressing their academic, career, and social/emotional needs (ASCA, 2016, A.1.e, A.1.h). Additionally, school counselors work diligently to, "develop and maintain professional relationships and systems of communication with faculty, staff, and administrators to support students," (B.2.a). These supportive relationships are vital for collaborative and collective efforts that not only support students, but also support staff and administrator efforts, both at the individual student level and the larger systemic school level.

There are dual needs to consider when approaching the handling of this case. The student in this situation is experiencing a lack of quality and efficiency in the teaching and delivery of math content from the teacher. The school counselor can assume that other students may be struggling as well. The first approach will take into account supporting the student's academic needs and providing support for remediating the grade deficits. The second approach takes into account the situation of the teacher. The teacher in this case is behaving in a manner that is unethical and damaging to the students' academic development. The *Code of Ethics* section E, "Maintenance of Standards," provides two steps for school counselors to follow when situations arise regarding ethical behaviors of colleagues.

   a. School counselors consult with professional colleagues to discuss the potentially unethical behavior and to see if the professional colleague views the situation as an ethical violation. School counselors understand mandatory reporting in their respective district and states.
   b. School counselors discuss and seek resolution directly with the colleague whose behavior is in question unless the behavior is unlawful, abusive, egregious or dangerous, in which case proper school or community authorities are contacted.

The ASCA Code of Ethics (2016) specifies that school counselors employ the legal and ethical principles of the school counseling profession (B-PF 3) and that an ethical decision-making model is utilized for navigating the process of remediating the ethical issue or dilemma. While further investigation of the situation is warranted, the school counselor can consider that she has a responsibility to determine the extent of the truth to what the student has reported about the teacher's behaviors, to address the situation with the teacher, and to determine a subsequent course of action after meeting with the teacher. Utilizing an ethical decision-making model as a theoretical framework provides a grounded approach to addressing and remediating the situation, with a higher likelihood of a successful outcome.

There are nine steps in the decision making model as presented by Stone (2001): (a) define the problem, (b) apply the ASCA Ethical Standards for School Counselors and the law, (c) consider the students' chronological and developmental levels, (d) consider the setting, parental rights and minors' rights, (e) apply the ethical principles of beneficence, autonomy, nonmaleficence, loyalty, and justice, (f) determine potential courses of action and their consequences, (g) evaluate the selected action, (h) consult, and (i) implement the course of action.

In this situation the school counselor understands that the mental and emotional wellness of the teacher is affecting her ability to teach efficiently and subsequently is hindering students' learning (step a). The ethical standards, for example the ones addressed earlier, (step b) are referenced and utilized when determining the purpose and rationale for addressing and intervening with the ethical dilemma. Steps c and d provide further context and understanding for elements that can be addressed and inform planning interventions and steps to address the ethical dilemma. The ethical principles (step e) serve as a lens for the planning and action steps and are applied to all individuals in the case. This step is critical because intervening action affects everyone immediately involved and can vicariously affect others around the situation. Careful consideration is given to everyone who may be impacted in order that potential courses of action (step g) are constructively analyzed for how the ethical principles are upheld for all persons immediately and vicariously involved. Through that consultation (step h) a final course of action to intervene and address the ethical dilemma is implemented (step i).

Multicultural Considerations

The conversation of mental health has become a critical element in our society. The mental-health culture is met with stigma, support, uncertainty, and perceptions, all of which are influenced by other cultural systems within our society (e.g. religion, human development, politics and law, and community systems, to name several). Depending on the sub-contextual influences, individuals who experience mental health challenges will feel empowered to seek care without shame or embarrassment or adversely will not have the self-efficacy and confidence to seek supportive services and interventions.

Emotional instability may be a by-product of an array of mental health issues and disorders: depression, anxiety, trauma, and personality disorders, to name a few. Life changes can influence the onset of the mental health issues that affect emotional stability. Emotional instability certainly intersects with holistic forces from community influences, family systems, mental health diagnoses, and workplace environments. The emotional instability in females, specifically, can be stereotyped for *time of the month*, hormones, and gender causes and thusly be completely disregarded for other serious and dire issues that are happening.

While the mental health phenomenon is continuing to have a presence in health care and insurance, many individuals are unaware of the resources and systems in place that they have access to get the care they need; these include health insurance reimbursement, medical-leave, government-funded organizations, low-cost/sliding scale facilities, technology tools, and more. While individuals may know of these support systems, feelings of shame and guilt inhibit many people from ever seeking those supports. Depending on the cultural system from which a person comes, the person can be supported, shamed, or steered away from receiving supportive services. Individuals may even hesitate to admit to someone that they have a problem. School counselors consider mental health as a culture. Therefore, when addressing mental health needs and identifying resources and supports, school counselors must consider the intersectionality of subcultural contexts (religion, society, politics, development, abilities, communities, family-structures, and identity) and their impacts on individuals' mental health and their self-efficacy and abilities to support their mental health.

Case Discussion Questions

1. Apply the ASCA ethical decision-making model to this case and determine a course of action that you would take as a school counselor.
2. How would you address the teacher to investigate the student's claims?
3. Utilizing a solution-focused brief therapy framework, how would you collaborate with the teacher to support her? Consider types of outside activities, in-school supports, and goals.
4. The information from the student about the teacher's behaviors is determined to be fully valid; describe how you would follow through with communicating to the parent about the situation while protecting confidentiality and advocating for the student.
5. What types of supports will you provide for not only the individual student but also the classes of students who may be struggling due to the teacher's performance? In particular, consider the impact the math competencies have on standardized tests and college admissions.
6. How will you address faculty mental health and wellness for the campus at large regarding this incident?
7. What types of resources and referrals should be prepared prior to meeting with the teacher?
8. How will you respond if the teacher pleads with you to not report to administration what is occurring and promises that it will get better?
9. How will you respond if the teacher is angry and denies all the allegations?

Resources

Teacher Burnout Solutions and Prevention:

www.thegraidenetwork.com/blog-all/teacher-burnout-solutions-prevention

References

Akca, F., & Yaman, B. (2010). The effects of internal-external locus of control variables on burnout levels of teachers. *Procedia Social and Behavioural Sciences*, *2*, 3976–3980.

American School Counselor Association. (2016). *Ethical standards for school counselors*. Alexandria, VA: Author.

American School Counselor Association. (2019). *ASCA School Counselor Professional Standards & Competencies*. Alexandria, VA: Author.

Bardoshi, G., Schweinle, A., & Duncan, K. (2014). Understanding the impact of school factors on school counselor burnout: A mixed-methods study. *The Professional Counselor*, *4*(5), 426–443.

Berg, I. K., & De Jong, P. (1996). Solution-building conversation: Co-constructing a sense of competence with clients. *Families in Society*, *77*, 376–391.

Bermejo-Toro, L., Prieto-Ursua, M., & Hernandez, V. (2015). Towards a model of teacher well-being: Personal and job resources involved in teacher burnout and engagement. *International Journal of Experimental Educational Psychology*, *36*(3), 481–501.

Carlson, M. (2017). Using solution-focused brief therapy in schools. *Communique*, *46*(2), 1–3.

Kim, J. S., & Franklin, C. (2008). Solution focused therapy in schools: A review of the outcome literature. *Children and Youth Services Review*, *31*, 464–470.

Pietarinen, J., Pyhalto, K., Soini, T., & Salmela-Aro, K. (2013). Reducing teacher burnout: A socio-contextual approach. *Teaching and Teacher Education*, *35*, 62–72.

Shen, B., Mccaughtry, N., Martin, J., Garn, A., Kulik, N., & Fahlman, M. (2015). The relationship between teacher burnout and student motivation. *British Journal of Educational Psychology*, *85*(4), 519–532.

Stone, C. (2001). *STEPS: Steps to ethical problems in schools*. Retrieved from https://www.schoolcoun selor.org/asca/media/asca/Ethics/EthicalStandards2016.pdf

Wright, T. A., & Hobfoll, S. E. (2004). Commitment, psychological well-being and job performance: An examination of conservation of resources theory and job burnout. *Journal of Business and Management*, *9*, 389–406.

Reflections: In the space provided, write your notes and reflections regarding this case study.

12 Serious Criminal Charges

Leigh Falls Holman and Kristi L. Nobbman

Background

Students' criminal behavior can occur both in the community and on school campuses. In fact, during the 2015–2016 school year, 78.9% of public schools reported having an incident of crime on campus, while only 47.4% reported the criminal behavior to law enforcement (McFarland et al., 2017). This may result in school counselors interacting with police officers or juvenile probation/parole officers who supervise juvenile offenders. However, many school counselors are intimidated by such interactions and often feel unsure of how to handle inquiries by law enforcement officials due to competing legal and ethical concerns.

When possible, school counselors attempt to prevent violent incidents, intervene when concerns arise about potential violence, and respond when violence occurs on campus (ASCA, 2019, p. 49). Although arrest rates for juveniles have declined since 2007, there were still about 1 million juveniles arrested in 2016 (Puzzanchera, 2018). While property crimes, robbery, and aggravated assault have decreased in recent years, during the same period, rates for murder committed by juveniles increased. Most juveniles arrested for violent crime tend to be male; however, 1 in 5 involves a female. Additionally, more than half of these arrests are ethnic minorities (Puzzanchera, 2018).

Among minorities, students who are undocumented pose unique challenges for schools, even when these students come into the country with their parents fleeing violence or persecution in their home countries. According to the 2014 and 2015 Census Bureau data, 42.4% legal and undocumented immigrants currently live in the United States, and 10.9 million are students in public schools, accounting for 23% of public school enrollment nationally (Camarota & Zeigler, 2016). Under *Plyer v. Doe* (1982), undocumented children are entitled to an education. For school counselors, accepted practice is not to identify these students to authorities.

Another complicated factor with youth that involves legal enforcement is students' gang activity. These associations often increase youth's criminal behavior, particularly in the community. Gang-involved youth can disrupt school order and create an unsafe school climate for other students and staff alike. Students in urban schools report gang activity in school at higher rates than in suburban schools. In fact, in 2015, 11% of students reported the presence of gang activity in their schools (McFarland et al., 2017). Although the case in this chapter is not typical, it is a composite example of several real cases that the author encountered as a school counselor in a large urban school environment.

Description of the Case

Ms. Smith is one of seven counselors at a large high school in an urban area. Her caseload averages around 500 students. It is not unusual for someone to leave the school in handcuffs or an ambulance on a daily basis due to drugs and gang activity. On a typical day, the secretary in the counseling office notifies Ms. Smith that two police officers are at the school to talk to her about a student. She invites the officers into her office, and they tell her that one of her students is being investigated for murder. The officers do not indicate that they have communicated with the student's assigned associate principal or the building principal. They want information about the student and specifically ask to see his records, although they do not present a court order allowing a release of the records. The officers' presentation is demanding and somewhat aggressive toward the school counselor. She believes they are attempting to use their power as officers to intimidate her into talking about the student and giving them information that they may not legally be entitled to access.

Ms. Smith knows the student they are investigating. When she has interacted with the student, he has always been respectful and has not caused trouble in classes or exhibited any behavioral problems in school. He seems to be an intelligent young man who is on track for graduation in spite of attendance issues. Additionally, the counselor is aware that Mario is likely an undocumented immigrant because he lives with a group of other students who have identified themselves as such. They live together in one apartment and take care of each other like a family. They report that they live with an aunt, and she is the adult who comes to school to address any issues that arise or to pick them up if they are sick; however, the counselor suspects that the woman is not actually a family member. The students' parents are all still in Mexico. Ms. Smith does not know if the officers are aware that he is undocumented or that he lives with other students who are also undocumented.

The counselor also does not know who the victim is or if he or she has any relationship to any other student at the school. However, there are at least five students in the school that she knows who have had a family member murdered this year. Mario has been involved extensively in gang activity and drug dealing, according to the school resource officers; however, he has never been caught doing so on the campus. The investigating police officers indicate that the murder may have been part of his gang affiliation. Historically, when a gang member has murdered a rival gang member, the rival gang retaliates with additional violence.

This is particularly concerning because at this week's Monday morning administrator meeting, the principal informed all the counselors and assistant principals about rumors around school that there may be an altercation between two gangs who have students on campus, but Ms. Smith does not know any details. The building administrator is concerned that parents are going to keep their children home during state-mandated testing that is coming up in order to keep their children safe from the violence. The principal directed everyone in the meeting to contact him directly with any potential information that may help shed light on what the disagreement is about, so he can try to intervene. The counselor does not know if this situation is related to this altercation, but she suspects it may be.

Strategies for Consideration

It is not unusual for school counselors to be involved in serious cases such as the one described here. Students and their parents or guardians have rights, and the school counselor recognizes that the demands of the officers will require that she follow appropriate protection of student data until otherwise informed by her superiors or a court order. Because cases like these are serious and complicated, school counselors need an arsenal of information and skills to respond appropriately.

Theoretical Frameworks

Bruce Perry's (2012) neurosequential model of education (NME) is helpful when counselors work in environments where students have to deal with frequent violence in their homes or neighborhoods. Simplified, NME teaches that the brain is organized from the bottom up, meaning from the brainstem to the cortex. Early childhood trauma, chronic stress, and unpredictable environments cause disorganization in the brain and maladaptive responses from students because they respond using the lower brain (i.e. flight, fight, or freeze). Given Mario's situation, it is likely he is unable to control his frustration or able to communicate while keeping eye contact. Additionally, he may demonstrate difficulty communicating calmly. Mario is presumably responding in reactive or reflexive cognitive states, which require intensive de-escalating skills from whomever he is interacting, especially when faced with accusations concerning his possible gang and /or illegal activity.

The NME model may also be helpful for faculty and staff. It teaches an interpersonal hierarchy. If teachers are able to identify where in the hierarchy they interact with their students, they are more able to make meaningful steps toward a safe and powerful relationship. Through NME, faculty and staff are given tools to decrease the power differential and de-escalate students' behavior. Additionally, NME can help faculty and staff manage their own secondary trauma reactions, in working with and caring for these students. It allows faculty and staff to make meaning out of the student's behavior and enables them not to take the behavior personally, as the behavior is a manifestation of reactions controlled by the lower brain.

Professional Experiences

School counselors can be leaders in the area of trauma-informed schools. They are trained specifically to understand how to identify potential trauma reactions and how to manage the affective and/or behavioral manifestations that may result from environmental stimuli. These stimuli might communicate potential danger to a student (e.g., a teacher raising her voice to get the students' attention may be perceived as a safety threat by a student who lives in a violent home and/or neighborhood and must be hyper-vigilant). Using a NME framework, Ms. Smith can use de-escalation and communication skills with the police officers, Mario, the administration, and faculty.

The counselor had multiple concerns raised during the conversation, which she made note of but did not share with the officers. The primary concern related to potential safety concerns for the students, staff, and faculty was whether someone in the building had committed a murder; and perhaps even more concerning, the potential for gang retaliation for the murder. Additionally, she was keenly aware of the Federal Educational Rights and Privacy Act of 1974 (FERPA), which is a federal law that protects the privacy of student educational records. She also knew that the student was likely an undocumented immigrant and that there had been a recent intensification of arrests and deportations in the area based on reports of other students. She was not certain that this situation might actually be the officers' way to gain information to arrest the student for illegally entering the country rather than an actual murder. Because the geographic area in which she worked had many immigrants, the counseling staff and building administrators were well aware that they were not mandated to report immigration status of students or their parents to authorities.

The authors of this chapter have experience working in both school and clinical mental health settings with justice-involved youth. This experience was helpful in dealing with the current situation. The counselor knew that the officers' presentation was a common approach to garner information from people during an investigation. Understanding that this was a tactic to get information, she was able to stay grounded in her professional responsibilities. She also knew that she did not have to provide an immediate response to the officers regarding information requested. Even if the officers ultimately would have access to the information, there would be no reason that the counselor could not consult with her counseling supervisor and the building administrator, and together they may even consult with the school board attorney on how to handle the matter. Her knowledge of the law, professional ethics, and experience professionally interacting with law enforcement informed how she approached the situation.

Counselor Impact

It makes sense that any counselor in this situation would feel a great deal of stress. Ms. Smith is caught between two moral imperatives—one involving safety of students, faculty, and staff and the other involving maintenance of privacy around educational records. Additionally, the counselor is potentially justified in fearing for her own safety if Mario or his fellow gang members become aware that the police are talking to the counselor about this case. In times of stress, school counselors need to have support from colleagues and supervisors.

The officers' aggressive, threatening presentation with the counselor seemed to be intended to increase pressure on the counselor to comply with their demands for information. However, these officers also chose not to speak with an educational administrator, rather coming to the counseling office directly. It would be easy for the counselor to become emotional or reactive in response to a perceived threat and fail to make good, well-thought-out decisions about how to handle the situation.

Therefore, it is important for the counselor to remain grounded in this situation. She can do this by sitting firmly in an office chair with her feet flat on the floor, intentionally feeling the chair beneath her and the floor under her feet. This will ground her in the room. Additionally, the counselor should be mindful to slow down her breathing. By doing these things, the counselor is more likely to be able to reduce her stress level and corresponding overactivation of the autonomic nervous system (ANS) response, so that she can access her ability to think through the events.

Mental Health Implications

If Mario actually murdered someone, and he presents as respectful and is careful in his criminal activity, such that he has not been caught on campus, it is likely that his behavior is well thought out and not impulsive. This indicates he may have some level of psychopathy, which potentially increases the danger risk for others at the school. While the ASCA Code of Ethics states school counselors do not make a diagnosis, they are trained in diagnostic criteria. It is important for the counselor to have some awareness of the characteristics of someone who has socialized into criminal behavior as a survival mechanism. This behavior would be different from someone who may have criminal behavior as his or her only goal in life, especially if he or she is working in a school and neighborhood where criminal activity is common. A counselor must be very careful in a situation where a student demonstrates strong executive functioning, allowing him to problem solve and develop plans to perpetrate violence, if he believes he has been *ratted out* to the police.

Additionally, there is a potential safety issue of which faculty, staff, and students are keenly aware. Parents are fearful enough, since they are reporting they will not send their students to school during the upcoming testing period next week because they heard through neighborhood conversation that a gang altercation is being planned to occur at the campus. Students are fearful which will affect their ability to concentrate and attend to what is going on in classes. For students who have had family members fall victim to violence, this information could trigger a transcrisis situation. A transcrisis situation happens when an unresolved issue from an earlier trauma emerges because of a current traumatic or stressful event (James & Gilliland, 2013). Therefore, students or parents may react in peri-traumatic anger/aggression or dissociation when interacting with this counselor and others on campus. Further, school is often the only safe place for the students in this neighborhood. Having a threat of violence at school removes this safe haven, thus increasing the likelihood for peri-traumatic reactions.

For people who live under an almost constant threat of violence, like the students at this school, it is not uncommon for them to experience over-stimulation of the ANS, which regulates blood pressure, body temperature, respiration, and glandular secretion of stress hormones. When people have an overactive ANS system, they are very sensitive to environmental stimuli that may be perceived as threatening. When someone perceives danger in the environment, the normal reactions are fight, flight, or freeze reactions. Some common affective and behavioral presentations are anger and aggression (fight) and dissociation (flight, escape). Reaction time is crucial in a situation where someone's life may be in jeopardy, so the ANS system is able to neuro-hijack the *thinking brain* where executive functioning occurs (attention, impulse control, problem solving, etc.). Therefore, when someone has an overactive ANS, he or she is using most of his or her energy scanning the environment for perceived dangers and defending against those (real or imagined) dangers. He or she does not have energy or attention to use on things like math or English instruction, which require the brain to be calm, focused, and attentive.

Ethical Considerations

There are several ethical and legal principles outlined by the American School Counselor Association's Ethical Standards for School Counselors (2016) that the counselor should consider. The first is:

> A.1.g. Are knowledgeable of laws, regulations and policies affecting students and families and strive to protect and inform students and families regarding their rights.

There are several potential legal issues that the counselor should be aware of in this situation to resolve it in a professional manner. These include the Family Educational Rights and Privacy Act (FERPA; 20 U.S.C. § 1232g; 34 CFR Part 99); any state laws related to schools notifying people on campus about a potential threat, also known as duty to warn laws; any state laws related to cooperating with a criminal investigation; and any state or federal laws, regulations, or school policies regarding reporting illegal immigrants to the authorities.

The following ASCA ethical principles are related to the same concern, which is confidentiality (ethical) and privacy (legal) concerns regarding records release.

> A.2.j. Protect the confidentiality of students' records and release personal data in accordance with prescribed federal and state laws and school board policies.
>
> A.12.a. Abide by the Family Educational Rights and Privacy Act (FERPA), which defines who has access to students' educational records and allows parents the right to review and challenge perceived inaccuracies in their child's records.
>
> b. Advocate for the ethical use of student data and records and inform administration of inappropriate or harmful practices.
>
> B.2. Responsibilities to the School.
>
> a. Develop and maintain professional relationships and systems of communication with faculty, staff and administrators to support students.

This student's records are protected under FERPA (20 U.S.C. § 1232g; 34 CFR Part 99). The most common way to provide these records to authorities is to have the parent/legal guardian sign a consent allowing for this to occur. However, it is unlikely that the officers want the counselor in this case to contact a parent/legal guardian for permission, and it is unrealistic in this scenario for the counselor to identify a responsible legal guardian for Mario. The officers may also obtain a court order for the records under which the counselor would be legally obligated to provide the records to the officers.

Finally, the school counselor in this situation is dealing with a very delicate situation, so another ethical standard that applies is:

> A.2.m. Advocate for appropriate safeguards and protocols so highly sensitive student information is not disclosed accidentally to individuals who do not have a need to know such

information. Best practice suggests a very limited number of educators would have access to highly sensitive information on a need-to-know basis.

The police investigation of Mario for a murder is sensitive information. It is crucial that the counselor not exacerbate the situation by speaking to people who are not directly involved in deciding how to handle the problem. If information that suggests a student may be under investigation for murder were to spread through the school, additional safety concerns may develop. It is best to contact the building principal and the director of counseling for the district, if one exists, to consult about the situation. These administrators are likely to consult with the district's legal counsel. Granted, this may result in the officers becoming angry or more demanding because it delays them in getting the information they want; however, it is the counselor's professional ethical and legal duty to take care in determining the right way to address the situation.

Multicultural Considerations

One of the primary multicultural concerns regarding this case is that counselors may have certain implicit biases related to undocumented immigrants, male students who grow up in violent neighborhoods, and/or students in impoverished communities. It is important for counselors to be aware of their biases and to be open to feedback about potential ethnic, religious, or gender biases. Using the American Counseling Association (ACA) competencies on working with special populations can help guide counselors in what they need to do to gain the awareness, knowledge, and skills necessary to be culturally competent.

Discussion Questions

1. What are your personal reactions to this incident? If you had a child who attended this school, would that change your reaction? How would you manage your own reactions in order to respond in a professional manner to the request being made?
2. What are your social locations related to race, gender, ethnicity, poverty, violence, etc., which might affect your perception of this student? How would you minimize the impact of your social locations on how you handle a student issue such as the one described in this case study?
3. How would you determine who in the school has a *need to know* what is going on with this student under the FERPA guidelines?
4. As a school counselor, how do you balance confidentiality of the student and his records, the needs of law enforcement to investigate a murder case, and the safety of self (from gang members) and everyone in the school?

Resources

Bluestein, J. (2001). *Creating emotionally safe schools: A guide for educators and parents.* Deerfield Beach, FL: Health Communications, Inc.

References

American School Counselor Association. (2016). *Ethical standards for school counselors.* Alexandria, VA: Author.
American School Counselor Association. (2019). *The ASCA national model: A framework for school counseling programs* (4th ed.). Alexandria, VA: Author.
Camarota, S. A., & Zeigler, K. (2016). *Immigrants in the United States: A profile of the foreign-born using 2014 and 2015 Census Bureau data.* Washington, DC: The Center for Immigration Studies.
Federal Educational Rights and Privacy Act of 1974 20 U.S.C. § 1232g; 34 CFR Part 99.

James, R. K., & Gilliland, B. E. (2013). *Crisis intervention strategies* (7th ed.). Belmont, CA: Brooks/Cole.

McFarland, J., Hussar, B., de Brey, C., Snyder, T., Wang, X., Wilkinson-Flicker, S., . . . & Hinz, S. (2017). *The condition of education 2017* (NCES 2017–144). U.S. Department of Education. Washington, DC: National Center for Education Statistics. Retrieved from https://nces.ed.gov/pubsearch/pubsinfo.asp?pubid=2017144

Perry, D. (2012). *Neurosequential model in education*. Houston, TX: The Child Trauma Academy.

Puzzanchera, C. (2018). *Juvenile arrests, 2016*. Juvenile Justice Statistics: National report series bulletin. Office of Juvenile Justice and Delinquency Prevention. Washington, DC: Office of Justice Programs. U.S. Department of Justice.

Reflections: In the space provided, write your notes and reflections regarding this case study.

13 Cutting

A Non-Suicidal Self-Injury

Shannon McFarlin

Background

In 2013, the American Psychiatric Association (APA) proposed criteria for a new mental health diagnosis termed *non-suicidal self-injury* (NSSI). Per the APA (2013), the hallmark feature of NSSI is repetitive and "intentional self-inflicted damage to the surface of [the] body . . . , with the expectation that the injury will lead to only minor or moderate physical harm" (p. 803). More specifically, NSSI behaviors are absent of the intent to end one's own life, which is confirmed when an individual overtly denies intent, or which others can infer from the presumably non-lethal nature of an individual's past self-injurious behaviors (APA, 2013).

Behaviors that constitute NSSI can include cutting, carving, burning, rubbing, and picking one's skin; stabbing and hitting oneself; inserting objects into one's body; and ingesting substances in large quantities (Glenn, Kleiman, Cha, Nock, & Prinstein, 2016; Madge et al., 2008), among others. Although these types of non-suicidal, self-injurious behaviors might seem unfathomable to most people, the individuals who enact them typically see them as means to desired interpersonal (i.e., social) and intrapersonal (i.e., cognitive/affective) outcomes (Nock & Prinstein, 2004). These outcomes include revenge against others, attention from others, relief from unwanted negative emotions, escape from intolerable conditions, increase in positive feelings, and self-punishment for perceived wrongdoings (McAuliffe, Arensman, Keeley, Corcoran, & Fitzgerald, 2007).

Early adolescence (ages 12–14) typically denotes the onset of NSSI behaviors (Whitlock et al., 2011), which tend to be more present in mid-adolescence (ages 15–16) and usually subside by late adolescence (age 18; Plener, Schumacher, Munz, & Groschwitz, 2015). Lifetime prevalence rates for adolescents vary by study and range from 17–60% (Kaess et al., 2013; Swannell, Martin, Page, Hasking, & St John, 2014), with NSSI behaviors occurring more often among females than males at a rate of 3:1–4:1 (APA, 2013). Factors identified as contributing or relating to the development of NSSI behaviors include bullying victimization; adverse childhood experiences, such as physical abuse by an adult; other mental health disorders, like borderline personality and depression; higher IQ; social contagion, which is learning via observations of others or exposure to media; substance use; poor body image; and a sexual minority or gender-variant identity (APA, 2013; Brown & Plener, 2017; Chang et al., 2014; Jarvi, Jackson, Swenson, & Crawford, 2013; Monto, McRee, & Deryck, 2018; Taliafarro, McMorris, Rider, & Eisenberg, 2019).

Results from Berger, Hasking, and Reupert's (2014) study that examined the need for NSSI training among educators indicated that a colossal majority of mental health professionals in schools has encountered one or more students who have enacted NSSI behaviors. Yet more than 3 out of 4 mental health staff members, including school counselors, reported a need for training about non-suicidal self-injury as well as a lack of knowledge about what and how to communicate with parents when their students are self-injuring (Berger et al., 2014). With this information in mind, consider the following case, which depicts a scenario that school counselors commonly face.

Description of Case

Gracie, a 14-year-old Caucasian female, was a freshman at a high school in a low socioeconomic area on the outskirts of a large city on the day that her mother contacted Mrs. Gupta, Gracie's school counselor, for assistance. When Mrs. Gupta answered the phone in her office on that October morning, Gracie's mother, Mrs. Allen, began the conversation by stating:

> "I'm hoping that you won't mind checking on Gracie today. When she was leaving for school this morning, I saw some marks on her left arm. They looked really red. But when I asked her to show them to me, she wouldn't. She just stomped out of the house. I don't know what to do. She's been out of control for a long time, and last year she had to be hospitalized for threatening to kill herself. I thought she was doing a little better since then, but I don't think she's stopped the cutting. Oh, and she ran away a couple of times over the summer when she got mad at me for telling her she couldn't hang out with her friends at the park. I honestly don't know what to do. I can't afford for her to go the hospital again. Her daddy lost his job three months ago, and we don't have health insurance now. I'm working two part-time jobs, and we just don't have the money. I've got three other kids to look after, and they're having troubles, too. I'm hoping that you will talk to Gracie to see what's going on."

Mrs. Gupta took a deep breath and mentally ran through her daily schedule. She knew that she was supposed to attend an Annual, Review, and Dismissal (ARD) meeting in 30 minutes for a student receiving special education services. Yet she also knew that she needed to address Mrs. Allen's concerns. She decided to send a quick email to her assistant principal to let him know that she would not be at the ARD meeting. Then she gave Mrs. Allen her full attention, requesting additional information about Gracie's history.

In her conversation with Mrs. Allen, Mrs. Gupta learned that Gracie had begun cutting herself on the arms, hips, and outer thighs at the age of 12. Mrs. Allen explained that when the cutting first began, she just thought that Gracie was participating in a fad that she learned from peers in middle school. She said that when she and Mr. Allen discovered Gracie's cutting, they responded by grounding her to her room, refusing to allow her to spend time with her peers at the park during after-school hours, and removing all sharp objects from the house. Yet afterward, Gracie found ways to smuggle razors into the house, keeping a stash of them in a pencil case that she kept in the top of her closet. Mrs. Allen explained that the impetus for Gracie's hospitalization at age 13 was an incident in which she walked into the bathroom to find Gracie carving the word *STUPID* on the inside of her arm. When Mrs. Allen confiscated the razor, Gracie became violent, hitting her mother repeatedly in the chest and yelling, "I hate you! I'm going to kill myself because *I hate you!*" Then Mrs. Allen called 911, and an ambulance arrived at the house to take Gracie to an inpatient mental health facility where Gracie was admitted for 10 days.

Mrs. Allen reported that, initially, Gracie's time in the hospital seemed to have helped her somewhat. While in the hospital, Gracie participated in group and individual therapy sessions as well as two family therapy sessions with her mother and father. Although Gracie was angry about the hospitalization at first, she seemingly embraced it after a couple of days. With a smile on her face, she told peers and providers outlandish stories of having been adopted from a Russian orphanage at birth, of having been sex-trafficked at the age of 7, and of having had a secret relationship online with one of the Jonas brothers, all of which were untrue. When others confronted her about her outrageous stories, she offered additional details to substantiate them, often contradicting information that she previously had shared. Mrs. Allen confessed to Mrs. Gupta that, yes, Gracie did have a habit of "making up stories and telling crazy lies," which two years previously resulted in a report to child protective services after Gracie told a teacher that her father was a drug dealer. Still, despite Gracie's propensity for untruthfulness during her time in the hospital, staff there had determined her to be stable and released her back to her parents with a recommendation that Gracie continue her treatment with outpatient therapy sessions.

Mrs. Allen disclosed that she had not followed up with outpatient therapy services for Gracie because Gracie had seemed to be doing well after she left the hospital. However, after the school year ended and summer vacation began, Gracie began to sneak to the park nearby to see her old friends from middle school. During the summer months, she ran away from home twice when her parents forbade her from going to the park, each time staying away for no more than 24 hours. Mr. and Mrs. Allen did not call the police either time, and Gracie returned home by her own volition on both occasions.

When Gracie entered ninth grade the following September, she struggled to find a new peer group. Her friends from middle school were zoned to other high schools, which pleased her parents but not Gracie. Searching for her new niche, Gracie floated from peer group to peer group, attempting to engage them with grandiose stories and attention-seeking behaviors. In a short period of time, scathing rumors about Gracie's scandalous past began to circulate the halls, and she met peer rejection around every corner.

After obtaining Gracie's history from Mrs. Allen, Mrs. Gupta agreed to check in with Gracie at school. Mrs. Gupta found Gracie in her third period class, physical education, and requested that Gracie escort her to her office. In the privacy of the counseling office, Mrs. Gupta informed Gracie of her mother's earlier call and asked Gracie if she had been cutting herself. Gracie responded with, "My mom is so dumb," but then pulled up her shirtsleeve and thrust her forearm forward for Mrs. Gupta to view. Scars and wounds crisscrossed up and down Gracie's arm. Although most of the scars were light in color and visibly healed, there were fresh cuts near her wrist that were crusted with dried blood. "I'm not suicidal," Gracie said obstinately. "I don't need to go to the hospital, so don't call my mom. She gets so crazy about this stuff. It just helps me feel better. I haven't done it in a long time, and I swear I'm not suicidal."

Strategies for Consideration

School counselors working with students who present with NSSI often do not have enough information on how to approach these behaviors. The following sections offer strategies and information that will assist school counselors in how to assess for NSSI and other co-occurring mental health issues; where and when to make referrals; and how to inform parents regarding the self-injurious behaviors.

Theoretical Frameworks

Researchers have identified mentalization-based treatment (MBT) as one of the most effective therapeutic modalities for the treatment of NSSI among both adults and adolescents (Calati & Courtet, 2016; Glenn, Franklin, & Nock, 2014). The purpose of MBT is to help students and clients think before reacting to their own internal experiences and interpretations of others' thoughts and feelings. By practicing mentalization (i.e., thinking through the meanings assigned to others' and one's own mental states), students can become more adept at regulating emotions and managing impulsive behaviors (Bateman & Fonagy, 2010).

A primary focus of MBT is students' transference responses toward the counselor, which are rooted in early attachment experiences (Bateman & Fonagy, 2010). Assisting students in mentalizing transference responses involves six sequential steps, which are (1) validating the student's transference feelings; (2) exploring the counselor's behaviors that engender the transference feelings; (3) acknowledging the ways that the counselor's behaviors are consistent with the student's interpretation of her or him; (4) collaborating with the student for other possible interpretations of events; (5) presenting an alternative perspective to the student; and (6) monitoring the reactions of both the student and the counselor.

Throughout all processes of MBT, the counselor conveys empathy, support, and positive regard for the student or client, always donning an inquisitive, not-knowing position (Bateman & Fonagy, 2010). Important to note is that, although similarities between the student's counseling relationship and relationships with others are identified and acknowledged during counseling processes, foraging through wounds from the past is not the intended goal of MBT. Instead, the premier intent is to teach students how to consider phenomena in different ways, making room for multiple understandings of them (Bateman & Fonagy, 2010).

Although the outlined process of guided mentalization is brief in nature, desired results usually are not achieved within only a few brief counseling sessions, especially when adolescents evidence symptoms of other coexisting mental health disorders (e.g., borderline personality; Bateman & Fonagy, 2010). Because school counselors generally do not provide long-term, clinical counseling services for the students they serve, they frequently refer students who require more intensive services to outside service providers (ASCA, 2016). With the latter statement in mind, a logical question to follow might be: Then what *can* school counselors do on their campuses to assist students who are or were engaging in self-harming behaviors? In response to this question, Humphreys, Risner, Hicks, and Moyer (2016) recommended that school counselors employ the following strategies immediately following a student's disclosure of (or the counselor's discovery of) the student's NSSI behaviors:

- Ensure the student's safety and welfare, facilitating immediate medical care when significant injuries are present.
- Assess for risk of suicide.
- Assess for escalation of NSSI behaviors since the first-known episode.
- Assess for co-occurring problems.
- Assess the necessity for referral to an emergency mental health facility.
- Inquire about the use of shared cutting devices, which can elevate risk for exposure to life threatening, communicable diseases (e.g., HIV), and document the information that is obtained.
- Solicit the student's consent for a parental contact plan.
- Work collaboratively with the student to formulate a plan for disclosure to parents.
- Seek input from other professionals for ethical decision making.
- Adhere to the ethical principle of nonmaleficence (i.e., do not harm) as the motivating guide in all decision-making processes.

For postcrisis follow-up encounters with the student, Humphreys et al. (2016) proffered these additional strategies:

- Invite the student to participate in weekly group counseling sessions with peers who share common challenges.
- Meet with the student frequently to assess risk for suicide.
- Equip the student with simple strategies that can be used to manage impulses to self-harm (e.g., breathing techniques to reduce anxiety, music and/or art to divert attention from triggering stimuli, ice cubes held to the skin to elicit outcomes once achieved with self-harming behaviors).

Finally, school counselors are encouraged to incorporate preventative strategies into their counseling programs that can benefit all students on campus (Humphreys et al., 2016). Strategies for the prevention of NSSI can include educating students about how to assist suicidal or self-injurious friends, as youth are more likely to disclose vulnerable aspects of themselves to close friends than they are to adults. School counselors also are advised to prepare themselves for unexpected events that require responsive services to students. Self-preparatory tasks that are proposed for all counselors include participating in trainings to increase counseling competencies, compiling and revising lists of updated referral resources, and managing work time to ensure availability for unexpected student crises.

Professional Experiences

School counselors often receive telephone calls, emails, and personal appearances from parents requesting socioemotional assistance for their students. Sometimes requests are for in-school counseling services; sometimes they are for referrals to community providers; and sometimes they are for student welfare checks, as was the case with Gracie's mother. When parents make these kinds of requests, school counselors sometimes lack clear courses of action. Schools often do not have established protocols for responsive services for individual students, and counselors commonly report feeling uncertain about confidentiality parameters and reporting responsibilities. Additionally, school counselors regularly are assigned multiple duties, many of which are unrelated to actual counseling practice, and most of which are time-consuming priorities of school administrators. Oftentimes, fulfilling assigned administrative duties sometimes means neglecting students' immediate needs, and meeting students' immediate needs often means failing to fulfill other assigned duties. Moreover, when classroom teachers resist interruptions to their instructional time with students, responding to students' immediate needs can prove to be even more challenging for school counselors.

School counselors are trained on methods of assessing and responding to student crises in their graduate programs. However, after they graduate from their programs and begin school counseling practice, they bear the responsibility of remaining current with research regarding mental health care for students. Remaining current with mental health trends can be challenging for many school counselors due to budget restrictions, time constraints, and lack of support from administrators, among other things.

Counselor Impact

Some school counselors report feeling incompetent to intervene with suicidal and self-harming students. Inadequate understanding of NSSI, inability to distinguish NSSI from suicidality, and low self-appraisal of risk assessment skills are all factors that contribute to feelings of ineptitude. Despite the courses of action that counselors employ when intervening on behalf of students, the uncertainties of their decisions weigh heavily on them, compelling them to question their own decision-making ability and to ruminate about possible repercussions for students.

School counselors who regularly over-identify with their students' struggles are at risk for professional burnout and compassion fatigue, the latter of which Figley (1982) described as the cost of caring for others who are in physical and emotional pain. Symptoms of compassion fatigue commonly include cynicism, stress-related illness, vicarious trauma, physical and emotional exhaustion, anger and irritability, substance abuse, and depression, which ultimately can result in diminished work satisfaction and the ability to feel compassion and empathy for others (Figley, 1982). To avoid compassion fatigue, school counselors must maintain appropriate boundaries with the students and families that they assist, taking care not to become too emotionally engaged with the subjects of their work and to enact strategies for their own self-care and wellness.

Not only can school counselors incur emotional afflictions from their work with students, but they also can experience increased hardships in their personal and familial lives when their work demands are too taxing. For example, just as do teachers, school counselors often encumber expenses for necessary work-related items and services that school district budgets will not support. Such expenses might include those incurred for counseling props, student supplies, and fees for professional training opportunities. Financial burdens, as well as burdens related to overtime work, can strain school counselors' familial and social relationships, further increasing their risk for burnout and compassion fatigue.

Mental Health Implications

Although it can occur in isolation, NSSI commonly occurs comorbidly with other psychiatric conditions such as borderline personality disorder, substance abuse disorders, post-traumatic stress disorder, affective disorders (e.g., major depressive disorder), anxiety disorders, behavioral disorders, and eating disorders (Cipriano, Cella, & Cotrufo, 2017), among others. In particular, borderline personality disorder (BPD), which is "a pervasive pattern of instability of interpersonal relationships, self-image, and affects, and marked impulsivity" (APA, 2013, p. 663), tends to be prevalent among those who struggle with NSSI. In fact, BPD is the only DSM-V (APA, 2013) disorder that includes NSSI as a diagnostic criterion, and NSSI is thought to be a possible precursor to BPD (Stead, Boylan, & Schmidt, 2019).

Whereas a lack of suicidal intent is a requirement for a formal diagnosis of NSSI, researchers have identified NSSI as a strong predictor of future suicidal behaviors among those who contend with it (Chesin et al., 2017). When multiple methods of self-harm have been employed, when there is a longer history of NSSI behaviors, and when NSSI behaviors occur with greater frequency, an individual's risk for a later suicide attempt is even greater (APA, 2013; Grandclerc, De Labrouhe, Spodenkiewicz, Lachal, & Moro, 2016). Because of its link to subsequent suicidal ideation, NSSI should be taken seriously, and early intervention should be sought.

Ethical Considerations

The following ethical considerations from the ASCA (2016) Ethical Standards for School Counselors are relevant to this case.

> A.1.b Aim to provide counseling to students in a brief context and support students and families/guardians in obtaining outside services if the student needs long-term clinical counseling.

School counselors can provide short-term counseling services to students for issues that impede their functioning at school. When working with students, school counselors must be able to differentiate between the need for short-term counseling and the need for more intensive therapy. When long-term, clinical counseling is necessary, school counselors provide students and parents with referrals to outside providers who can assist students with their specific therapeutic needs.

> A.1.c Do not diagnose but remain acutely aware of how a student's diagnosis can potentially affect the student's academic success.

School counselors do not diagnose students with mental health disorders. Yet they must remain knowledgeable of current mental health conditions that afflict students, as well as the ways that mental health symptoms can interfere with academic success.

> A.1.h Provide effective, responsive interventions to address student needs.

School counselors are compelled to provide responsive services to students who are in need. The interventions that are employed must be best practices that are grounded in research and theory.

    A.6.a Collaborate with all relevant stakeholders, including students, educators and parents/ guardians when student assistance is needed, including the identification of early warning signs of student distress.

When school counselors assist students who evidence distress, collaboration with others is key. Counselors collaborate with teachers and administrators to monitor students at school, and they collaborate with parents to devise plans for students' safety outside of school. In all cases, students are involved in safety planning to the greatest extent possible, based on developmental level.

    A.9.a Inform parents/guardians and/or appropriate authorities when a student poses a serious and foreseeable risk of harm to self or others. When feasible, this is to be done after careful deliberation and consultation with other appropriate professionals. School counselors inform students of the school counselor's legal and ethical obligations to report the concern to the appropriate authorities unless it is appropriate to withhold this information to protect the student (e.g. student might run away if he/she knows parents are being called). The consequence of the risk of not giving parents/guardians a chance to intervene on behalf of their child is too great. Even if the danger appears relatively remote, parents should be notified.

When a student is deemed to be at risk for harming self or someone else, the school counselor must inform parents, school stakeholders, and authorities, if necessary. Before breaching confidentiality, the school counselor needs to consult with other professionals to ensure ethical and legal decision making, taking care to document the results of those consultations. When a breach is necessary, the school counselor should inform the student of the mandate that requires the disclosure of information to others, if doing so is not likely to result in additional harm to the student. Even if the school counselor determines that the student does not pose an immediate risk to self or others, the counselor should follow through with reporting information about the student's risk to parents.

    A.9.b Use risk assessments with caution. If risk assessments are used by the school counselor, an intervention plan should be developed and in place prior to this practice. When reporting risk-assessment results to parents, school counselors do not negate the risk of harm even if the assessment reveals a low risk as students may minimize risk to avoid further scrutiny and/or parental notification. School counselors report risk assessment results to parents to underscore the need to act on behalf of a child at risk; this is not intended to assure parents their child isn't at risk, which is something a school counselor cannot know with certainty.

School counselors must be knowledgeable about risk assessments, and they must use assessment instruments and procedures that are well established. School counselors must know how to interpret results of risk assessments, and they must have follow-up interventions identified prior to assessing students for risk. Even when a student's assessment yields evidence of low risk, school counselors acknowledge that the need for risk assessment was enough to warrant concern for the student's welfare, and they convey that concern to parents when reporting results to them.

    A.9.c Do not release a student who is a danger to self or others until the student has proper and necessary support. If parents will not provide proper support, the school counselor takes necessary steps to underscore to parents/guardians the necessity to seek help and at times may include a report to child protective services.

When a school counselor determines that a student is at risk for harming self or others, the school counselor is not to leave the student alone. If the counselor must leave the student momentarily, then she or he must first ensure the student's safety by soliciting another professional to stay with the student in her or his absence. Students who are at high risk are not to be returned to their classrooms. Instead, the school counselor is to contact the student's parent/guardian and/or authorities to report the risk and to request assistance. The school counselor is to stay with the student until a responsible party arrives to withdraw the student from school. If the school counselor does not feel safe being alone with the student, then the counselor can request the presence of a colleague while waiting for parents and/or authorities to arrive.

> B.1.h Provide parents/guardians with accurate, comprehensive and relevant information in an objective and caring manner, as is appropriate and consistent with ethical and legal responsibilities to the student and parent.

In Gracie's case, her mother contacted the school counselor with concerns for Gracie's welfare. Per this ethical code, the school counselor, Mrs. Gupta, should follow-up with Gracie's mother to report on her findings.

Multicultural Considerations

Native American, Hispanic, and white students have the highest reported rates of NSSI behaviors (i.e., 20.79%, 19.9%, and 17.71%, respectively), which are least reported among African American and Asian students (i.e., 12.10% and 14.98%, respectively; Monto et al., 2018). Rates among students who identify as bisexual tend to be higher than they are among students who identify as either straight or gay (Fraser et al., 2018). Although NSSI is more common among females, it does occur among male students, with one in 10 boys reporting past self-injurious behaviors (compared to 4 in 10 girls; Monto et al., 2018). Furthermore, rates among youth whose religious identities are salient tend to be much lower than those among youth who identify as atheist or agnostic (Whitlock & Rodham, 2013).

Regarding gender, researchers have noted differences in self-injuring behaviors among males and females. Cutting and scratching are more common among girls, who tend to inflict injuries to their arms and legs (Sornberger, Heath, Toste, & McLouth, 2012). In contrast, boys are more prone to burning and hitting themselves, and they are more likely to incur injuries to the chest, face, and and/or genitals (Sornberger et al., 2012). Bakken and Gunter (2012) noted that males' NSSI behaviors also tend to be more impulsive and painful, and that suicidal thoughts are more prevalent among males who self-injure than they are among females who enact self-harming behaviors (Bakken & Gunter, 2012).

Case Discussion Questions

1. Based on what you have read in this chapter, what other information would be important to obtain about Gracie's history? How would you obtain that information? What makes that information important to consider?
2. In your words, what is the primary difference between NSSI behaviors and suicidal behaviors?
3. If you were Mrs. Gupta, what would be your next steps in assisting Gracie? List them in the order that you would enact them.
4. Do some research to find sources of training on the topic non-suicidal self-injury. Provide a short synopsis of one of the training opportunities and explain its potential benefit for you.

5. Brainstorm one campus-wide strategy that you might implement to help prevent NSSI among students. What resources would you need for its implementation? How feasible would it be? What kind of impact can you see it having on students?

Resources

National Suicide Prevention Lifeline:

   Phone:1-800-273-TALK (1-800-273-8255) and 1-800-SUICIDE (1-800-784-2433)
   Website: suicidepreventionlifeline.org
   Twitter: @800273TALK

References

American Psychological Association. (2013). *Diagnostic and statistical manual of mental disorders* (5th ed.). Arlington, VA: American Psychiatric Association.

American School Counselor Association. (2016). *Ethical standards for school counselors*. Alexandria, VA: American School Counselor Association.

Bakken, N. W., & Gunter, W. D. (2012). Self-cutting and suicidal ideation among adolescents: Gender differences in the causes and correlates of self-injury. *Deviant Behavior*, *33*(5), 339–356. doi:10.1080/016 39625.2011.584054

Bateman, A., & Fonagy, P. (2010). Mentalization based treatment for borderline personality disorder. *World Psychiatry*, *9*(1), 11–15. Retrieved from www.ncbi.nlm.nih.gov/pmc/articles/PMC2816926/

Berger, E., Hasking, P., & Reupert, A. (2014). "We're working in the dark here": Education needs of teachers and school staff regarding student self-injury. *School Mental Health*, *6*(3), 201–212. doi:10.1007/ s12310-014-9135-7

Brown, R. C., & Plener, P. L. (2017). Non-suicidal self-injury in adolescence. *Current Psychiatry Reports*, *19*(3), 20. doi:10.1007/s11920-017-0767-9

Calati, R., & Courtet, P. (2016). Is psychotherapy effective for reducing suicide attempt and non-suicidal self-injury rates? Meta-analysis and meta-regression of literature data. *Journal of Psychiatric Research*, *79*, 8–20. doi:10.1016/j.jpsychires.2016.04.003

Chang, S. S., Chen, Y. Y., Heron, J., Kidger, J., Lewis, G., & Gunnell, D. (2014). IQ and adolescent self-harm behaviours in the ALSPAC birth cohort. *Journal of Affective Disorders*, *152–154*, 175–182. doi:10.1016/j.jad.2013.09.005

Chesin, M. S., Galfavy, H., Sonmez, C. C., Wong, A., Oquendo, M. A., Mann, J. J., & Stanley, B. (2017). Nonsuicidal self-injury is predictive of suicide attempts among individuals with mood disorders. *Suicide and Life-Threatening Behavior*, *47*(5), 567–579. doi:10.1111/sltb.12331

Cipriano, A., Cella, S., & Cotrufo, P. (2017). Nonsuicidal self-injury: A systematic review. *Frontiers in Psychology*, *8*(8). doi:10.3389/fpsyg.2017.01946

Figley, C. R. (1982). *Traumatization and comfort: Close relationships may be hazardous to your health*. Paper presented at the Keynote address for Families and Close Relationships: Individuals in Social Interaction Conference at Texas Tech University in Lubbock, TX.

Fraser, G., Wilson, M. S., Garisch, J. A., Robinson, K., Brocklesby, M., Kingi, T., . . . & Russell, L. (2018). Non-suicidal self-injury, sexuality concerns, and emotion regulation among sexually diverse adolescents: A multiple mediation analysis. *Archives of Suicide Research: Official Journal of the International Academy for Suicide Research*, *22*(3), 432–452. doi:10.1080/13811118.2017.1358224

Glenn, C. R., Franklin, J. C., & Nock, M. K. (2014). Evidence-based psychosocial treatments for self-injurious thoughts and behaviors in youth. *Journal of Clinical Child & Adolescent Psychology*, *44*(1), 1–29. doi:10.1080/15374416.2014.945211

Glenn, C. R., Kleiman, E. M., Cha, C. B., Nock, M. K., & Prinstein, M. J. (2016). Implicit cognition about self-injury predicts actual self-injurious behavior: Results from a longitudinal study of adolescents. *Journal of Child Psychology and Psychiatry*, *57*(7), 805–813. doi:10.1111/jcpp.12500

Grandclerc, S., De Labrouhe, D., Spodenkiewicz, M., Lachal, J., & Moro, M.-R. (2016). Relations between nonsuicidal self-injury and suicidal behavior in adolescence: A systematic review. *PLoS One*, *11*(4), e0153760. doi:10.1371/journal.pone.0153760

Humphreys, K. D., Risner, W., Hicks, J. F., & Moyer, M. (2016). Non-suicidal self-injury: Cutting through the pain. *VISTAS Online*. Retrieved from www.counseling.org/docs/default-source/vistas/article_4486fd 25f16116603abcacff0000bee5e7.pdf?sfvrsn=4;Non-Suicidal

Jarvi, S., Jackson, B., Swenson, L., & Crawford, H. (2013). The impact of social contagion on non-suicidal self-injury: A review of the literature. *Archives of Suicide Research, 17*(1). doi:10.1080/13811118.2013. 748404

Kaess, M., Parzer, P., Mattern, M., Plener, P. L., Bifulco, A., Resch, F., & Brunner, R. (2013). Adverse childhood experiences and their impact on frequency, severity, and the individual function of nonsuicidal self-injury in youth. *Psychiatry Research, 206*(2–3), 265–272. doi:10.1016/j.psychres.2012.10.012.

Madge, N., Hewitt, A., Hawton, K., de Wilde, E. J., Corcoran, P., Fekete, S., . . . & Ystgaard, M. (2008). Deliberate self-harm within an international community sample of young people: Comparative findings from the Child & Adolescent Self-harm in Europe (CASE) Study. *Journal of Child Psychology and Psychiatry, and Allied Disciplines, 49*(6), 667–677. doi:10.1111/j.1469-7610.2008.01879.x

McAuliffe, C., Arensman, E., Keeley, H. S., Corcoran, P., & Fitzgerald, A. P. (2007). Motives and suicide intent underlying hospital treated deliberate self-harm and their association with repetition. *Suicide and Life-Threatening Behavior, 37*(4), 397–408. doi:10.1521/suli.2007.37.4.397

Monto, M. A., McRee, N., & Deryck, F. S. (2018). Non-suicidal self-injury among a representative sample of US adolescents, 2015. *American Journal of Public Health, 108*(8), 1042–1048. doi: 10.2105/ AJPH.2018.304470

Nock, M. K., & Prinstein, M. J. (2004). A functional approach to the assessment of self-mutilative behavior. *Journal of Consulting and Clinical Psychology, 72*, 885–890. doi:10.1037/0022-006X.72.5.885

Plener, P., Schumacher, T., Munz, L., & Groschwitz, R. (2015). The longitudinal course of non-suicidal self-injury and deliberate self-harm: A systematic review of the literature. *Borderline Personality Disorder and Emotional Dysregulation, 2*(2). doi:10.1186/s40479-014-0024-3

Sornberger, M. J., Heath, N. L., Toste, J. R., & McLouth, R. (2012). Nonsuicidal self-injury and gender: Patterns of prevalence, methods, and locations among adolescents. *Suicide and Life-Threatening Behavior, 42*(3), 266–278. doi:10.1111/j.1943-278X.2012.0088.x

Stead, V. E., Boylan, K., & Schmidt, L. A. (2019). Longitudinal associations between non-suicidal self-injury and borderline personality disorder in adolescents: A literature review. *Borderline Personality Disorder and Emotional Regulation, 6*(3). doi:10.1186/s40479-019-0100-9

Swannell, S. V., Martin, G. E., Page, A., Hasking, P., & St John, N. J. (2014). Prevalence of nonsuicidal self-injury in nonclinical samples: Systematic review, meta-analysis and meta-regression. *Suicide & Life-Threatening Behavior, 44*(3), 273–303. doi:10.1111/sltb.12070.

Taliafarro, L. A., McMorris, B. J., Rider, G. N., & Eisenberg, M. E. (2019). Risk and protective factors for self-harm in a population-based sample of transgender youth. *Archives of Suicide Research, 23*(2), 203–221. doi:10.1080/13811118.2018.1430639

Whitlock, J., Muehlenkamp, J., Purington, A., Eckenrode, J., Barreira, P., Baral Abrams, G., . . . & Knox, K. (2011). Nonsuicidal self-injury in a college population: General trends and sex differences. *Journal of American College Health, 59*, 691–698. doi:10.1080/07448481.2010.529626

Whitlock, J., & Rodham, K. (2013). Understanding nonsuicidal self-injury in youth. *School Psychology Forum: Research in Practice, 7*(4), 1–18. Retrieved from www.counseling.org/docs/default-source/ vistas/article_4486fd25f16116603abcacff0000bee5e7.pdf?sfvrsn=4;Non-Suicidal

Reflections: In the space provided, write your notes and reflections regarding this case study.

14   Homeless Students

Linda M. Hart

Background

One of the most unsettling issues in the United States is that of homelessness, and research con-ducted on this topic is immense. The growing number of homeless youth in the United States is alarming. Although it is impossible to determine the exact number, it is estimated that more than 2 million children in the United States are identified as homeless (National Alliance to End Homelessness, 2009; Slesnick, Dashora, Letcher, Erden, & Serovich 2009), and the number has grown significantly in recent years (National Association for the Education of Homeless Chil-dren and Youth [NAEHCY]/First Focus, 2010). The challenges faced by school districts con-cerning homeless students include how best to serve the students' according to their needs as the homeless student population continues to grow (Aviles de Bradley, 2011). Many homeless students go unidentified for various reasons, including (a) embarrassment, (b) family secrets, (c) fear, and (d) shame. For this reason, many homeless students do not receive the resources and opportunities available to them, resulting in poor academic achievement (Toro, Dworsky, & Fowler, 2007).

Although the homeless population faces many challenges, homeless youth face additional challenges, including poor academic achievement (Hardy, 2009; Toro et al., 2007). Students facing the hardships of homelessness experience personal challenges. Personal challenges include economic hardships, lack of proper medical care, food insecurity, psychological dis-tress, difficulties within the family, and lack of decent clothing (Berliner, 2009). Students fac-ing these hardships often consider school to be their safe haven; a place of comfort, belonging, and security. Although many of these students may not actively participate in risky behaviors, they are exposed to several risk factors, including emotional and behavioral problems, physi-cal and/or sexual victimization, criminal activity, and high school dropout rates, which are risky behaviors related to homelessness (Fowler, Toro, & Miles, 2009). The following case study reveals the experiences of unaccompanied teenage sisters who are citizens in both the United States and Mexico, but who want to live in the United States and take advantage of the educa-tional system.

Description of Case

Camila, 17, and her sister Ana, 15, lived with their mother and older sister in Oaxaca, Mexico, up until two years ago. Most of their family members are citizens of Mexico, except the two girls. Camila and Ana were both born in Texas, making them dual citizens of the United States and Mexico. Their mother came from Mexico to visit her sister in Texas during her pregnancies and intentionally to give birth in the United States with the hopes of offering her children a better life as U.S. citizens. After their births, the family returned to Mexico. As Camila grew up, she longed for an education in the United States and dreamed of attending college. When she was a high school freshman, she pleaded with her mother to let her move to live with her aunt in Texas so she could attend school in the United States. Her mother reluctantly agreed but knew this was a great opportunity for Camila.

Although she knew little English, it did not take Camila long to assimilate to her new surroundings and explore all the new opportunities introduced to her. She quickly found a job at a local confectionary so she could have her own spending money and not add financial burdens for her aunt. She studied the city's transportation system so she could catch the city bus to work and school. She began her sophomore year in a large, multiculturally diverse, Title I public high school along the Gulf Coast of Texas. Camila did not know one person in the high school with a student body of over 2,000. She felt alone. During her first year at the school, she joined several student organizations, including the student council, the biomedical club, and the choir. She also joined a local church youth group down the street from her aunt's home.

Camila's sister, Ana, was impressed with Camila's determination and wanted to join her sister in Texas. Although she was quite young, Ana talked her mother into letting her move to Texas to be with Camila and their aunt in Texas the following school year. Ana would begin high school as a freshman, while Camila was now a junior. Ana followed her sister's example and started working and going to a church youth group as well. Things appeared to be going well for the girls until their aunt asked Camila for the girls' social security numbers. She told the girls she needed them to open a bank account. It was not long before Camila realized that her aunt was planning to use them fraudulently. A family argument ensued, and their aunt kicked the girls out of her home. They were devastated and knew they had to make it work in the United States, somehow. Although they loved their mother and family in Mexico, they knew if they returned, it would destroy their dreams of attending college.

Without adult supervision or custodianship, the girls were considered unaccompanied youth. Camila quickly found housing she and her sister could afford, which was a run-down, rodent- and bug-infested garage apartment above an old house in the lower socioeconomic part of town. The apartment was bare, and the girls slept on the floor with blankets and pillows. They were willing to make personal sacrifices in exchange for the opportunity to attend school. For the next few months, the girls continued working, going to school, and participating in their church youth group. As a junior, Camila began looking into the college application process and sought out her professional school counselor for assistance. The two formed a bond right away, and her counselor helped Camila with the application process including her academic résumé, letters of recommendation, community service, college applications, and financial aid.

Camila received permission to take an office aid position for the following semester so she could use that period to work on college plans. As her counselor assisted Camila with the Free Application for Federal Student Aid (FAFSA), Camila's living arrangements were revealed, identifying her as independent. Camila admitted that she and her sister failed to tell anyone for fear of being deported to Mexico because they were unaccompanied minors. Her counselor contacted the district's homeless liaison, who immediately processed the paperwork to have Camila and Ana enrolled in the McKinney Vento Act program. Once identified as homeless, the district liaison was able to assist the girls with clothing, furnishings for their apartment, and school transportation. They also registered for the Supplemental Nutrition Assistance Program (SNAP) and Medicaid to help with medical needs. Once trust was established between Camila and her counselor, she was more outspoken about her plans and was eager to pursue her dreams.

As an unaccompanied youth, Camila was eligible (under the McKinney Vento program for homeless students) to receive the maximum amount allowed by the federal Pell Grant, as well as many financial need-based scholarships. Because she was ranked in the top 10% of her class, she was also eligible to receive merit-based scholarships. By the time she graduated from high school, Camila earned enough scholarships to cover her entire four years at a major public university in Texas. She spent her first year as a college freshman studying abroad in England. Her academic resilience, determination, and dedication to education served as a path for her younger sister to follow.

Strategies for Consideration

Homelessness is a reality for many families including school-aged children. School counselors will most likely encounter the issue of homelessness in their routine counseling duties and will need information on how to assist students who are homeless. The following sections provide legal and common-sense approaches school counselors can use as they help homeless students navigate the school environment.

Theoretical Frameworks

While working with students, school counselors often use specific theoretical frameworks to form a foundation from which to work. Considering the girls' situation, their counselor felt the solution-focused brief (SFB) counseling was best suited to move forward, while identifying specific goals.

The SFB counseling model is an ideal framework for working with students with specific goals. In Camila's case, her school counselor helped her determine college and career goals, then set forth a plan to achieve such goals. Because SFB counseling is a positive-oriented therapy, it is based on the optimistic assumption that students can formulate their own solutions (Corey & Corey, 2016). Solution-focused therapy employs techniques that begin with establishing a collaborative relationship with students. Assuming the student is the expert about her life, the school counselor worked with her to set clear goals and create a plan to attain them in a minimal space of time. Using techniques such as the miracle question, scaling, and exception finding, the school counselor can help the student formulate plans that are within reach.

Professional Experiences

The author has a wide range of professional colleagues from around the United States. Through networking with her counseling colleagues, she had the opportunity to have extensive discussions concerning at-risk, homeless, or unaccompanied students. The experiences and challenges of the homeless students were quite similar. School counselors reported various challenges themselves, such as having huge student caseloads, lack of knowledge of the students' living arrangements or family situations, and extra duties. The vast majority stated that with the many extra duties they are given, they do not have enough time to spend counseling the students and learning more about them. According to colleagues, extra duties given to school counselors include (but are not limited to) testing coordinator, coordinator of special programs, hall and bus monitor, lunch duty, master scheduler, scholarship coordinator, management of report cards and progress reports, and college fair planning.

School counselors reported additional duties other than those listed; however, the point was well taken that they are not given enough time to provide appropriate counseling services for each student. While school counselors cannot provide long-term counseling to individual students, the major concern is that students may have serious issues that are often overlooked or not addressed because school counselors are not allowed enough time to address them. Although school counselors do not set their student caseloads, they can and should advocate for appropriate numbers in order to provide the best services possible to all students. The counselors' discussions concerning homeless students led to ideas for future awareness toward the students' concerns, including (a) having access to information regarding students' living arrangements, (b) having time to get to know each student in her caseload to create relationships, and (c) having fewer non-counseling duties to spend more time counseling.

Counselor Impact

School counselors often are given large student loads, along with many extra non-counseling duties for which they are responsible. Although every student should have a relationship with his or her school counselor, at-risk, homeless, and unaccompanied students may require more attention to their personal situations in order to help them realize their potential. One of the biggest challenges that counselors face, in regard to homeless students, is the fact that the students' situations may be inadvertently unknown. When school counselors find that they have missed important information regarding students' situations, they might feel upset, angry, or guilty. Unfortunately, school or district level administrators who might not understand the role of the school counselor usually determine large caseloads and the assignment of inappropriate duties.

Advocating for appropriate roles and reasonable caseloads is one of the ways to combat the misuse of the counselor's time. Advocacy is an ongoing professional necessity. School counselors can meet with administrators before the beginning of school and provide them with a yearly calendar that outlines the important duties of the comprehensive school counseling program (CSCP). If possible, the counselor should suggest that the principal sign off on the calendar as a way to support the plan. Additionally, counselors can make presentations to students, staff, parents, and community members to promote the role of the school counselor. The next step in this process is to collect data on the counseling interventions and programs that are a part of the CSCP. Gradually, school counselors should be able to show the impact that these interventions and programs make on the total school community.

Mental Health Implications

In Camila's case, the school counselor worked with her for quite a while before she was aware of Camila's situation. Camila had been very anxious and was relieved to be able to share her story and experiences. Camila had been experiencing anxiety and stress related to her living arrangements and the uncertainty of possible deportation. Additionally, she felt disappointed and depressed that her aunt would engage in illegal behavior and put the entire family at risk.

Her counselor reiterated confidentiality, which prompted Camila to become more open about her situation. The counselor would assess for mental health issues that might need professional attention outside of the school. She could also provide resource information to the sisters if needed. Only when Camila's situation was revealed and her mental health was stable could she and her counselor work on significant goals. In order to assist her fully, her counselor (with Camila's permission) spoke with the student's teachers and some scholarship donors to make them aware of her situation, which prompted more support, assistance, and consideration. Her counselor realized that Camila's situation was unique, but might not be as uncommon as she thought.

Ethical Considerations

The ASCA (2016) Ethical Standards for School Counselors provides standards of behavior for cases involving homeless students.

> A.1. Supporting Student Development. School counselors: a. Have a primary obligation to the students, who are to be treated with dignity and respect as unique individuals.

In this case study, the counselor knew that Camila's situation and circumstances required support and a team approach to helping her continue being academically successful. Camila's homelessness was not viewed as a stigma in the eyes of the counselor but rather a situation that needed to be addressed effectively and immediately.

b. Aim to provide counseling to students in a brief context and support students and families/guardians in obtaining outside services if the student needs long-term clinical counseling.

The counselor chose to use solution-focused brief counseling in this case, which was positive, short-term, and focused on getting Camila through school with plans for postsecondary options.

e. Are concerned with students' academic, career and social/emotional needs and encourage each student's maximum development.

Before learning that Camila was an unaccompanied minor, the counselor helped Camila with the college application process including her academic résumé, letters of recommendation, community service, college applications, and financial aid. Once the counselor learned of the two sisters' difficult living situation, she devised a plan that would continue the girls on a path toward college after high school.

f. Respect students' and families' values, beliefs, sexual orientation, gender identification/expression and cultural background and exercise great care to avoid imposing personal beliefs or values rooted in one's religion, culture or ethnicity.

The school counselor understood Camila's familial and cultural values. The counselor was bound to help the sisters within the parameters of the school's policies and state and federal laws, setting aside any potential personal biases or preconceived notions.

g. Are knowledgeable of laws, regulations and policies affecting students and families and strive to protect and inform students and families regarding their rights.
h. Provide effective, responsive interventions to address student needs.
i. Consider the involvement of support networks, wraparound services and educational teams needed to best serve students.

Each school district has regulations and policies regarding homeless students. Some districts may even have a liaison who works directly with students whose housing is compromised. In this case, the district liaison for homeless students was contacted and was able to help the sisters access basic services that provided food, clothing, and medical assistance through the McKinney Vento Act.

A.2. Confidentiality. School counselors: a. Promote awareness of school counselors' ethical standards and legal mandates regarding confidentiality and the appropriate rationale and procedures for disclosure of student data and information to school staff.

School counselors are challenged to determine how much information should be disclosed to teachers and staff based on the rule of a *need to know*. With the approval of Camila and Ana, the school counselor might want to let teachers know some information about the students' living situation, but it probably is not necessary to discuss the entire story. Teachers who have information about students' life challenges often can be helpful to the counselor in looking out for crises, depression, anxiety, and other helpful information that may not come to the attention of the school counselor otherwise. Additionally, teachers can be the front line of support for those students who struggle academically or with mental health issues.

A.4. Academic, Career and Social/Emotional Plans. School counselors: b. Provide and advocate for individual students' preK–postsecondary college and career awareness, exploration and postsecondary planning and decision making, which supports the students' right to choose from the wide array of options when students complete secondary education. c. Identify gaps in college and career access and the implications of such data for addressing both intentional and unintentional biases related to college and career counseling. d. Provide opportunities for all students to develop the mindsets and behaviors necessary to learn work-related skills, resilience, perseverance, an understanding of lifelong learning as a part of long-term career success, a positive attitude toward learning and a strong work ethic.

The school counselor in this case focused on the essential role of her profession, which was to support Camila in her desire to attend college after high school in spite of the many barriers that were present in her life. Camila's goals were honored by the counselor; any biases related to homelessness or undocumented children were overcome; and the counselor helped Camila pursue her goals until they were obtainable.

> A.6. Appropriate Referrals and Advocacy. School counselors: c. Connect students with services provided through the local school district and community agencies and remain aware of state laws and local district policies related to students with special needs, including limits to confidentiality and notification to authorities as appropriate.

As soon as Camila's counselor was aware of her housing situation, she contacted the liaison for homeless students, who was able to provide services for the sisters to make sure they could finish school and realize their goals of attending college. Under the McKinney Vento Act, school districts are required to have a homeless education liaison who works with young people, schools, and service providers to make sure that homeless youth receive the support services for academic achievement they are guaranteed under law.

> A.10. Underserved and At-Risk Populations. School counselors:f. Advocate for the equal right and access to free, appropriate public education for all youth, in which students are not stigmatized or isolated based on their housing status, disability, foster care, special education status, mental health or any other exceptionality or special need.

School counselors are charged with advocating for students and their rights as well as showing students how to advocate for themselves. In this case, clearly the school counselor did not attach any stigma to the fact that the sisters were homeless and undocumented. She advocated for Camila by guiding her through the process of applying for college.

Multicultural Considerations

Having dual citizenship had implications for Camila and Ana. For example, some services that were offered in the United States might not have been offered had they not had U.S. citizenship (food assistance, financial aid, etc.). Camila was allowed to apply for financial aid and was awarded government assistance based on her personal situation and financial status. In her case, she was considered independent and was awarded assistance accordingly.

Camila also joined a student-led organization and was very active in the group that supported her culture. Additionally, the church youth group she was a part of was very diverse, which allowed her and her sister to assimilate to the diversity of her community. According to Sue and Sue (2013), there is a great deal of pressure for racial and ethnic minorities to adapt to the ways of the dominant culture. That is exactly what the girls were trying to do. Not only did they adapt, they excelled.

Case Discussion Questions

1. How might you counsel the older sister regarding serving as both an older sister and sur- rogate parent to the younger sibling?
2. What are the implications for the younger sister once Camila goes to college? How might you counsel Ana?
3. Some teachers and administrators hold biases regarding homelessness and immigrants. How would you talk to them about homeless students in your school, and how would you advo- cate for their support on behalf of these students?
4. Group counseling is often effective in the school setting. It provides a safe place for students with similar problems to discuss their situations and options as well as their feelings sur- rounding these issues. Plan a series of six group-counseling sessions with eight homeless students. What will be the main topic of each session, and what activities might you include?
5. When students are homeless, parents may be inaccessible. Discuss with your peers how to get permission for these students to participate in group counseling; to complete forms that provide access to services; and to discuss academic goals and needs.

Resources

American School Counselor Association (2016). *Ethical standards for school counselors.* Alexandria, VA: American School Counselor Association.

Hallett, R. E., Skrla, L., & Low, J. A. (2015). That is not what homeless is: A school district's journey toward serving homeless, doubled-up, and economically displaced children and youth. *International Journal of Qualitative Studies in Education, 28*(6), 671–692.

National Center for Homeless Education. (2010). *Education for Homeless Children and Youth program data collection summary.* Washington, DC: U.S. Department of Education.

Wright, S. (2018). How does coping impact stress, anxiety, and the academic and psycho- social functioning of homeless students? Dissertation Abstracts International: Section B: The Sciences and Engineering. ProQuest http://search.ebscohost.com.ezproxy.shsu.edu/ login.aspx?direct=true&db=psyh&AN=2017–33539–139&site=ehost-live&scope=site

References

American School Counselor Association. (2016). *Ethical standards for school counselors.* Alexandria, VA: American School Counselor Association.

Aviles de Bradley, A. (2011). Unaccompanied homeless youth: Intersections of homelessness, school experi- ences, and educational policy. *Child & Youth Services, 32,* 155–172. doi:10.1080/0145935X.2011.583176

Berliner, D. C. (2009). *Poverty and potential: Out-of-school factors and school success.* Boulder, CO: Edu- cation and the Public Interest Center & Education Policy Research Unit. Retrieved from http://epicpolicy. org/publication/poverty-and-potential

Corey, M. S., & Corey, G. (2016). *Becoming a helper.* Boston, MA: Cengage Learning.

Fowler, P. J., Toro, P. A., & Miles, B. W. (2009). Pathways to and from homelessness and associated psycho- logical outcomes among adolescents leaving the foster care system. *American Journal of Public Health, 99,* 1453–1458. doi:10.2105/AJPH.2008.142547

Hardy, L. (2009). The changing face of homelessness. *American School Board Journal,* (6), 18–20.

National Alliance to End Homelessness. (2009). *America's homeless youth: Recommendations to congress on the runaway and Homeless Youth Act.* Retrieved from http://www.endhomessness.org

National Association for the Education of Homeless Children and Youth (NAEHCY). 2010. *A criti- cal moment: Child & youth homelessness in our nation's schools.* Retrieved from http://firstfocus.net/ resources/report/a-critical-moment-child-youth-homelessness-in-our-nations-schools/

Slesnick, N., Dashora, P., Letcher, A., Erden, G., & Serovich, J. (2009). A review of services and inter- ventions for runaway and homeless youth: Moving forward. *Children and Youth Services Review, 31,* 732–742. doi:10.1016/j.2009.01.006

Sue, D. W., & Sue, D. (2013). *Counseling the culturally diverse: Theory and practice.* Hoboken, NJ: John Wiley & Sons, Inc.

Toro, P. A., Dworsky, A., & Fowler, P. J. (2007, March*). Homeless youth in the United States: Recent research findings and intervention approaches.* Paper presented at The 2007 National Symposium on Homeless Research, Washington, D. C. Retrieved from http://aspe.hhs.gov/hsp/homelessness/symposium07

Reflections: In the space provided, write your notes and reflections regarding this case study.

15 Undocumented Immigrant Students

Eunice Lerma and Clarissa Salinas

Background

In the past five years, there has been an influx of immigrants from Latin America, accounting for 38% of U.S. immigrants (Pew Research Center, 2017). Central American countries' widespread poverty, an abundance of weapons, a legacy of societal violence, and overwhelmed yet inactive law enforcement and judicial systems can all be attributed to reasons people leave their countries to seek asylum in the United States. Immigrants fleeing from their countries due to war or human devastation, natural events, or other conditions that make it dangerous to live in their home country can file for Temporary Protection Status (TPS). Immigrants from El Salvador (27%) and Honduras (13%) are reported to have the highest requests for TPS (Pew Research Center, 2019).

Children can be put into three different categories: *undocumented* children are often brought very young to the United States by unauthorized immigrant parents, *unaccompanied* children enter the United States alone and are detained and provided care through federal custody, and U.S.-born *citizen-children* of undocumented immigrants who are affected by their parents' immigration status. All three groups may live in *mixed-status families*, where family members hold different legal/immigration status (Zayes et al., 2017). Many laws have determined the immigration status and safety of those who migrate to the United States. One executive order issued by the Obama administration to ensure undocumented children would have an educational path is the Deferred Action for Childhood Arrivals (DACA). The DACA program has been jeopardized with the Trump administration order to the Department of Homeland Security (DHS) to expand groups of immigrants prioritized for removal, expediting hearings, and enlisting local law enforcement to help make arrests. These guidelines have dramatically increased deportation for undocumented students and their parents (Nakamura, 2017). Ongoing immigration law changes have caused a state of emergency and incited instability for undocumented immigrant students.

Description of Case

Wilson is an undocumented immigrant from Honduras. His single mother raised him and his younger brother. Wilson's mother sent him, at 12 years old, to the United States on his own. He came on top of the Beast, a train that travels from Central America through Mexico. His trip on the Beast was over 10 days. He was caught and deported to Honduras twice before finally making it into the United States. Once he crossed into the United States, he immediately was placed in a human trafficking home by his coyote. A coyote or *coyotaje* (Spanish term) is a person who guides undocumented migrants across the border. There is a range of services provided from acquiring false documents or paying officials to let them pass illegally to physically transporting them through the border (Bailey, 2014). Once they were in the United States, Wilson and other young boys had to do intensive labor as gardeners and construction workers for long hours each day. Wilson lived this life for three years and was not enrolled in school. He was 15 years old when Immigration and Customs Enforcement (ICE) raided his job site.

All the other undocumented workers were adults and were detained for deportation, but Wilson was placed into the state foster system. Wilson was given a new family to care for him. The family that took him in was an affluent, Caucasian, non-Spanish-speaking family living in a high socioeconomic suburb. Wilson's English was limited to yardwork and painting terminology, making it very difficult to communicate with his foster family. Further, he missed his family back in Honduras and had a difficult time identifying with his new family and the American culture.

Upon school enrollment, Wilson was tested for English language learner (ELL) services and qualified for everything that the state offered regarding ELL. Wilson had one ELL course; all his other courses were general education courses where ELL accommodations were offered. None of those teachers were Spanish-fluent or even Spanish-speaking, making it extremely difficult for him to communicate with them. Additionally, teachers did not see the need to learn Spanish to be able to offer the courses in the Spanish language. Consequently, Wilson was discouraged. At 16 years of age, Wilson was an older freshman compared to his 14-year-old classmates. Wilson wanted to stay in school and graduate with his corresponding class, but he felt that he was too old and would rather start working full time. He mentioned to the counselor that he came to the United States to work and needed to provide for his family at home. The counselor did not speak Spanish and used a translator to communicate with Wilson. He did not have the proper paperwork to stay in the United States, so he was hoping to remain undocumented in the United States as long as possible. Recently, teachers reported that he has lost interest in activities and schoolwork.

Strategies for Consideration

Working with undocumented students presents unique challenges for school counselors. These challenges can be navigated using a theoretical framework, their own professional experiences and those of supervisors or consultants, knowledge of mental health considerations, codes of professional ethics, and multicultural considerations. These considerations are discussed in the following sections to provide counselors with tools that will be helpful when working with undocumented students.

Theoretical Frameworks

Bronfenbrenner (1977, 1979, 1986) developed the ecological systems theory to describe how a child's environment and their interaction with this environment affects how they will develop. The individual, his or her context and culture, and time interactions make up the social ecological views of human development. Multiple environments or ecological systems interact and influence every aspect of the child's life. A child is concurrently enmeshed in different ecosystems from the home/intimate system (microsystem) to the larger school system and then to the largest (macrosystem), which is society and culture. The smallest and immediate environment in the child's life is the *microsystem*, which includes their daily home, school, peer group, and community. The *mesosystem* incorporates the relationships between microsystems such as between school and home, peers and family, family and community. The *exosystem* pertains to the connection between two or more settings that may not directly interact with but indirectly affect the child such as caregiver's workplace, neighborhood, and extended family.

The *macrosystem* is the largest most detached group yet still has significant impact on a child's central beliefs and ideas; this includes political and economic influences. The impact of both change and constancy in a child's environment is the *chronosystem*. Changes in family structure, home, country, caregiver's employment status, and any political/economic cycles or wars substantially affect the lives of children. A social-ecological framework considers the numerous factors that affect potential behaviors and outcomes of children and youth with an immigrant status in the United States. For immigrant children, these factors can include developmental changes at the microsystem, documentation status and acculturation at the macrosystem, immigration reform acts and laws at the exosystem or forced migration, and war in the home country and economic stressors at the macrosystem (Serdarevic & Chronister, 2005).

Schools and a child's interaction with the school system fall under the microsystem. Many immigrants find themselves in under-resourced, highly segregated, limited engaging opportunity schools (Orfield & Lee, 2006; Suárez-Orozco, Suárez-Orozco, & Todorova, 2008). Racially and linguistically isolated schools put students at academic risk, leading immigrant students to have limited resources, low teacher expectations, poor achievement test outcomes, high dropout rates, and minimal academic/career assistance (Gándara & Contreras, 2009).

Professional Experiences

The authors reached out to school counselors through an association email listserv and interest groups where they were able to describe the experiences and issues related to working with undocumented students. This was very important in gathering up best practices and recommendations from practicing counselors. This humanitarian crisis is growing rapidly, and so is the need for school counselors to become aware of best practices with working with undocumented students.

Based on the experiences of these school counselors, the following suggestions regarding undocumented students emerged:

1. Empower them to advocate for themselves and their rights as students. Dr. J created a psychoeducational group to educate them on the American school system and their requirements. This allowed them a space to meet students from different countries and connect with students that might speak their own language and/or are from their home country.
2. Educate them thoroughly regarding state and federal laws: for example, substance use, rights as minors, domestic violence, and sex education.
3. Family and culture are very important. Immigrant children may put the family's needs before their own. Some are sent to the United States to work and provide finically for their families in their home countries. Be aware of this and respect it as a cultural imperative.
4. Be open and understanding to cultural beliefs about mental illness.
5. Take an interest in the child and show that you care.
6. Be aware of best practices in academic counseling. Become familiar with their home country educational system and how you can recover some credits toward graduation.

Counselor Impact

Upon entrance to the United States, unaccompanied minors are usually provided a temporary sponsor and enrolled in the public-school system. The number of immigrant students that enroll in school is rapidly growing and is a source of media attention most recently. School counselors are witness to news coverage of children in detention centers and painful stories of the separation from their biological families. Oftentimes, those same children enroll in schools where the counselor works. It can be extremely difficult for school counselors to avoid the risk of countertransference in such circumstances. Thus, it is helpful for school counselors to engage in their own counseling to process the countertransference, as well as to seek consultation from fellow clinicians.

In addition to the risk of countertransference, school counselors can become discouraged to work with immigrant students because of the limited time they have with them and the decisions that are made for their final placements. This is similar to the frustrations experienced by private clinicians who work with children in foster care. Oftentimes, school counselors meet with new students and begin to build rapport and make progress but then learn that the student moved away to be placed with a foster family or extended biological family. Nevertheless, while under their care, school counselors work to provide these students with psychoeducation about the American school systems and coordinate peer support. Again, school counselors could benefit from attending their own counseling to process such frustrations and to prevent burnout.

Mental Health Implications

In this scenario, Wilson had not ever received counseling services before, nor had he been diagnosed with any mental illness. It is important to consider, however, the trauma that Wilson experienced as a citizen of Central America as well as his migration to America. Commonly, immigrants from Honduras are exposed to war-related trauma and political violence. Further, Wilson's journey to America was marked by violence, deprivation of basic resources, and fear. Thus, Wilson should be screened for post-traumatic stress disorder (PTSD) and depression to determine the severity of his symptoms and its impact on his daily functioning. Wilson could benefit from a referral to a counselor and attend weekly sessions to process his traumatic experiences, as well as work to build a better relationship with his foster family. The school counselor should obtain a *release of information* to communicate with Wilson's counselor and treatment team. Finally, the school counselor should meet with Wilson's teachers to educate them on *trauma-informed care* and recommend that they use this approach when interacting with Wilson to ensure that he feels supported and nonthreatened.

Ethical Considerations

School counselors are bound by strict ethical standards that are provided by ASCA (2016) to guide counselors in their daily work with students. The following standards are relevant to working with undocumented students.

> A.1.e Are concerned with students' academic, career and social/emotional needs and encourage each student's maximum development.

The school counselor has a duty to ensure that every student has the necessary support and resources to advance. Wilson has lost interest in his schoolwork and is emotionally conflicted about his need to support his family back in Honduras and graduate from school.

> A.2.m Advocate for appropriate safeguards and protocols so highly sensitive student information is not disclosed accidentally to individuals who do not have a need to know such information. Best practice suggests a very limited number of educators would have access to highly sensitive information on a need-to-know basis.

The school counselor can disclose to Wilson's teachers that he has been impacted by traumatic experiences but does not need to describe the details. For example, teachers should be aware that he is from Honduras but not that he is undocumented. The Family Educational Rights and Privacy Act (FERPA) protects the citizenship status. With the use of this law, school counselors would keep the status of citizenship confidential just as they would maintain the confidentiality of other aspects of a student's records (U.S. Department of Education, 1974). Wilson's undocumented status would be considered highly sensitive information that the school counselor should keep confidential. In the event that Wilson's status became public to members of his school, then Wilson would be put at risk for more scrutiny and isolation from his peers.

> A.3.c Review school and student data to assess needs including, but not limited to, data on disparities that may exist related to gender, race, ethnicity, socio-economic status and/or other relevant classifications.

It is important for the school counselor not only to review Wilson's academic performance in his classes but also to be aware of his enrollment in foster care and separation from his biological family.

> A.4.c Identify gaps in college and career access and the implications of such data for addressing both intentional and unintentional biases related to college and career counseling.

Wilson reported a desire to drop out of school so that he could work and provide for his family living in Honduras. The school counselor has an obligation to help Wilson make an informed decision about which direction he should take.

> A.6.c Connect students with services provided through the local school district and community agencies and remain aware of state laws and local district policies related to students with special needs, including limits to confidentiality and notification to authorities as appropriate.

Wilson qualified for all the English language learner services that the state had to offer. However, his particular school did not employee teachers who could speak to Wilson in Spanish, which made it extremely difficult for him to succeed in the courses offered. In such cases, the student has a legal right to a translator, and the school has the responsibility to provide one for the student in need.

> A.10.f Advocate for the equal right and access to free, appropriate public education for all youth, in which students are not stigmatized or isolated based on their housing status, disability, foster care, special education status, mental health or any other exceptionality or special need.

Although an undocumented immigrant and a foster child, Wilson has the right to free public education in America and equal treatment from his peers and teachers.

> A.13.d Consider the student's developmental age, language skills and level of competence when determining the appropriateness of an assessment.

Wilson could benefit from completing an assessment for PTSD and depression. In selecting the assessment, however, the school counselor must be mindful of Wilson's developmental age, language skills, and level of competence. Thus, finding an assessment that is offered in Spanish and verbally administering the assessment could help Wilson complete it appropriately.

> B.2.a Develop and maintain professional relationships and systems of communication with faculty, staff and administrators to support students.

The school counselor should be in contact with Wilson's teachers to ensure that he receives the support he needs in the classroom. The counselor can make recommendations to teachers for appropriate interventions to use in the classroom based on the symptoms that Wilson reports in counseling.

Multicultural Considerations

There are several multicultural aspects to consider when working with Wilson. First, very common in the Latin culture, he has a strong sense of responsibility to provide for his family back home. He demonstrates a strong tie to his family, known as *familismo*. Although he has not seen his biological family in several years, he understands that his sole purpose is to work and earn money for them. Unfortunately, when ICE raided his job site, Wilson was mandated to live with a foster family and attend school. Without the freedom to work, Wilson loses his sense of purpose and is unable to concentrate in school. His limited ability to speak English and the resistance from teachers to learn Spanish also contributes to his poor academic performance and sense of discouragement. Ultimately, if Wilson chooses to finish school and graduate, he would be limited in the work he finds due to his undocumented status. Thus, the school counselor must respect Wilson's strong desire to provide for his family while also advocating that he receive all the necessary accommodations to be successful in school. It could be helpful for the school counselor to refer Wilson to a support group or refugee center where Wilson could meet other individuals with similar experiences to his own.

Second, Wilson was placed with a foster family that does not speak Spanish. The family is of a different cultural background and socioeconomic status, which makes it difficult for Wilson to acculturate and identify with his new family. Under the Constitution and under the law, children in foster care have the right to an appropriate, stable placement in the least restrictive situation possible. Wilson could benefit from having a child advocate who is familiar with such laws and who can support his need for a more appropriate placement. Meanwhile, his school counselor can include Wilson's foster parents in his case planning and educate them on the effects of trauma so that they can better understand his lack of motivation in school and depressed presentation.

Case Discussion Questions

1. How would you advocate for your students? What role would you take?
2. How can the school counselor help maintain personal/social, academic, and career goals of undocumented students?
3. What information does the school counselor need to provide students, parents, staff, and administration to help undocumented students?
4. How would you handle a student who does not speak your language?
5. Where can you find the most current laws and policies regarding undocumented minors?

Resources

The Haas Jr. Fund: www.haasjr.org/perspectives/topics/immigrant-rights
The College Board: https://professionals.collegeboard.org/guidance/financial-aid/undocumented-students
National Association of Secondary School Principals: www.nassp.org/policy-advocacy-center/nassp-position-statements/undocumented-students/

References

American School Counselor Association. (2016). *Ethical standards for school counselors*. Alexandria, VA: Author.
Bailey, C. (2014). Creating a Coyote Cartography Critical Regionalism at the border. *European Journal of American Studies, 9*(3), 1–19.

Bronfenbrenner, U. (1977). Toward an experimental ecology of human development. *American Psychologist*, *32*, 513–531.

Bronfenbrenner, U. (1979). Contexts of child rearing: Problems and prospects. *American Psychologist*, *34*(10), 844–840. doi:10.1037/0003-066X.34.10.844

Bronfenbrenner, U. (1986). Ecology of the family as a context for human development: Research perspectives. *Developmental Psychology*, *22*, 723–742.

Gándara, P., & Contreras, F. (2009). *The Latino educational crisis: The consequences of failed policies*. Cambridge, MA: Harvard University Press.

Nakamura, D. (2017). Trump administration issues new immigration enforcement priorities, says goal is not "mass deportations". *Washington Post*. Retrieved from June 14, 2019, from www.washington post.com/politics/trump-administration-seeks-to-prevent-panic-over-new-immigration-enforcement-policies/2017/02/21/a2a695a8-f847-11e6-bf01-d47f8cf9b643_story.html?utm_term=.df636c1c6dfb

Orfield, G., & Lee, C. (2006). *Racial transformation and the changing nature of segregation*. Cambridge, MA: The Civil Rights Project at Harvard University.

Pew Research Center. (2017). *Recently arrived U.S. immigrants, growing in numbers, differ from long-term residents*. Retrieved June 1, 2019, from www.pewresearch.org/fact-tank/2019/06/03/recently-arrived-u-s-immigrants-growing-in-number-differ-from-long-term-residents/

Pew Research Center. (2019). *Many immigrants with temporary protected status face uncertain future in the U.S.* Retrieved June 1, 2019, from www.pewresearch.org/fact-tank/2019/03/08/immigrants-temporary-protected-status-in-us/

Serdarevic, M., & Chronister, K. M. (2005). Research with immigrant populations: The application of an ecological framework to mental health research with immigrant populations. *International Journal of Mental Health Promotion*, *7*(2), 24–34.

Suárez-Orozco, C., Suárez-Orozco, M., & Todorova, I. (2008). *Learning a new land: Immigrant students in American Society*. Cambridge, MA: Harvard University Press.

U.S. Department of Education. (1974). *The Family Educational Rights and Privacy Act (FERPA)*. Retrieved November 10, 2019, from https://www2.ed.gov/policy/gen/guid/fpco/ferpa/index.html

Zayes, L. H., Brabeck, K. M., Hefforon, L. C., Dreby, J., Calzada, E. J., Parra-Cardona, R., . . . & Yoshikawa, H. (2017). Charting direction for research of immigrant children affected by undocumented status. *Hispanic Journal of Behavioral Sciences*, *39*(4) 412–435.

Reflections (for students or counselors to write): In the space provided, write your notes and reflections regarding this case study.

Section III

Critical Cases Involving Inappropriate Adult Behavior

"Cherish and love your children so as not to create bad adults."

Dr. Judy A. Nelson

"The old adage, hurting people hurt people, has been parroted in effort to explain why people take harmful and egregious actions toward others. My son Austin believes, 'If a man has a conscience, he will suffer from his mistakes.' The pain I have witnessed many of our youth to encounter was inevitably at the hand of an adult."

Dr. Lisa A. Wines

Adults are supposed to know right from wrong and serve as roles models for our youth. However, what happens when the adults gifted with the grace to influence, teach, or raise our children are also broken? They have unresolved traumas, or they selfishly use their power over children to get their needs met. Perhaps they cannot control or manipulate another adult person, thereby taking advantage of a young person who is considered a part of a vulnerable population. The mind is warped, thinking is skewed, and because of it, egregious acts or mistakes are made. Because adults are often trusted persons in the lives of our youth, an underage person may think they are at fault for the adult's heinous act. This section introduces cases where adults' behavior with our youth is inappropriate.

16 Sexual Abuse by a Parent

Leigh Falls Holman and Kristi L. Nobbman

Background

According to the Rape, Abuse & Incest National Network (RAINN, 2018), child protective services (CPS) finds evidence to support claims of child sexual abuse, on average, every nine minutes. In 2016, 57,329 cases of child sexual abuse were substantiated by CPS (Children's Bureau, 2018). Children experience sexual abuse perpetrated by adults and by their siblings, peers, or other relatives. In fact, the Children's Bureau (2018) reported that 80% of perpetrators of sexual abuse are parents. Lifetime prevalence of an adolescent female experiencing sexual abuse by an adult is 11.2%, with a 95% confidence interval, and 1.9% for males (Finkelhor, Shattuck, Turner, & Hamby, 2014). This includes 1 in 9 girls and 1 in 53 boys assaulted by an adult (Finkelhor et al., 2014). However, risk of sexual victimization for girls increases significantly in adolescence to 26.6% (Finkelhor et al., 2014). Therefore, statistically speaking, it is likely that school counselors will interact with victims of sexual abuse.

Further, according to a seminal Adverse Childhood Experiences (ACEs) study, children who experience abuse are at increased risk for addiction, depression, and suicide attempt (Felitti et al., 1998). More recently, a study found that victims are four times more likely to develop substance use disorders (SUD) and post-traumatic stress disorder (PTSD) and three times more likely to develop more depressive episodes in adulthood (Zinzow et al., 2012). Therefore, it is important to be aware that the students you engage with behavioral issues or mental health concerns may, in fact, have an underlying history of child abuse. It is important that school counselors understand that students rarely come to their offices intending to disclose such abuse; rather, it may be other issues that bring them into the counselor's office that unexpectedly lead to a report of sexual abuse, as is illustrated in this case study.

Description of the Case

Ms. Jonas is a first year high school counselor at a larger suburban high school. Twin sisters beginning their junior year, Anna and Ava, ask to see the counselor about graduating early. Initially, Ms. Jonas reviews each girl's transcript prior to the meeting. She notices that Anna has made good grades throughout her freshman and sophomore years and has taken summer school classes each summer. Her GPA is 3.95. In reviewing the transcript, it is clear that she is able to meet the requirements for early graduation.

However, when Ms. Jonas reviews Ava's transcript, she sees Ava's academic progress is much more concerning. Ava has her basic credits from the first two years of high school, and she has also taken summer coursework, although some of it is to make up for courses she did not pass during the regular school term. Ava has a GPA of 2.15. In order to graduate early, she will need to take coursework by correspondence in addition to a full load this year. Given her academic performance thus far, the counselor would not recommend the early graduation route to Ava. However, since her twin sister is likely to move to that path, it is important to discuss the options with both girls.

They insist on coming to see Ms. Jonas together. Anna is clearly the dominant twin. She speaks for both girls initially, so that the counselor needs to stop and ensure that Ava's voice is also heard. When the counselor explores the twins' individual reasons for choosing early graduation, they both state they want to enter the Air Force in order to allow the military to pay for college in the future. They have spoken with a recruiter who told them they are eligible for service as soon as they graduate.

Upon further discussion about their urgency to graduate early, the girls look at each other tentatively, and Ms. Jonas senses that something else is going on. After some prompting, the girls report that they are being sexually abused by their father. They report this has been going on since they were 12 years old, and they want out of the house. They say they have 8- and 10-year-old sisters, as well, about whom they are worried, and they plan to petition for custody of their sisters when they have jobs with the Air Force. They believe they need to be in the position to gain custody of their sisters soon because they are approaching the age Anna and Ava were when they were first victimized by their father.

When Ms. Jonas begins to discuss the need to report the abuse to child protective services (CPS), the twins become quite angry and state that Mrs. Jensen (another counselor at the school) did not report it last year. When Ms. Jonas asks what they mean, they reported that they talked to Mrs. Jensen last year about early graduation, and she decided not to report the abuse. Ms. Jonas tells the girls that she will discuss this with Mrs. Jensen and the other counselors at the school and would meet with the girls again at the end of the day. The counselor knows that she has to report the abuse, but she also knows that when reporting, one of the questions she will be asked is whether the students had disclosed to anyone else. Therefore, she would also have to report the previous disclosure to Mrs. Jensen. Since Mrs. Jensen is her colleague, Ms. Jonas wants to talk with her and potentially make the call together.

Strategies for Consideration

In this situation, the counselor needs to gain enough information to file the report but not appear to be investigating the abuse. Open-ended questions, utilized in most therapeutic interventions, allow students to provide details without being led to a specific answer. Additionally, the counselor will need to confront and/or challenge the girls in their ambivalence to disclose the abuse to CPS. However, this disclosure must be done in a highly sensitive way, considering the topic. Strategies such as affirming, reflecting, and communicating genuineness are necessary to help the girls feel safe as they disclose the abuse.

Given that school counselors are mandated reporters of abuse, it is important that they understand the process for reporting abuse and how to manage the discussion with the child regarding the report that is forthcoming. When working with children or adolescents who experience child sexual abuse, it is important that school counselors be informed about common signs and symptoms and behavioral manifestations of the abuse. This information may be helpful in managing any potential behavioral manifestations a child may engage in at school. Additionally, the information can be helpful if communicated to the various stakeholders for a school counselor's services, including the child, parents, teachers, and/or administrators.

Many school counselors engage in limited direct services, and most would not engage in counseling students on sexual abuse issues. Therefore, they must know the available resources for referrals for counseling, both for the child victim and for the parents or siblings, who may need additional support. Although disclosing details of the abuse to teachers may not be appropriate, it would be prudent to let the victim's teachers know that she or he is dealing with a stressful life event. Furthermore, this life event may affect their emotional state, behavior, and/or academic performance, and it is fitting to request that teachers notify you if they observe any concerning changes in the child's mood or behavior so that you may intervene appropriately. It also is good practice for school counselors to work with the child, non-offending parents, and/or the child's mental health provider to provide additional support at school.

Theoretical Frameworks

A humanistic, person-centered therapy (PCT; Rogers, 1957) approach is likely the most helpful theoretical framework to use initially with the girls. They need a place where they feel psychologically safe to discuss what happened to them. The counselor can facilitate each girl's process of disclosure by creating the core conditions in the counseling relationship including remaining congruent, demonstrating nonjudgmental unconditional positive regard, and communicating empathy. To ensure accurate empathy, a feedback loop must occur where the counselor hears the student, then reflects back to the student her understanding of the issues/feelings, and the student confirms that the counselor is correct (e.g., yeah, right! or exactly!).

Ava seems to be following her sister's lead on early graduation and joining the Air Force. Using motivational interviewing (MI) techniques regarding her academic and career decisions might also be helpful (Miller & Rollnick, 2013). However, MI may be useful with both girls because they both experience ambivalence about disclosure and reporting the abuse and have chosen to attempt to take control of the situation by graduating early, joining the Air Force, and parenting their younger sisters. Motivational interviewing is humanistic and person-centered, so it can be integrated into a PCT approach. Motivational interviewing includes a set of techniques using the acronym OARS to help the student talk about the situation. This model includes asking open-ended questions (O), like "What is your plan after graduation?"; affirming (A) Ava's self-efficacy in making her own decisions about her future; using reflective (R) listening techniques similar to PCT (e.g. "I hear fear in your voice when you talk about your younger sisters"); and summarizing (S) to reinforce what has been said, communicate that the counselor has been listening, and prepare the student to move forward. An example of summarizing in this situation would be "After graduation, you plan to join the Air Force and petition custody of your younger sisters, so you can keep them safe."

Motivational interviewing (Miller & Rollnick, 2013) has four principles. The first is to express empathy using skillful reflective listening and to normalize ambivalent feelings. Even the report of abuse causes the girls' ambivalence. They want to get out of the situation and want to save their younger sisters from abuse, but they do not necessarily want to get their dad in trouble. The next MI principle is to develop the discrepancy between the student's goals and values (I want myself and my sisters to be safe) and what is currently happening (we are not safe). Talking about the pros and cons of a situation can help the student move forward with making a decision consistent with his or her values. The next principle is to roll with the resistance and avoid the *righting reflex* (e.g., you should . . .). By avoiding telling the student what she should do (e.g. making the argument that early graduation may not make the most sense for Ava because she has more trouble with schoolwork and may need more time), the counselor also avoids having the student take the opposite side of this argument, thus becoming more entrenched in the decision to pursue early graduation, even if it doesn't make sense. By rolling with the resistance, the counselor helps the student explore her reasons for the decision, even if the counselor does not agree with it. Finally, MI's fourth principle is to support the students' self-efficacy by using reflective listening, summaries, and affirmations to validate frustrations with the current situation while remaining optimistic that things can be different in the future.

Professional Experiences

There are several school counseling issues to address in this scenario. The school counselor needs to report the abuse. She also needs to address the potentially unethical and illegal behavior by her colleague. She needs to provide a referral to the school's mental health counselor to address mental health concerns. Finally, she needs to work with Anna and Ava independently to talk about their academic and postsecondary goals and develop an individualized plan to help each as she progresses.

The counselor in this situation first consulted the school's mental health counselor, who agreed that the abuse must be reported, but she stated that she would advise talking to Mrs. Jensen prior to the report in order to clarify her perception of what occurred. She reminded the school counselor that when using an ethical decision-making model applied to potential unethical behavior of a colleague, counselors should first discuss the concern with the counselor personally.

The counselor met with Mrs. Jensen immediately and told her about the abuse disclosure and that she was going to make the CPS report. She stated that she knew that CPS would ask if the abuse had been disclosed previously to anyone. Mrs. Jensen, a 10-year school counseling veteran, acknowledged the girls reported sexual abuse by their dad last school year. She stated that this is common with *the kinds of kids we get at this school* and states that you will understand it better after you get more experience. The counselor inferred that Mrs. Jensen was referring to either the girls' low socioeconomic status or their ethnicity, but she did not clarify.

Mrs. Jensen stated that following the girls' previous disclosure, she met with their older brother, and he denied they were being abused. Therefore, she did not think abuse occurred and did not report it to CPS. The newer school counselor was surprised and concerned when her colleague acknowledged what happened, and she stated that her understanding is that the law requires school counselors to report any suspected or known child abuse to CPS. At that time, Ms. Jonas stated that she would have to report the girls' previous disclosure and expressed concern that Mrs. Jensen could be in some legal and ethical peril. Mrs. Jensen did not seem to be concerned and told the counselor to go ahead and report it to CPS, and that she stands by her decision not to report. Mrs. Jensen then said, "They won't do anything anyway."

Ms. Jonas met with the girls after lunch and told them that she discussed last year's disclosure with Mrs. Jensen. The counselor also told them what the law requires. She stated that she consulted the school mental health counselor, who agreed she was required by law to report the disclosure. She asked the girls individually if they wanted to be in the room when she made the report or if they wanted her to make the report and let them know afterward that it was done. They both stated that they wanted her to do it after they left the office and went back to class. The counselor informed Anna and Ava that it was possible that a CPS investigator may want to talk with each of the sisters separately at school. Each girl acknowledged understanding and went back to class.

Child protective services placed a high priority on the case and sent an investigator to both the high school and the younger sisters' school to interview each girl separately. The twins later told their counselor that their 10-year-old sister also reported abuse, but she stated she did not know that it had happened to anyone else in the family. Ultimately, all four girls were removed from the home. Anna graduated one semester later and ended up going into the Air Force as planned, and Ava graduated at the end of the school year. After being placed with her maternal grandmother and getting mental health counseling, Ava's grades improved, resulting in her ability to move forward academically faster than anticipated. The counselor disclosed the situation with her colleague to the district's director of student services, also a counselor, who remediated Mrs. Jensen's error in judgement.

Counselor Impact

When counselors deal with sexual abuse of a student, they may develop countertransference reactions or vicarious trauma. Countertransference occurs when the counselor has an emotional reaction to the student, or in this case to the students' father or toward the counselor who didn't report the abuse last year. This emotional reaction refocuses the counselor on her thoughts and feelings about the situation rather than remaining focused on the students' needs.

Vicarious or secondary trauma is another potential outcome of working with kids who have suffered abuse. Hearing stories of traumatic events and witnessing the fear these girls are experiencing can leave an *emotional residue* that the counselor has difficulty dealing with. In this case, the counselor may continue to think and worry about the girls after she has made the CPS call. However, doing so may result in her inability to be fully engaged in her own relationships outside of work.

Over time, experiences of vicarious trauma can lead to compassion fatigue and burnout. This may be part of why Mrs. Jensen demonstrated some cynicism and apathy about the girls' abuse report initially. When counselors experience burnout, they are impaired professionals. A counselor may experience symptoms of burnout including emotional exhaustion, depersonalization, and having a low sense of personal accomplishment. If a counselor is unable to *let go* of the stories of abuse or frustrations about how the system works, she is likely to become emotionally exhausted as repeated exposure to students' traumas affect her life. As a protective measure, it is normal for a counselor experiencing emotional exhaustion to defend against this through depersonalization or avoidance of working with students. She may do this by being *too busy* to meet with students; by staying in her office so that no one can access time with her; or by reflexively responding to a student in a manner that is not helpful, thus increasing the likelihood that students stop reaching out to the counselor for help. This can then lead the counselor to develop a low sense of personal accomplishment because she no longer believes she is an effective counselor.

If a counselor cannot acknowledge or refuses to acknowledge burnout, other professionals may have to step in and bring this to the counselor's attention. Then the counselor must take action to access the resources that can help remedy the burnout. Some possible strategies include participating in personal counseling, consulting with colleagues on difficult cases, seeking supervision for cases that cause burnout, and asking for help in the counseling office until the counselor feels secure in working with students again.

Mental Health Implications

There are several common responses people have following chronic sexual abuse. The autonomic nervous system (ANS), which developed evolutionarily to protect animals (people) and help them survive environmental threats, is activated when someone experiences a threat to his or her emotional, psychological, or physical safety. Since the victim's survival mechanisms are primed for protecting them from additional assaults, they experience chronically hypersensitive physiology. This results in high levels of stress hormones such as cortisol and adrenalin.

Elevated stress hormones can produce anxiety symptoms. Anxiety symptoms can manifest in many types of disorders, including panic attacks with or without agoraphobia, other specific phobias, or generalized anxiety disorder. Each of these types of anxiety can affect school performance. Panic attacks may prevent a student from being able to attend to school assignments, and in the case of agoraphobia, this includes attending school. A specific phobia may relate to an environmental trigger associated with the abuse. It helps if the counselor can facilitate the student's identification of the environmental trigger, which can lead to problem solving to minimize or eliminate the environmental trigger. Generalized anxiety can result in slow processing time because the student is focused on the anxiety rather than schoolwork. As a result, she may do poorly in school, particularly if timed.

Students who have experienced chronic incest, like Anna and Ava, commonly develop post-traumatic stress disorder (PTSD). Manifestations of PTSD include hypervigilance to external stimuli that the person perceives as threatening. As a result, they may demonstrate anger and aggression that is protective but may seem irrational. They also may dissociate some or all parts of the sexual abuse. As a result, they may have difficulties with *zoning out* in school and missing important material being discussed. These symptoms can also be easily confused for attention deficit hyperactivity disorder (ADHD); however, they are actually trauma reactions. It may be helpful for counselors to educate teachers about how PTSD can mimic the behavioral manifestations of ADHD.

Finally, some sexual abuse survivors develop physical manifestations of the abuse. For instance, they may clench their stomach due to chronic stress, resulting in physical symptoms of stomach pain, difficulty digesting food, vaginismus, and constipation. These are real physical symptoms, but they are psychological in origin. We call these symptoms somatization or psychosomatic symptoms. The physical symptoms may need medical care, but they are unlikely to go away with medical intervention alone because they are motivated by the psychological issues the person is (not) dealing with.

Ethical Considerations

The first set of ethical standards (ASCA, 2016) listed (A.11.c, A.11.b, A.9.d, and A.11.e) address the child abuse reported by the twins.

> A.11.c. Are knowledgeable about current state laws and their school system's procedures for reporting child abuse and neglect and methods to advocate for students' physical and emotional safety following abuse/neglect reports.
> A.11.b. Report suspected cases of child abuse and neglect to the proper authorities and take reasonable precautions to protect the privacy of the student for whom abuse or neglect is suspected when alerting the proper authorities.

It is important for school counselors to follow the state laws on mandated reporting and also to follow the school's policies and procedures on reporting abuse. School policies may require the counselor to inform the principal if she makes a child abuse report or to complete internal paperwork related to the disclosure and report.

> A.9.d. Report to parents/guardians and/or appropriate authorities when students disclose a perpetrated or a perceived threat to their physical or mental well-being. This threat may include, but is not limited to, physical abuse, sexual abuse, neglect, dating violence, bullying or sexual harassment. The school counselor follows applicable federal, state and local laws and school district policy.

This standard might apply to the need to make the child abuse report, not only in order to protect the twins but also to protect their younger sisters from being abused.

> A.11.e. Guide and assist students who have experienced abuse and neglect by providing appropriate services.

This standard addresses the need to make appropriate referrals, for instance a referral to the school mental health counselor, to address the psychological effects of the incest. One might also perceive CPS as a resource as well because they will ensure the students have a safe place to live and that their basic health, educational, psychological, and physical needs are addressed.

The second set of standards (E. a-c) address behavior of the counselor's colleague, Mrs. Jensen.

> E. Maintenance of Standards. When serious doubt exists as to the ethical behavior of a colleague(s) the following procedures may serve as a guide:
>
> a. School counselors consult with professional colleagues to discuss the potentially unethical behavior and to see if the professional colleague views the situation as an ethical violation. School counselors understand mandatory reporting in their respective district and states.

In this situation, the counselor consulted the school's mental health counselor and the district's director of student services, who supervises school counselors in the district.

> b. School counselors discuss and seek resolution directly with the colleague whose behavior is in question unless the behavior is unlawful, abusive, egregious or dangerous, in which case proper school or community authorities are contacted.

The school counselor met with Mrs. Jensen to discuss the situation and her concerns. She maintained that by law she had to make a CPS report and that she would have to answer honestly when they asked if the abuse had been disclosed to anyone else. Mrs. Jensen did not seem to be concerned that she may have broken the mandated reporting law or violated the ASCA standards discussed here.

    c. If the matter remains unresolved at the school, school district or state professional practice/standards commission, referral for review and appropriate action should be made in the following sequence:

- State school counselor association

    - American School Counselor Association (Complaints should be submitted in hard copy to the ASCA Ethics Committee, c/o the Executive Director, American School Counselor Association, 1101 King St., Suite 310, Alexandria, VA 22314.)

The counselor addressed the concern with the director of student services who remediated the situation with Mrs. Jensen. Since this occurred within the district, a report was not made to the state or national professional association.

Multicultural Considerations

Child sexual abuse/incest is a delicate issue regardless of multicultural considerations; however, it can be further complicated if the student or the perpetrator comes from a cultural background that does not define sexual abuse in the same manner that we do in the United States. In an effort not to generalize about entire groups of people, we will not go into specific instances of this occurrence. However, it is important that school counselors are aware of the diversity of ethnic and religious groups to which his or her students are a part. Some religions, for instance, believe it is acceptable for a 12-year-old girl to marry a grown man. Some countries that students' families immigrate from may not define sexual abuse the same way that we do in the United States. An international exchange in which one of the authors participated resulted in new awareness that a country where many of her students' families immigrated defined sexual abuse only as *penetration*. As such, any other type of molestation would not be perceived as sexually abusive. Some cultures blame the victim in sexual abuse situations, believing that the victim encouraged the abuse. Other cultures simply do not discuss sexuality at all, and therefore, any discussion of sexual abuse can be perceived as problematic.

Where a student is culturally situated can affect the student's understanding of his or her own victimization and whether he or she reports abuse. An educator's cultural situation may affect his or her perception of abuse and therefore should be a topic of in-service training that counselors conduct with teachers at the beginning of every school year. The counselor's own beliefs about sex and sexual abuse can affect how the counselor perceives a disclosure and how he or she addresses that disclosure. Therefore, counselors must continually explore their own cultural biases about sexuality and sexual abuse and attend relevant continuing education to improve their self-awareness and gain information relevant to this topic.

Discussion Questions

1. What are the salient pieces of information that need to be communicated to child protective services when you make the report? Why do you think this is important?
2. What is your reaction to the colleague's handling of this situation the previous year? Role-play how you would address these concerns with a colleague and the expectations you have of a colleague's response. How do you envision this incident affecting working relationships between colleagues? What is the next step if you believe your discussion was unsuccessful?

3. Other than CPS, do you need to report your colleague's behavior to anyone else? Explain your reasoning.
4. Does anyone else need to be informed about your CPS report or the disclosure of abuse? Explain your reasoning.
5. Are there potential countertransference issues that you need to be cognizant of when dealing with an abuse report? How would you manage countertransference?
6. How might this type of case affect a school counselor's level of job stress? Vicarious traumatization?

Resources

Childhelp: www.childhelp.org/story-resource-center/child-abuse-education-prevention-resources/
National Child Abuse Hotline: 1-800-422-4453
Prevent Child Abuse America: https://preventchildabuse.org/resources/

References

American School Counselor Association. (2016). *Ethical standards for school counselors*. Alexandria, VA: Author.

Children's Bureau (2018). *Child maltreatment 2016*. Washington, DC: U. S. Department of Health and Human Services, Administration for Children and Families, Administration on Children, Youth and Families, Children's Bureau. Retrieved from www.acf.hhs.gov/cb/research-data-technology/statistics-research/child-maltreatment

Felitti, V. J., Anda, R. F., Nordenberg, D., Williamson, D. F., Spitz, A. M., Edwards, V., Koss, M. P., & Marks, J. S. (1998). Relationship of childhood abuse and household dysfunction to many of the leading causes of death in adults: Adverse Childhood Experiences (ACE) Study. *American Journal of Preventative Medicine*, *14*(4), 245–258. doi:https://doi.org/10.1016/S0749-3797(98)00017-8

Finkelhor, D., Shattuck, A., Turner, H. A., & Hamby, S. L. (2014). The lifetime prevalence of child sexual abuse and sexual assault assessed in late adolescence. *Journal of Adolescent Health*, *55*, 329–333. https://doi.org/10.1016/j.jadohealth.2013.12.026

Miller, W. R., & Rollnick, S. (2013). *Motivational interviewing: Helping people change*. New York, NY: The Guilford Press.

Rape, Abuse & Incest National Network. (2018). *Children and teens: Statistics*. Retrieved from www.rainn.org/statistics/children-and-teens

Rogers, C. (1957). The necessary and sufficient conditions of therapeutic personality change. *Journal of Consulting Psychology*, *21*, 95–103.

Zinzow, H. M., Resnick, H. S., McCauley, J. L., Amstadter, A. B., Ruggiero, K. J., & Kilpatrick, D. G. (2012). Prevalence and risk of psychiatric disorders as a function of variant rape histories: Results from a national survey of women. *Social Psychiatry and Psychiatric Epidemiology*, *47*(6), 893–902.

Reflections: In the space provided, write your notes and reflections regarding this case study.

17 Violence in the Home

Frannie E. Neal and Judy A. Nelson

Background

Child maltreatment encompasses physical, sexual, and psychological abuse; neglect; and exposure to family violence. It occurs across all social, economic, racial, and cultural categories. In the United States, more than 15 million children witness domestic abuse annually (https://ctccfv.org/evidence-of-need/), and a report of child abuse is made every 10 seconds involving 6.6 million children each year (www.childhelp.org/). According to the study on adverse childhood experiences (ACE) (www.cdc.gov/violenceprevention/), intimate partner violence (IPV) in the home and violence toward children are risk factors that often negatively impact children immediately and over an entire lifetime. Children who observe or are included in IPV, along with children who experience abuse themselves, are at risk for the following: injury, mental health issues including suicide, unintended pregnancy and maternal health problems, infectious and chronic disease, risky behaviors such as alcohol and drug abuse, and a lack of educational and career opportunities (www.cdc.gov/violenceprevention/).

School counselors are often the first to know about violence in a child's home, including the maltreatment of children, because either the child reports this directly to the counselor or a staff member brings it to the counselor's attention. Therefore, a discussion of the important roles that school counselors play in protecting the health, welfare, and safety of children is critical. These roles can include but are not limited to reporting child abuse, training staff on how to recognize and report child abuse, and advocacy of child victims of violence and abuse.

Mandatory reporting of child abuse generally is spelled out in state law. Counselors must adhere to the specific laws governing their respective states. In some states, teachers can refer cases of abuse to a designee such as the school counselor, but other states mandate that the first responder must report the incident. Mandatory reporters must report suspected abuse, whether reported by students or others who have knowledge of a situation. Those who do not feel confident in their reporting skills or hesitate to report for other reasons by waiting until the final hour put children at risk of physical, sexual, and psychological harm.

Mandatory reporting of child abuse is clearer than the reporting of domestic violence. There are, however, good reasons to report domestic abuse whether a counselor's state mandates this reporting or not. Children can be caught up in the violence and become victims of direct violence themselves by trying to help the non-offender or just by being in the home. Mandatory reporting of children exposed to domestic violence varies from state to state, so again, school counselors must be aware of the laws governing their states. It is important to remember that the law supersedes school district policy. Some counselors choose to reach out to the non-offending parent rather than contact the authorities in domestic violence situations. This involves risks because most victims carry a great deal of shame about their situation, which might mean that they will deny what the child has told the counselor or will be angry and refuse to talk to the counselor. Counselors should be careful not to advise the parent what course of action to take but simply provide the parent with resources that could be helpful. There are some websites included in the resources section of this chapter that would be useful resources.

Training regarding recognizing and reporting child abuse must be consistent with the laws of each state and is essential to reduce the potential injury of children who attend school. Training is critical for school counselors, as well as all other school staff, to build skills and knowledge regarding how and when to report child abuse and child victimization. School counselors might receive training provided by their states, in their graduate training programs, or simply from other experienced counselors or supervisors. They often are looked to as the expert for child abuse reporting on a school campus and thus have a responsibility to their colleagues and to the children they serve to provide training on how to identify child abuse and what to do if it is suspected, according to state guidelines. School counselors are poised to offer staff development on a regular basis regarding the important issues of child abuse identification and reporting. Some states mandate that all school personnel receive training each academic year.

Advocacy, along with leadership and collaboration (American School Counselor Association [ASCA], 2019), is a mainstay of the ASCA National Model (2019) and is often related to disadvantaged or marginalized populations. Children who experience violence in the home are decidedly disadvantaged and often marginalized (Barrett, Lester, & Durham, 2011). Advocacy is one of the most important roles that school counselors play regarding violence in the home. The notion that school counselors are agents of change and promote social justice is not new (Griffin & Steen, 2011; Toporek, Lewis, & Crethar, 2009; Trusty & Brown, 2005). Advocating for children who are maltreated can be done at individual, systemic, and broader community levels. Teaching a child methods of coping based on interpersonal strengths empowers the child to solve problems, think creatively, and act to stay safe and healthy. Systemic advocacy includes creating a multidisciplinary team to address issues of maltreatment and training staff on the signs of abuse and how to report. School counselors can also make community presentations that raise the awareness of the impact of the maltreatment of children.

In addition to child abuse reporting and training, school counselors can be instrumental in assisting students who are exposed to or directly experience violence in the home (Fontes, 2000). Fontes (2000) described methods of helping students cope with child maltreatment. Identifying students who might be experiencing parental or marital violence can be accomplished by simply asking the question directly if there is reason to suspect this problem. Counselors can also be aware of changes in students' behaviors and sudden aggression, particularly in boys toward female students and teachers. Some children will act out their experiences in play.

Additionally, the school counselor can be most helpful when the child is in school by collaborating with teachers and other school staff on how to provide a low stress environment for the child. Reducing competition, encouraging collaboration, and providing ample opportunities for the child to be successful are ways that teachers can provide a loving and nurturing environment. The counselor can also offer individual counseling to the student by teaching pro-social skills and providing time for the child to reflect on what is going on at home—making sure that the child understands that the situation is not his or her fault. The following case study describes a case of maltreatment of a young child and how the school counselor was able to intervene.

Description of Case

Maria is an 8-year-old Caucasian female and second-grader in a small, rural elementary school in the southwestern United States. When the school counselor met with Maria, the child described feeling depressed as she missed school earlier in the week as punishment. Maria shared a recent experience at home and began to open up about her home environment.

Maria began by explaining her family system and dynamics. Maria recalled from an early age watching her father beat her mother repeatedly. Maria's father abandoned her at the age of 5, and she was taken from her drug-addicted mother at the age of 6. Despite feeling brainwashed by her mother, Maria deeply missed and loved her mother. After she was taken from her mother, Maria was forced to live with her father and his new family. Maria's father met her stepmother at a drug rehabilitation center, where she unknowingly became pregnant, not realizing it until eight months into her pregnancy. Maria's stepbrother was born with heroin in his system.

The family recently relocated to the current city and school district. Maria discussed her step-mother's abusive behavior and passive aggressive tendencies toward her and her father. Maria also felt scared watching her father beat another woman. Maria's stepmother frequently threat-ened Maria and forced her to the corner of the living room as punishment, where she would then beat her. Maria's stepmother told Maria how much she hates her, that no one loves her, and that her father would choose her over Maria. Maria described frequently being left home when the rest of her family went out of town or went out as a family without Maria. Maria's family nick-named her the *ghost of the house*.

During the weekend preceding this session, Maria's stepbrother told his mother that Maria said something, which Maria did not recall. Maria's stepmother forced Maria to stand in the corner again, where she beat Maria with a book. Maria's father, stepmother, and stepbrother then left to go to the park without her. Maria described how her parents let her out of the corner before they left her alone. The next day, Maria's stepmother forced Maria to stay home from school as punishment. According to Maria, school is the only thing she enjoys.

After discussing these events, the counselor provided a worksheet for Maria while she took notes. The counselor asked Maria to draw the feeling she had during this incident and the cause of these feelings. Maria described her feelings as *frustrated* and *depressed*, drew the feelings on paper, and described the cause. The counselor asked Maria how she takes care of herself through-out these incidents. Maria described how she tried to zone out, push it down, but somehow it comes back to haunt her at times. Maria began to panic when the counselor informed her that a call was made to child protective services (CPS). The counselor assured Maria that the call was made to support and protect her and explained to Maria that she could speak to her whenever she needed. Maria described how she felt much better after the session. Maria mentioned how she previously saw a counselor but never felt understood. The counselor checked in with Maria later that day.

In the following weeks post the incident, the counselor checked in consistently with Maria to offer support. The CPS agency visited the school and the home to interview Maria and her family. Maria no longer slept on the floor after the CPS visit, when the CPS officer requested that Maria sleep in a bed. After this visit, Maria and her family spent the weekend away and then came to school late that Monday morning due to her parents' frustration with the CPS call. The counselor invited Maria to check in whenever needed and requested that Maria keep her updated.

Strategies for Consideration

The following sections consist of recommendations and considerations for school counselors when dealing with children who experience violence in the home. Whether the student is the victim of the violence or is exposed to the violence of others, children can be harmed irreparably if no one intervenes. School counselors are expected to know how and when to intervene in these situations.

Theoretical Frameworks

We have considered two theoretical frameworks for this case in order to conceptualize the cases involving the maltreatment of children accurately. Interventions were chosen that are appropriate for children who experience maltreatment either in the form of intimate partner violence to which they are exposed or child abuse or neglect of any type. These frameworks are narrative therapy and play therapy. Both of these theoretical perspectives are well suited to the school setting.

Coordinating efforts with outside counselors and parents (as appropriate) can help maintain consistent and positive messages to the student as healing begins.

Narrative therapy suggests that change happens by paying close attention in therapy to unique outcomes, which are narrative details outside the main story (White & Epston, 1990). Narrative therapy can be a path to healing for children and adolescents who are willing and able to engage in talk therapy. Focusing on a child's strengths and resilience and exploring the times when a child experienced power and control can be addressed in the school setting and will not interfere with any outside counseling that the child might be receiving. Feelings of shame might develop and be maintained as a result of child maltreatment (Deblinger & Runyon, 2005). The school counselor can help mitigate feelings of shame that are common with child maltreatment by encouraging the student to *talk out loud* about the experiences and to create a new narrative of hope and healing. School counselors can enlist teachers and administrators to support ongoing positive encounters with students who have experienced maltreatment. The new narrative eventually becomes *I am a worthy person valued by the adults at school who love and care for me.*

For very young students, play therapy can be applied for similar results as with narrative therapy. Play therapy can foster a sense of control in children who have experienced maltreatment and uses symbolism to help children make sense of their experiences (Landreth, 2001). By playing out a scenario repeatedly in the playroom, children can test out and ultimately master their realities. Nondirective play therapy requires counselors to accept the child unconditionally, to believe that the child has the capacity to solve personal problems, and to allow the child to lead throughout the therapeutic process. School counselors in elementary schools often have training in play therapy, and many have created makeshift or portable playrooms in their offices to use when working with young children. Some graduate programs include play therapy as part of their school counseling training, and post-graduate continuing education is available in the form of workshops and intensive instruction.

Professional Experiences

Forging a relationship with state agencies such as CPS is critical for school counselors but can also be disappointing and frustrating. Recognizing that case managers of these agencies are overworked and may experience vicarious trauma based on the cases they investigate might put the plight of the investigators in perspective. Case overloads and high career turnover of case managers and other CPS workers might be reflected in the attitudes and behaviors of caseworkers. While it has been the experience of school counselors interviewed for this chapter that CPS workers are in place to serve the best interests of children and families, they did express concern that sometimes workers did not appear to feel the urgency for the child's plight that the school counselor felt. Cooperating with the employees of the state agencies is one way to assist in the investigations brought to their attention. Providing a private place for CPS workers to interview possible victims and having all pertinent information (home address, parents' names and phone numbers, siblings' names and ages, etc.) available for the workers can be a great help to them.

Reporting child abuse or domestic violence that might affect a child is one of the roles that school counselors take very seriously, since they are mandated reporters. As stated earlier, every state has laws, rules, and regulations regarding how and when to report child abuse. One counselor reported that when she first made a CPS referral, she wanted to be involved and even considered that she was an investigator of sorts herself. She quickly learned that once the report is made, the school counselor must allow CPS workers to do their job for the best outcome for the child. It is certainly appropriate to continue to check on the child at school and to include the child in any appropriate services under the guidelines of the comprehensive school counseling program (CSCP). However, interviewing the child to obtain a case against the alleged offender is the role of CPS.

Although mandated reporters supposedly are anonymous, it is not unusual for parents or guardians to find out from their child who the reporter actually was. This can make future contacts with the family strained and challenging. Being familiar with and able to cite state law can be helpful in these situations. School counselors can also request that a CPS worker meet with the parents at school to assure the family that the school counselor was bound by law to make the referral to the agency. Parents may even request that the school counselor no longer have access to the child. In this situation, the administrators might be able to intervene on behalf of the counselor and explain to the parents that the CSCP is an integral part of every student's school experience.

Counselor Impact

The probability for school counselors to become overly involved emotionally with students who suffer from violence in their homes is quite high. Counselors who monitor their own behavior and emotional state can continue to have appropriate professional boundaries and be the best advocate possible for the child and the family. Consultation and supervision can assist counselors as they navigate the rough waters of child abuse and domestic abuse.

As stated previously, school counselors can become frustrated with the system and feel that not enough is being done for the child. Bryant and Baldwin (2010) stated that 59 of 61 comments to an open-ended question in their study on child abuse reporting were negative. Four themes emerged from a question regarding the effectiveness of reporting child abuse: "understaffed and lacking resources, negative follow-up, children and families not helped, and does more harm than good" (p. 181). Continuing to make reports consistently and with as much information as possible can help CPS do the best job possible for each child. As an advocate for students, school counselors can persist in their goal of having the best possible outcomes for the clients they serve.

Mental Health Implications

Some of the unfortunate outcomes of violence in the home are depression and anxiety in children who experience these issues. These mental health problems can result in poor academic performance, isolation, and an unwillingness to make friends, acting out behaviors at home and at school, and refusal to engage in class activities, and can even lead to self-harm or suicide. When school counselors suspect that a child suffers from depression, anxiety, or both, it is critical that CPS workers are aware so that they can alert the parents to these serious mental health issues as they work with the family. Referrals to outside counseling are appropriate, but it is important to work with CPS to avoid confusion and redundancy.

Some CPS agencies offer their own counseling services or contract with licensed professionals to provide counseling to children who are at risk and in their systems. In some cases, social workers or licensed counselors will come to the school to provide these services. Helping teachers and administrators understand the importance of counseling for children who have experienced violence in the home is an important role for school counselors to play. When these counseling sessions occur during academic time, the school counselor can help both the student and the teachers understand the importance of flexibility. Providing a private place for the counseling sessions will enhance the counselor's relationship with CPS workers and will ensure confidentiality on the part of the student.

Ethical Considerations

Violence in the home presents unique ethical considerations for school counselors. This section will discuss the ethical considerations school counselors must gauge when a student experiences violence in the home. Primarily, school counselors are mandatory reporters. School counselors must report suspected abuse of vulnerable populations to the authorities. School counselors have a duty to protect the safety and privacy of students, which includes keeping them at school until CPS and/or police arrive if there are immediate safety concerns. School counselors also could create safety plans for students and families if necessary. As a forefront of the counseling alliance, confidentiality must be maintained and only broken if there is immediate harm to the student. It is imperative for school counselors to inform students of the limitations of confidentiality in these situations at the start of the counseling alliance and then remind them of the limitations when a report is made. If a report is made, school counselors can assure students that the report was made to protect the student. If the student feels as though trust is broken with the information reported, school counselors must continue to build trust in the counseling alliance with the student.

It is important for school counselors to err on the side of caution when reporting violence in the home. School counselors report suspected abuse in good faith. While school counselors have an ethical duty to protect students, reporting suspected abuse may cause uncomfortable situations and strained relationships with the student's family. This balance between being a counselor and being a mandated reporter can be difficult.

Several ethical principles are involved in cases of violence in the home. First, school counselors have a responsibility to ensure non-maleficence, or do no harm. Second, school counselors must ensure beneficence and the welfare of the students. Third, school counselors have a responsibility to serve as advocates for students and fight for justice. It is equally important to validate students' experiences, acknowledge the injustice that occurs when there is violence in the home, and assure students that the violence is not their fault. Last, school counselors must respect and promote the autonomy of students and their families. School counselors have a unique opportunity to empower students and families, as well as connect them with necessary resources, support, and outside counseling.

Finally, school counselors have an ethical duty to document and consult. Consultation is especially important for school counselors when there is an issue of violence in the home. School counselors must consult with professional colleagues in the case of an ethical dilemma. It is also imperative to document when a report is made in the school's student information system for future reference. Likewise, school counselors must practice self-care when there are difficult ethical dilemmas to prevent counselor burnout or compassion fatigue.

The American School Counselor Association (ASCA) Ethical Standards (2016) described the following responsibilities of school counselors pertaining to domestic violence and abuse:

A.9. Serious and Foreseeable Harm to Self and Others

School Counselors

a. Inform parents/guardians and/or appropriate authorities when a student poses a serious and foreseeable risk of harm to self or others. When feasible, this is to be done after careful deliberation and consultation with other appropriate professionals. School counselors inform students of the school counselor's legal and ethical obligations to report the concern to the appropriate authorities unless it is appropriate to withhold this information to protect the student (e.g. student might run away if he/she knows parents are being called). The consequence of the risk of not giving parents/guardians a chance to intervene on behalf of their child is too great. Even if the danger appears relatively remote, parents should be notified.

b. Use risk assessments with caution. If risk assessments are used by the school counselor, an intervention plan should be developed and in place prior to this practice. When reporting risk-assessment results to parents, school counselors do not negate the risk of harm even if the assessment reveals a low risk as students may minimize risk to avoid further scrutiny and/or parental notification. School counselors report risk assessment results to parents to underscore the need to act on behalf of a child at risk; this is not intended to assure parents their child isn't at risk, which is something a school counselor cannot know with certainty.

c. Do not release a student who is a danger to self or others until the student has proper and necessary support. If parents will not provide proper support, the school counselor takes necessary steps to underscore to parents/guardians the necessity to seek help and at times may include a report to child protective services.

d. Report to parents/guardians and/or appropriate authorities when students disclose a perpetrated or a perceived threat to their physical or mental well-being. This threat may include, but is not limited to, physical abuse, sexual abuse, neglect, dating violence, bullying or sexual harassment. The school counselor follows applicable federal, state and local laws and school district policy.

Parents have a right to know when their child is at risk of self-harm or harm from others. If parents are the perpetrators of such harm, then the appropriate authorities must be alerted. Students who are abused or who witness violence in their homes are at risk for threats to their mental health and physical safety, and the counselor must intervene by reporting the danger.

A.11. Bullying, Harassment and Child Abuse

School Counselors

b. Report suspected cases of child abuse and neglect to the proper authorities and take reasonable precautions to protect the privacy of the student for whom abuse or neglect is suspected when alerting the proper authorities.

c. Are knowledgeable about current state laws and their school system's procedures for reporting child abuse and neglect and methods to advocate for students' physical and emotional safety following abuse/neglect reports.

d. Develop and maintain the expertise to recognize the signs and indicators of abuse and neglect. Encourage training to enable students and staff to have the knowledge and skills needed to recognize the signs of abuse and neglect and to whom they should report suspected abuse or neglect.

e. Guide and assist students who have experienced abuse and neglect by providing appropriate services.

The sections of the code cited here refer to reporting incidences of child abuse to the appropriate authorities. When a student reports to the counselor that he or she has been harmed or is in danger of being harmed, the school counselor does not investigate but rather makes the report to the appropriate persons. School counselors must be aware of the most current laws, regulations, and policies regarding the reporting of instances of child abuse to the authorities. Additionally, school counselors train school staff on how to identify students who may be victims of abuse or of violence in the home.

A.12. Student Records

School Counselors

f. Establish a reasonable timeline for purging sole-possession records or case notes. Suggested guidelines include shredding paper sole-possession records or deleting electronic sole-possession records when a student transitions to the next level, transfers to another school or graduates. School counselors do not destroy sole-possession records that may be needed by a court of law, such as notes on child abuse, suicide, sexual harassment or violence, without prior review and approval by school district legal counsel. School counselors follow district policies and procedures when contacting legal counsel.

School counselors keep school records up to date according to school district policy and legal counsel. However, sole-possession notes regarding child abuse and other safety concerns are separate and might be required in a court of law. These notes belong solely to the counselor, who should either destroy them at a designated time or transition them to the next grade level counselor.

Multicultural Considerations

In counseling alliances, school counselors must respect their students' cultures. It is not only our ethical responsibility but also key to building trust in a counseling alliance. School counselors must seek professional development if unaware or uneducated about a client's culture. Ongoing multicultural training is also vital for school counselors to stay updated and informed, and school counselors must seek consultation if necessary. Additionally, school counselors must understand how their own identity (race, ethnicity, gender, SES status, etc.) may affect students from marginalized populations. It is crucial for school counselors to continue to gain multicultural awareness and skills, as well as to confront how their identity may affect their students. This process is vital in order to build trust within the counseling alliance.

School counselors should be aware of the school demographics and be educated about the strengths and challenges each culture faces. For instance, violence is accepted as part of life in various cultures, and speaking out against the violence is looked down upon. It is imperative for school counselors to be cognizant of the culture's family roles and expectations of those roles. There may be certain cultural barriers and perspectives that prevent women and/or men from seeking help or from leaving a violent situation at home. Furthermore, school counselors must be aware of how violence is viewed in the family and how reporting violence is viewed. For instance, if the culture values men as the patriarch of the family and head of the home, it may be expected for women to obey men and tolerate the violence. Finally, school counselors must be aware of how the culture views counseling and whether or not there is trust in school counselors. If the client identifies with a culture that does not approve of counseling services, it may be difficult for the school counselor to intervene. Again, if there are cases of discrepancy or difficulty, it is necessary for the school counselor to seek consultation, professional development, and/or additional resources.

School counselors have the opportunity to observe how the violence affects the student in the classroom. Violence at home manifests differently in children of various cultures. For instance, some students may respond by shutting down, while others respond by reacting to everything in the classroom. It is imperative for school counselors to understand the student's culture and how the counselor might help the student. School counselors are able to consult with teachers and staff, host professional development meetings on this subject, meet with the student individually, meet with the student in small group settings, and create behavior plans if necessary to help the student succeed in school.

> Association of Multicultural Counseling and Development Multicultural Counseling Competencies (Arredondo et al., 1996): Counselors must examine their attitudes/beliefs, knowledge, and skills
>
>   I. Counselor Awareness of Own Cultural Values and Biases
>   II. Counselor Awareness of Client's Worldview
>   III. Culturally Appropriate Intervention Strategies

Case Discussion Questions

1. Research the child abuse reporting system in your state. Be sure to be aware of the phone numbers and internet sites to contact if you need to report a case of child abuse.
2. Research the laws in your state regarding the reporting of child abuse. Create a staff development workshop on identifying child abuse and reporting child abuse according to the laws in your state. Work in small groups and make your presentations to the entire class.
3. What are your thoughts and feelings about reporting child abuse, and how might those affect the decisions that you make when a child reveals that he or she has been physically, emotionally, or sexually abused?
4. Neglect is considered child maltreatment and is reportable in most states. Think about what constitutes neglect as a reportable offense. Remember that your own value system might affect the types of parenting behaviors that seem neglectful to you. How will you determine what is actually neglect?
5. Determine if your state has laws that govern the reporting of domestic violence. If there are such laws, find out how they might affect you as a school counselor.
6. If there is no mandatory reporting of domestic violence in your state, discuss what you would do if a child reported to you that her parents' fighting often becomes physical and very frightening to the child.

Resources

The Children's Center on Family Violence: https://ctccfv.org/

The Adverse Childhood Experiences (ACE) Study www.cdc.gov/violenceprevention/childabuseandneglect/acestudy/aboutace.html

National Domestic Violence Hotline: 1-800-799-7233 and TTY 1-800-787-3224

National Child Abuse Hotline/Childhelp: (1-800-422-4453) www.childhelp.org

National Suicide Prevention Lifeline: 1-800-273-8255 www.suicidepreventionlifeline.org

National Resource Center on Domestic Violence: 1-800-537-2238 www.nrcdv.org INCITE! Women of Color Against Violence: www.incite-national.org

Casa de Esperanza: 651–772–1611 www.casadeesperanza.org

References

American School Counselor Association. (2019). *ASCA national model.* Alexandria, VA: American School Counselor Association.

American School Counselor Association. (2016). *Ethical standards for school counselors.* Alexandria, VA: American School Counselor Association.

Arredondo, P., Toporek, M. S., Brown, S., Jones, J., Locke, D. C., Sanchez, J., & Stadler, H. (1996). *Operationalization of the multicultural counseling competencies.* Alexandria, VA: AMCD.

Barrett, K., Lester, S. & Durham, J. (2011). Child maltreatment and the advocacy role of the professional school counselors. *Journal for Social Action in Counseling & Psychology, 3*(2), 86–203. https://doi.org/10.33043/JSACP.3.2.86-103

Bryant, J. K., & Baldwin, P. A. (2010). School counsellors perceptions of mandatory reporter training and mandatory reporting experiencing. *Child Abuse Review, 92,* 172–186.

Deblinger, E., & Runyon, M. (2005). Understanding and treating feelings of shame in children who have experienced maltreatment. *Child Maltreatment, 10,* 364–376.

Fontes, L. A. (2000). Children exposed to marital violence: How school counselors can help. *Professional School Counseling, 3,* 231–237.

Griffin, D., & Steen, S. (2011). A social justice approach to school counseling. *Journal for Social Action in Counseling and Psychology, 3,* 74–85.

Landreth, G. L. (2001). *Innovations in play therapy: Issues, process, and special populations*. New York, NY: Taylor & Francis.

Toporek, R. L., Lewis, J. A., & Crethar, H. C. (2009). Promoting systemic change through the ACA advocacy competencies. *Journal of Counseling and Development, 87*, 260–268.

Trusty, J., & Brown, D. (2005). Advocacy competencies for professional school counselors. *Professional School Counseling, 8*, 259–265.

White, M., & Epston, D. (1990). *Narrative means to therapeutic ends*. New York: W. W. Norton.

Reflections: In the space provided, write your notes and reflections regarding this case study.

18 Custody Issues

Helena Stevens

Background

School counselors support parents in matters that are consistent with the scope of practice like providing child-behavior resources, academic support meetings, behavior and academic intervention meetings, and referral resources. Parental support and buy-in to the importance and capacity of the school counselor is a vital element for any service or intervention to be successful. Unfortunately, with the high rates of divorce, school counselors face barriers and challenges due to the changing family dynamics, contentious divorces, and legal parameters to custodial rights. With family changes and difficult situations, the children experience an array of emotional, behavioral, and academic issues. Given these dynamics, school counselors must think critically about maximizing the collaborative and consultation pillars of their comprehensive programs in order to mitigate barriers and reach parents in order to support students holistically and support the work parents do. The following case is an example of a contentious divorce situation and potential methods for working through difficulties.

Description of Case

As an elementary school counselor, Mr. Darwin is working with a third-grade boy who is 9 years old. He was referred to the school counselor by his mother via a phone call and email, due to a recent separation and ongoing divorce and custody case between the child's mother and father. The mother wants the counselor to meet with her son to provide emotional support to him, as she is worried that the custody battle, specifically, is affecting him negatively. Mom is a first generation Mexican-American, and the father is of Mexican descent.

Dad is supportive of the counselor meeting with the student and does not contest it. Mr. Darwin consults with the teacher to learn more about the student, and the teacher has noticed that the student is frequently off task and often talks over the teacher and other students. She feels his behaviors are more juvenile than his peers are and that he behaves in immature ways with communication and wanting help from the teacher. She agrees to let the student leave class once a week for 30 minutes to meet with the counselor in his office.

In working with the student, Mr. Darwin comes to understand more about the situation. The student's mother is in the process of remarrying and is pregnant. The student comments that he does not like his soon-to-be stepdad very much and does not feel like his mom pays much attention to him. He expresses that he wished he could spend more time with his biological dad, specifically because his dad lets him play more video games. The counselor asks the student to do an activity in an effort to understand his feelings and thoughts about either parent as well as to strategize ways the student can connect more meaningfully with both parents. The student reflects on his struggles with his mom and specifies that his mom spends a lot of time on her phone and on social media. Mr. Darwin plans to have the student reflect on his dad in the next session.

Within that same week, the mother and soon-to-be stepdad arrive at Mr. Darwin's office to receive consultation and support on how to handle the custody case. Mom would like advice on how to appear and what to do during court meetings, as she desires full rights as the full-time or primary custodial parent. She spends time venting about dad's parenting and explaining why he should not have custodial rights. She also does not want dad to be a part of the decisions or communication regarding the services her son is receiving from the school counselor. Her partner does not say much during the meeting. Mom is sincere and emotional during the meeting, while her partner is supportive and actively listens. Mr. Darwin is aware that he cannot provide legal advice to either parent, nor can he voice an opinion about custodial rights. Those decisions are determined by the court. He does, however, listen empathically and reflect an understanding of how difficult the situation is for the entire family. He assures the parent that his top priority is to support her student academically, socially, and emotionally. Mr. Darwin is transparent about the rights of both parents to have access to school records, communications, and services unless otherwise instructed by the courts. He also gently suggests that children whose parents are divorcing generally have better outcomes in school when co-parenting is mutual and in the best interest of the child. The meeting ends after an hour or so, and mom asks to schedule a follow-up meeting with the counselor to discuss things further. Being aware of boundaries in his role at the school, Mr. Darwin responds that he will follow up with her later in the week regarding setting up a meeting.

Strategies for Consideration

Custody issues are prevalent in school settings. Some of these issues are conflictual while others are simply a matter of logistics. School counselors often are called upon to advocate for students involved in custody situations that are harmful or uncomfortable for children. The following sections offer interventions and considerations for school counselors who work with students and families in the process of custody arrangements.

Theoretical Frameworks

Consultation is an evidence-based theoretical framework and collaborative action that school counselors employ to both formally and informally support the individuals they serve (parents, teachers, administration, students) when a problem arises in which the individual is unsure of the solution (Solmonson, 2019). In consultation work, there are three key players: consultant, consultee, and client. Consultees seek consultation to remediate an issue occurring with a client. In a school system, school counselors serve as consultants for students, teachers, parents, administrators, and staff. Clients can be any of the school-wide stakeholders. The consultation work focuses on understanding the consultee's views and perceptions of the issues in order to provide an indirect service to support reconciliation, growth, or remediation between the consultee and the client (Dougherty, 2014). As this indirect service is provided, the school counselor continuously considers the school-system and surrounding systems to understand the situation holistically.

The *American School Counselor Association* includes consultation as a critical service component of successfully implemented comprehensive school counseling programs (CSCP) (Brigman, Webb, Mullis, & White, 2004). This specific professional practice empowers individuals who influence and affect the educational experiences that students have (ASCA, 2019). Consultation has a primary focus of providing the consultee resources and help in order to support their development and action in specific situations, situations that affect third parties (Warren & Baker, 2013). The school counselor provides this service to the consultee to determine an appropriate intervention to address the concerns brought forward. Consultation has the capacity to support the consultee in learning new skills and knowledge that will empower his or her self-efficacy and initiative taking when similar problems arise in the future. Specifically, consultation can empower parents and help them develop effective strategies for parenting.

There are varieties of consultation models that school counselors can utilize. These models also have a variety of theoretical orientations foundational to each model: cognitive, behavioral, multimodal, and developmental. The choice of model and theory depends on the situation in which consultation is applied. An Adlerian approach can be effective for supporting students holistically. Adlerian theory reflects an emphasis of understanding individuals from a holistic lens and understanding how current actions influence future outcomes. There are seven key principles in Adlerian focused consultation in schools: (1) equality between the consultant and consultee, (2) encouragement, (3) respect, (4) the mistaken goals of behavior, (5) logical consequences, (6) family atmosphere, and (7) faith in the client (child) and consultee (parent, teacher, and administrator). In a seminal piece by a student of Alfred Adler, four main psychological goals of children's misbehavior were identified (Dreikurs, 1948). The goals are to get attention, to get power or control, to get revenge, and to display inadequacy. When considering the current behaviors that are occurring with the student client (step 4), the consultant (counselor) and consultee (parent) consider the goals behind the behaviors.

The Adlerian approach is a form of mental health consultation with specific foci on education and training for parents and teachers. There are four described steps, sequential in nature, in the Adlerian approach (White & Mullis, 1998). The length of the consultation work will depend on the needs of the situation, time needed for the plan of action, and any other items or issues that come up.

1. A respectful, encouraging relationship must first be developed to promote a sense of working together.
2. Problems are then identified, and there is agreement as to what to work on.
3. An exploration of the child's functioning within the social contexts of home and school and sibling and peer relationships, along with an exploration of strengths and weaknesses, provides a better understanding of what might help.
4. Finally, the consultant and consultee work together to formulate a plan built on cooperation and encouragement.

In this current case study, the school counselor is the consultant, with the parent as the consultee. The consultative relationship centers on supporting the student, who is the client in this case. The behaviors the student exhibits in class is more than likely a result of the environmental changes and contention between the parents during their divorce and custody battle. Given that the parent is seeking support because of the child's behavioral issues, the work done with the parent can provide new learning and understanding of how the divorce is affecting the child and what strategies the parent can use to provide emotional care.

Professional Experiences

Experience A: As a school counselor, working with children of divorced parents happened more often than not. The students experienced a lot of anger and bitterness between the divorced parents, differences in parenting styles (that often clashed with each other), and a variety of system changes and transitions (remarrying, stepsiblings, moving). The emotional impact was evident and influenced behaviors both socially and academically. Supporting students who were in the alternative setting because of behavioral and academic issues was very difficult without parental support. The divorce element created further barriers with legal stipulations because legal custody dictates who has full or joint rights to education information and permissions. The school counseling position was complicated and challenging at times when working with parents who both had legal rights but did not work well with each other. Another challenge was the situation in which one parent had legal rights and the other did not, and the one without legal rights wanted to be involved. Finally, it was also difficult to work with stepparents who were supportive and wanted to make decisions about the student but did not have legal rights.

One case example in particular involved a male student who failed in his regular high school and was moving back and forth between his mother and father frequently. His father had visitation but no legal custody. He wanted more custody rights and was in the process of taking the mother back to court. The father had lost his custodial rights due to substance abuse. The student wanted to spend more time with his dad and reflected to the principal and myself that his mom was never around, and he spent more time with his dad anyway.

The student's mother was in the process of remarrying a partner who had two children, middle-school aged. When she could be reached, she had many derogatory comments to say about dad. The primary purpose of contacting the mother was for academic support, and as a support team, school personnel learned more about the home situation. The student had great capacity, and because of the divorce and household situations, his emotional wellness suffered and academic work declined. The team felt strongly that if the mother was able to support our academic interventions and understand her child's emotional needs more, the student could thrive in school.

After some persistence with contacting the mother, the team was able to bring her in to the support team meeting to talk about how her child was doing. We used it as an opportunity to present the different options the student had based on academic progress: community college, industry employment, and night school. The school support team wanted to objectively express how current academic deficiencies would affect his options and what remediation was needed to increase his future options. The school counselor spent time asking the mother what she hoped to see her son doing in the future and what she thought needed to happen for him to reach those aspirations. The team explored what was going on comprehensively for mom remarrying, family additions, divorce, and how that affected her relationship with her child. Through some open conversation and gentle nudging, the mother had increased awareness of how the environmental changes were impacting the student. This initial meeting lasted almost two hours.

The school counselor set up three additional meetings to meet with mom and the student to talk about strategies for supporting the student academically and emotionally. She did not focus the time on the divorce or custody situation. The time they spent together, each session about 30 minutes, focused on grade progress, what types of support the student wanted from his mom and the school, and how the student was doing emotionally. At first the student was not happy about these meetings, but his mom was willing and wanted to work better with her child, which helped the student buy into the meetings. The consultative approach in this situation was supportive and was a big factor in having the mother (consultee) and the student (client) meet together to have a collective work approach.

Experience B: The counselor worked with a student whose parents were recently divorced. The parents had joint physical and legal custody. The student had some digestive issues that affected his ability to attend school regularly. Both parents wanted to be involved in the collaboration and decisions about school accommodations and support. Given the legal arrangement, both parents needed to be a part of the conversations, and both parents had the right to decisions regarding their son. While this was a strength, the parents also did not see eye to eye on everything, which made it challenging to come to a consensus about accommodations for the student's learning needs given the medical issues. Specifically, mom wanted a battery of accommodations and considerations (removing P.E. requirements, more time after the semester ended to finish classwork, late start days), and dad felt he was being babied and needed to learn to toughen up. Between the different parental approaches and medical needs, the student's grades had dropped to C's/D's/F's by the middle of the year.

The initial meetings started with just the parents. The student would be either at home with a family member or in classes. The counselor decided at midyear to have a meeting with both the parents and the student. She felt that during the consultations about the supportive interventions that could be put into place (eventually a 504), the student needed to be a part of the decisions which might affect him. From the individual meeting in the fall, the student didn't reflect much beyond what mom thought was needed for his academic success. The counselor met with the student again individually before the group meeting to make sure he was comfortable and would be able to speak for himself without deferring to mom instinctively. Doing this was important because the student was not prepared for participating in a group meeting.

In the individual meeting, the counselor asked him what he wanted to do about P.E., homework time, and late starts. The student did not have many ideas but was very open to different ideas. He wanted to participate in P.E. still, but was worried that if a digestive issue hit him during P.E., it would be a crisis for him. He knew most of his issues happened in the morning, so he thought P.E. could continue in the afternoon. Because he was at different parental homes during the week, a late start was difficult to consistently implement because dad did not think it needed to happen and because digestive issues did not happen every morning. The parents were working with a dietician to decrease issues as well. The student was willing to try to show up on time with the option of coming to the nurse in the morning and rest if the situation was not too severe or to stay home if it was. The counselor agreed to work with the first period (which was intentionally an elective class) teacher to develop a system for recovering work if the student needed to rest.

When the student met with the parents, the counselor talked about different options they had and re-discussed them with the student and asked how everyone felt. Because of the legal rights of both parents, the counselor needed to get everyone on the same page. She reinforced that it was a way to begin and could be modified as needed, which could be no P.E. and late starts, if outcomes of the first intervention supported that next level of intervention. From the guided consultation efforts, the parents came to a consensus on the plan to keep P.E. later and to allow the student to see the nurse when needed, with the counselor talking to the first period teacher. The student's wishes were respected in a way that did not cause confrontation with the parents. The reinforcement was exactly what the student felt comfortable trying, and the parents agreed to a middle ground. The interventions were successful, and while there were days that the student did need to stay home, the absences were not extensive, and his grades steadily improved to B/C averages with teacher support. Sometimes the counselor has to work behind the scenes with the student to navigate difficult parents.

Counselor Impact

The situation in this case study has several elements that affect the school counselor. The first to consider is the boundary of the counselor's role and scope of practice. The mother referred her son to the counselor and wants services to support the emotional well-being of the student, given the current divorce proceedings. This falls well within the scope of practice. The mother also wants consultation on how to navigate the custody hearing and advice on what to say and do. This does not fall within the scope of practice. The school counselor must consider how to establish a boundary line with the mother, one that is clear and specific, about how the counselor can support the student, keep the mother apprised of the work being done, and provide resources for supporting the student's emotional well-being outside of the school. Being mindful of asserting the boundary in a gentle and supportive manner is imperative in order not to damage the working relationship with mom.

Working with the dad is another element to consider. Since a custody order has not been finalized, the dad has full custodial rights and a right to information about the services the son is receiving. Despite mom's wishes against this, the counselor has a responsibility to communicate to both parents and to be clear about that responsibility to mom, as she expresses wishes against it. Ideally, both parents will be able to work together to provide support and care for their child. However, until a custody order is finalized and things settle down, the counselor will be communicating back and forth with both parents.

A third consideration is confidentiality in the sessions with the student. The mother is adamant that she should have full custody and has depicted dad in a specific manner that is not necessarily congruent with how the son has reflected his relationship with his parents. Both parents have a right to information (FERPA), and the counselor must be careful with what is shared and what information to protect with confidentiality. Additionally, state educational codes vary from state to state and can inform what records and information pieces need to be available to both the school and the parents.

Mental Health Implications

Bitter and contemptuous divorces have negative impacts on children. Unfortunately, it is not uncommon in divorces for the parents to have interparental acrimony. Acrimony includes bitterness, hostility, and animosity and can result in verbal and sometimes physical altercations. Children might witness and hear parents fighting, angry and hateful comments, destruction to property, and sometimes physical abuse between parents. The stress and anxiety that comes from the tumultuous and difficult times is a lot, especially given the developmental life stage the child is in, for children to manage and deal with. Children in those situations are likely to suffer poor academic achievement, behavioral and emotional disorders, and antisocial and/or criminal conduct (Dunstan, Talbot, & Pozo de Bolger, 2017). No one divorce is the same, but Dunstan and colleagues (2017) found that interventions that provided parents and children with the following to be helpful: opportunities to build connections and explain loss and grief in divorce, mental health impacts of divorce, child behavior management, communication skills, single and co-parenting, and how to address impacts of divorce at its different stages, significantly reduced acrimony between parents and improved the child(s) well-being. School counselors, thus, can consider how to provide resources to parents and connect families to divorce support groups. Additionally, school counselors can consider how to incorporate these topics (as appropriate) into individual and group school-based sessions.

Ethical Considerations

The *American School Counselor Association Code of Ethics* (2016, Section A.2) provides the ethical guidelines for addressing, maintaining, and protecting the confidentiality of students. However, school counseling is a state-by-state practice, and only the state laws can recognize the school counseling sessions as a privileged communication interaction. If privileged communication is not recognized and the parents want to know what work is being done in sessions (as they have consented for the child to attend), the school counselor must balance the legality of the parents' rights and protecting the safety of the student. Section A.5 specifies that school counselors, "avoid dual relationships that might impair objectivity and increase the risk of harm to students." Practicing outside the scope of the practice (legal consultation) creates a dual relationship that is unethical and outside of the legal parameters of the school counseling license. Taking action to define the boundary line for the parents is imperative in the work being done.

Multicultural Considerations

In this specific case, consideration is given to the Mexican-American identity and the first-generation identity of the parents. Cohesion, acculturation, and the construct of the family influence and affect the family roles and interpersonal relationships (River et al., 2008). Families born outside of the United States experience acculturation issues from integrating values, lifestyles, and norms that are not congruent with U.S. society. Mexican Americans account for a high population of the Latino society in the United States, and with continued high rates of immigration, the cultural identity base continues to be a strong force (Guzman, 2001). The acculturation issues can create high levels of stress and angst in the family structure, with specific consideration given to the children who assimilate more with U.S. culture than is desired by the family (Smokowski, Rose, Bacallao, Cotter, & Evans, 2016).

The patriarchal influence in Hispanic families is an element that is important when considering this case. Strong emphasis is placed on the family in Hispanic families, with specific strength given to religious and father-headship elements. Additionally, high context communication is reflective of interpersonal interactions in Hispanic families. When supporting the student and parents in this case, the school counselor must take careful consideration of the affect that divorce has on the family structure and family identity within the Hispanic communities, the patriarchal system that may be in place, and how other cultural systems influence and impact communication, parenting, and interpersonal relationships.

Case Discussion Questions

1. Apply the consultation model to this case and address how you would work with the mother to support the student's needs.
2. How will you include the father in the work, and how will explain to the mother parental rights and the importance of having her ex-husband involved?
3. How will you respond to the mother's request to meet again to gain legal advice?
4. Mother wants to know what her son and the counselor talk about in the sessions, and privileged communication is not recognized for school counselors in your state. How will you balance confidentiality and the parents' right to information?
5. What types of case notes will you keep, given the statutes mentioned in question four?
6. How will you consider the cultural elements of this case, and what areas will you need to understand/learn about further?
7. What developmental considerations will you take into account when discussing divorce with the student, given that he is 9?
8. What communication style will you employ as the consultant, given the high context communication style of Hispanic families? Write a few examples of what that will look like.

Resources

Divorce Magazine: www.divorcemag.com/blog/school-resources-children-of-divorce
Help Guide: www.helpguide.org/articles/parenting-family/children-and-divorce.htm
Sesame Street: www.sesamestreet.org/toolkits/divorce?language=en

References

American School Counselor Association. (2016). *Ethical standards for school counselors*. Alexandria, VA: Author.
American School Counselor Association. (2019). *ASCA School Counselor Professional Standards & Competencies*. Alexandria, VA: Author.
Brigman, G., Webb, L., Mullis, F., & White, J. (2004). *School counselor consultation: Developing skills for working effectively with parents, teachers, and other school personnel*. Hoboken, NJ: Wiley.
Dougherty, A. M. (2014). *Psychological consultation and collaboration in school and community settings* (6th ed.). Belmont, CA: Cengage.

Dreikurs, R. (1948). *Challenge of parenthood.* New York City, NY: Duell, Sloan, and Pearce.

Dunstan, D. A., Talbot, C. J., & del Pozo de Bolger, A. (2017). Supporting children's well-being: Outcomes of a rural child-focused education program for separating or divorced parents. *The Australian Journal of Rural Health, 25,* 132–133.

Guzman, B. (2001). *The Hispanic population: Census 2000 brief.* Washington, DC: U. S. Department of Commerce.

River, F., Guarnaccia, P., Mulvaney-Day, N., Lin, J., Torres, M., & Alegria, M. (2008). Family cohesion and its relationship to psychological distress among Latino groups. *Hispanic Journal of Behavioral Sciences, 30*(3), 357–378.

Smokowski, P. R., Rose, R. A., Bacallao, M., Cotter, K. L., & Evans, C. B. R. (2016). Family dynamics and aggressive behavior in Latino Adolescents. *Cultural Diversity and Ethnic Minority Psychology, 23*(1), 81–90.

Solmonson, L. (2019). Collaboration and consultation. In L. A. Wines & J. Nelson (Eds.), *School counselors as practitioners: Building on theory, standards, and experience for optimal performance.* Upper saddle River, NJ: Pearson.

Warren, J. M., & Baker, S. B. (2013). School counselor consultation: Enhancing teacher performance through rational emotive-social behavioral consultation. *Vistas Online, 69,* 1–15.

White, J., & Mullis, F. (1998). A system approach to school counselor consultation. *Education, 119*(2), 242.

Reflections: In the space provided, write your notes and reflections regarding this case study.

19 Gay and in a Relationship With an Adult Male

Shannon McFarlin, Lisa A. Wines, and Ronda L. Henry

Background

Before contemporary technologies, many controversial topics were tucked away and out of the social eye. There were explanations for this conservatism due to the social rejection of certain behaviors and styles of life. Because of technological advancements in the 21st century, we are now able to obtain information about phenomena invisible to us and to connect with others who once were inaccessible. For members of the lesbian, gay, bisexual, transgender, queer, Intersex, Asexual, and Ally (LGBTQIAA) populations, the ability to connect with like-others online has opened doors to self-acceptance and greater self-understandings. With increased access to information and venues for self-expression, sexual minority populations are more visible among American society, with 4.5% of U.S. adults openly expressing an LGBT identity (Gallup, 2018) and 10.4% of high school youth identifying as gay, lesbian, or bisexual (U.S. Department of Health and Human Services, 2018).

The adolescent years are a time for self-expression, making friends, and finding identity. During these years, adolescents learn about themselves and compare their experiences to earlier learned lessons and messages from others in their environments. They try to find their social circles and begin to develop strategies for navigating life (Russell & Fish, 2016) that may or may not align with values and morals taught within the home.

Peer acceptance is crucial during the adolescent years. Adolescents look to peers in hopes of finding acceptance, belonging, and understanding. Yet students who identify as gay or bisexual sometimes struggle to find peer groups that accept them (Russell & Fish, 2016). For many of these youth, donning a sexual minority identity entails bullying, harassment, ridicule, and violence from both peers and adults, and some attempt to minimize rejection from others by exploring heterosexual relationships. When attempts to pass as heterosexual fail, others might feel confused and retaliate against the sexual minority youth in anger (Russell & Fish, 2016). In the face of rejection from peers, and with few same-sex role models available to them (Human Rights Campaign, 2019), some gay and bisexual youth turn to social media outlets in search of partners and acceptance (Russell & Fish, 2016). When this occurs, the youth can be lured into relationships with older partners who might abuse or exploit them (Human Rights Campaign, 2019).

Other prevalent issues in our society is this idea of sexually grooming young males and forming rings for prostitution. This form of grooming can begin online (Winters, Kaylor, & Jeglic, 2017), where mental engagement first takes place (e.g., where the mind goes, the body will follow). In the field of counseling, grooming is considered a crisis where sexual predators make an effort to prepare these minors for corroboration in their own sexual abuse (Jackson-Cherry & Erford, 2017). These individuals present as coy, caring, and full of compliments, using flattery, with high levels of sexual deviancy. The topic of sex is introduced early in the conversation, with some form of pornography included, teaching techniques of masturbation and engaging in cybersex (Winters et al., 2017). Additionally, there are several identified risk factors for creating prostitution rings in adolescents or juveniles in general. These factors consist of belonging to dysfunctional families, experiencing mental health issues, having poor social skills, suffering from an abuse history, and performing inadequately in school (Twill, Green, & Traylor, 2010).

Some adolescent males are longing for a relationship with their father. Some youngsters have not had a father in the home, leaving a void to contend with, and could convey opportunity for a predator. Fatherless homes can be a result of alcohol or drug dependency, physical and emotional abuse, divorce, infidelity, parental alienation, or decisions made to be in a noncommittal relationship (e.g., one-night stand or being a mistress). This sort of yearning for fatherly influence can make these males vulnerable and quick to welcome the attention of any adult male.

Description of Case

Savion, a 13-year-old, heavy-set eighth-grader, had been spending time in the office of the school counselor, Mr. Palicki, because he constantly experiences rejection and isolation due to other students' perception of his sexual orientation as a gay male. Savion, who is a rather vibrant and outgoing individual, was quite expressive in his pursuit and sexual interest in heterosexual male athletes, often resulting in physical violence, verbal threats, and acts of intimidation. These athletes were furious, yet they were punished for their less-than-kind responses to Savion's unwanted advancements.

One day, Nurse Capello contacted the school counselor because a male student was visiting her office restroom excessively due to a prognosis of irritable bowel syndrome (IBS). This syndrome caused the student embarrassment and a desire for privacy, which seemed to be a frustration for the school nurse. Mr. Palicki asked the name of the student, only to discover that it was Savion, who had missed several classes, was not performing well academically, and was not socially accepted by many.

School counselor Palicki decided to meet with Savion to offer support via counseling services. Mr. Palicki was concerned with this student's safety, attendance, academics, social experiences, and his overall health. After a few sessions, the school counselor built great rapport and trust with Savion, who disclosed there were a couple of non-truths in his current circumstances. Savion told Mr. Palicki that because he liked these athletes and was proud to be gay, he enjoyed upsetting and sexually harassing them. Mr. Palicki also learned during their time together that his IBS and trips to the restroom were because the student was severely stressed. This was due to multiple decisions regarding skipping school and the sexual encounters he was having with a 20-year-old adult male, Dorian. Savion met Dorian online on a website for teenage dating, and because of constant daily communication, grew an affection for Dorian that incited acceptance, hypersexuality, and a desire to recruit other boys into a form of a grooming ring. Dorian wished to establish himself locally with other young males within the community but knew he had to remain inconspicuous.

Mr. Palicki knows he needs to meet individually with the athletes responsible for the verbal and physical assaults, along with addressing the acts of intimidation. Additionally, learning about the 20-year-old online predator (Dorian), a report must be made to law enforcement to reduce the potential number of victims. Mr. Palicki shares his plan with Savion and makes sure he also understands his responsibility to report this to his parents.

Strategies for Consideration

The strategies discussed here provide a theoretical foundation to enhance school counselors' knowledge and skills, along with professional experiences as a medium for consideration and reflection. Other relevant strategies are inherent in the discussion of counselor impact, because understanding the potential impact can create mindfulness and prevent certain outcomes from occurring. Although diagnosing mental health conditions is not a part of the school counselor role, exposure to these implications creates opportunity to connect with students via counseling services within the school, along with providing continuity of care referrals to law enforcement, other mental health specialists, and medical professionals.

Theoretical Frameworks

Scholars have proposed several homosexual identity stage models to outline common developmental experiences among lesbian women and gay men (e.g., Cass, 1979; Coleman, 1981; Gock, 2001; Troiden, 1989). Most of the models denote preadolescence as the beginning of the identity development process, which the models purport to conclude typically in individuals' mid- to late 20s. Among the models in the literature, Cass's (1979) linear stage model is cited most frequently. The stages of Cass's model are outlined here to aid in the assessment of Savion's gay identity development.

Stage 1: Identity Confusion

The first stage is the stage at which an individual gains an initial awareness of feelings, thoughts, and behaviors that others might interpret as gay. Inner strife is common among individuals at this stage, who often isolate themselves from others as they ponder the question, "Could I be gay?" (Cass, 1979).

Stage 2: Identity Comparison

The defining characteristic of the second stage is social alienation. At this stage, an individual provisionally consigns to the idea, "Maybe I *am* gay." For some, the new self-understanding might create distress, and individuals might make attempts to present a heterosexual image to others, blame others for their circumstance, or alter self-perceptions. Risk for self-harm is high at this stage, and feelings of self-hatred are common among those in this phase of development (Cass, 1979).

Stage 3: Identity Tolerance

"I probably am gay" is the prevailing thought among individuals at Stage 3, which is when the loneliness of alienation catalyzes many to seek out other sexual minority individuals. The emotional quality of their first social interactions with members of sexual minority groups dictates the extent to which individuals experience distress at this stage. Negative interactions can reinforce pejorative views of self; positive interactions can affirm a gay identity and propel them to the next stage in the developmental process (Cass, 1979).

Stage 4: Identity Acceptance

Increased contact with others who identify as gay helps individuals to experience greater feelings of normalcy at this stage. However, incongruence between presentations of self to others and one's own understandings of self commonly wells at this stage, mustering individuals forward to the next stage of development (Cass, 1979).

Stage 5: Identity Pride

The defining characteristic of individuals at this stage is ethnocentrism (Cass, 1979), or an "Us versus Them" mentality (Altemeyer, 2003). Activism is common among individuals at this stage, who become increasingly cognizant of heterosexist discrimination. The gay identity becomes the master status that supersedes all other identities, and individuals at this stage commonly rebel against the heterosexual community by openly flaunting their homosexuality (Cass, 1979).

Stage 6: Identity Synthesis

Attaining the understanding that sexual orientation is only one facet of an individual's overall identity and relinquishing an ethnocentric attitude are the hallmarks of Stage 6, the final stage in the developmental process. As Cass (1979) purported, full self-acceptance cannot be truly realized until these two things happen. It is at this stage that individuals can again develop and maintain positive relationships with members of the heterosexual community (Cass, 1979).

Professional Experiences

School counselors experience a range of complexity when assisting students similar to the one discussed in this case. To start, school counselors should have a theory to operate within to conceptualize situations and to articulate professional decisions made to support students. Additionally, school counselors should realize when working with an individual like Savion that there are other persons involved who would benefit from immediate attention and counseling services. All too often, the depth and gravity of everyone impacted may be overlooked inadvertently. The heterosexual male athletes are important to work with because, for them, the experience of being pursued and groomed by a same-sex person can be confusing, off-putting, and infuriating, all while having to sort through their own internal thoughts and emotions. In this case study, it could be that harassment reports were made because of the unwanted advances leading them to no other choice. It is clear that Savion misunderstood appropriate ways to express his interest in male students, and he did not have a sense of their receptiveness prior to his decision to pursue them.

An additional priority is the relationship that exists between the 20-year-old male and the adolescent student. From a professional standpoint, school counselors are aware of laws around statutory rape and molestation of a minor. Most school counselors do not experience the interceding of the grooming of adolescent males and perhaps a ring of adolescent exploitation. However, counselors are adept at gathering information (counseling), making proper reports to parents and law enforcement, and documenting the process, as these tasks are all vital to providing the necessary continuity of care.

Counselor Impact

The potential impact on a school counselor, regarding a case such as this, may be insurmountable. The values and moral compass of the school counselor might not align with the mindset surrounding the development of sexual orientation in young persons. School counselors often have beliefs regarding the type of experiences youth should have, and although they come from a place of compassion, their convictions may suggest it is wrong to engage in same-sex relationships. The impact of placing values onto another person could be quite overwhelming, and to greater extremes, initiate a desire to control and save students from themselves. The focus in this study first must be to protect the minor student from a predator; when that is resolved, it might be appropriate for the school counselor to offer resources to the family regarding sexual identity development and gay relationships.

Further, if school counselors have ever had vicarious or actual experience with sexual abuse, sexual trauma, or molestation, they may become overinvested in students' remediation and healing process. From an ethical standpoint, counselors run the risk of blurring professional boundaries. Counselors can experience re-traumatization (e.g., flashbacks and upsetting memories), particularly if the school counselor did not seek treatment for the original trauma. It is quite possible in such circumstances to experience a cognitive or emotional relapse due to the exposure encountered while working with these students' circumstances.

Mental Health Implications

According to Russell and Fish (2016), sexual minority youth are at high risk for poor mental health. These youth commonly experience discrimination from others, higher exposure to HIV and other sexually transmitted diseases, homo-prejudice, increased levels of stress, and humiliation. These experiences often contribute to depression, anxiety, low self-esteem, suicidal ideation, and many other mental health disorders among this population of students (Russell & Fish, 2016). On the note of suicide, the Centers for Disease Control and Prevention (CDC; U.S. Department, 2018) reported that in 2017, 23% (i.e., almost one out of four) of lesbian, gay, and bisexual youth had attempted suicide, compared to only 5.4% (i.e., approximately one in 20) of their heterosexual counterparts. Mental health problems are exacerbated forms of *dis-ease* (e.g. feeling discomfort, anguish, or agony), which can cause disease, an illness, ailment, or complication. Mental health conditions that could become of concern are generalized anxiety disorder (GAD), major depressive disorder (MDD), stress-related disorders, bipolar, and substance use disorders.

Sexual minority youth can also experience medical conditions such as irritable bowel syndrome (IBS, Kinsinger, 2017). Irritable bowel syndrome is a chronic gastrointestinal ailment that causes pain and irritation, leading to diarrhea and/or constipation. As Kinsinger (2017) stated, the severity and disability of IBS directly relate to the presence of psychological problems and deficits in cognitive processing. What this means for sexual minority youth is that the trials of coming out and discovering self-identity can result not only in mental health complications but also in behavioral and physiological problems. Likewise, when an individual experiences stress of this magnitude, the body reacts to a demand or challenge. Stress is an emotional or physiological reaction and can have a grave impact on adolescents. Evidence of feeling frustration, anxiety, and anger may be present, along with symptoms of nervousness. Acute stress is short term and helps anyone in dangerous situations, whereas chronic stress is over time and long term.

Ethical Considerations

There are several ethical considerations (ASCA, 2016) appropriate for a case such as this. School counselors are charged to make decisions grounded in ethics regarding the student's sexual orientation, a commitment not to impose personal bias or values onto students, and a requirement to report sexual abuse and harassment of a minor.

Regarding the student's sexual orientation:

A.1.f Respect students' and families' values, beliefs, sexual orientation, gender identity/ expression, and cultural background and exercise great care to avoid imposing personal beliefs or values rooted in one's religion, culture, or ethnicity.

School counselors are not to impose their personal beliefs and values onto students. When working with Savion, the school counselor must not allow any personal tenets that discriminate against sexual minorities to cloud her judgment of him or to guide his work with the student.

A.6.e Refrain from referring students based solely on the school counselor's personal beliefs or values rooted in one's religion, culture, or personal worldview. School counselors maintain the highest respect for student diversity. School counselors should pursue additional training or supervision in areas where they are at risk for imposing their values on students, especially when the school counselor's values are discriminatory in nature.

> School counselors do not impose their values on students and/or families when making referrals to outside sources for student and/or family support.

The school counselor must provide Savion with appropriate services, if necessary. If the school counselor's values and beliefs system collide with Savion's right to autonomy in his decisions about his sexual orientation, then the school counselor must refrain from referring Savion to another school counselor or to an outside provider solely because of the values conflict. Instead, the school counselor must seek training and/or supervision to increase cultural sensitivity and to moderate the risk of doing harm to the student. When making referrals to outside providers, the school counselor must not intentionally refer the student and family to providers who practice conversion therapy, which can be harmful for sexual minority minors (Beer, 2015).

Regarding the duty to report abuse and neglect:

> A.9.d Report to parents/guardians and/or appropriate authorities when students disclose a perpetrated or a perceived threat to their physical or mental well-being. This threat may include, but is not limited to, physical abuse, sexual abuse, neglect, dating violence, bullying, or sexual harassment. The school counselor follows applicable federal, state, and local laws and school district policy.

In this case study, Savion reported to the school counselor that he was having sex with a 20-year-old male. In all U.S. states, the sexual relationship between the two males constitutes child abuse due to Savion's status as a minor, to his partner's status as an adult, and to the age difference between them. The school counselor must follow through with notifying the parents and the authorities of the suspected abuse.

> A.11.b Report suspected cases of child abuse and neglect to the proper authorities and take reasonable precautions to protect the privacy of the student for whom abuse or neglect is suspected when alerting the proper authorities.

This ethical standard speaks to Savion's privacy rights in reporting processes. When making the report to authorities, the school counselor should proffer important identifying information about both Savion and his adult partner, while simultaneously taking care to reveal only the need-to-know information that will assist authorities in their investigation of child abuse.

> A.11.e Guide and assist students who have experienced abuse and neglect by providing appropriate services.

When the suspected child abuse is reported to authorities and to Savion's parents, Savion might experience negative emotions such as anger, resentment, embarrassment, or guilt. If necessary and appropriate, the school counselor should assist Savion in processing his experience of the incident in the aftermath of the report to others.

Regarding the duty to report sexual harassment:

> A.11.a Report to the administration all incidents of bullying, dating violence, and sexual harassment as most fall under Title IX of the Education Amendments of 1972 or other federal and state laws as being illegal and require administrator interventions. School counselors provide services to victim and perpetrator as appropriate, which may include a safety plan and reasonable accommodations such as schedule change, but school counselors defer to administration for all discipline issues for this or any other federal, state, or school board violation.

Savion confessed to the school counselor that he has a history of sexually harassing male peers at school, which he continues to do and to enjoy. The school counselor has the charge of advocating for the well-being of all students. When Savion violates the rights of other students, then the school counselor must report his transgressions to school administrators, who can proceed with disciplinary procedures. If other students report that Savion's sexual harassment of them causes them distress, then the school counselor should arrange accommodations for these students that will increase their sense of safety and comfort at school.

Multicultural Considerations

According to the Centers for Disease Control and Prevention (CDC, 2019), regarding new diagnoses of human immunodeficiency virus (HIV) in 2017, youth ages 13 to 24 constituted 21%. Among the youth who were diagnosed with HIV, 87% were young men, and 93% of the diagnosed young men were males who were having sex with males. As the CDC (2019) noted, prevention challenges for this population include inadequate sex education, low testing rates, substance abuse, low rates of condom use, and increased numbers of partners. Moreover, the risk for HIV infection is larger for young men who have sex with older partners, who are more likely to have had greater numbers of sexual partners (CDC, 2019). The CDC (2019) also stated that youth ages 20 to 24 have some of the highest reports of other sexually transmitted diseases (STDs), especially youths of minority groups and low socioeconomic status, and that the risk for HIV infection increases when another STD is present.

With this information in mind, and considering that "[y]outh with HIV are the least likely of any age group to be linked to care in a timely manner" (CDC, 2019, para. 1), the school counselor in this case study should consider the probability that Savion's irritable bowel symptoms could be related to a sexually transmitted infection. Several STDs can cause anorectal (i.e., relating to the anus and rectum) and gastrointestinal problems, including chlamydia, chancroid, shigella, syphilis, and gonorrhea (Whitlow, 2004). A referral to the school nurse and/or to an outside medical doctor for testing should be strongly considered.

Case Discussion Questions

1. If you were school counselor Palicki, what would be your course of action? List the steps that you would take to assist Savion in the order that you would execute them.
2. How would you enlist Savion's cooperation in reporting processes? With a partner, role-play the discussion that you would have with him about your duty to report his relationship with the adult partner both to authorities and to his parents.
3. When discussing Savion's predicament with his parents, what would you say to them?
4. Considering Cass's (1979) model of homosexual identity formation, where would you say that Savion is in his process of developing a gay identity? What are his strengths and challenges at his current phase of development? What counseling interventions might you use to aid him in a successful developmental process?
5. Make a list of referrals that might be appropriate for Savion and his family. Provide a justification for each referral.

Resources

Parents, Families, and Friends of Lesbians and Gays: https://pflag.org/needsupport
Child Welfare: www.childwelfare.gov/topics/systemwide/diverse-populations/lgbtq/lgbt-families/
Human Rights Campaign: https://www.hrc.org/explore/topic/children-youth

References

Altemeyer, B. (2003). Why do religious fundamentalists tend to be prejudiced? *International Journal for the Psychology of Religion, 13*, 17–28. doi:10.1207/S15327582IJPR1301_03

American School Counselor Association. (2016). *Ethical standards for school counselors.* Alexandria, VA: American School Counselor Association.

Beer, J. (2015). Testimony on sexual orientation change efforts. *Journal of Gay & Lesbian Mental Health, 19*, 94–95. doi:10.1080/19359705.2014.960780

Cass, V. C. (1979). Homosexual identity formation: A theoretical model. *Journal of Homosexuality, 4*, 219–235. doi:10.1300/J082v04n03_01

Centers for Disease Control and Prevention. (2019). *HIV and youth.* Retrieved from www.cdc.gov/hiv/group/age/youth/index.html

Coleman, E. (1981). Developmental stages of the coming-out process. *Journal of Homosexuality, 4*, 31–43. doi:10.1300/J082v07n02_06

Gallup. (2018, May 22). *In U.S., estimate of LGBT population rises to 4.5%.* Retrieved from https://news.gallup.com/poll/234863/estimate-lgbt-population-rises.aspx

Gock, T. S. (2001). Asian-Pacific Islander issues: Identity integration and pride. In B. Berzon (Ed.), *Positively gay: New approaches and gay and lesbian life* (3rd ed., pp. 334–341). Berkeley, CA: Celestial Arts.

Human Rights Campaign. (2019). *Teen dating violence among LGBTQ youth.* Retrieved from www.hrc.org/resources/teen-dating-violence-among-lgbtq-youth

Jackson-Cherry, L. R., & Erford, B. T. (2017). *Crisis assessment, intervention, and prevention* (3rd ed.). New York, NY: Pearson.

Kinsinger, S. W. (2017). Cognitive-behavioral therapy for patients with irritable bowel syndrome: Current insights. *Psychology Research and Behavior Management, 10*, 231–237. doi:10.2147/PRBM.S120817

Russell, S. T., & Fish, J. N. (2016). Mental health in lesbian, gay, bisexual, and transgender (LGBT) youth. *Annual Review of Clinical Psychology, 12*, 465–487. doi:10.1146/annurev-clinpsy-021815-093153

Troiden, R. R. (1989). The formation of homosexual identities. *Journal of Homosexuality, 17*, 43–73. doi:10.1300/J082v17n01_02

Twill, S. E., Green, D. M., & Traylor, A. (2010). A descriptive study on sexually exploited children in residential treatment. *Child & Youth Care Forum, 39*(3), 187–199. doi:10.1007/s10566-010-9098-2

U.S. Department of Health and Human Services, Centers for Disease Control and Prevention. (2018). *Youth risk behavior surveillance—United States 2017* (MMWR Surveillance Summary Vol. 67 No. 8). Retrieved from www.cdc.gov/healthyyouth/data/yrbs/pdf/2017/ss6708.pdf

Whitlow, C. B. (2004). Bacterial sexually transmitted diseases. *Clinics in Colon and Rectal Surgery, 17*(4), 209–214. Retrieved from www.ncbi.nlm.nih.gov/pmc/articles/PMC2780056/

Winters, G. M., Kaylor, L. E., & Jeglic, E. L. (2017). Sexual offenders contacting children online: An examination of transcripts of sexual grooming. *Journal of Sexual Aggression, 23*(1), 62–76. doi:10.1080/13552600.2016.1271146

Reflections: In this space, provide your notes and reflections for this case.

20 Inappropriate Sexual Advances From a Teacher

Lisa A. Wines, Sherrie K. Grunden, and Natalie Alfonso Welsch

Background

Each year, parents send their children back to school around the country, trusting school personnel with each child in their care. It is true that teachers often spend more time with their students than parents spend with their child. Teachers build healthy relationships with students and, when this is done correctly, help them to gain valuable information helpful toward their education. Educators have a tremendous responsibility, and as trained professionals, teachers have high standards and are expected to be role models for the students assigned to their classrooms. This means that educators must maintain a level of professionalism that does not cross the boundary of the teacher/student relationship. However, when that boundary is crossed, teachers are at risk of allegations being made against them.

All educators should take special precautions to evade any situation in which the professional boundary is not clearly maintained. Specifically, teachers should avoid inviting students to their homes, engaging in activities away from school that are not school sponsored, and having conversations that divulge personal information about the teacher or student. When this happens, the relationship can become more personal than necessary for both parties involved. An inappropriate relationship occurs when teachers cross the line and begin to pursue a more personal exchange with a student, which can vary from allowing the student to share information that is sexual or provocative in nature to the teacher requesting a physical relationship (Professional Boundaries with Students, 2019).

According to Chang and Chang (2018), relationships between teachers and students that have become inappropriate or sexual in nature are on the rise. In fact, teacher and student relationships have made a steady increase each year for the past nine years, with the year 2018 seeing a 36% increase from the previous year (Chang & Chang, 2018). Due to the nature of a student and teacher relationship, the age of the victim or student is inconsequential. Regardless of the age of the student, the teacher is aware of the boundary that must be maintained due to the power differential in the relationship and must recognize that no student can consent to a relationship with an educator that is sexual in nature. To protect students, there are mandates by both lawmakers and education agencies in place that are enforced. An educator found guilty of indecent exposure or any sexual act with a student is usually charged with a felony. If convicted, the offender can be required to register as a sex offender, even if the student has reached the age of consent. The consequences of a teacher/student inappropriate relationship can be detrimental for either involved and can affect them for years following the relationship.

For this reason, there are also stronger laws now in place that require school administrators to notify parents of any suspected relationship between their child and a district employee under investigation. In addition to parent notification, administrators must ensure that the investigation is reported to future school districts that may attempt to employ the teacher that was investigated for inappropriate relations. With the new regulations approved to safeguard other students from falling victim, any administrator that is guilty of covering the investigation or assisting a terminated teacher from gaining new employment at a different school district can also be charged with a felony or fined up to $10,000. This new law was enacted after a study indicated that teachers who have sexual relationships with students often resign to avoid legal issues and then secure a new position with a different school district. So while teacher misconduct with students is certainly not a new issue for lawmakers and administrators, these additional measures mean the consequences are more severe to deter such a relationship from occurring. Now it does not simply mean that a teacher must find a new job and quietly resign from a school district that suspects an inappropriate relationship between an educator and a student.

Aside from criminal charges, some state boards of education, as in Texas, can issue sanctions on a certified teacher if they are guilty of pursuing a romantic involvement with a student. These can occur if a teacher is found to have made sexually degrading comments, comments about a student's body, or comments regarding a student's sexual performance or sexual history. Additionally, if convicted, the teacher more than likely will have their teaching certificate revoked and also will forfeit the fund paid into the teacher retirement system. Furthermore, a teacher can be sanctioned for inappropriate hugging, touching, or kissing or initiating a relationship with the student to be consummated after graduation. Even if the relationship does not progress to one that involves sexual acts, the teacher can still be charged with online solicitation of a minor if communication through text messaging or social media has occurred and a sexual act has been requested by the teacher (Professional Boundaries with Students, 2019). Although the state of Texas was the source of this information, each state will have its own laws governing these types of occurrences.

Description of Case

At the time of this incident, the student, William, was a 17-year-old senior in high school attending a small, rural school. Only a couple of months prior to the start of his senior year, his older brother was killed in a car crash that was witnessed by their mother. William and his family were struggling with the loss of his older, outgoing brother. The two brothers were close in age, and William struggled with depression and guilt. William always wished he were close to his mother but often felt empty inside when it came to his relationship with her. Following his brother's accident, he began drinking and smoking marijuana to deal with the pain of his loss. He also began experimenting with other high-risk behaviors, often driving at high rates of speed. He reported seeking out feelings that would lessen the hurt and anger of losing his brother.

Ms. Thomas, William's English teacher, was a 34-year-old mother of two who was involved in a physically and emotionally abusive relationship with the father of her children. At the time of the incident, Ms. Thomas was married to a man who exhibited narcissist behavior. He made unreasonable demands of her and her children and was often verbally abusive. Ms. Thomas was withdrawn, felt isolated, and suffered from poor self-image. Having recently relocated due to her husband's employment, she socialized little outside of school. The stress of her home life led her to spend long hours at school working away from home. She attended sporting events, class meetings, and special school sponsored events in the community and grew close to the students in her classes, one of whom was William.

William was below grade level and was at risk for not meeting graduation requirements. Mrs. Loredo, the school counselor, contacted William due to his low performance and risk of not graduating. William shared his current circumstance, and Mrs. Loredo knew she must support William and began to see him for counseling sessions. Additionally, Mrs. Loredo wanted to add another layer of support. With permission from William and his parents, the counselor asked one teacher, Ms. Thomas, to begin working with him and other students after school in effort to help them with these academic deficits.

Initially, William saw Ms. Thomas as a supportive adult that he enjoyed as a teacher, and she saw him as a young man who was grieving and needing support. After a night of drinking with friends, he called her from his brother's grave and said that he was contemplating suicide. She went to his aid and counseled him through this episode, contacted Mrs. Loredo for a follow-up, and even reported the events to his mother. However, following these reports, William began flirting and seeking further attention from her. Rather than dissuade him and report the behavior, Ms. Thomas allowed it to continue. The two grew closer during that time and began talking on the phone and exchanging text messages. Over time, the messages became more personal in nature, and eventually they became inappropriate and sexual in nature. The messages continued until graduation, at which time the relationship became physical, and the two were sexually intimate. The two met secretly for over a month before William mentioned the meetings in one of the counseling sessions with Mrs. Loredo, who exposed the relationship to the school administration.

Ms. Thomas resigned from her position and surrendered her teaching certificate. In retrospect, she does not feel like a predator but simply someone who made a grave judgment error. "If I had it to do over, I would have immediately put a halt to his behavior and reported him to the principal," she said. "I realize now that my own dysfunctional relationship led me to seek acceptance and affirmation elsewhere; I am just so sorry that I found it where I did." In the aftermath of the fallout from this relationship, Ms. Thomas' marriage suffered, and she and her husband divorced.

William later shared that he felt his older brother sought a relationship with a former teacher at their school. After his brother's death, he wanted to emulate his brother and said he was conscious of pursuing his teacher. He stated that he did not feel as though he were a victim and rarely thought of the occurrence in any manner. Mrs. Loredo, however, considered William to be a victim of child abuse, and she referred the family to an outside therapist.

Strategies for Consideration

The case study presented is complex and has many layers available for a school counselor to explore and develop a deeper understanding. The following sections provide theoretical ideas for case conceptualization, professional experiences of practicing teachers and counselors, counselor impact, and mental health implications. Additionally, the ethical and multicultural implications of such a case are discussed.

Theoretical Frameworks

John Bowlby's (1965) attachment theory is a theoretical framework applicable to this case for school counselors' use, as a lack of attachment and/or inability to facilitate attachment between a child and significant caretakers might be a precipitating factor in an intimate relationship between a student and teacher. This theory is not only about the secure relationships formed with a caretaker as an infant but is equally about human connection over time. It is obvious that both William and Ms. Thomas are unsatisfied with the relationships in their personal lives and thus have sought the attention and support of each other to fill the void.

As the case spans the student's senior year, it should not go without notice that there was no account of William's family showing support during that period in his life. His experienced symptoms were severe, and his grief, over time, was insurmountable. Relationships can begin with an emotional friendship and escalate into a physically intimate affair as the individuals involved struggle with the imbalance between an ideal circumstance and reality (Reibstein, 2013). Within the perspective of the teacher, partaking in this behavior with her student can be identified as supplemental to an unfulfilling marriage and can be induced by "high arousal situations" (Reibstein, 2013). With the formation of an inappropriate attachment between student and teacher, there is potential for psychological damage to the student who is the charge of the teacher and the school community.

The presence of attachment ruptures (Reibstein, 2013) provides the backdrop for William's lack of emotionality and Ms. Thomas's emotional overcompensation in the relationship. She allowed the communication between herself and the student to become inappropriate and expressed that by doing so, it disguised her lack of attachment with her husband. In reference to the state of William's mental health, his formulation of attachments and his relational expectations moving forward are in jeopardy of distortion and could result in self-sabotaging interpersonal and intrapersonal habits.

Professional Experiences

Area school counselors who understood the dynamics of students' and teachers' relationships met to discuss professional boundaries. One counselor described the aftereffects of inappropriate professional boundaries on the part of teachers as heartbreaking for the student, the family, and the teacher. The stigma for the family of the teacher, she noted, was especially traumatic for their own children.

One aspect that all counselors agreed upon is that teachers and students both need more education on the dangers of inappropriate relationships. Both families and school personnel need to be vigilant for the signs of an inappropriate relationship between a teacher and student, particularly when both parties have dysfunctional home circumstances. One high school counselor summarized a case in which a high school coach was arrested for his relationship with a high school cheerleader. While the community was shocked when the events were exposed, the students in the school did not share those feelings. They reported that they had known for months, and yet no one came forward to report the relationship.

By educating the students and providing a confidential method to report a suspected relationship, administrators would be notified sooner, and the teacher could be monitored closely to see if professional standards were maintained with all of their students. Likewise, by providing a more detailed professional development for educators, schools administrators could not only reinforce the need for each teacher to develop and maintain the highest ethical standards, but they could also highlight the consequences for breaking the trust that parents, students, and schools place in them. This should include the requirement to report any comment or action by a student, even if the teacher is unsure if the student is joking. Based on the input from the counselors in the interview, these suggestions were presented:

1. Professional development, primarily in secondary schools, is needed each school year with detailed examples of cases and consequences for educators who have been involved in inappropriate teacher/student relationships. The school counselor is well positioned to provide this type of staff development.
2. Student body assemblies should be held early in the year, with administrators educating the students on what the appropriate behavior to be expected from adults and teachers is. Again, the school counselor is the person who students trust and who can provide this type of assembly for students.
3. A confidential method of reporting suspected inappropriate behavior between a teacher and student, such as a phone app or online method, is necessary.
4. Administrators should employ careful monitoring and frequent administrative presence in the schools.

Counselor Impact

One counselor felt that as the school year progresses, teachers and students become more familiar with one another, and that is when the professional boundaries are likely to become blurred. She stated that counselors could maintain the education throughout the school year by meeting with different extracurricular groups and teams to continue to educate the students on appropriate contact and behaviors to be expected from all the adults in their lives. She also stressed that this includes all adults, so as not to just focus on particular adults in the students' lives.

Counselors should also be prepared to work with students who experience any inappropriate advances or contact from an adult to one of their students. Due to the age and psychological development of the students, they may not even realize how detrimental this can be and how it may affect them later. Counselors should allow students to share their experiences and discuss how they feel without offering their personal thoughts and feelings on the subject.

Mental Health Implications

In this case, William presented with undiagnosed symptoms of both depression and grief. It is evident that the student was unaware of resources available to him to aid in the mental or psychological processing of his brother's death and instead sought both the attention and comfort from a trusted adult in his life. Rather than report these symptoms, his teacher (an academic professional) negated the signs and saw the student as an option of support for the grievances she faced in her own life. After the relationship was reported and the student was removed from the situation, it was crucial that the school counselor initiated counseling processes and referrals for mental health services.

An inappropriate relationship with a teacher, regardless of who initiated it, can result in a variety of mental and emotional consequences. While school counselors do not diagnose mental health disorders, they are trained to recognize them and to report the concerning behaviors to a licensed professional. In this particular case, a diagnosis for consideration is major depressive disorder, moderate, recurrent, as the student experiences a depressed mood, a loss of interest, diminished ability to think, and suicidal ideation. An important thing to consider is the difference between a major depressive episode and symptoms appropriate to the loss of a family member.

The combination of the loss of a sibling and an intimate relationship with a teacher can put copious amounts of stress on an individual; thus, William, is a good candidate for post-traumatic stress disorder. He was directly exposed to a death of a close family member and shortly after was sexually exploited by a trusted adult. As a result of the traumatic event with the addition of an inappropriate relationship with his teacher, William experienced intrusive symptoms such as prolonged distress, avoidance of any negative feelings associated with both the loss and the intimate relationship, and drastically altered cognitive functioning.

Other symptoms that can affect William's health, safety, and quality of life must be considered. William could lose all respect he had for himself and continue to act out in impulsive and psychologically and physically damaging ways. The rejection he experienced at the end of the intimate relationship, despite his claims that he was only acting as his brother, could set him up for failed relationships in the future. Depression and its associated symptoms can distort cognitive ability and functionality in different aspects of an individual's life. If William is unable to process through his experiences and process how his emotions, feelings, thoughts and behaviors are connected, what could the potential be for a repeated experience?

Ethical Considerations

The following standards from the American School Counselor Association (2016) are relevant to this case.

> A.1.a Have a primary obligation to the students, who are to be treated with dignity and respect as unique individuals.

The counselor's primary role is to support the student who has been sexually abused by an adult who was charged to care for him, teach him, and mentor him. Regardless of William's age (he may be 17 or 18 as a senior), his status as a student in high school indicates that a sexual encounter with a teacher is abuse due to the hierarchical nature of the relationship. Mrs. Loredo probably has a professional relationship with Ms. Thomas; however, the teacher's case is going to be handled by administrators and law enforcement.

> A.2.a Promote awareness of school counselors' ethical standards and legal mandates regarding confidentiality and the appropriate rationale and procedures for disclosure of student data and information to school staff.

Confidential student information is on *a need-to-know* basis. While other teachers and staff may be aware of an inappropriate relationship between William and Ms. Thomas, the school counselor must not discuss, gossip, or provide details regarding the situation. In this case, only the administrators had a *need to know* to protect other students from a teacher without professional boundaries.

> A.2.f Recognize their primary ethical obligation for confidentiality is to the students but balance that obligation with an understanding of parents'/guardians' legal and inherent rights to be the guiding voice in their children's lives. School counselors understand the need to balance students' ethical rights to make choices, their capacity to give consent or assent, and parental or familial legal rights and responsibilities to make decisions on their child's behalf.

William's parents are privy to all of his school records and information pertaining to his development because he is currently attending high school; therefore, Mrs. Loredo must contact his mother to apprise his family of the situation.

> A.2.i Request of the court that disclosure not be required when the school counselor's testimony or case notes are subpoenaed if the release of confidential information may potentially harm a student or the counseling relationship.

If Ms. Loredo is subpoenaed to appear in court regarding this case, and she determines that releasing William's confidential information will be harmful to him, she can make a request to the court that disclosure of that information not be required.

Multicultural Considerations

Teachers and counselors must approach the classroom understanding that not all students come from the same background as themselves. Students may come from a home lacking a parental figure and seek the attention and affection of teachers of that same sex. Recognizing this fact and striving to maintain a relationship that does not include physical affection or sharing of personal details is paramount in maintaining a professional relationship with all students. Inappropriate relationships can begin as legitimate concern and care on a professional level, but if those boundaries are not maintained, the relationship can develop into deeper feelings that are then acted upon.

Additionally, teachers must be aware that students from different cultures may show respect and present themselves to an authority figure differently than that of the teacher's culture. Despite this, teachers must expect the same professional integrity from themselves with all students and maintain that professionalism at all times. All contact must be documented and should only involve school-related information.

Discussion Questions

1. In this case study, the school counselor advocated for professional development for teachers each school year on the importance of maintaining an ethical teacher/student relationship. What role do you feel a school counselor could play in this professional development?
2. What student groups might be more vulnerable to developing an inappropriate relationship with a teacher? How could a school counselor work with those students to help alleviate that threat?
3. In what ways could a school counselor educate the student body about appropriate adult/ student contact and how to report what is inappropriate?
4. What role might a school counselor play in a suspected inappropriate student/teacher relationship?
5. How might a school counselor provide care for a victim of an inappropriate relationship with a teacher?

References

American School Counselor Association. (2016). *Ethical standards for school counselors*. Alexandria, VA: Author.

Bowlby, J. (1965). *Childcare and the growth of love* (2nd ed.). Harmondsworth, England: Pelican Books.

Chang, J., & Chang, J. (2018, September 25). *Statesman exclusive: Improper teacher-student relationship cases soar*. Retrieved May 30, 2019, from www.statesman.com/news/20170915/statesman-exclusive-improper-teacher-student-relationship-cases-soar

Professional Boundaries with Students. (2019). Retrieved May 12, 2019, from https://tcta.org/node/12941

Reibstein, J. (2013). Commentary: A different lens for working with affairs: Using social constructionist and attachment theory. *Journal of Family Therapy*, *35*(4), 368–380.

Reflections: Use this space to write your notes and reflections on this case study.

21 A Confidante to a Pregnant Middle School Student

Lisa A. Wines, Deborah Webb Johnson, and Jasmine S. Akrie

Background

In the field of education today, teachers often have to do more than just teach the district-provided curriculum. In some cases, students are facing so many challenges in their homes and social lives that they are not able to be present in the classroom. These students require more than just a teacher who stands at the front of the classroom to deliver a lesson. Whether it is a hug, a listening ear, or just someone to talk to, these moments lead a teacher to wear the hat of a confidante. Other terminology similar to a confidante is that of a mentor. The effectiveness of mitigating behavioral and emotional problems depend largely on the relationship between a teacher and student (Kern, Harrison, Custer, & Mehta, 2019).

Some studies have shown the importance of building a relationship with students and how that leads to academic success. In a study by Dr. Canute S. Thompson (2018), the researcher found that students place significant importance and value on being and feeling respected by their teachers. Researchers have also demonstrated that when students feel cared about and a sense of connection to the adults within their school, they perform better academically (Anderman, 2002). This response to care and a sense of connection is human nature. When a person feels as though someone cares about him or her as important and valued, that person tends to strive to please and make that other person happy with his or her actions.

In another study related to this topic, Russell (2018) shared the personal experience of a teacher who expressed the fact that students must have a voice in order to be successful academically and personally. This statement demonstrates that teachers have to cultivate a culture in their classrooms that is safe and inclusive and that also allows students the opportunity to share and feel heard in order to excel academically. This article purports that the development of a supportive and nurturing teacher–student relationship is essential to the success of the student, both academically and beyond.

While supporting students in the classroom is vital to the success of the student, the risk of lines blurring is possible. As the relationship of respect and trust grows between teacher and student, it is not uncommon for the student to begin to confide in the adult. There is no way for the teacher to predict the nature of the issues shared by students. Part of the criteria for being a great teacher simply requires supporting the student as a whole person. This type of relationship can open the door to critical situations not easily handled by school counselors and administrators. The following case study details how a trusting relationship between a student and teacher developed into something beyond just academics.

Description of Case

At the time of this incident, Valerie, a 14-year-old Caucasian female, was an eighth-grade student in a middle school in a small, rural school district in the southeastern region of the United States.

Valerie was an A-B honor roll student who participated in many extracurricular activities such as band, student council, and cheerleading. Her school counselor encouraged her to participate fully in school clubs and programs. The counselor viewed Valerie as a student who was bright, socially well liked, admired by her teachers, and bound for college. Valerie relied on her school counselor to help her choose the courses on her initial high school four-year plan that would prepare her for college.

Valerie was an avid member of the robotics club. Mr. Townsend, the robotics instructor, valued Valerie's passion for the organization and her leadership skills. Valerie was among 12 students (three females and nine males) who participated in the after-school robotics activities to prepare for the state robotics competition. Frequently, Mr. Townsend depended upon Valerie to supervise the group activities; therefore, it was not unusual for the two of them to meet about the club's activities on Saturdays and even after school. Mr. Townsend would often call Valerie out of class during his conference period to assist him in preparing for the upcoming leadership competition. Mr. Townsend interrupting their classes irritated some teachers, but most did not complain because Valerie would always get her work in on time and was an exceptional student.

One day during class, Mr. Townsend noticed that Valerie was not her normal vivacious self. She appeared to be withdrawn and was not even prepared for the class presentation that they had discussed over the last week. After class, Mr. Townsend questioned Valerie about her disposition, but she quickly brushed off his concerns, stating only that she had not gotten enough rest the night before and thought she was coming down with the flu. Mr. Townsend was not satisfied with Valerie's answer; therefore, he approached Valerie during the lunch period and asked her to visit with him in the classroom. Valerie hesitantly followed Mr. Townsend to his classroom.

During the course of the conversation, Mr. Townsend discovered that Valerie was four weeks pregnant. She begged Mr. Townsend not to say anything to anyone, especially to the nurse or the school counselor. Valerie cried and told Mr. Townsend that if her parents knew, they would make her put the baby up for adoption or make her have an abortion. Valerie told Mr. Townsend that the father of the baby was a high school athlete in the district who was 17 years old and did not want him to have any problems with the law. Mr. Townsend thought about his own baby that had been born only four months before and was emotionally upset about the thought of Valerie not being able to birth and raise her own child. Out of initial empathy, Mr. Townsend gave Valerie his personal cell phone number and told Valerie that she could call him at any time—day or night. He complied with Valerie's request and did not disclose what Valerie had told him to anyone at the school, especially not her parents.

Three days later, at 2:00 a.m., Mr. Townsend answered Valerie's phone call to his personal cell phone. Valerie was emotionally distraught and wanted to come up with a plan of how to live on her own and raise the baby. Mr. Townsend talked with his wife about the situation, and they decided that they would help Valerie without her parents' knowledge. It was evident that responding empathically was their goal, but unfortunately, empathy quickly turned into a lack of boundaries and professionalism.

It was not unusual for Mr. Townsend to call or text Valerie at home to check on her in the early morning hours so that he could make sure she was OK. Throughout the next two weeks, Valerie and Mr. Townsend communicated via text during school and after hours. Valerie became very close to Mr. Townsend to the degree that other students began to notice how they were always together. Mr. Townsend provided Valerie with transportation to and from the local crisis pregnancy center in the area on Saturday when they were supposedly meeting at the school to work on the state project. Mr. Townsend told Valerie about the center and the confidential counseling they provided. Because Valerie was rather mature for her age, Mr. Townsend told her to tell the counselor at the center that she was 18 years old to avoid any problems.

Mrs. Sharp, the science teacher, had also noticed how often Valerie was in Mr. Townsend's classroom alone. She had even witnessed Mr. Townsend hugging Valerie. Mrs. Sharp talked with

Mr. Townsend's mentor teacher about his camaraderie with many of his students, especially since he was only in his second year as a classroom teacher. While Mrs. Sharp appreciated Mr. Townsend's creative teaching style, she was concerned that he was establishing himself more as a friend to his students than an instructor. A few times Valerie would be late to class, and some of the students on the robotics team mumbled about how she was always getting to work on a special project for Mr. Townsend.

Mrs. Sharp questioned one of Valerie's closest friends about the situation after class and discovered that Valerie was pregnant. Mrs. Sharp quickly contacted the school counselor, who then contacted the school nurse. Both the nurse and the school counselor met with Valerie and confronted her about her pregnancy. Valerie had still been attending the cheer class, and Mrs. Sharp was concerned for Valerie's safety. After much discussion, Valerie admitted that she was two months pregnant and that her parents were not aware of the situation. Valerie even disclosed how Mr. Townsend had been helping her by allowing her to go to the local pregnancy crisis center.

The nurse called Valerie's parents and asked them to come to the school, and they listened as Valerie disclosed that she was pregnant and that she had been leaving campus to go to the crisis center. She also admitted how frequently Mr. Townsend and she were communicating. Valerie's parents contacted their cell service provider and had their daughter's cell phone communication of calls and text messages printed. They presented this record to the school administrator. After looking over the cell phone communication and text records and listening to Valerie's story, Mr. Townsend was placed on administrative leave for the duration of the investigation.

Strategies for Consideration

Students often depend upon the school counselor to assist them in developing a new way of thinking, processing information, and dealing with the changes within their environment (Wright, 2012). The following sections present counseling theories that are appropriate to develop interventions and counseling approaches in response to the need for abbreviated student-focused interventions. Additionally, the professional experiences of counselors and the impact of counseling issues such as the one described here are discussed. Ethical and multicultural implications also are addressed.

Theoretical Frameworks

Cognitive behavior therapy and reality theory are effective theoretical frameworks for school counselors to implement in the school setting because they provide strategies for students to implement that address personal situations. By utilizing these two theories, school counselors are able to work collaboratively with the student to establish the goal(s) within the counseling sessions. By establishing a trusting and caring counseling environment, the school counselor is able to teach the student how to challenge irrational beliefs they may have developed in response to incidents occurring within their environment (Wright, 2012). School counselors tend to focus more upon situations the student is facing in the here and now; therefore, they rely upon Glasser's reality theory, which purports that "the only behavior each of us can control is our own" (Wright, 2012, p. 205). School counselors strive to teach students that they are the change agents for the unpleasant situations they encounter and to accept the consequences for their own actions.

In the case scenario mentioned earlier, the classroom teacher was not equipped to address the social and emotional problems that were affecting the middle school student. If the teacher had contacted the school counselor, the consultation model would have been effective in addressing the student's pregnancy. The school counselor would have been able to meet with the student and serve as an advocate for the student to tell her parents about the pregnancy. School counselors can also utilize the consultation method to provide strategies and interventions that will directly affect teacher–student relationships. Teachers and school counselors can collaborate to address classroom problems and to assist in connecting family members with outside counseling support to address the family system.

Professional Experiences

The authors of this chapter have each witnessed the negative effects and consequences of school personnel becoming too emotionally involved with students. It is quite easy for school counselors to find themselves in compromised professional positions due to becoming an inappropriate confidante to students. In a roundtable discussion with counselors and teachers, they shared several scenarios with the authors of this chapter.

One teacher within the school forum questioned the role the school counselor assumed in working with a student who was dealing with the financial consequences of a family member's unexpected death. The school counselor utilized a great deal of school time to assist the student in obtaining personal information through local agencies to assist him in becoming more independent. This teacher's example depicted the caring nature of the counselor; however, many colleagues felt that the counselor went beyond the role of a school employee. The members of the forum further discussed the amount of time some counselors have invested to address the personal needs of only a select number of students and how that is not appropriate for a comprehensive school counseling program (CSCP), which is for all students. When a counselor spends a great deal of time securing outside assistance for a student beyond the realm of his or her responsibilities, other students within the school are deprived of counseling services related to academic and emotional needs, and the CSCP itself is compromised.

The discussion among the teachers and counselors within the forum about various scenarios led to the conclusion that often a counselor's or teacher's sympathy for the student can lead to crossing a professional boundary and promoting emotional involvement with a student. Some teachers stated that, often, knowing too much about a student's personal life caused them to lose objectivity when it came to grades and due dates. Becoming overly involved with a student emotionally can also lead to *burnout* and even personal problems because they often felt obligated to take their work home with them. Teachers stated that they knew of at least one coworker who spent her own personal money to assist needy students in the classroom.

One teacher described how another teacher with whom she worked spent an exorbitant amount of her own personal money for clothes, shoes, school supplies, and even school lunches for low-income students. Rather than contacting the school counselor to assist the parent in obtaining assistance from community programs, the teacher, who was raised in a dysfunctional home himself as a young child, took on the financial responsibility for many students within the school. Some of his fellow teachers lauded his efforts publicly; however, others realized the emotional and financial consequences of assuming responsibility for the personal needs of so many individuals.

Based upon many of the numerous shared experiences and recollections, members of the forum discussed the rationale that causes teachers, counselors, and support staff to become overly involved with students. One factor that contributes to excessive involvement is the amount of time staff members spend with students. Many extracurricular activities and after-school programs cause students to spend a lot of time after school and even hours during the weekend with students. Some teachers serve multiple roles to students; that is, they are not only a classroom instructor, but a coach, student council sponsor, drill team sponsor, and so forth. The small membership of many of the clubs, organizations, or activities often create a more intimate setting where students and even staff members begin to share more personal information than would be shared in the classroom atmosphere.

Teachers and counselors agreed that often staff members have their own personal baggage that contributes to the propensity of biases toward helping students that have a similar background.

Spending extra time with students and getting to know them on a more intimate, personal level creates a role confusion between the student and the teacher or other staff member. Some teachers stated that they have even heard students refer to staff members by their first name because the student no longer viewed the teacher as their instructor, but as a close friend.

Another significant factor that leads to teachers crossing the professional line and engaging in a more personal relationship with a student is the presence of advanced technology. School staff members and students often open up lines of private communication through Facebook accounts, Twitter, Snapchat, and other social media. One teacher shared how she had received many requests on her Facebook account to *friend* several of her students, and parents even made these requests. Some teachers stated that they no longer utilize Facebook, or they make most information *private* on their Facebook account because they want to keep their personal lives private from their students and parents. Another member of the group shared that the school counselor had posted a public Facebook request for diapers to be brought to the school for teen-age mothers, which she felt was inappropriate.

Sometimes young, first-year teachers want to befriend their students because they believe this will create the rapport required within the classroom. One member of the forum shared that there is one teacher's classroom in her school where all the students hang out in the morning. The teacher even brings snacks for them in between classes. Students have been known to convince their other teachers to allow them to go to this particular classroom teacher's room to work on a project when they are mainly going there to just *hang out*. Members of the forum agreed that there should be professional development within the schools to address blurred boundary lines and to establish professional boundaries to prevent emotional involvement. It is critical for staff members to be informed of the dangers of becoming overly involved with students.

Counselor Impact

School counselors should assume the role of a supporting adult, that is, providing the student with coping strategies, time management assistance, conflict resolution, anger management strategies, positive behavior strategies, and other information related to school success. School counselors are often not equipped to address the mental health problems of students who seek assistance from them. Many times, the student's problem is related to the family system and is beyond the scope of practice in the school setting.

The school counselor may experience countertransference because of becoming emotionally involved with a student's personal problems. This can cause a change in roles to that of a caring parent rather than an empathetic counselor. The student's situation might even trigger unresolved feelings from the counselor's past that cause a loss of objectivity and a blurring of professional boundaries. Counselors might have family members who have struggled with addictions, mental health issues, poverty, sexual identity, or self-esteem problems that contribute to their propensity for crossing a professional boundary with a student. By crossing the professional boundary line and becoming overly involved with a student, the counselor loses professional insight and becomes biased. The counselor's insight is blurred by their own emotions and countertransference.

School counselors may possess a psychological construct that causes them to feel the need to save other people. Counselors who have a *savior complex* begin to take extreme measures to assist or save others to the degree that they actually enable students. While others may view these counselors as being altruistic and unselfish, they are actually internally motivated to help others fulfill their own personal need for self-satisfaction rather than enabling students to take responsibility for their own actions and empower them to solve their own problems. School counselors operating under a *savior complex* are often unable to separate their personal lives from their professional lives. They sacrifice their time with their own family members and friends to assist students because they feel this is a noble cause. Not only do these counselors endanger their personal relationships to *save* their students, they also ignore their own needs for self-care.

Mental Health Implications

School counselors can find becoming involved in the personal problems of students to be extremely exhausting. Many counselors have stated that after talking with a student with suicidal ideations, family problems, pregnancy, and other intense situations, they are physically drained. It is imperative for the school counselor to find the means to help students work through their problems without becoming lost in others' personal issues. School counselors who are unable to limit the emotional involvement with students may even become discouraged by their inability to fix the students' problems. School counselors may begin to view their efforts within the school setting as unproductive and ineffective; therefore, this may cause them to leave the profession. As in any profession, it is vital for the school counselor to maintain personal recreation and hobbies to provide outlets from the stresses of work.

Some school counselors enter the profession believing that they are going to be able to have individual and group counseling sessions much like a community counselor. However, there are a number of non-counseling duties such as state testing, cafeteria duty, bus duty, response-to-intervention (RTI) meetings, and 504 meetings that consume a lot of a school counselor's time. Many problems students face are related to family problems that the school counselor is not equipped to address because of the parameters of the school counseling position. Some counselors may even enter the helping profession as a means of fulfilling a void that exists within their own personal lives. These counselors may assume that the satisfaction of helping others will help them resolve feelings of loneliness, dissatisfaction, and even rejection. The economic background, dysfunctional home life, or lack of self-satisfaction may contribute to the emotional involvement that a school counselor may develop.

Ethical Considerations

> The professional educator has a primary obligation to treat students with dignity and respect. The professional educator promotes the health, safety and well-being of students by establishing and maintaining appropriate verbal, physical, emotional and social boundaries.
>
> (National Association of State Directors of Teacher Education and Certification [NASDTEC], 2015)

School counselors should serve as a consultant to teachers. When teachers are uncertain on how to deal with a situation with a student or a parent, the school counselor can provide resources as well as support for students struggling with social-emotional issues (Warren & Baker, 2013). School counselors are equipped to provide teachers on how to respond appropriately with students and specific classroom situations (Warren & Baker, 2013).

> A.2.d. Inability to give consent when counseling minors, incapacitated adults, or other persons unable to give voluntary consent, counselors seek the assent of clients to services and include them in decision making as appropriate. Counselors recognize the need to balance the ethical rights of clients to make choices, their capacity to give consent or assent to receive services, and parental or familial legal rights and responsibilities to protect these clients and make decisions on their behalf.
>
> (ACA, 2014)

A.1.d. Acknowledge the vital role of parents/guardians and families.

The school counselor is ethically required to contact Valerie's parents even though the student has requested that her family not be told about her pregnancy. Since Valerie is a minor, the counselor is responsible for protecting her from harm. As a 14-year-old, Valerie is not capable of acquiring the prenatal assistance that is required, and she is possibly not mentally or emotionally prepared for dealing with a full-term pregnancy. Had the teacher, Mr. Townsend, contacted the school counselor regarding Valerie's pregnancy, the school counselor would have provided adequate consultation and served as a supportive advocate for Valerie as she told her parents about her pregnancy. While teachers and counselors show that they care for students, they must be careful to avoid crossing professional boundaries. In the case study, it was the ethical and correct decision for Mrs. Sharp to report her concern that Mr. Townsend had crossed a professional boundary with one of his students.

Multicultural Considerations

> Seeking to understand students' educational, academic, personal and social needs as well as students' values, beliefs, and cultural background.
>
> (NASDTEC, 2015)

> A.2.c. Developmental and Cultural Sensitivity Counselors communicate information in ways that are both developmentally and culturally appropriate.
>
> (ACA, 2014)

> A.15.d. Are culturally competent and sensitive to diversity among families. Recognize that all parents/guardians, custodial and noncustodial, are vested with certain rights and responsibilities for their children's welfare by virtue of their role and according to law.
>
> (ASCA, 2016)

The case study indicates that Valerie is Caucasian; however, the reader does not know her socioeconomic status, family values, or religious beliefs. The school counselor and the classroom teacher should not allow their own personal beliefs or values to cloud their decision to communicate with the parents about their daughter's pregnancy. It is imperative that the school district provide guidance for teachers to identify when their own personal views may be affecting their students. By law, parents have the right to determine the outcome of the pregnancy and to determine the health services and counseling services for their child. The well-being of the child must be the focal point in every decision of a school counselor and teacher.

Case Discussion Questions

1. How has the advancement in communication technology created potential pitfalls in school staff maintaining appropriate professional boundaries between themselves and their students?
2. What proactive measures could be provided to teachers like Mr. Townsend so that they would be prepared to handle a situation similar to Valerie's?
3. What are the advantages and disadvantages of being an empathetic teacher?
4. Discuss a situation where the boundary lines could have or did become blurred between yourself or a colleague with a student. What was the outcome of the situation, and what did you learn from the experience?

5. Discuss how self-care techniques are crucial in maintaining a positive and effective professional career in teaching and counseling.
6. Describe the role school counselors play in assisting classroom teachers in maintaining professional boundaries with their students.

Resources

How Teachers Maintain Healthy Relationships with Students: https://www.aassa.com/uploaded/Educational_Research/Child_Protection/UE_Guideposts_for_TeacherstoMaintain_Healthy_Relationships_With_Students.pdf
Reproductive Health: Teen Pregnancy: https://www.cdc.gov/teenpregnancy/about/index.htm

References

American School Counselor Association. (2016). *Ethical standards for school counselors.* Alexandria, VA: Author.
American Counseling Association (ACA). (2014). *ACA code of ethics.* Alexandria, VA: Author.
Anderman, E. (2002). School effects on psychological outcomes in adolescence. *Journal of Educational Psychology, 94,* 795–809. doi 10.1037/0022-0663.94.4.795
Kern, L., Harrison, J. R., Custer, B. E., & Mehta, P. D. (2019). Factors that enhance the quality of relationships between mentors and mentees during check & connect. *Behavioral Disorders, 44*(3), 148–161. https://doi-org.ezproxy.lib.uh.edu/10.1177/0198742918779791
National Association of State Directors of Teacher Education and Certification [NASDTEC]. (2015). *Model code of ethics for educators (MCEE).* (n.d.).
Russell, M. (2018). Teachers empowering students by building relationships and fostering agency. *California English, 23*(4), 6–9.
Thompson, C. S. (2018). The construct of "respect" in teacher-student relationships: Exploring dimensions of ethics of care and sustainable development. *Journal of Leadership Education, 17*(3), 42–60. https://doi-org.ezproxy.lib.uh.edu/10.12806/V17/I3/R3
Warren, J. M., & Baker, S. B. (2013). School counselor consultation: Enhancing teacher performance through rational emotive-social behavior consultation. *Ideas and Research You Can Use: VISTAS, 69.*
Wright, R. J. (2012). *Introduction to school counseling.* Thousand Oaks, CA: Sage Productions, Inc.

Reflections: Use this space to write your notes and reflections on this case study.

22 Intimacy Between an Adult and a Minor Student

Lisa A. Wines, Amanda Rohrbach, and Kayla P. Gaddy

Background

The national Centers for Disease Control and Prevention (CDC) [2017] found that 40% of high school students engaged in sexual intercourse, and 10% had more than four partners. Additionally, they found that 7% were forced to have sexual intercourse when they did not want to (CDC, 2017). A study completed by Townsend and Rheingold (2013) found that about 1 out of 10 children will be sexually abused before their 18th birthday. This type of sexual abuse can vary from unwanted sexual advances to unwanted sexual intercourse.

To understand the prevalence of sexual abuse and sexual assault, specific information regarding statutory rape statistics were reviewed. However, as the *age of consent* varies from state to state, global statistics regarding what constitutes *statutory* is difficult to ascertain. In Texas, for example, the age of consent is 17 years old. However, in Georgia, the age of consent is 16 years old. A study for the Department of Justice, completed by Hines and Finkelhor (2006), specifically addressed adolescent male and adult female sexual relationships. They noted that "relationships between adolescent males and adult females are the statutory relationships most likely to be viewed by youth and society as sexual initiation rather than sexual exploitation" (Hines & Finkelhor, 2006, p. 305).

Additional analysis found that only around 5% of men reported that they had a consensual sexual relationship as an adolescent male with an older female. This dynamic occurs in about 25% of all heterosexual statutory rape cases, and over 65% of males indicated that the relationship was consensual. Hines and Finkelhor (2006) were also able to ascertain how adolescent males emotionally view their relationships, indicating that a majority viewed them as positive, a third were neutral, and a small minority (>5%) viewed them as negative. Further attention is needed to understand societal attitudes that endorse a sexual relationship between an adolescent male and an adult female who also happens to be a student. This support can hinder the reporting of not only the abuse but the symptomatology that can come from that abuse or relationship. Stemple and Meyer (2014) found that the majority of the remaining sexual assault paradigm are men being perpetrators and women being victims and that the male victim may not feel masculine in deciding to make a report.

As stated earlier, not all relationships are nonconsensual. In fact, school is a place where young boys and girls meet, beginning various types of relationships. Platonic relationships are among the options, but so are sexual relationships. According to Carver, Joyner, and Udry (2003), romantic relationships among youth are critical to their development. It is believed that these types of relationships assist with autonomy, secure attachment, understanding their dating and sexual behavior, and mate selection. More importantly, pair bonding and reproduction are inevitably the crux of these formations. When these bonds form, there is jurisdiction that makes the adult student, in the age for and still registered for school, run the risk of breaking the law and obtaining a record for doing so.

Description of Case

The school counselor became aware that Jessica, a Caucasian female who is 18 years of age, was in need of her assistance. The senior was raised in a middle-class family in a suburban school district. Jessica began visiting with the school counselor intermittently, due to her teacher's concerns of self-harm, which was later confirmed by the counselor, who stated that the minor cuts did not require medical intervention. Leading right up to winter break, Jessica had previously visited with the school counselor four times. During her visits, Jessica indicated that she felt like a failure and wanted to be accepted by her peers. As a result, the counselor worked with Jessica to develop and practice coping strategies.

Also during their time together, Jessica had a secret she was hesitant to disclose to the school counselor. She had been molested as a child and believed this was affecting her all the time. She feels vulnerable all too often and constantly wants to be in a relationship with a male student. Like many of her friends, Jessica was not currently seeing any outside professionals for medical attention or therapy. She was able to attend all of her classes and was scheduled to advance to the next grade level. Ralph, her father, had been inconsistent in her life and had difficulty with substance use. Further, her mom was not around due to working nights and sleeping during the day.

Several weeks after returning from winter break, Jessica visited the school counselor. She reported having difficulty sleeping after attending a party several weeks ago, in which she engaged in sexual relations with Javier, a 15-year-old Hispanic male who attends the same school. She reported that she thinks he has been her only sexual partner and that she is worried, as he is a relatively popular student with great potential for an athletic scholarship. Similar to her father, she often abused alcohol but was really attracted to Javier. Since then, they engaged in sex frequently, but Jessica began to question the frequency and normalcy of such habits. Jessica added that the difficulty sleeping was due to nightmares regarding her own previous sexual abuse by a family friend who was caring for her while her parents were away. She reported that she was only 10 years old at the time but is starting to have vivid memories that leave her anxious and unable to sleep.

Javier's family, in light of his being a male and the inherent rights that come with such, believed in him having a sexual relationship with Jessica, regardless of her being a legal adult. His parents viewed Javier as a young man who was lucky to date and engage in an early sexual relationship. His family were even talking about Jessica becoming a mom to their future five grandchildren. Although illegal, it was very unlikely that his parents would have made a report against Jessica because their expectation was culturally based and celebrated within Javier's family.

Strategies for Consideration

The strategies for consideration help school counselors to change maladaptive patterns of thought and self-harming behaviors and to address the traumatic experience of sexual abuse. This section outlines the theoretical frameworks used to help treat and stabilize students struggling with statutory rape and childhood sexual abuse. The professional experiences of the school counselor related to the case are included, along with the counselor's impact and mental health implications.

Theoretical Frameworks

The efficacy of cognitive behavior therapy (CBT) for both parties of the sexual relationship is based firmly in research findings (Pifalo, 2007). The specific changes or outcomes of treatment can be a different way of acting, thinking, and feeling. Techniques can include journaling, relaxation, and unraveling cognitive distortions. In clinical settings, this therapeutic technique typically lasts about ten sessions, being clustered in the beginning of treatment. In schools, session numbers can be reduced for the sake of time. This focus on the present as opposed to the past can increase the integration of skills into current thinking, allowing the student to experience change in processing their situation.

Trauma-focused cognitive behavior therapy (TF-CBT) is applicable for both the adult perpetrator and minor victim (Pifalo, 2007). This therapeutic intervention is focused on the impact of trauma and is targeted for individuals who have experienced a traumatic event between the ages of 3 and 21 years old. This intervention usually lasts for about 12 to 25 sessions and incorporates an individual and family therapeutic approach. As a result of the length of time, it may be beneficial to locate a referral to an outside therapist that focuses his or her treatment on TF-CBT. The goals of the intervention are to decrease emotional and behavioral reactions to the trauma, challenge cognitive distortions related to the trauma, increase family protective factors, and process the trauma through narrative and in-vivo techniques.

TF-CBT is applicable to Jessica because she has been through sexual assault in her past and has also been a perpetrator in sexual assault. After experiencing childhood trauma, Jessica is more likely to exhibit self-destructive behavior, feelings of depression, and interpersonal relationship problems and to engage in risky or inappropriate sexual behavior. This intervention could help her process through her trauma and address the negative distortions that are present. After focusing on the core childhood sexual abuse, Jessica would then need to address her role in the sexual abuse of Javier and what distortions led her to want to have a sexual relationship with him.

Javier, as the minor victim, would also benefit from TF-CBT. A counselor would be able to form a supportive therapeutic relationship that allows Javier to feel comfortable discussing and processing through his trauma. Masculinity and the societal implication that men are not sexually assaulted are cognitive distortions that Javier might have surrounding the inappropriate sexual relationship. These cognitive distortions would then be addressed and unraveled. Through family sessions, the counselor would also be able to offer psychoeducation to Javier and his family on statutory rape, trauma, and their long-term effects. School counselors would have to locate the perfect niche to work in because of Javier's cultural considerations and his family's support in having a relationship with Jessica.

Professional Experiences

The author's experiences in working with male students who have been a victim of statutory rape by an adult female student is vast. For many, gender roles are reversed, and the older student is typically male, with the younger student being female. Unfortunately, this situation becomes exposed when either student is hurt and/or is in trouble. One reflection is when the sexual experience of a 15-year-old female with an 18-year-old male and a 17-year-old male was documented (i.e. in either text or photographs) and posted without her knowledge and/or consent to social media. The older male student inadvertently disclosed this statutory situation, which was ultimately resolved via police intervention. An additional investigation was conducted regarding distribution of child pornography and to the limitations of Romeo/Juliet laws when another participant existed. The experience, however, for the female is the aftermath of the video's distribution. She displayed signs of depression, as she withdrew from her peers, as well as having difficulty in her academic classes. She experienced several instances of suicidal ideation, having no clear plan. She spent significant time in the counselor's office, and through counseling interventions and the teachers' commitment to her emotional lability, the student was able to remain in school and ultimately began to thrive.

The second experience involves a younger female student and an older male student with special needs (15-year-old female, 20-year-old male). The extent of the older male's special needs prevented him from appropriately understanding the social cues and inappropriateness of his actions. Once the students broke up after a short engagement, the male student began *stalking* the female student. The female student sought assistance from the counseling office due to her inability to feel safe at school. The older male student would find her in class throughout the day, would attempt to talk with her in the hallways, and texted and requested social media attention multiple times throughout the day and night. The student's schedule was changed, and the counselor had a discussion about the use of firm language to discourage his advances and assisted her with a *cease and desist* agreement through administration. Furthermore, the female student was provided a crisis safety plan as to what steps she should take in the event that she felt unsafe in school. This included seeking assistance from the counseling office, administration office, school resource officer, and several teachers located strategically throughout the building.

Counselor Impact

At first glance, the case study described in this chapter would seemingly only apply to counselors at the secondary level in which adult students and minor students are educated in the same building. However, as of 2013, 1 out of 10 children are sexually abused in some capacity prior to the age of 18. However, given the recent reports that child sexual abuse has increased, the number is likely to be higher. Even if the perpetrator of the sexual abuse is not in the same building as the victim, the counselor is likely to interact with a student that is a victim of sexual abuse.

This case highlights the interaction between education and community stakeholders, including the parents of both students, the police, child protective services, and private counseling service providers. The counselor's ability to maintain these connections, as well as ensuring the campus administration is aware of the issues surrounding not only the mental health of the students but their safety as well, are equally vital. Further, a multidisciplinary approach that includes the counselor from the alternative campus (if necessary for the perpetrator) and other on-site mental health professionals can assist with safety planning, academic expectations, interventions, and the possibility for additional related services that can be provided by the school.

Counselors that serve campuses where adult students are in the same building as minor students should also consider preemptive education. This step can ensure the older students (17–21) understand their state's expectations regarding the age of consent, the parameters of statutory rape, and the potential consequences of such relations. This preventative measure can assist students with making positive decisions regarding their romantic relationships.

Mental Health Implications

In this case, the school counselor had previous knowledge of self-harm behavior with Jessica and participated in several sessions, developing a relationship. Furthermore, Jessica was able to learn and practice coping strategies. Assuming Jessica remains in school, as opposed to going to juvenile detention, she is likely to transition to a new school, such as disciplinary alternative education placement (DAEP) to separate her from the victim, Javier. The school counselor could facilitate the transitioning of relationship dynamics to the new school counselor. As this school counselor develops a relationship with Jessica, she can continue to assist her with further use of her coping strategies (including journaling cognitive restructuring, how to worry constructively, and acceptance practices) and reflection on decision making and consequential outcomes. The school counselor should also consider a safety plan in the event that Jessica indicates a desire to self-harm during the school day.

The counselor should speak with Javier to ascertain his mental and emotional response to his sexual engagement with Jessica. The counselor should offer differing perspectives regarding how some might feel victimized. Should Javier not feel victimized, the counselor should ensure that Javier understands that these feelings can change over time and to seek support if necessary. The counselor may also check back in with Javier prior to the end of the school year to ascertain his emotional well-being.

If Javier does feel victimized, the counselor can make every effort to normalize his feelings related to sexual abuse. The counselor needs to work closely with Javier's family to assist with finding local resources to assist with further intervention. Further, the counselor could check in with Javier regularly to assess his well-being and academic success.

Ethical Considerations

The following ASCA (2016) standards apply to the case study in this chapter.

> A1.i. Consider the involvement of support networks, wraparound services, and educational teams needed to best serve students

For both students presented, the provision of additional resources would be beneficial for both families. For Jessica, who may or may not have legal issues with which to contend, it might be advantageous to have the provision of long-term counseling for being both the victim and perpetrator of sexual abuse. Additionally, Javier may or may not see himself as a victim. However, his family may have need for seeking services outside of the educational system to assist with the preservation of Javier's self-esteem.

> A2d. Explain the limits of confidentiality in developmentally appropriate terms through multiple methods such as student handbooks, school counselor department websites, school counseling brochures, classroom curriculum and/or verbal notification to individual students.

The counselor, who already has a relationship with Jessica, would need to carefully explain the limitations of confidentiality upon learning of the inappropriate sexual relationship with a minor. This does not mean the dissolution of the relationship. However, the potential ramifications can be a topic of discussion when meeting with Jessica.

> A9d. Report to parents/guardians and/or appropriate authorities when students disclose a perpetrated or a perceived threat to their physical or mental well-being. This threat may include, but is not limited to, physical abuse, sexual abuse, neglect, dating violence, bullying or sexual harassment. The school counselor follows applicable federal, state and local laws and school district policy.

In this particular case, the school counselor had a duty to report to both the police and child protective services upon learning the nature of the inappropriate sexual relationship between Jessica and Javier. It is equally important that the school counselor report and notify parents of both students. Counseling the families through the complexities and aspects of statutory rape, perpetrator, or victimization aspects is a priority.

Multicultural Considerations

Jessica already had a relationship with the counselor. But what if that was not the case, and Jessica was brought to the school counselor's attention through notification from the police to the school? Jessica's previous history of accepting assistance for relational difficulties with peers and self-harm might have been exacerbated if she had not received prior assistance. Additionally, what about the students who do not have the means to access additional outside services?

Students may need ongoing intensive therapy that is outside the scope of practice for the school counselor. These topics can include some of the issues that Jessica presented, such as an addiction within the family, prior history of sexual abuse, self-harm, substance abuse, and peer relational problems. Given this possibility, strictly discussing the aspect of any ramifications of the sexual relationship between the two students may open a completely new variety of concerns that affect the social and emotional health of the students. Counselors who are familiar with the symptomology of sexual abuse victims and of children of addicts could be better equipped to identify the students that may need interventions and or long-term/intensive counseling interventions (Hall & Hall, 2011). Furthermore, developing relationships with outside agencies or service providers that offer reduced or sliding scale fees may increase the student's ability to receive assistance.

Working with Javier's parents to better understand the potential legal issues with having a relationship with Jessica is recommended. From a cultural perspective, his parents are not opposed to such relationships. In counseling Javier, perhaps exploring the effect of this relationship, the impact on his academic performance, or the idea of exploring his postsecondary goals or career options is necessary for proper development.

Providing information to other educators within the school may increase awareness as to the ways in which a student with a previous history of sexual abuse may have developed unhealthy coping mechanisms. The use or abuse of substances in conjunction with self-harm, peer-relational problems, and engaging in risky sexual activities are just some of the ways in which a student may be attempting to cope. Educating fellow staff within the school can assist the counselor with identifying the students that may need some additional support in a proactive way.

Case Discussion Questions

1. In the case study, the school counselor is required to report the inappropriate relationship to the school and to the authorities. In what way do you think the counselor is obligated to inform the perpetrator and the victim of the requirement to report?
2. In the case study, the adult student is moved to a different school. How should her school counselor facilitate the process of introducing her to the new counselor?
3. In what way could a school counselor psychoeducate students about statutory rape and its consequences?
4. How might a school counselor implement a proactive approach to identifying at-risk students of sexual abuse?
5. How should a school counselor respond to a student's disclosure of sexual abuse?

Resources

Statutory Rape: A Guide to State Laws and Reporting Requirements: https://aspe.hhs.gov/report/statutory-rape-guide-state-laws-and-reporting-requirements-summary-current-state-laws/sexual-intercourse-minors

References

American School Counselor Association. (2016). *Ethical standards for school counselors*. Alexandria, VA: American School Counselor Association.
Carver, K., Joyner, K., & Udry, R. (2003). National estimates of adolescent romantic relationships. In Flosheim, P. (Ed.), *Adolescent romantic relationships and sexual behavior: Theory, research, and practical implications* (pp. 23–56). Mahwah, NJ: Psychology Press.
Centers for Disease Control and Prevention (CDC). (2019, March 11). National Center for HIV/AIDS, Viral Hepatitis, STD, and TB Prevention (NCHHSTP) | CDC. Retrieved from www.cdc.gov/nchhstp/
Hall, M., & Hall, J. (2011). The long-term effects of childhood sexual abuse: Counseling implications. *Pobrane z*. Retrieved from http://counselingoutfitters.com/vistas/vistas11/Article_19.pdf

Hines, D. A., & Finkelhor, D. (2007). Statutory sex crime relationships between juveniles and adults: A review of social scientific research. *Aggression and Violent Behavior*, *12*(3), 300–314. doi:10.1016/j.avb.2006.10.001

Pifalo, T. (2007). Jogging the cogs: Trauma-focused art therapy and cognitive behavioral therapy with sexually abused children. *Journal of Art Therapy Association*, *24*(4), 170–175.

Stemple, L., & Meyer, I. H. (2014). The sexual victimization of men in America: New data challenge old assumptions. *American Journal of Public Health*, *104*(6), e19–e26. doi:10.2105/AJPH.2014.301946

Townsend, C., & Rheingold, A. A. (2013). *Estimating a child sexual abuse prevalence rate for practitioners: A review of child sexual abuse prevalence studies*. Darkness to Light, Charleston, SC. Retrieved from www.D2L.org/1in10

Reflections: In the space provided, write your notes and reflections regarding this case study.

23 Incarcerated Parent

Natalie Fikac

Background

Children are affected by the choices, situations, actions, and inactions of their parents. Most often children are powerless over divorce, adult substance use, parents who refuse to get help, adult financial situations, and the list goes on. However, parental incarceration is probably one of the most complex and devastating situations for children due to the loss, grief, and trauma of experiencing a parent who is absent because of being in jail or prison. Additionally, there is an element of embarrassment, shame, or stigma for the child when a parent is incarcerated. Some unique issues can arise from a family situation such as incarceration, and children with incarcerated parents (mothers in particular) are at increased risk for failing academics and school dropout (Dallaire, Ciccone, & Wilson, 2008).

Parental incarceration is considered one of the adverse childhood experiences (ACEs), or experiences defined as stressful or traumatic such as abuse or neglect in a child's life. Turney (2018) used data from the 2016 National Survey of Children's Health (NSCH) to examine the relationship between parental incarceration and exposure to six additional ACEs: parental divorce or separation, parental death, household member abuse, violence exposure, household member mental illness, and household member substance problems. Results suggested that "children of incarcerated parents are exposed to nearly five times as many other ACEs as their counterparts without incarcerated parents (2.06 compared to 0.41, on average), and these statistically significant differences persist after adjusting for demographic and socioeconomic characteristics" (p. 218).

Additionally, in one qualitative study (Saunders, 2018), 16 children were interviewed, and results demonstrated that the stigma of parental incarceration was expressed in children's lives in diverse ways. Despite these differences, three key strategies for managing the stigma emerged from the data including keeping information private, relying on one's self to manage everyday life rather than counting on others, and handling peer relationships. The following case is an example of the impact of parental incarceration on a middle school student.

Description of the Case

Kimberly is a typical eighth-grade Caucasian female 13-year-old student. She has been in the school band for the past three years and plays the flute. Ms. Connally has been her counselor for over two years, as she has moved grade levels with her students and began working with Kimberly during her sixth-grade year. Kimberly is the oldest child in her family. She has a sixth-grade brother, a fifth-grade sister, and a second-grade brother. Kimberly lives with her grandmother and has little recollection of her father, as he died when she was 5 years old.

Over the past two years that Ms. Connally has worked with Kimberly, she has come to know her grandmother and her mother very well. Life has not been easy for Kimberly or her siblings, as Kimberly's mom is unable to hold a job for an extended period, and finances are always a stressor. Kimberly has taken on the *motherly role* with her three siblings because of her mother's issues. Kimberly stops by Ms. Connally's office at least once a day to check in, and over time, Ms. Connally has encouraged her to participate in clubs on the junior high campus and serve in leadership roles. Kimberly has a close-knit set of friends that has disbanded multiple times over her junior high career and then rejoined as typical drama has settled down.

It is early fall in October, and Kimberly has missed several days of school. Ms. Connally calls home to check on Kimberly, and her grandmother informs her that Kimberly and her siblings have not been in school because their mother was involved in a car accident while she was intoxicated. She goes on to explain that she was drunk and tested positive for methamphetamines. Kimberly's mom is in the county jail at this time. Grandmother is distressed and crying and explains that Kimberly and her siblings are scared and not ready to return to school.

Strategies for Consideration

The following sections will provide tools and strategies for assisting a student like Kimberly who has a parent who breaks the law and subsequently is incarcerated. Suggestions on appropriate theories and counseling techniques are discussed, as well as the professional experiences of the author of the chapter. Additionally, ethical and multicultural considerations will provide insight in how to assist students in similar situations.

Theoretical Frameworks

Kimberly is frightened and traumatized by what is happening to her mother and will need support if she is to be successful in her academic and social life. There are several forms of therapy that are appropriate when working with a student who has experienced grief and trauma. Cognitive behavioral therapy (CBT) (Beck, 2011), trauma and grief component therapy (TGCT) (Saltzman, Layne, Steinberg, & Pynoos, 2003), and practicing mindfulness are all effective forms of therapy for working with students who have experienced trauma and grief. The TGCT model is an evidence-based, manualized treatment used in group or individual counseling and has been used successfully in schools with adolescents who experience trauma and/or grief (www.nctsn. org/sites/default/files/interventions/tgcta_fact_sheet.pdf). School counselors can use the four modules of TGCT in sequence or separately as determined by need. The first module includes foundational information and skills related to the trauma and typical grief reactions; module two provides ways to work through the trauma; module three helps students work through grief; and module four focuses on the future. Counselors also might use these modules in classrooms when an entire school has been disrupted by a traumatic event. Depending on the level of trauma and loss experienced by the student(s), it would be important to refer a student to a licensed professional such as a licensed professional counselor or licensed clinical social worker.

Professional Experiences

The author of the chapter reached out to many colleagues who have worked with students affected by trauma, loss, and grief. One theme that emerged was the need for support for families in which children are living with grandparents and for whom one or more parent is incarcerated. Support for students who have had similar experiences include placing these students in individual counseling, group counseling, assigning mentors, providing opportunities on the campus for leadership roles for the student, involvement in extracurricular activities as appropriate, and connecting the student and their siblings and family with outside agencies and therapeutic supports. It is also imperative that Kimberly's school counselor reach out to the school counselors of Kimberly's siblings to ensure that their needs are being met.

Oftentimes a team approach is appropriate in meeting everyone's needs, even if they are on different campuses. There are situations where the court, child protective services, and the police department crime victims' liaison can assist with connecting the family with supports that are needed. In this situation, there is a definite need for wraparound services. The school community and larger community in which the student lives need to offer their individual specific levels of support. School or community social workers can be instrumental in this process. Oftentimes the school counselor serves as the *wraparound specialist* to ensure that the needs of the student are met while on campus and in the community. The school counselor can coordinate these efforts to ensure that services are effective, consistent, and not duplicated. The school counselor is the one person on the team who will have the most contact with the student and can assess how the interventions are working.

Counselor Impact

School counselors can easily become overwhelmed when confronted with heart-wrenching situations with their students. This is especially true when there is a relationship developed over many years and with students and families. In this particular situation, the student and her siblings are suffering trauma and loss due to decisions made by their mother.

School counselors can experience vicarious trauma and countertransference in situations such as these. It is important for school counselors to practice self-care and to have colleagues and supervisors both to debrief and to process situations such as these. A fellow school counselor, a district level director of guidance and counseling, a lead counselor, or a mentor counselor can offer support in extremely tense situations. Supervision, consultation, and self-care are essential for the success of a school counselor.

Mental Health Implications

In this particular case, there are no known signs of mental health concerns directly stated. There are still some concerns for Kimberly's mental well-being. Kimberly has experienced multiple losses in her life: her father's death, in a sense the loss of her childhood, the loss of a *normal* home life being raised by her grandmother, and the loss of her mother. Compounding these losses, Kimberly is an adolescent female in the midst of puberty, when life can be difficult even for a teenager with a seemingly normal childhood. As part of the grief cycle, Kimberly will likely experience anger and hostility, depression and sadness, and joy. The grief cycle is not predictable, especially when compounded with hormones; thus, she could feel all of these emotions in one day or even within a few hours.

The amount of stress that Kimberly has experienced for her age could easily aid in a diagnosis of post-traumatic stress disorder (PTSD). Kimberly's teachers should be on alert for the signs and symptoms associated with these mental health concerns and ready to provide consultation and referral to the school counselor and possibly outside resources. It will be equally important for Ms. Connally to be well versed in the symptomatology of anxiety, depression, and PTSD to ensure that appropriate supports are in place on the campus and that appropriate referrals are made.

Ethical Considerations

School counselors understand that their actions must be guided by the ethical standards of their profession (ASCA, 2016). The following standards are relevant to this case study.

A. RESPONSIBILITY TO STUDENTS A.1b. Aim to provide counseling to students in a brief context and support students and families/guardians in obtaining outside services if the student needs long-term clinical counseling.

School counselors are not therapists. In this case, Kimberly's needs are beyond the level of care needed by a student and extends beyond the scope of practice for the school counselor. Therefore, Kimberly's needs warrant a referral to an outside clinical counselor. Ms. Connally should make a referral to Kimberly and her family for further therapy. However, the school counselor can continue to offer Kimberly the same services under the umbrella of the comprehensive school counseling program.

f. Respect students' and families' values, beliefs, sexual orientation, gender identification/ expression and cultural background and exercise great care to avoid *imposing personal beliefs or values rooted in one's religion, culture or ethnicity*

The experiences that Kimberly has had during her life are unique to her; it is important that Ms. Connally be mindful that her own personal experiences may be very different from those whom she serves.

h. Provide effective, responsive interventions to address student needs.

Ms. Connally should take the time to research, consult, and learn more about the best way to support Kimberly and should suggest the same for Kimberly's siblings' counselors. Seeking supervision from other school counselors, a mentor, or a former professor is appropriate in this situation. School counselors must develop tools via professional development and training in order to respond appropriately to the needs of the students they serve.

i. Consider the involvement of support networks, wraparound services and educational teams needed to best serve students.

In this situation, it would be helpful to have many supports in place for Kimberly and her siblings. A team of individuals housed at the campus, in the district, and in the community would best be able to wrap around this family and provide services and supports. Ms. Connally should be the coordinator of this effort on Kimberly's behalf. School counselors must think differently about the various stakeholders on their campuses and in the community that can provide supports needed for their students. The school counselor can accomplish this by bringing various stakeholders to the table regularly to brainstorm and action plan around high needs students.

A.2. a. Promote awareness of school counselors' ethical standards and legal mandates regarding confidentiality and the appropriate rationale and procedures for disclosure of student data and information to school staff.

In Kimberly's situation, there are many pieces to this story, and it is important that Ms. Connally know the legal mandate around confidentiality. As school counselors are working with students, staff members, students, families, and community members, policies and procedures should be reviewed regularly via handbooks, department meetings, staff meetings, and any other means of communicating the appropriate steps to take when dealing with a crisis.

e. Keep information confidential unless legal requirements demand that confidential information be revealed or a breach is required to prevent serious and foreseeable harm to the student. Serious and foreseeable harm is different for each minor in schools and is determined by students' developmental and chronological age, the setting, parental rights and the nature of the harm. School counselors consult with appropriate professionals when in doubt as to the validity of an exception.

It is important that Ms. Connally knows the legal mandate around confidentiality. School counselors must be mindful of each individual situation and incident that students bring to them and how this plays out in regard to confidentiality. Additionally, there may be conflicting rules if the school counselor is also a licensed professional counselor.

A.6. Appropriate Referrals and Advocacy School counselors: a. Collaborate with all relevant stakeholders, including students, educators and parents/guardians when student assistance is needed, including the identification of early warning signs of student distress.

Kimberly's needs are unique, and relevant staff at her campus as well as her siblings' campus should be on alert for signs of distress. A *check in-check out* is a great way to ensure this happens. Allowing the student to check in with the school counselor when she enters the building in the morning and to check out before going home provides an observational tool for the counselor to assess how the student is doing. School counselors must be aware of how to identify early warning signs, signs and symptoms of mental health concerns, and steps for both campus and district level student needs.

b. Provide a list of resources for outside agencies and resources in their community to student(s) and parents/guardians when students need or request additional support. School counselors provide multiple referral options or the district's vetted list and are careful not to indicate an endorsement or preference for one counselor or practice. School counselors encourage parents to interview outside professionals to make a personal decision regarding the best source of assistance for their students.

In this case, it is important that the referral list include therapists that are trained in trauma and loss therapy as well as grief therapy. School counselors must have a vetted list that is reviewed regularly to ensure that students and families receive the best treatment, depending on the situation. It is customary to provide at least three names to a family during the referral process.

d. Develop a plan for the transitioning of primary counseling services with minimal interruption of services. Students retain the right for the referred services to be done in coordination with the school counselor or to discontinue counseling services with the school counselor while maintaining an appropriate relationship that may include providing other school support services.

In Kimberly's case, it is imperative that the school counselor maintain relations with the outside therapist. School counselors develop relationships with community referral agencies and follow local policy and procedures to ensure that services are not interrupted in support for the student.

f. Attempt to establish a collaborative relationship with outside service providers to best serve students. Request a release of information signed by the student and/or parents/guardians before attempting to collaborate with the student's external provider.

A release of records is essential in Kimberly's case, as there are many supports needed for her family on the campus and in the community. School counselors develop relationships with community referral agencies and follow local policy and procedures to ensure that services are not interrupted in support for the student. The release of information (ROI) is signed first. It is imperative that the appropriate forms are in place before contacting other mental health professionals involved in a case. Parents and guardians have a right to approve or disapprove the counselor's contact with an outside agency or therapist.

> g. Provide internal and external service providers with accurate, objective, meaningful data necessary to adequately assess, counsel and assist the student.

School counselors develop relationships with community referral agencies and follow local policy and procedures to ensure that necessary data is available and shared as appropriate.

> A.11. Bullying, Harassment and Child Abuse. School counselors: b. Report suspected cases of child abuse and neglect to the proper authorities and take reasonable precautions to protect the privacy of the student for whom abuse or neglect is suspected when alerting the proper authorities.

As details of Kimberly's living situation unfold, Ms. Connally must remain vigilant to ensure that Kimberly and her siblings are taken care of. School counselors are mandated reporters for suspected cases of child abuse and neglect. Ms. Connally is familiar with Kimberly's home situation and can be on alert for signs of neglect such as not attending school in order to care for her siblings and her grandmother and signs of abuse due to the tension and frustration on the part of the adults in the family.

> c. Are knowledgeable about current state laws and their school system's procedures for reporting child abuse and neglect and methods to advocate for students' physical and emotional safety following abuse/neglect reports.

School counselors are mandated reporters for suspected cases of child abuse and neglect and are knowledgeable about systems in place.

> d. Develop and maintain the expertise to recognize the signs and indicators of abuse and neglect. Encourage training to enable students and staff to have the knowledge and skills needed to recognize the signs of abuse and neglect and to whom they should report suspected abuse or neglect.

As school personnel are mandated reporters, schools counselors are charged with recognizing signs and symptoms of abuse and neglect and helping to educate the staff members on their campus. School counselors regularly attend training to serve as an expert on recognizing the signs and indicators of abuse and neglect and share this knowledge with their staff to ensure they can recognize the signs and symptoms as well.

> B. RESPONSIBILITIES TO PARENTS/ GUARDIANS, SCHOOL AND SELF: B.2. Responsibilities to the School. School counselors: b. Design and deliver comprehensive school counseling programs that are integral to the school's academic mission; driven by student data; based on standards for academic, career and social/emotional development; and promote and enhance the learning process for all students.

When a comprehensive school counseling program is in place, school counselors have the time and space to meet the academic, social and emotional, and college and career readiness needs of their students. To ensure that the needs of students are met, the school counselor designs and delivers a comprehensive school counseling program.

B.3. Responsibilities to Self. School counselors: f. Monitor their emotional and physical health and practice wellness to ensure optimal professional effectiveness. School counselors seek physical or mental health support when needed to ensure professional competence.

In this case, the school counselor must actively monitor her mental, emotional, and physical health to ensure she is able to support her students and staff. The school counselor knows where to seek support to ensure she is ethically competent.

g. Monitor personal behaviors and recognize the high standard of care a professional in this critical position of trust must maintain on and off the job. School counselors are cognizant of and refrain from activity that may diminish their effectiveness within the school community.

Mrs. Connally must be cognizant of her own social and emotional needs so that she can best meet the needs of Kimberly and her other students.

h. Seek consultation and supervision from school counselors and other professionals who are knowledgeable of school counselors' ethical practices when ethical and professional questions arise.

As Mrs. Connally is working with Kimberly, she should seek consultation from her counseling supervisor, counseling colleagues, and campus administration as needed and appropriate.

Multicultural Considerations

In addition to the considerations discussed, school counselors are trained to understand the cultural differences in responding to trauma and grief. Kimberly, who is Caucasian, lives in a low socioeconomic home in which the grandmother is the head of the household. Currently, Kimberly's mother is incarcerated. One of the cultural considerations of having an incarcerated parent is that of secrecy and isolation. Kimberly might want to keep her family situation private to avoid gossip and rumors about her and her family. She may be embarrassed to admit to her peers what is going on right now in her family. The school counselor can help Kimberly prepare statements to be shared with peers that do not reveal her mother's incarceration. Ms. Connally can also discuss with Kimberly that her mother's choices do not reflect poorly on the children; those choices are her mother's alone.

Case Discussion Questions

1. In this case study, the school counselor plays an important role in ensuring that Kimberly's needs are met on the campus. What talking points would you use to educate and advocate on Kimberly's behalf with her teachers, band teacher, school nurse and administration?
2. Make a list of students that you know who may have experienced a similar situation with a parent or family member. How can the school counselor help to ensure that their needs are being met on the campus?
3. What information should students, parents, and staff have about parent and/or family incarceration, and how would this information be disseminated in your district?
4. In groups of three or four, role-play the conversation you would have with Kimberly and her grandmother once you learn of her mother's impending jail time. What steps need to be taken, and who is in charge of each step?

5. Role-play talking to Kimberly's teachers. What points would the school counselor need to make to ensure the teachers are best able to support Kimberly upon her return to school?

Resources

ACE Study:

> https://stopabusecampaign.org/faq-the-ace-study/what-are-adverse-childhood-experiences-aces/did-a-household-member-go-to-prison/

Programs for Children of Incarcerated Parents:

> https://web.connectnetwork.com/programs-for-children-of-incarcerated-parents/
> Department of Justice: https://nicic.gov/children-of-incarcerated-parents
> Children of Incarcerated Parents: https://youth.gov/youth-topics/children-of-incarcerated-parents#:~:text=These%20children%20require%20support%20from,experiences%20leading%20up%20to%20it.

References

American School Counselor Association. (2016). *Ethical standards for school counselors*. Alexandria, VA: American School Counselor Association.

Beck, J. (2011). *Cognitive behavioral therapy: Basics and beyond* (2nd ed.). New York, NY: Guilford Press.

Dallaire, D., Ciccone, A., & Wilson, L. (2008). Teachers' experiences with and expectations of children with incarcerated parents. *Journal of Applied Developmental Psychology, 31*, 281–290.

Saltzman, W. R., Layne, C. M., Steinberg, A. M., & Pynoos, R. S. (2003). School based trauma-and grief-focused intervention for adolescents exposed to community violence. *The Prevention Researcher, 10*, 8–11.

Saunders, V. (2018). What does your dad do for a living? Children of prisoners and their experiences of stigma. *Children and Youth Services Review, 90*, 21–27.

Turney, K. (2018). Adverse childhood experiences among children of incarcerated parents. *Children and Youth Services Review, 89*, 218–225.

Reflections: In the space provided, write your notes and reflections regarding this case study.

Section IV

Critical Cases Impacting the School Community

"How do we explain tragedies to children with their limited experiences and naïve ideas? The innocence of children can be a protective factor or put them at risk. So much depends on how the adults in the community help children integrate tragedy into their lives."

Dr. Judy A. Nelson

"Having community is a gift and, in an instance where it's traded for anarchy and chaos, the culture of a school community is compromised, because it is perceived as unsafe and not secure."

Dr. Lisa A. Wines

The African proverb "It takes a village to raise a child" means the child can grow in a rich soil of healthy and secure environments. In fact, the book of Proverbs provides us with instructions on how to live moral and peaceful lives. The term community radiates this ideal of order, cohesion, and bonding shared by commonalities and values. When the flow of community is interrupted by death, natural disaster, or persons who may have gone astray or become too individualistic, then, inevitably, incidents of crises can occur, which directly and tangentially affects everyone—children and adults alike. In this section, cases that affect the school community are described.

24 The Death of a Beloved Teacher

Le'Ann Solmonson

Background

A critical incident in a school setting has the potential to negatively affect students' academic performance, as well as social and emotional development (Studer, 2015). The death of a teacher would be an example of a critical incident. The school counselor has a significant leadership role in collaborating with administrators and other school staff to plan for and respond to a crisis in order to minimize the stress felt by students and staff. When the crisis affects the entire school, well-thought-out crisis plans provide for a systematic response and minimize decision-making when emotions may escalate. Crisis intervention is intended to support students through a difficult event that is interfering with normal functioning. Erford (2019) suggests the goals of crisis intervention are to assist students in managing emotions, understand what has happened, integrate the event into one's life, and interpret the event in a way that is meaningful.

Experiencing death is a stressful event. Individual students respond differently to stress based upon temperament, coping skills, internal and external resources, and available support systems. The school counselor is uniquely trained to assess stress responses and determine the level of support that is needed by students. When dealing with death, a student's personal values and cultural beliefs can also influence his or her reactions to the loss. The school counselor may be working with a variety of beliefs among the student population. Being supportive of the individual belief system may present challenges when dealing with a loss that impacts a large number of students. In addition, this may be the first death some students have experienced. Those students will need assistance in processing the grief response and understanding what is being experienced. The following case study describes one school's response to an accident and resulting death involving a widely loved and respected teacher.

Description of Case

Mr. Howard was a large man with a gentle but authoritative presence in a room. He was an experienced teacher who served as a grandfather figure to many students. He worked in a small magnet high school in a large suburban school district. He taught social studies to every ninth- and tenth-grader in the school. The structure of the school included an advisory program in which students were assigned to a *Family* with approximately 25 other grade 9–12 students. Two adults led the Family, and older students mentored younger students. The adults served as advisors to the students and monitored their academic progress and also were the first contact for any concerns about the students. Close relationships developed during the daily Family period, and rituals were developed to recognize celebrations and achievements.

Mr. Howard instilled in his Family a strong sense of honor and integrity. Mr. Howard was one of those teachers who commanded respect without ever asking for it. He rarely raised his voice or showed negative emotions in front of students. He had high expectations of students academically, personally, and socially. He had a way of developing relationships with students that resulted in them being intensely loyal to him, and he was dedicated to his students.

Students were aware that Mr. Howard had several health problems, including diabetes. On more than one occasion, he became ill at school and had to leave. One particular incident was serious enough that the school nurse called an ambulance, and students witnessed EMTs taking him out of the school for transport to the local hospital. Those students were visibly shaken and were very concerned about their beloved teacher. A number of students went to the hospital to check on him after school ended for the day. He returned to school a few days later, much to the relief of his students.

Mr. Howard was an avid outdoorsman in his spare time. Over the Thanksgiving holidays, he was preparing some of his equipment for the upcoming hunting season and fell off a deer stand, resulting in serious injuries. He was hospitalized in critical condition and underwent surgery. Despite the accident occurring over a holiday, word spread among the students about Mr. Howard's serious condition. The school counselor was also notified and reached out to the principal to discuss how to respond. Together, they made the decision to notify all of the school staff first. The other adult in Mr. Howard's Family and the school counselor made phone calls to all of the students and parents in the Family to be sure they were notified prior to returning to school on Monday.

On Monday, the principal made an announcement to inform the entire school about Mr. Howard's accident and to give an update on his medical condition. He had not regained consciousness and was still in serious condition. The school counselor attended his classes on Monday, as well as being with his Family during advisory period. She answered questions with information and corrected any misinformation students may have heard. Several times during the day, a student asked if Mr. Howard was going to die. The school counselor answered honestly and stated that his condition was very grave. She stated the doctors were doing all they could to take care of him. The school staff was supportive of students and tried to prepare them for a negative outcome. On Wednesday morning shortly after the school counselor arrived on campus, a member of Mr. Howard's family called her to inform her he had died in the early hours of the morning. The school counselor immediately notified the principal. The staff members were called to the library and were informed. Because of the seriousness of Mr. Howard's injuries, most of his colleagues were prepared for the news. The school counselor notified the district crisis team to have additional counselors on campus if needed.

As students arrived, they were told to report to their Family rather than to first period. The principal and school counselor felt this was the most appropriate place for students to be when they were told of Mr. Howard's death. It would allow his Family to be together and support one another. The other advisor was the one who informed the students, with the support of the school counselor. The advisors in the other Families were the ones that informed the other students. Students were made aware of counselors being available in the library throughout the day if they wanted to talk. The majority of the students wanted to be with their peers and with the adults with whom they had a relationship. However, several of the adults in the building did make use of the counselors for their own support, as well as resources for how to respond to the grieving students. After an extended time in Family, the students returned to a normal schedule for the remainder of the day.

The school counselor was in Mr. Howard's classroom throughout the day. Many of the students were tearful as they entered the classroom. There was a brief processing time, and then students spent the remainder of the period making cards and writing letters to Mr. Howard's family. There were a few moments when students were sharing memories of Mr. Howard that laughter was heard. The school counselor was present but did not intervene unless a student became overly emotional. She allowed them to share their grief and comfort each other. She checked in on his Family and his classes each day for the remainder of the week but only stayed as long as needed.

The Howard family scheduled the funeral on Saturday to allow the school staff and students to attend without disrupting the school day. A visitation was held at the funeral home on Friday evening, and the school counselor attended in order to be there to support the students. For some, it was their first experience with a visitation that included an open casket. There were a few that asked the school counselor to be with them while they viewed Mr. Howard's body. She helped them to process their fears and grief as needed. At the funeral, the Howard family had designated a reserved area for Mr. Howard's Family members and former students who had been in his Family. The school counselor was again close by for support but allowed the students to comfort one another.

When students returned to school the Monday following the funeral, a well-known long-term substitute teacher was in Mr. Howard's classes. It was determined he would remain until the end of the semester, which was only a few more weeks. The school counselor worked with Mr. Howard's Family to organize a tribute to him that would be displayed in the front hall of the school. In addition, the student government association, which Mr. Howard advised, planted a tree in front of the school in his memory. The school counselor checked in with his Family on a regular basis and provided information regarding the normal grieving process.

It has been over ten years since Mr. Howard's death. Students have remained connected through social media. Several times a year, someone will post a tribute to Mr. Howard, recognizing the impact he had on his or her life.

Strategies for Consideration

The following sections will cover the theoretical frameworks for working with individuals who have experienced a loss, the knowledge gained from the professional experiences of the author, the impact of a death on the counselor who is responsible for the crisis interventions, and overall mental health implications when a school is dealing with a death.

Theoretical Frameworks

Grief counseling is intended to help the individual understand and manage the feelings associated with the loss in a healthy manner. J. W. Worden (2009) suggested there are four tasks to mourning: to accept the reality of the loss, to work through the pain of grief, to adjust to life in which the deceased is missing, and to establish a lasting connection to the deceased while moving forward with life. From the case of Mr. Howard, there is evidence of each of these tasks in the work of the school counselor. Allowing his students to talk through their feelings and share their memories of Mr. Howard would be examples of accepting the reality of the loss. Making the cards for the Howard family, attending the visitation, and attending the funeral were the first stages of working through the pain of grief. The counselor was available if students needed her. However, she allowed the students to work through their pain with each other and in their own way. The selection of a familiar substitute to fill in until the end of the semester assisted the students in adjusting to life without Mr. Howard. The substitute also knew Mr. Howard and was sensitive to the loss the students experienced. In addition, the lasting connection was made through the tribute in the hallway and the planting of a tree. Those memorials would maintain Mr. Howard's presence in the school for years to come.

While psychological first aid (PFA) is intended as a response to individuals who have experienced a trauma or a disaster, the supportive and practical assistance utilized in PFA can be helpful in dealing with a less traumatic death. It entails nonintrusive, practical care and support; assessing needs and concerns; listening, but not pressuring those affected to talk; and being a comforting and calming presence. The goal is to establish a nonintrusive and compassionate connection. When using PFA, the counselor asks the individual who has experienced a crisis to tell what they need, and then the counselor provides practical support and assistance. In the case of Mr. Howard's death, the counselor allowed the students to connect with one another while making sure they were aware she was available if needed. Throughout the time described in the case, the school counselor was respectfully observing and only intervened when the need was expressed.

Professional Experiences

This author has 14 years of experience as a school counselor and has dealt with at least one death of a student, parent, or staff member every year. The first couple of incidents brought about great anxiety and feelings of not being prepared to deal with such an intense situation. These feelings were common among a national sample of school counselors surveyed in 2013 by Solmonson and Killam. Of the counselors surveyed, 60.3% reported feeling not very prepared to deal with the death of a teacher. Only 4.8% reported feeling prepared, and 34.9% reported feeling some-what prepared. The average number of years of experience within the sample population was three years. From personal experience, those feelings of incompetence decreased with each crisis intervention in which this author was involved. In addition to responding as the campus school counselor, this author has also been a part of a district crisis team and a regional response team serving in a rural area. The following suggestions are based upon those experiences.

1. Ensure open lines of communication exist with administrators, school staff, and parents. Regardless of the age of the students, all parents should be notified of a death that impacts a large number of students. Provide information that has been verified by the family of the deceased.
2. Do not proceed in a business-as-usual manner. Provide affected students the opportunity to process their feelings. It is helpful to give them something to do that can be seen as helpful, like making cards or writing letters. However, return to a normal schedule as soon as possible to provide students with a sense of routine and structure. This is supportive of Worden's first task of accepting the reality of the loss, as well as the second task of working through the pain.
3. Consider developmental and cultural differences in the response of students. Different people respond to grief in different ways and have different ways of coping.
4. If professional support is coming from outside the building, the school counselor should be leading the efforts. Outside counselors do not know the culture of the school or the students. The students see them as strangers. Most students want to be with a caring adult with whom they already have a relationship. They find security and comfort in those relationships. If there is a counselor still employed with the district from a previous campus that the students know, attempt to have that counselor available for support. This is also an example of Worden's first and second tasks.
5. Allow students to talk and grieve together with an adult monitoring and intervening if a student becomes too emotionally dysregulated. Do not pressure a student to talk or share feelings with others. Some may not be comfortable expressing emotions in the school setting. The ability to talk through their grief is supportive of Worden's second task.
6. Have a counselor in the teacher's room throughout the first day to provide support and assistance to students. Assess the students' responses to determine how long this will need to continue. Add reminders to your calendar to follow up on regular intervals with the students who are the most impacted by the death.
7. Be mindful of death language and platitudes that are frequently offered. Do not use euphemisms like lost, passed, or crossed over, but use concrete words like death, dead, and died. Avoid saying things that are value driven such as "He's in a better place now" or "He is with God now."

8. Identify an individual who is known to the students to take over the teacher's class. It can be another teacher in the building, a frequent substitute that the students know, or a former teacher. This is aligned with Worden's third task of adjusting to live without the individual.

9. Work with the family on the timing of removing the teacher's belongings from the classroom. If possible, leave them until a natural break in the school year or the end of the year. This is also evidence of Worden's third task.

10. Allow students to participate in planning a memorial or tribute to the teacher. This is congruent with Worden's fourth task of establishing a lasting connection while moving forward with life.

Counselor Impact

The school counselor is likely to have an emotional response to the death of the teacher. He or she has lost a colleague. In addition, he or she is dealing with the emotions of students and other staff members. In a leadership role, the school counselor will have to compartmentalize personal emotions in order to provide crisis interventions for others. It is often helpful to identify someone on the outside crisis team to be available for the school counselor. Even something as simple as making sure the school counselor has lunch, gets a cup of coffee, has water available, or takes a break—all can be helpful. Plan for a time to process with administrators and school staff at the end of the day and grieve together. This is also a time to identify students who appear to be struggling more than others and plan for the next day. The school counselor should work closely with the administrator to continue to monitor students and staff, as well as assessing the effectiveness of their interventions. Consider providing small group counseling for the students who are having the most difficult time coping with the loss.

Mental Health Implications

Ongoing monitoring of students will assist in identifying any student who may have a complicated grief response. Students who have recently experienced another loss or have experienced numerous losses are particularly vulnerable. Watch for significant changes in behaviors, attitudes, socialization, and academic performance that continue long after most other students have returned to normal functioning. Maintain open lines of communication with parents related to any concerning behavior exhibited by students. Provide parents with a list of common indicators of mental health issues that may arise because of grief and provide resources in the community for outside support.

Ethical Considerations

The following ethical considerations are relevant to this case (ASCA, 2016).

A.1.b. Aim to provide counseling to students in brief context and support students and families/guardians in obtaining outside services if the student needs long-term clinical counseling.

A.1.e. Are concerned with students' academic, career, and social/emotional needs and encourage each student's maximum development.

A.1.h. Provide effective, responsive interventions to address student needs.

In this case, the counselor was available to students prior to and immediately after the death, including supportive actions through the funeral process. She worked with those students who had closer relationships to Mr. Howard to assist in processing their grief. She was aware of the emotional needs of the students and provided appropriate interventions to encourage healthy strategies for coping with death. If a student continues to exhibit problematic behaviors, an out-side referral may be necessary.

> A.7.a. Facilitate short-term groups to address students' academic, career, and/or social/emotional issues.
> A.7.b. Inform parent/guardian(s) of student participation in small group.
> A.7.c. Screen students for group membership

Grief counseling is an appropriate small-group intervention in the school setting. For students who may demonstrate a need for additional assistance, the school counselor would follow all ethical guidelines related to engaging in group work in a school setting.

> B.3.f. Monitor their emotional and physical health and practice wellness to ensure optimal professional effectiveness. School counselors seek physical or mental health support when needed to ensure professional competence.

A school counselor is going to have a personal response to a death of a colleague. In order to be able to provide effective services for the students, the school counselor must attend to his or her own grief response. Having a support system that is not involved in the loss will provide the school counselor space to process his or her emotions and mental health needs.

Multicultural Considerations

A student will respond to death from within their own cultural perspective. This includes how they conceptualize death and what happens when a person dies. Counselors should be knowledgeable about how different cultural and religious groups respond to death and the associated rituals. There are some common cultural coping mechanisms that appear to be useful in working with children and adolescents (Kuehn, 2013). Those include maintaining some type of bond with the deceased that include something physical like a memory book or a memorial item like a plaque or a tree that is planted. It can also be some type of spiritual connection, such as seeing death as a transition to a place where reunification will occur.

Another common theme that crosses cultures is some type of meaning making related to the death. The meaning can vary, but the purpose is to make coping with the death easier. Different stages of experiencing grief is also a concept that is common among various cultures. All cultures also have rituals associated with death, and those rituals are often a celebration of life. The final universal concept is the idea of community support and avoiding isolation. School counselors should ultimately accept these cultural differences and know that prioritizing your own values or culture as the focus of providing services limits counselors' ability to be accepting and open.

Discussion Questions

1. What are your own personal experiences with death that may affect your responses as a school counselor?
2. This case study occurred in a small school with a unique advisory structure that created close relationships with adults and students, as well as student to student. How do you think that affected the case? Do you think this environment was more beneficial than a traditional school environment? Why or why not?
3. Several of the students were involved in a local youth group associated with a church. As word of Mr. Howard's death got out, the youth pastor from the church wanted to come into

the school to provide support for students. Do you think this is something the school should allow? Why or why not? If you think it should be allowed, what parameters would you put in place for the youth pastor's involvement?
4. Your district has a crisis response team that is involved in all campus crises. The leader of the team comes into the school and begins to take control of the response activities. How would you, as the campus school counselor, intervene on behalf of your campus?

Resources

School Crisis Center: www.schoolcrisiscenter.org/wp-content/uploads/2017/04/ncscb-guidelines-responding-death-student-or-school-staff.pdf

Counselingbyheart: www.schoolcounselingbyheart.com/2012/03/25/when-a-staff-member-dies/

U.S. Department of Education Emergency Response and Crisis Management Technical Assistance Center: https://rems.ed.gov/docs/copingw_death_studentorstaff.pdf

Grief Speaks: www.griefspeaks.com/id97.html

References

American School Counselor Association. (2016). *Ethical standards for school counselors*. Alexandria, VA: American School Counselor Association.

Erford, B. (2019). *Transforming the school counseling profession* (5th ed.). New York, NY: Pearson.

Kuehn, P. D. (2013). Cultural coping strategies and their connection to grief therapy modalities for children: An investigation into current knowledge and practice. *Master of social work clinical research papers: Paper 215*. St. Paul, MN: St Catherine University. Retrieved from https://sophia.stkate.edu/cgi/viewcontent.cgi?article=1217&context=msw_papers

Solmonson, L., & Killam, W. (2013). A national study on crisis intervention: Are school counselors prepared to respond? *VISTAS 2013, Summer Issue, American Counseling Association*. Retrieved from www.counseling.org/docs/vistas/a-national-study-on-crisis-intervention.pdf?sfvrsn=2

Studer, J. (2015). *The essential school counselor in a changing society*. Thousand Oaks, CA: Sage.

Worden, J. W. (2009). *Grief counseling and grief therapy* (4th ed.). New York, NY: Springer.

Reflections: In the space provided, write your notes and reflections regarding this case study.

25 Coping With a Disaster

Judy A. Nelson and Benny Malone

Background

Natural disasters are impossible to predict; they destroy property, cause injury and death, and traumatize survivors in families, neighborhoods, communities, towns, or even in an entire country. Disasters cause serious disruptions in day-to-day living, and sometimes extreme numbers of lives are lost to those experiencing such an event. Natural disasters, such as hurricanes, flooding, extremes in temperatures, cyclones, and tsunamis destroy property and end lives. Man-made disruptions and accidents include airplane crashes, explosions, infrastructure failures such as collapsing bridges and towers, and nuclear incidents are considered forms of disaster.

The effects of disasters can last for years or even decades. Children are particularly vulnerable to the trauma of disasters as often they lose family members, friends, and teachers, and their homes and schools might be destroyed. Children do not have the personal resources or capacity to integrate disasters into their lives. Researchers (Baggerly & Exum, 2008; Rank & Gentry, 2003; Webb, 2004) reported the extent to which children tolerate the disruption and destruction of disasters depends on how well parents and other significant adult caretakers handle and model responses to these situations.

In addition to the destruction of property and loss of lives, the natural disasters that have become common around the world have provided lessons in culture, class, poverty, and power. In an editorial in the *Journal of School Violence*, Gerler (2006) called these disasters another form of violence in which children are powerless in the face of significant losses. Based on literature, Burham (2009) cited global events such as disasters as one of the main contemporary fears of children. In her own study, Burham identified hurricanes and tornadoes as number 18 on the list of most common fears generated by 1,033 participants from 23 schools including elementary, middle, and high school students.

Additionally, these disasters often affect areas that are already poverty-stricken with very little means of restoring the loss of electricity, crops and other food sources, and housing and various infrastructures. This was evident in the destruction of Ward 5 in New Orleans after Hurricane Katrina, earthquakes and hurricanes in Haiti, and extreme drought in some countries in Africa. In light of these types of disasters, thousands of people have migrated to other parts of their own country or to other countries as a way to cope with impossible situations. This migration of thousands of people has been problematic for receiving countries many of which have placed bans on opening their borders to the refugees.

In 2005, Hurricane Katrina, a Category 5 storm, almost destroyed the city of New Orleans and resulted in approximately 250,000 evacuees who migrated to Houston, Texas (The Guardian, 2015). Most of those who landed in Houston were poor African American families whose children had experienced inadequate educational systems for many years. These children entered schools in Houston Independent School District and the surrounding school districts and overwhelmed those systems with hundreds of new enrollees. The new students had no school records, were most likely traumatized by the hurricane and the abrupt move to another city miles from their homes, and faced ridicule from students and families who had lived in Houston all of their lives. The following case study describes how one school district's director of guidance and a university professor collaborated with each other and additional community resources to assist displaced students as they transitioned to their new schools.

Description of Case

In the aftermath of Hurricane Katrina in mid-September of 2005, parents began to enroll their children in one suburban school district just miles from the inner city of Houston, Texas. As displaced families looked for temporary housing arrangements in shelters, children were enrolled in local schools in order to normalize life in some small way. School counselors were normally finished with the task of enrolling new students by this time of the school year; however, they enrolled hundreds of new students from New Orleans and worked with administrators to place the students in appropriate classes and welcome them to their new city. District officials and school staff had to rework the infrastructure of the already overcrowded schools to accommodate the new students. As school counselors registered these students and talked to parents, it became clear that these families needed emotional and psychological support. Social services were doing their best to find food, lodging at shelters, and clothing for the displaced families, but who would provide the emotional support that they needed?

   To answer this question, the director of guidance of the district and a professor at a nearby university began collecting information and collaborating to provide these much-needed counseling services to the families. The two professionals formed crisis response teams composed of school counseling interns from the university who were also employees (teachers) of the school district. These teams were led by students in the doctoral program at the university or graduates of the master's program who worked in the school district. All of the team members were connected to both the university and the school district, and they were charged with providing emotional support at the shelters where most of the families were housed. Potential team members were emailed requesting their participation followed by a planning and organizational meeting. The purpose of the planning meeting was to assign tasks and responsibilities to all of those volunteers who would ultimately be working in some capacity with the displaced families. The topics covered at the meeting included

- the make-up of the teams;
- the role of each team member;
- The assignment of a team leader to each team;
- the names of the shelters that had been contacted by the director of guidance regarding the emotional support teams;
- the shelter that was assigned to each team;
- the contact information for the shelters and the team members;
- a plan of action to for identifying the needs of the evacuees living in the shelters; and
- guidelines for responding to the families, and particularly those with young children.

   In a separate meeting, the team leaders discussed how to provide crisis response information to their team members. The director of guidance agreed to upload resources to the school district intranet global drive for all school counselors to access. The university professor sent out articles regarding crisis response to the school counseling trainees and included these as required reading for their courses. The school counselors conducted the responses, the role of the student trainees was to be observers and co-facilitators, and these students received group supervision from their professor. In addition to the counseling, the school district provided funding for parent training and support groups.

Strategies for Consideration

Natural and man-made disasters can impact entire communities for long periods of time. Because these disasters usually involve so many victims, school counselors must seek out community partners to help with what is certain to be the overwhelming task of responding to the students and families associated with the school system. The following sections highlight interventions, considerations, and challenges involved in responding to natural disasters.

Theoretical Frameworks

Because of the extreme losses experienced by survivors of natural and man-made disasters, counselors must use a theoretical framework that is based on empathy and unconditional regard. Person-centered counseling (Rogers, 2003) is appropriate for clients who are struggling with existential questions about their lives and their futures. Being present as adult survivors struggle to grasp their situations and to plan for the future of their families is the most effective way of being a helper at such a time of crisis. Additionally, counselors can provide lists of appropriate resources to parents to access the basic needs that they have, including food sources and lodging. Children, on the other hand, do not have the capacity to make decisions about the future or to access resources, nor should they. Believing that parents, teachers, and other adults will take care of them is necessary for their safety and their ability to return to normal childhood behaviors.

According to researchers (Baggerly & Exum, 2008), children's fears and anxiety can be mitigated when parents and teachers are able to provide emotional support. School counselors can provide training to both parents and teachers so they can respond to children in ways that are helpful and soothing. Harper, Harper, and Stills (2003) reported that due to the large numbers of children often impacted by natural disasters, training parents and teachers to intervene is an efficient way to meet the needs of more clients. These types of workshops are an effective way for school counselors to make the best use of their time and efforts. The ripple effect of training adults can affect the lives of many more children than simply meeting one-on-one with parents, teachers, and students. Included at the end of this chapter are resources that can assist school counselors as they plan informational meetings for parents and teachers regarding the best ways to help children in the recovery process.

Play therapy is one way for counselors to help children express their fears and worries in a safe environment with any judgment withheld (Baggerly & Exum, 2008). Play therapy is appropriate, particularly for children who experience continuing symptoms long after the disaster and that interfere with daily functioning at school and in the home. The nondirective nature and unconditional regard of play therapy provides opportunities for the child to begin to feel competent and have a sense of control over his or her environment in the playroom. These feelings of empowerment can transfer to home and school in time. Many school counselors have training in play therapy and have travel therapy kits that easily can be used in the school counseling office. Some school counselors have a portion of their offices designated as the *play therapy room*.

Professional Experiences

Two colleagues, the authors of this chapter, who actually worked on a project like the one described, elicited a list of best practices for future university and school district partnerships and responding to crises such as hurricanes, tornadoes, flooding, explosions, crashes, and infrastructure failures. According to Nelson and Malone (2008), those best practices are as follows:

- Identify a project director in both the school district and the university.
- Expect a sharing of power and support by the leadership of both organizations.
- Create a climate of respect and trust in the project.
- Nurture a collaborative spirit among all participants.
- Establish a willingness to be flexible among all participants.
- Use a team approach to divide up the tasks.
- Designate leaders for each team.
- Provide the necessary supervision of school counselors and counselors-in-training.

The result of the willingness to create partnerships in the aftermath of a crisis enables a pooling of resources that would otherwise not be possible. This means that more individuals and families can receive the help they need quickly. The willingness of two entities to work together with a common goal rules out any participant being the best or holding a higher position than the other. This is true collaboration.

Counselor Impact

One of the most difficult assignments for counselors is to respond to clients who have lost everything including loved ones, property, jobs, and the ability to provide for their families. These clients might feel hopeless and that there is no solution to their situations. Counselors can help clients focus on processing cognition and feelings, with reflections on their lived experiences. This is in opposition to having answers to their crisis in the moment. It is not unusual for counselors to begin to feel a need to find solutions or to believe that they must do something to make the situation all better, which of course is not possible. Additionally, school counselors often are victims of the very disasters that have affected their clients and might have experienced loss and trauma themselves.

Self-care is of the utmost importance in these cases. School counselors can become exhausted and dysfunctional if they do not know when to say "no" or if they are not self-aware enough to realize their own limitations or to know that they are impaired from overwork and emotional upheaval. In the case example in this chapter, teaming was the most prudent way for counselors to remain functional and capable of carrying out their responsibilities as trainees, school counselors, and leaders. Consultation and supervision were the primary outlets for possible impairment, particularly for the student trainees, who probably were experiencing this type of trauma for so many clients for the first time. Supervision of these students was mandatory and provided by experienced school counselors, and the two leading colleagues were available to assist with supervision and consultation as needed. Additionally, the trainees were able to process their experiences each week during class time at the university.

Mental Health Implications

Fear, depression, self-blame and guilt, loss of interest in school and other activities, regression, bad dreams, eating disturbances, aggression, inability to concentrate, and separation anxiety are typical symptoms in children after a natural disaster (Speier, 2000) and are dependent on the developmental level. Many children recover from these symptoms with basic family and school support. However, according to Baggerly and Exum (2008), some children experience symptoms that are long lasting and disrupt daily living. Clinical symptoms may result in a diagnosis of acute stress disorder, post-traumatic stress disorder, or other anxiety and depression disorders. Referring these children to outside counseling is appropriate. Additionally, as referenced earlier, training parents and teachers to approach displaced children in ways that offer support, love, nurturing, and hope will affect large numbers of students and families.

Ethical Considerations

School counselors must approach their work from a lens of ethical behavior. The following standards (ASCA, 2016) apply to this case.

> A.1. Supporting Student Development. School counselors: A.1a. Have a primary obligation to the students, who are to be treated with dignity and respect as unique individuals. A.1.b. Aim to provide counseling to students in a brief context and support students and families/guardians in obtaining outside services if the student needs long-term clinical counseling. A.1.c. Do not diagnose but remain acutely aware of how a student's diagnosis can potentially affect the student's academic success. A.1.d. Acknowledge the vital role of parents/guardians and families. A.1.h. Provide effective, responsive interventions to address student needs. A.1.i. Consider the involvement of support networks, wraparound services and educational teams needed to best serve students.

School counselors primarily are obligated to protect the interests of students; thus, in the aftermath of a disaster, the counselor will implement as many strategies and interventions as possible to assist students in their recovery. Many students will recover with the help of parents and teachers, but others will continue to have symptoms of trauma long after the event. While the school counselor can provide individual and group counseling in the short term, those students needing longer term clinical care should be referred to outside services. While it is not the role of the school counselor to diagnose mental health disorders, they are trained and informed regarding these disorders and can describe symptomology that will help outside mental health professionals make diagnoses and inform treatment.

> B.1. Responsibilities to Parents/Guardians. School counselors: B.1.a. Recognize that providing services to minors in a school setting requires school counselors to collaborate with students' parents/guardians as appropriate. B.1.d. Are culturally competent and sensitive to diversity among families. Recognize that all parents/guardians, custodial and noncustodial, are vested with certain rights and responsibilities for their children's welfare by virtue of their role and according to law.

After a disaster, it is critical for school counselors to be knowledgeable on the community resources that can help families recover. Keeping an up-to-date list of support networks and other services will help counselors provide descriptions of services, phone numbers, and addresses to families. Providing culturally responsive assistance to families in their time of need is expected of the school counselor.

Multicultural Considerations

As reported by Shillingford, Oh, and DiLorenzo (2018), in some circumstances families are forced not only from their homes but from their countries of origin. In the case of the people of Haiti, families there experienced not only political unrest and upheaval but also devastating natural disasters in 2010, 2016, and 2017. These disasters resulted in increased migration to the United States due to loss of lives, jobs, homes, schools, and infrastructure.

When schools in the United States experience an influx of new students due to disaster, often these students are traumatized and possibly experiencing PTSD. However, when these students have been dislocated from their home country, the need for culturally appropriate responses is critical. Stressors experienced by displaced immigrant children include feeling isolated in the new school setting (Chhuon, Hudley, Brenner, & Macias, 2010) and the differences in school culture and climate (Cone, Buxton, Lee, & Mahotiere, 2014). Language barriers, cultural identity, and acculturation are some of the cultural difficulties that immigrant children might face in a new school setting (Shillingford et al., 2018).

School counselors are leaders in the school environment, and teachers and administrators should naturally look to counselors to help integrate new students into the school culture. Training all staff to be culturally responsive and appropriate is one way to ensure that everyone has basic information about students from another culture. Ongoing staff development will be needed to check in with teachers and staff for feedback and additional training. Counselors can also meet with new students to assure them that the counselor's office is a place that is safe and can provide help. If the number of new immigrants is not too large, the school counselor can meet regularly with the students to provide an outlet for fears, complaints, and problems.

Case Discussion Questions and Activities

1. Discuss in small groups the possible natural and man-made disasters that have occurred in your communities. How were responsive services implemented in school counseling offices at the time? If you do not know, contact several school counselors and inquire about their roles in the time(s) of disaster.
2. Choose one of the following and make a plan of responsive services using the information from this chapter: (1) a tornado destroys homes in a neighborhood near the school where you work as the school counselor; (2) the electric grid in your school and surrounding area is compromised, and no one seems to know why, but families will be at least three weeks without electricity; (3) a small aircraft carrying the parents of one of the children in your school crashes, and all passengers are killed; (4) a hurricane destroys almost every building in a small school district on the Gulf Coast.
3. What are the support services that you would rely on after a natural disaster?
4. Design a workshop for teachers on how to help traumatized students recover from a disaster.
5. Design a workshop for parents and guardians on how to help their traumatized children recover from a disaster.

Resources

FEMA Children and Disasters: www.fema.gov/children-and-disasters

American Academy of Child and Adolescent Psychiatry Disaster Resource Center www. aacap.org/AACAP/Families_and_Youth/Resource_Centers/Disaster_Resource_Center/ Home.aspx

National Institute of Mental Health Helping Children and Adolescents Cope with Disasters www.nimh.nih.gov/health/publications/helping-children-and-adolescents-cope-with-disasters-and-other-traumatic-events/index.shtml

The National Child Traumatic Stress Network: Disasters www.nctsn.org/what-is-child-trauma/ trauma-types/disasters

References

American School Counselor Association. (2016). *Ethical standards for school counselors*. Alexandria, VA: American School Counselor Association.

Baggerly, J., & Exum, H. (2008). Counseling children after natural disasters: Guidance for family therapists. *The American Journal of Family Therapy, 36*, 79–93.

Burham, J. (2009). Contemporary fears of children and adolescents: Coping and resiliency in the 21st century. *Journal of Counseling and Development, 87*, 28–36.

Chhuon, V., Hudley, C., Brenner, M. E., & Macias, R. (2010). The multiple worlds of successful Cambodian American students. *Urban Education, 45*, 30–57.

Cone, N., Buxton, C., Lee, O., & Mahotiere, M. (2014). Negotiating a sense of identity in a foreign land: Navigating public school structures and practices that often conflict with Haitian culture and values. *Urban Education, 49*, 263–296.

Gerler, E. (2006). Editorial: Another kind of school violence. *Journal of School Violence, 5*, 1–4.

Harper, F. D., Harper, J. A., & Stills, A. B. (2003). Counseling children in crisis based on Maslow's hierarchy of basic needs. *International Journal for the Advancement of Counseling, 25*(1), 10–25.

Nelson, J., & Malone, B. (2008). Case study: Pooling resources. *ASCA School Counselor*, 33–35.

Rank, M. G., & Gentry, J. E. (2003). Critical incident stress: Principles, practices, and protocols. In M. Richard, W. Hutchinson, & W. Emener (Eds.), *Employee assistance programs: A basic text* (3rd ed., pp. 208–215). Springfield, IL: Charles C. Thomas Publisher.

Rogers, C. R.(2003). *Person-centered therapy: Its current practice, implications, and theory*. London, England: Constable & Robinson Ltd.

Shillingford, M. A., Oh, S., & DiLorenzo, A. (2018). Using the multiphase model of psychotherapy, school counseling, human rights, and social justice to support Haitian immigrant students. *The Professional Counselor, 8*(3), 240–248.

Speier, A. H. (2000). *Psychosocial issues for children and adolescents in disasters*. Rockville, MD: U.S. Department of Health and Human Services, Substance Abuse and Mental Health Services Administration, Center for Mental Health Services. Retrieved from http://cretscmhd.psych.ucla.edu/nola/Video/MHR/Governmentreports/Psychosocial%20Issues%20for%20Children%20and%20Adolescents%20in%20Disasters.pdf

The Guardian. (2015). *New Orleans West: Houston is home for many evacuees 10 years after Katrina*. Retrieved from https://www.theguardian.com/us-news/2015/aug/25/new-orleans-west-houston-hurricane-katrina

Webb, N. B. (Ed.). (2004). *Mass trauma and violence: Helping families and children cope*. New York: Guilford Press.

Reflections: In the space provided, write your notes and reflections on this case study.

26 Active Shooter Lockdown Practice

Judy A. Nelson and Danny Holland

Background

Active shooter drills in schools have become commonplace, with 95% of schools in 2015–2016 participating in these drills, according to the U. S. Department of Education National Center for Education Statistics (2018–036). The alert, lockdown, inform, counter, and evacuate (ALICE) training leads the way in active shooter defense instruction, and business is booming with rapid growth. Active shooter drills are the new normal for public school safety. However, do these drills help, or are they doing more harm than good to some students who experience these some-times very realistic active shooter simulations?

Very little research has been conducted on these experiences, and according to Jonson (2017), school personnel should be looking for evidence-based practices to provide the best response to school safety issues. Most experts agree that preparing for an active shooter by *hardening* school protocol and policy is not nearly as effective as threat assessments that identify potentially harmful students to self and others as well as prevention programs (NASP, 2017; Zhang, Musu-Gillette, & Oudekerk, 2016). School counselors have been trained to assess threats and recognize thoughts and behaviors indicative of potentially dangerous situations. However, in canvassing school counselors across the country, most of them appreciated the idea of preparedness and had experienced drills that ranged from simply locking down the classrooms to very realistic drills with fake blood, actors who played dead students, and law enforcement who came with full emergency paraphernalia. The following case study describes in detail how an active shooter drill backfired for one student and caused him and his family to lose faith in the system that was supposed to keep students safe. Real-life experiences from school counselors provide insight into how this could have been avoided.

Description of Case

At the time of this incident, Tim, a 17-year-old Caucasian male, was a junior in high school in the western United States in a large suburban school district that borders on a densely populated metropolitan area. A psychiatrist diagnosed Tim with *anxiety disorder not otherwise specified* due to extreme anxiety, panic attacks, restlessness, and irritability that had lasted three months prior. Tim is currently taking medication for his anxiety and attends group counseling with the school counselor because his anxiety has affected his ability to concentrate in classes, and his grades are lower than in the past.

The precipitating event responsible for the onset of the anxiety problems might have been the break-in at his home while he and his family were out having dinner. When the family returned home, the front door was kicked open, with furniture and household items strewn about the floor. The missing items included all medication from the medicine cabinets in each bathroom, two lap-top computers, one iPhone that had not been used in a while, and a tablet. Additionally, the glass on the locked gun cabinet in which the father's gun collection was displayed had been broken, and all nine guns were missing. The guns were probably the most valuable of all that was stolen, as the collection included antique and rare guns.

Since the event, Tim has had nightmares and terrors about the break-in that enacted visualization of the family returning while the intruders were in the house. His greatest fear was that these people would return to harm him and his family members. Tim and his family are addressing their mental health issues with a therapist recommended by the psychiatrist who is also treating Tim. Tim and his parents visited with the school counselor shortly after the break-in, explained Tim's anxiety diagnosis and medication support, and asked the school counselor to monitor his progress in school for a few weeks while he worked through his fear and anxiety over the event at home. The school counselor agreed and asked permission to provide Tim's teachers with a short version of the problem so that they would be on the alert for any changes in behavior. The parents and Tim agreed. Additionally, the school counselor obtained permission for Tim to meet in a group once a week during lunch with other students who also experience anxiety. Although it can be powerful work to discuss the source of his anxiety, Tim would not need to reveal any of the background to his anxiety problems. Perhaps his healing and support could derive from hearing how other students were coping.

Two weeks after the meeting with the school counselor, approximately 2,500 students participated in a lockdown drill in order to practice response procedures of an active shooting incident. Students and teachers were aware that the lockdown would occur, but they did not know exactly when; however, they did have instructions to lock the doors to the classrooms and not let anyone in during the drill. Parents were notified about the drill in a letter home about a week before it was to occur. The administrative team, which did not include the school counselors, worked with local law enforcement and an active shooter defense instruction team led by a private company to plan this event. They decided to have all classrooms locked down, but they chose one classroom that would experience more serious repercussions from the actors who portrayed the active shooter as well as law enforcement.

Unfortunately, the classroom chosen to receive the more serious drill was the science room in which Tim was taking Biology II. When the drill was announced, Tim's teacher directed all of the students to come away from the door, which she locked, and to get under the tables at the front of the classroom. The students were cooperative and took the drill seriously. About two minutes after the drill was announced, Tim and his classmates heard loud banging on the door to their classroom and two or three voices demanding to be let in. The shouting continued for about a minute, with a good deal of profanity and talk about killing. The teacher continued to reassure the students that this was a drill, not a real active-shooter event. After a minute or so, the shouting grew worse with other voices, presumably the police, yelling for the original voices to drop their weapons. Finally, there were fake gunshots and then silence. It was impossible to know if the police or the active shooters had been shot during this role-play.

All of the students in Tim's class were visibly shaken, but the teacher continued to be relatively calm and reassuring. However, Tim was in a full-blown panic attack, which the teacher recognized, immediately calling for help. The nurse and an administrator arrived quickly and took Tim to the nurse's office, where he was able to take some medication and recover. He was able to sleep on one of the nurse's cots until his mother arrived to take him home for the rest of the day. Tim did not return to school for several days but was able to do so after visiting with his therapist and psychiatrist. Tim's medication was adjusted, and he was able to continue with his education with a great deal of support.

Strategies for Consideration

Active shooter drills are becoming more common in all grade levels, and some students may experience fear and trauma because of these drills. The school counselor has many available tools to respond to students, teachers, and parents who have concerns about active shooter drills. The following sections provide school counselors with information on interventions and considerations for responding to those who need assistance before, during, or after an active shooter drill.

Theoretical Frameworks

Cognitive behavioral therapy (CBT) (Beck, 2011) is generally considered an effective framework for working with students in schools, as well as helping students cope with emotional and social problems that might affect their academics and career planning. In the case presentation offered here, the school counselor is conducting a group that focuses on helping students maintain positive outlooks and behaviors in school. Techniques such as journaling, behavior charts, and rewards for improved behaviors help students work toward maintaining appropriate classroom and homework activities. For example, the counselor might help Tim chart his feelings of panic, including where and when they occur and how he would rate their intensity. This activity could be in the form of journaling or simply a chart that he shares with the counselor and discusses his progress or lack thereof. Additionally, parent and teacher support are instrumental in assisting students to stay motivated to continue to make good choices.

Professional Experiences

The first author reached out to counselors around the country by posting on the Counselor Education and Supervision Network Listserv (or CESNET-L) and the American Counseling Association School Counseling Interest Network for School Counselors, where she was able to ask for comments from school counselors who had experienced an active shooter drill and how that experience had impacted them and their students. This was a worthwhile exercise because she heard from many counselors who had participated in an active shooter drill, all of which had important lessons they learned from each of these events. Their comments are relevant as to how the active shooter drill in this case study could have prepared for students like Tim who might be traumatized by such an experience. Here are the professional experiences of school counselors summarized:

Most school counselors who responded to the author's queries recognize the benefits of active shooter drills and felt that it was necessary to prepare students for the best outcome possible if a real active shooter was on campus. However, they also reported that they spent time responding to teachers and students who felt traumatized by the drills. The active shooter drills experienced by these counselors ranged from a simple lockdown procedure to a role-play involving shooters, dead bodies, fake blood, and the simulation of law enforcement intervention. For those school counselors who reported that some students had an experience of feeling traumatized during an active shooter drill, they stated that, in all of these cases, the staff learned something about how to proceed and improve during the next drill.

Some school counselors stated that they were left out of the planning of these drills, which proved to be detrimental in the outcomes of the experiences of certain students. If school counselors had been included, they could possibly have paved the way for better experiences for students who were more likely to be traumatized by such an event. School counselors know students and their situations and have the training and skills in mental health to assist in critical cases. Therefore, it is essential for school counselors to advocate for their role in implementing emergency plans and to educate administrators regarding their mental health training and expertise. One school counselor reported that there was a threat made to the school, which did not result in any action, but the following day, the whole school participated in an active shooter lockdown. This counselor reported that students were visibly shaken the day of the drill based on the scare that they had the previous day. Some counselors reported that they were aware of active shooter situations in other schools near their own, in university settings, or in their towns.

According to Dr. Danny Holland, one of the authors on this chapter, who has conducted several types of drill trainings and safety audits in large school districts in Virginia, school counselors are a critical part of an event and thus know the protocols to handle those events. The major focus of emergency protocols is triaging the event and containing the threat to reduce casualties. One factor that causes some difficulty with this process is that much of the development of protocols is done out of local school buildings at a district level. During active shooter drills, most of the focus is on lockdowns, shelter in place, and so forth. At the time of a real event, seconds count to reduce access to potential victims while those trained to stop the threat do so. Therefore, the drill itself is about immediate safety. It could be argued that school counselors play a vital role, primarily due to their relationship with potential victims, knowledge of the building facilities, and their training, which provide a very important piece to post-event care. Most of the focus regarding active shooter drills will be based on post-event examination of shooting trends and best practices to maintain physical safety. Essentially, those procedures will be law enforcement initiated. Once the threat is neutralized, school counselors are essential.

Based on the experiences of these counselors from around the nation, the following suggestions emerged:

1. The school counselor must be a part of emergency planning and training.
2. School counselors should advocate for active roles in emergency planning with their administrators.
3. The key for a successful drill is to have a well-understood and planned guide for conducting the drills. Each adult in the building must have a strong understanding of the procedures before attempting the drill. Department heads can brief teachers as well and funnel questions back to the appropriate staff. For example, P.E. teachers may have to adapt, and the clearer they know what to do if they are outside or in the locker room, the easier the drill will proceed.
4. Dr. Holland recommends teachers take ten minutes to discuss the drill procedure before the drill. Next, the administrator provides an announcement explaining the drill, and then the drill takes place. Afterwards, there is a recovery period from the drill. Last, a debriefing ensues from those in the hall observing, teachers with challenges (windows, doors that don't lock, locations of the phone in the room, how to know when to recover from a real scenario, etc.). At one school, once the lock down was initiated, only someone with the key to the door could release the lock down. There was no all-call or overhead announcement.
5. The emergency team should work diligently to decide how realistic the active shooter drill needs to be. Using a private company with expertise in active shooter defense and drills might be helpful in making these decisions. Some school districts have district-wide emergency planning that must be taken into consideration.
6. While all students need to be involved in drills designed to increase their safety (fire drills, tornado drills, active shooter drills, etc.), it is important to note that some drills are designed for emergency services to also practice response. These are often more realistic in design. For students to gain familiarity with a safety procedure, it is important for pre- and post-communication as well as actual drill procedure communication.
7. Parents should be made aware of an active shooter drill. If a child wishes to be a part of a training exercise involving law enforcement and emergency medical simulations, parents should sign permission for their children to participate. The permission should include warnings about possible side effects and characteristics of students who might be traumatized by these types of drills.
8. Alternate classrooms for students who opt out of the drill must be secure and out of the way of the activity and sounds of the drill. The challenge is greater for special needs children, and special accommodations may need to be put in place for these students.
9. Ideally, school counselors should work with other school personnel to create effective threat assessment tools and procedures to create a proactive response to more significant threats,

to triage trauma-related injuries to students who may experience such an event, and to create effective strategies to assist students with post-event recovery. This should also include talking to all students during classroom guidance lessons about the role of students in reporting dangerous threats or behaviors to appropriate school personnel.

Counselor Impact

School counselors can be overwhelmed by the large number of students for which they are charged and must have plans of self-care that allow them to debrief with others and also have time alone to meditate, exercise, play, or just relax. A plan is clear and definitive. Knowing when and where a school counselor needs debriefing or downtime is part of an effective plan. Supervision and consultation are essential elements of crisis response, and school counselors should have easy access to supervisors, mentors, and consultants.

One of the challenges of active shooter drills is the sheer number of students and staff who might need support before, during, or after the event. One counselor whose school experienced a threat one day and an active shooter drill the next day (in response to the threat) stated that numerous students and teachers were traumatized during the drill. How can one person cope with these numbers? One possibility is to create a response team from other schools or from the community that can help with situations involving many victims. Since the school counselor may also be a victim of trauma, that person can stay on the sidelines and allow others who were not in the drill to conduct the response to the trauma. These types of teams require pre-planning and organization well before the actual event. This strategy worked well in one large suburban district in Texas in which any crisis (including suicide, other deaths, violence, and terroristic threats) included a response from a district response team. The school counselor(s) who were personally involved in the situation planned where the team was needed but remained outside of the work of the team.

Mental Health Implications

In this particular case, the school counselor was aware of Tim's diagnosis, medication, and need for some space to heal after the break-in at his family's home. She had agreed to monitor him and received permission from Tim and his parents to provide limited information to Tim's teachers so that they could alert the school counselor if he experienced any behavior changes. These actions are typical protocol for the school counselor as she assisted Tim to continue to be successful in his academics, his college and career goals, and his healthy social and emotional states. The school counselor realized that anxiety, including panic attacks, can be devastating in all of the domains that the school counselor monitors (academic, college/career, and social/emotional).

Another possible check on Tim's progress would be for the school counselor to have the parents and Tim sign a two-way *release of information* so that the school counselor and the therapist and/or the psychiatrist could talk to each other. This action would open up the path for the school counselor to discuss the active shooter drill and Tim's response with the other mental health professionals involved in Tim's case, along with allowing the psychiatrist to discuss helpful strategies learned in therapy to implement throughout the course of the school day.

Ethical Considerations

School counselors must adhere to the ethical standards (ASCA, 2016) of their profession. The following standards apply to the case in this chapter.

A.1.c Do not diagnose but remain acutely aware of how a student's diagnosis can potentially affect the student's academic success.

The school counselor does not diagnose mental health disorders; however, the school counselor has training to understand and mitigate such diagnoses. In this case study, the school counselor was able to work with the student, parents, and teachers to help the student adjust to school after two disturbing events related to the student's anxiety issues.

> A.2.m Advocate for appropriate safeguards and protocols so highly sensitive student information is not disclosed accidentally to individuals who do not have a need to know such information. Best practice suggests a very limited number of educators would have access to highly sensitive information on a need-to-know basis.

The school counselor determined that the student's teachers had a *need to know* regarding the student's anxiety and how debilitating that diagnosis was. The school counselor was able to make suggestions for how to help the student continue to be successful in his academics, career goals, and social/emotional state. By providing some basic information, the school counselor created a working partnership among the student, parents, and teachers.

> A.7.a Facilitate short-term groups to address students' academic, career and/or social/emotional issues.

The school counselor conducts groups using best practices of group counseling including screening potential participants and obtaining parent permission for group participation. Tim was included in a group for academic success. The group members had a variety of reasons for struggling with their academics, and it was not a requirement of the group to discuss why the members struggled. Instead, the focus was on how to make changes that would help students maintain academic success.

Multicultural Considerations

Tim was fortunate to have excellent mental health services available to him through his family's insurance plan as well as supportive parents. What happens in the case of students from low socioeconomic school districts who experience anxiety due to unsafe neighborhoods, violence, abuse, and/or neglect and who do not have support from parents or the ability to access mental health services? In these cases, it is conceivable that the number of critical incidents that take place throughout the day makes it impossible for school personnel to address all of them. It might even be that a student experiencing anxiety would be the least important case to address in any given counselor's day. Being well versed in the symptomology of anxiety might help the counselor identify students who need support in groups or in individual counseling. Referrals to community agencies that offer low co-pays or sliding scales might be one path the school counselor could investigate for students with severe anxiety.

Additionally, students who are coping with anxiety but have not been diagnosed might use some forms of coping detrimental to healthy progress. For example, laughing or acting out during an active shooter drill may simply be the way some students cope with fear and anxiety during times of tension. The main issue here is to insist that parents, teachers, and administrators take the mental health problem of anxiety seriously. This can be done through the school counselor's confidence in his or her own expertise, staff development conducted by the school counselor, knowledge about community resources, and an ongoing respectful relationship with all stakeholders.

Discussion Questions

1. In this case study, the school counselor was not included in the important pre-planning of the active shooter drill. How would you advocate for such a role? What talking points would you use to convince administrators that you should be an integral part of a school safety team?

2. Make a list of the groups of students who might be negatively impacted by an active shooter drill in your school or district. How can the school counselor help maintain the safety and well-being of these students?
3. What information should students, parents, and staff have before an active shooter drill, and how would this information be disseminated in your district?
4. In groups of three or four, role-play the pre-planning of an active shooter drill. What steps need to be taken and who is in charge of each step?
5. Role-play talking to a group of students before an active shooter drill. What points would the school counselor need to make to help students feel more comfortable about such a drill?

Resources

National Center for Education Statistics: https://nces.ed.gov/
National Association of School Psychologists: www.nasponline.org/armed-assailant-drills
School Survey on Crime and Safety: http://nces.ed.gov/surveys/ssocs
Indicators of School Crime and Safety: 2017

References

American School Counselor Association. (2016). *Ethical standards for school counselors.* Alexandria, VA: American School Counselor Association.

Beck, J. (2011). *Cognitive behavioral therapy: Basics and beyond* (2nd ed.). New York, NY: Guilford Press.

Jonson, C. L. (2017). Preventing school shootings: The effectiveness of safety measures. *Victims & Offenders: An International Journal of Evidence-Based Research, Policy, and Practice, 12*, 956–973. doi:10.1080/15564886.2017.1307293

National Association of School Psychologists. (2017). *Questions to ask when considering armed assailant training.* [Factsheet]. Bethesda, MD: National Association of School Psychologists.

U.S. Department of Education, National Center for Education Statistics. (2018). *Indicators of school crime and safety: 2017* (NCES 2018-036), Indicator 20. Retrieved from https://nces.ed.gov/pubs2018/2018036.pdf

Zhang, A., Musu-Gillette, L., & Oudekerk, B. A. (2016). *Indicators of school crime and safety: 2015.* Washington, DC: National Center for Education Statistics, U.S. Department of Education, and Bureau of Justice Statistics, Office of Justice Programs, U.S. Department of Justice.

Reflections: In the space provided, write your notes and reflections regarding this case study.

27 A School Shooting

Danny Holland and Jamie Holland

Background

Just the words *school shooting* stir powerful emotions, fears, vulnerabilities, and reactions among a culture dedicated to protecting its youth. It is the nature of these types of egregious acts of murder and malice against the most vulnerable in our society that it tends to be one of the greatest fears, each day, for those who work with children and adolescents in schools. While we all agree that one student senselessly murdered on school property (or any other property) is too many, the data surrounding these incidents may be surprising. According to the FBI's Criminal Investigation Division and the Advanced Law Enforcement Rapid Response Training (ALERRT) Center at Texas State University, in 2018, there were 27 active shooter incidents causing 85 fatalities and wounding 128 others. Five of these events occurred within educational environments, resulting in 29 deaths and 52 wounded.

As high profile and unsettling as these numbers are, one of the first studies on the topic reported 85 school-associated homicides from July 1, 1992, through June 30, 1994 (Kachur et al., 1996). The Centers for Disease Control and Prevention (2019) reported that between July 1994 and June 2016, school-associated homicides consistently represented less than 2% of all youth homicides in the United States (Holland et al., 2019). They reported that a majority of those homicides occurred from the illegal use of firearms, and many were consistent with youth homicide rates unrelated to schools, involving male, racial/ethnic minority youth victims in urban settings. While a majority of those deaths involved illegal firearm use, the FBI reports that in 2018, of the 14,123 murders that occurred, 6,603 were firearm related (297 were from all types of rifles), which is down from 18,253 in 1993 (BJS, 2013). It also reported that 1,515 were from knives, 443 from blunt objects, and 672 from personal weapons (FBI, 2019). This report indicated an overall drop in homicides from 2016 and 2017, yet highlights that no matter what method of choice a homicidal person selects, the need is ever present for further examination of violence prevention strategies and the implementation of behavioral and systemic strategies within our communities, specifically with our youth.

While the data indicate that mass killings within schools are infrequent, the multiple-victim nature of these events combined with the cultural vehicles of information dissemination tends to create a widespread ripple effect throughout our families, schools, communities, and nation. While many caring individuals and organizations try to bring peace to communities by homogenizing these violent acts to certain methods or characteristics, the fact remains that these acts of mass murder are complex and often leave professional school counselors with the post-event fallout for months and sometimes years to come.

Description of Case

It was anything but the typical day at this Midwest high school. The hallways were quieter than usual as a limited number of students began trickling in after their unplanned break from school following a violent attack from a former student. The fresh smell of paint and repaired doors and windows drew the attention of students who last saw them fractured and destroyed by the violent attack. The heavy media presence across the street from the building marked the significance of students returning to the building for the first time since the shooting.

Beth was a professional school counselor at this high school for 11 years and was a good friend of many of the faculty members. She knew most of the students by name and was a favorite among them for her wit, kindness, and support during many seasons of their high school experience. Beth was also close with all of the victims, including the faculty members who were wounded and the families who lost their loved ones. She had arrived at the school hours earlier to set up rooms for crisis and grief counselors from other schools, city agencies, and other community agencies. The entire week seemed surreal, and her own grief surfaced periodically throughout the morning. The perceived need to *keep it together for the students* was her only motivation to suck back her own strong emotions and her overwhelming thought that things would never be the same at her beloved school. The lives permanently changed. Innocents lost. A new vulnerability surfaced and was nearly palpable.

As the morning light began to lighten familiar hallways as if nothing unusual happened, final preparations were made to memorials in key locations sure to draw the attention of students and staff. Beth checked her voicemails, which ranged from parents, support from the school division, caring professionals in the community, and of course, multiple national news sources wanting an interview. The additional police presence and additional counseling support on scene were a welcome sight to students and parents. Teachers, administration, and support staff consoled each other and attempted to comfort one another in the midst of the awkward struggle: to balance grief with tears while striving for hope in the future. As the buses began to arrive, the students who returned held each other, cried, and grieved together as they slowly entered the building. The sea of caring professionals and new adults in the building confirmed the significance of this day. As appreciative as students were to have them there, the line to receive support was wrapped around Beth. She was overwhelmed with the task of providing care to all of these students yet understood that she was the one they had developed a relationship with over the years.

Her relationship with students and the pre-crisis understanding of their functioning made Beth the perfect lead to begin some grief groups for those struggling the most. She thought, "How am I supposed to triage the hurting?" With the hurricane of her own emotions and losses surfacing similar to everyone else in the building impacted by this violent act, she began to educate faculty and families on the signs of acute stress and post-traumatic stress disorder symptoms. Beth began to evaluate needs, find natural connections, and place students into process groups that she could continue facilitating for six to eight weeks in order to assist students in processing feelings of grief and loss, which were rather foreign to them.

Day-by-day, week-by-week, additional grief support slowly began to thin. With her self-care and compassion fatigue closely monitored, she continued to connect with students and continued to process through deep feelings of hurt and pain. When she returned home at night, she wrestled to get to sleep, often waking up thinking about her students and their struggles. Many, she thought, would have difficulties; most seemed to have developed an unexpected resilience returning to a state of mental and physical homeostasis while others appeared *stuck*. Beth would process through her challenges weekly in her own time with her therapist. The critical incident stress debriefing techniques offered by her therapist were welcomed new additions to their time together that seemed to help with the vicarious trauma and her personal aftermath.

Week to week, students continued to process. Outside referrals were made for several parents to provide additional support, while Beth continued to walk through a life-changing event with students, faculty, families, and her community. Her pre-event typical duties seemed impossible to consider with the unplanned demand for other counseling services within the building. The *new normal* seemed like an impossible consideration. Until that day, she would continue to instill hope, inspire post-traumatic growth, and walk with the hurting through one of the most unfathomable events of their lives.

Strategies for Consideration

The case study reveals how overwhelming the school counselor's role might be in the aftermath of a school shooting. So many students, teachers, administrators, and parents needed support in this scenario. The following strategies will assist school counselors who have the daunting task of responding to such a horrific event. Clearly, the relationship a counselor has with the clientele in a school setting will determine the effectiveness of a variety of interventions.

Theoretical Frameworks

The advantage the school counselor has in the outcome of an event is the relationship and shared experience of the environment and event with the students needing care. In the immediate aftershock and the entire process of recovery, basic counseling skills are necessary for healthy care of students. Core counseling skills include active listening or a basic listening sequence. The ability for the school counselor to remain present with students who are experiencing a vast array of unwanted feelings and symptoms is critical to maintain their openness and trust. Empathy and empathic responses are also critical to progress. Empathy and sympathy are two completely different responses. An empathic response, one that taps into a feeling or experience in the counselor's life or past that is similar to experience what the student is feeling in that moment, helps the counselor walk with the student through it. Unconditional positive regard is also important to assist clients with maintaining openness as they process the hurt and pain. Confidentiality is critical, as their story being entrusted to you may be one of their most vulnerable and painful moments, all of which should be treated as sacred.

Cognitive behavioral therapy (CBT) (Beck, 2011) is a strong evidence-based approach to enable counselors to help students process through their hurt and pain that they cannot control. Counselors can assist students as they regain control over the parts of their lives over which they have influence. The techniques of CBT can assist school faculty and other persons in the building as they continue to help each other walk through pain and suffering related to the losses associated with the event. These techniques might include journaling, charting feelings over time, setting goals that focus on returning to previous activities and rituals, and creating memorials for the deceased.

Trauma-focused cognitive behavioral therapy (TF-CBT) (U.S. Department of Health and Human Services, 2012) is one treatment protocol that counselor researchers have demonstrated to be effective for treatment of PTSD and other related issues. A hybrid model, TF-CBT integrates trauma sensitive interventions with cognitive behavioral principles. It also utilizes attachment theory, developmental neurobiology, family systems, empowerment, and humanistic therapy. It involves components related to psychoeducation, parenting skills, relaxation, affect control, cognitive processing, trauma narrative work, and in vivo desensitization.

Professional Experiences

The first author has worked with victims of several recent mass shootings across the country and most recently provided death notification for more than half of the families of a recent mass shooting event, as well as continued care for some families and individuals. Both authors worked directly at the notification and reunification center of a recent mass shooting from 6 p.m. until 1 a.m. in the morning, walking with numerous families through one of the most painful situations they will likely ever experience.

It is important in the first moments after a traumatic event for school counselors to be comfortable working with many different levels of impairment within their students outside the comforts of their office and typical environment. During the immediate moments, core clinical skills and empathy are necessary to allow people to process. One of the most critical skills that a school counselor can use in those events is to remain present emotionally with the client while they process through struggles and events. During the periods immediately following the most recent mass shooting event, the relationship with victims' families was of paramount importance and was protected with the highest level of confidentiality and privacy. The high-profile nature of these events causes those who report on these events to seek any source to gain a soundbite or quote. These *opportunities* can cause those you are trying to reach to question your motivation for hearing details from their experience. Reassurance that you are only with them to provide comfort and support is important.

Critical incidents such as a mass shooting involve significant grief and loss for many individuals and stakeholders. From the individuals who knew the deceased to those who are watching and following the story closely through the media, losses may range from physically losing contact with a good friend and support to the loss of innocents with a new vulnerability. It is important to understand both losses and the process of grief. A loss is being deprived of or ceasing to have something that one formerly possessed or to which one was attached. A loss could be material, relational, psychological, systemic, or functional, such as a physical ability or loss of health. While some individuals possess a significant level of resilience toward losses, almost everyone involved in a mass shooting within a school will experience some level of loss. An individual's reaction to a loss can be impacted by many different factors including the person's age, gender, religion, personality, and experiences with previous losses.

Grief is the normal, dynamic process that occurs in response to any type of loss (Kubler-Ross, 1970). It may encompass physical, cognitive, emotional, social, and spiritual responses to loss. Grief is a process and not a single event. It is not unusual for students who are experiencing grief to have a wide array of somatic complaints such as headaches, nausea, appetite disturbance, fatigue, or insomnia. They may experience feelings of sorrow, anxiety, anger, numbness, and even helplessness. Memory disturbances and inability to concentrate often mark the experience of those moving through the grieving process. Complicated grief happens when an individual becomes *stuck* in the grieving process. They may struggle with delaying the integration of the loss into the present or even completely deny it occurred. Sometimes grief can be distorted by those who are stuck and can be viewed as a positive event or a relief.

While there are many models of grief, it is important to understand that processing grief is not a linear process. Kubler-Ross's (1970) stages of grief include denial, anger, bargaining, depression, and acceptance. Many professionals share these stages with individuals to assist with explaining the complexity of the process. Rando (1993) developed the Six R Process that counselors can use to process grief with clients. First, the client *recognizes* the loss. Then they react to the separation from the loss. Next, they *recoll*ect and *reexperience* the deceased and their relationship with them. Then they *relinquish* old attachments, *readjusting* to move adaptively into the new world without forgetting the old. Finally, they *reinvest* in the future. This takes time to process, and everyone moves at their own pace. This process can be adapted to an understanding of the nonlinear process of grief.

It is important for the counselor to be available to students after a traumatic event. The school counselor does not need to be intrusive but rather available when students want to talk. It is important for students to tell their stories of loss, wounds, and the deceased. Students need to have permission to grieve and express anger and sadness in ways that are not harmful to themselves or others. As counselors, it is also important that we do not attempt to offer stories of our own or self-disclose, as it can be experienced as demeaning and invalidating of the students' own experiences. The school counselor may encourage journaling, creative expression, support groups, talking with other professionals, and monitoring individuals' self-care.

Counselor Impact

The first author has seen and personally found significant benefit from critical incident stress debriefing after working with victims of mass shootings. It is highly likely that school counselors would become overwhelmed with the needs of everyone in school after an event, attempting to meet as many needs as possible. This systemic overload would be difficult to bear even without any personal impact from a mass shooting. In the case study scenario, Beth knew the teachers and students affected most by this event and was herself at risk of harm during the event in the building. While she may possess very strong resilience, she needs to monitor herself for compassion fatigue in the upcoming weeks and months to make sure she is avoiding burnout and is able to continue to provide the highest level of care to her students.

An individual therapist should be considered immediately following an event such as this. Trauma informed therapists would be able to provide critical incident stress debriefings as well as administer assessments such as the ProQOL, a quality of life measure. Self-care is critical to all school counselors and other counseling professionals, especially those who are experiencing the synergistic weight of helping their school through a mass shooting or other traumatic event. Beth may choose to use a plan such as Myers and Sweeney's (2005) personal wellness plan, which provides a structure for the development of five factors of self-care which include the creative self, coping self, social self, essential self, and physical self.

Coauthor Dr. Jamie Holland reports that when it comes to stress and trauma response, one cannot cut the head off the body or cut the body off the head. It is almost impossible for stress to be in the mind if the body is relaxed or vice versa. Therefore, it is critical to focus on mindfulness, deep breathing relaxation, progressive relaxation, and other wellness activities for the physical body in order to maintain emotional wellness during the critical moments that occur immediately after an event, such as a mass shooting. Dr. Jamie Holland's work with mass shooting victims focused immediately on meeting Maslow's hierarchy of needs, with an emphasis on physical needs during the moments when she participated in notifying families that they would not be seeing their loved ones again. In this case study, the focus should be on Beth's overall wellness to create positive habits and patterns of wellness that could sustain the increased level of stress experienced during her post-critical incident work.

As long as Beth can provide a solid boundary between her processes and those around her, she would be effective at assisting others with processing through the pain and event. She would need to obtain support through collaboration with other trusted professionals to assist her with identifying blind spots of self-care since she may become stuck from her own trauma processing as well as potential vicarious trauma processing. She is likely to notice the direction students may go as they work through their own issues to identify those who are struggling more significantly and those who have an increased level of resilience, differentiating between unhealthy processes and resilience. For this reason, it is critical that she demonstrate a high level of self-care while meeting the needs of others around her as one of the most effective tools in the system.

Mental Health Implications

Post-traumatic stress disorder will likely occur in those who are struggling with events they have witnessed or experienced that are understandably beyond their level of resilience. They may be experiencing intrusive and repetitive ideation, denial or some level of emotional guilt, increased nervous symptom arousal, or some level of disassociation. Some individuals may experience maladaptive patterns such as survivors' guilt, a clear vision of their own death, desensitization, emotional fixation, or feelings of potential insignificance in future relationships.

Symptoms in children may include regressive behaviors, agitation, generalized nightmares, and somatic complaints such as headaches and stomachaches. They may also experience comorbid anxiety, phobias, depression, or panic attacks. They are likely to go through reexperiencing symptoms, hyperarousal, and avoidance behaviors.

Students may benefit from several different types of groups that may be led by a school counselor during the post-event phase of recovery. Support groups can help students adjust emotionally and socially through psychoeducation and the processing of shared experiences. Some students may benefit from life adjustment groups that focus on integrating the past experiences into a new way of coping and creating a new direction as a group. Due to the uniqueness of the school environment, these may prove to be effective ways to help one another create new directions and meaning.

It is important to continue to monitor the progress of students who have experienced these types of events well beyond the initial phases of recovery. School counselors should not hesitate to screen for suicidal ideation or other harmful behaviors if they feel a student is not adequately recovering. Additionally, outside resources should be utilized. Referrals to outside therapists and resources can deeply benefit students, and the relationship the school counselor has with them can be the needed motivation to create buy-in for treatment.

In this scenario, Beth was able to bridge the gap between supportive care coming from other agencies, school divisions, and different parts of her state to assist her with services provided to students. She would act more in the role of a facilitator of care than direct provider in many situations and eventually bridge over to providing primary care as outside resources began to leave the building. As the school counselor, Beth had the best relationship with students and therefore would have the easiest access to them processing their pain, grief, and losses. Conversely, Beth would also have the most difficult time among workers of parallel process, with her own grief and loss process running concurrently to those with whom she is working.

Ethical Considerations

Working in an environment that has experienced the unimaginable requires school counselors to maintain the highest level of ethical standards (ASCA, 2016).

> A.1.c Do not diagnose but remain acutely aware of how a student's diagnosis can potentially affect the student's academic success.

The school counselor does not diagnose mental health disorders; however, the school counselor is one of the best resources to identify when somebody is processing grief and loss in a more healthy way, demonstrating higher resilience, or becoming stuck in struggling, needing a higher level of care.

> A.2.c. Are aware that even though attempts are made to obtain informed consent, it is not always possible. When needed, school counselors make counseling decisions on students' behalf that promote students' welfare.

In the mist of critical incident response in triage work, school counselors are unlikely to obtain informed consents to be able to do brief work with as many students as would need services. While the attempt would be made to obtain informed consent, it is important to understand that school counselors need to act with the information they have to provide the best safety and care to students.

> A.2.j Protect the confidentiality of students' records and release personal data in accordance with prescribed federal and state laws and school board policies.

School counselors must do all they can to protect the identity of students involved in critical incidents in mass shootings. This includes providing names to those who call to extract information to which they ethically or legally should not have access. In the past, parties have posed as victims' family members in order to obtain contact information and other news about victims. It is critical that information only be given to proper authorities under the correct legal processes and policies.

> A.7.a Facilitate short-term groups to address students' academic, career and/or social/emotional issues.

The school counselor conducts groups using best practices of group counseling, including screening potential participants and obtaining parent permission for group participation. Engaging in group process related to various levels of struggle with loss would be an excellent way for the school counselor to identify students who are struggling at a deeper level while assisting students with creating new narratives to move ahead into the future.

Multicultural Considerations

It is important to understand that most events that occur within the community manifest within the school in some way. It is impossible to separate the school environment from the community. In many low socioeconomic status (SES) communities, violence and losses are regular occurrences. Students in these areas may struggle from reduced resilience or unhealthy coping strategies to process painful events. It is also relevant to note that many individuals in different communities may lack access to services. Language barriers and cultural differences need to be respected and adjusted to be able to provide the proper support to all students. Likewise, various ethnicities and cultures have additional supports that may be utilized to help the greater community to work through critical events. These unique traits can be an excellent asset to the greater community as they continue to work together through moments of tragedy and loss.

Case Discussion Questions

1. Recall a time you experienced grief. What did individuals say that helped you? What were some things that were said that were not helpful? Is there anything you would have liked to have been handled differently?
2. Describe support that you have in place if needed for your own self-care during a critical incident or immediately following. What is your self-care plan to prevent burnout in process through vicarious trauma?
3. Who are the stakeholders within your building regarding the emotional and mental health care of students following a critical incident? Set up a time to connect and process through resources that may be available and familiarize yourself with your crisis plan in your school.
4. What additional training can you pursue to help your students in the event of critical incidents within the community or the school?
5. What are three pieces of advice that you would give Beth if you knew her and made contact with her by phone as she is experiencing this incident?

Resources

American School Counselor Association: www.schoolcounselor.org/school-counselors/professional-development/learn-more/shooting-resourcesThe National Child Traumatic Stress Network: www.nctsn.org/what-is-child-trauma/trauma-types/terrorism-and-violence/school-shooting-resources

Youth.govhttps://youth.gov/feature-article/federal-resources-helping-youth-cope-after-school-shooting

References

American School Counselor Association. (2016). *Ethical standards for school counselors*. Alexandria, VA: American School Counselor Association.

Beck, J. (2011). *Cognitive behavioral therapy: Basics and beyond* (2nd ed.). New York, NY: Guilford Press.

Bureau of Justice Statistic. (2013). *Firearm violence 1993–2011*. Retrieved October 20, 2019, from www. bjs.gov/content/pub/press/fv9311pr.cfm

Centers for Disease Control and Prevention. (2019).*Characteristics of school-associated youth homicides – United States*. Retrieved from https://www.cdc.gov/mmwr/volumes/68/wr/mm6803a1.htm

Federal Bureau of Investigation. (2019). *2018 crime in the United States report*. Retrieved October 20, 2019, from https://ucr.fbi.gov/crime-in-the-u.s/2018/crime-in-the-u.s.-2018/tables/expanded-homicide-data-table-8.xls

Holland, K. M., Hall, J. E., Wang, J., Gaylor, E. M., Johnson, L. L., & Shelby, D. (2019). Characteristics of school-associated youth homicides-United States, 1994–2018. *Morbidity and Weekly Report Center of Disease Control and Prevention, 68*(3). Retrieved from www.cdc.gov/mmwr/volumes/68/wr/pdfs/mm6803a1-H.pdf

Kachur, S. P., Stennies, G. M., Powell, K. E., Modzeleski, W., Stephens, R., Murphy, R., Kresnow, M., Sleet, D., & Lowry, R. (1996). School-associated violent deaths in the United States, 1992 to 1994. *JAMA, 275*(22), 1729–1733. doi:10.1001/jama.1996.03530460033027

Kubler-Ross, E. (1970). *On death and dying*. London: Tavistock.

Myers, J. E., & Sweeney, T. J. (2005). *The five factor well inventory*. Greensboro, NC: Authors.

Rando, T. A. (1993). *Treatment of complicated mourning*. Champaign, IL: Research Press.

U.S. Department of Health and Human Services. (2012). *Trauma-focused cognitive behavioral therapy for children affected by sexual abuse or trauma*. Child Welfare Information Gateway. Retrieved from http://www.ncsby.org/sites/default/files/resources/TF-CBT%20for%20Children%20Affedcted%20by%20Sexual%20Abuse%20or%20Trauma%20-%20Child%20Welfare%20Info.%20Gateway.pdf

Reflections: In the space provided below, write your notes and reflections regarding this case study and chapter.

28 A Pandemic

Judy A. Nelson

Background

Just as we were about to *put this book to bed*, a worldwide pandemic spread around the globe at lightning speed, impacting children and families throughout the world. While we still do not know how many people ultimately will be affected or when a vaccine will be ready that will help humans fight this disease, we thought that we should include a short chapter on this phenomenon, which most likely will not be the last pandemic we will experience.

In brief, the following describes how this pandemic began and what is happening to date. According to *Scripps Research Institute* (2020), on December 31, 2019, Chinese authorities alerted the World Health Organization (WHO) of an outbreak of a novel strain of coronavirus causing severe illness. Specifically, this virus is named SARS coronavirus-2, and the disease caused by the virus is COVID-19. Chinese authorities rapidly detected the epidemic and posited that the number of COVID-19 cases was increasing because of human-to-human transmission after a single introduction into the human population.

Coronaviruses are a large family of viruses that can cause illnesses ranging widely in severity (Deutsches Primatenzentrum (DPZ)/German Primate Center, 2020). The first known severe illness caused by a coronavirus emerged with the 2003 severe acute respiratory syndrome (SARS) epidemic in China. A second outbreak of severe illness began in 2012 in Saudi Arabia with the Middle East respiratory syndrome (MERS). The origin of the virus in humans most likely was the result of a human coming in contact with an animal that carried the virus. No vaccines or drugs are currently (at this writing) available to stop the spread of the virus; however, doctors and scientists all over the world are hoping to find a viable vaccine for the COVID-19 as quickly as possible.

School counselors in the United States have never had to respond to a pandemic, but some may have responded to flu epidemics or measles outbreaks that affected their school community. In general, being sick is—at the very least—annoying and, in some cases, fear and anxiety provoking or even deadly. In the case of a pandemic, students, parents, and school personnel may find that they are depressed and anxious about the future. They might experience school and other public venue closures, a shortage of supplies including food, mandates to *shelter in place*, job termination, and other changes in daily living that they have not experienced before.

Some families may experience fear for the safety of their loved ones who live in other states or countries. Families with elders may worry that their loved ones are especially compromised due to old age and other health issues. Some parents might lose their jobs or be temporarily laid off due to closures or lack of consumer traffic in stores, restaurants, and other businesses. Those who are lucky enough to keep their jobs may be working remotely from home in order to avoid the spread of the disease. Working from home can cause feelings of isolation and, more specifically, cause high levels of frustration because having to perform a job remotely (i.e., the use of multiple technology platforms) is not comfortable and creates a substantial learning curve. If parents do have to go to work, they might be concerned about leaving their children who are out of school at home alone, or they might not be able to find appropriate childcare for very young children. Clearly, a pandemic changes life in ways we never imagined. The following is a brief description of a possible case involving a school counselor and subsequent ideas about how to assist students, parents, and school staff during these unprecedented times.

Description of the Case

Mrs. Wright, the counselor at Remy Elementary, was somewhat alarmed to read the news in January of 2020 that a new virus had spread to thousands of people in China. While she knew of other fast-spreading viruses, according to the news, this virus was spreading very quickly, and doctors and scientists were working tirelessly to stop the flow of the virus before it reached other parts of the country. The counselor went about her usual school day and forgot about the COVID-19 disease caused by the virus until the next morning, when she read that the disease had spread to other countries. During the next couple of weeks, Mrs. Wright, along with other school personnel and parents of the students they served, became more alarmed. Finally, it was obvious that this was a pandemic of great proportions and that the United States would not be spared.

As state governments, counties, cities, and townships grappled with how to halt the spread of COVID-19 in the United States and how to protect the most vulnerable people in their communities, Mrs. Wright decided to create some resources for her staff, parents, and students. Her goal was to help them cope with the impending dangers and inconveniences of a pandemic, a situation that none of them had experienced until now. She knew that her time was limited because the governor of her state was talking about the closing of all public meeting places, including schools, to ward off the human-to-human contact as much as possible. The following sections discuss the ideas and strategies that Mrs. Wright considered and implemented to help her community deal with this pandemic.

Strategies for Consideration

Like most school counselors, Mrs. Wright wants to continue to assist her students and their parents throughout the pandemic. She will be creative and take great initiative in order to provide counseling services to her clientele. The following sections review some of the strategies that school counselors like Mrs. Wright might consider or might even be implementing now.

Theoretical Frameworks

A pandemic requires information that is factual and current to ward off rumors and mistaken ideas about the disease. School counselors can assist in informing the school community with accurate information by staying connected to sites like the Centers for Disease Control and Prevention (CDC), professional organizations such as the American Counseling Association (ACA) and the American School Counselor Association (ASCA), school district communication, and other verifiable entities. The next step is to use psychoeducational strategies to help students, parents, and teachers understand their feelings during the crisis. Assuring clients that it is normal to be worried and frustrated about the future, about how long the outbreak might last, and about the disruption to everyday life should be some of the school counselor's goals. Counselors also can help students understand that it is normal to worry about loved ones with compromised health issues, about financial problems, and about missing plans that were made before the pandemic.

In addition to psychoeducational strategies, school counselors know that techniques that are evidence based will provide the most help for students during a crisis. For example, students might respond well to cognitive behavioral therapy (CBT) [Beck, 2011] to dispel anxiety and depression. Keeping journals, charting feelings, challenging cognitive distortions, and relaxed breathing exercises are some of the techniques used in CBT, and counselors can use these techniques in either face-to-face or virtual sessions with student clients.

Another theory that would be helpful for school counselors in working with children or adolescents is relational-cultural theory (RCT). This theory is quite relevant because of the dangers of bigotry, discrimination, ostracism, and ageism during a pandemic. Relational-cultural theory explains the social implications of psychological theory. In this case, it would bring together the focus of the influence of the larger culture (i.e., non-sick persons) versus the minority or marginalized persons (i.e., those who could be infected) and looks deeply at the effects of this power differential on the ability to have healthy coexistences. The school counselor uses RCT to increase empathy in working with students and families. Helping students understand that the ramifications of social pain (i.e., separation and rejection) and physical pain are similar and equally devastating.

Professional Experiences

The author reached out to school counselors across the United States to find out how they are coping with this pandemic. Specifically, she wanted to know what interventions school counselors have employed to continue to assist students who may be experiencing challenges due to school closures, parents who are anxious, and everyone isolated from friends, coworkers, and teachers. As always, school counselors are creating interventions and programs as the need arises. Some of those interventions include

- making virtual counseling appointments through social media;
- checking in with students regarding their physical and mental health;
- using all available media to continue to provide counseling services and important information to all students, particularly when schools are closed for long periods;
- providing fact sheets to staff and parents to dispel myths and to remind everyone how to stay safe and healthy;
- providing staff development to help teachers watch for signs of extreme duress in students;
- providing help to teachers and students moving their classes online; and
- advocating for the school district to continue providing free and reduced breakfast and lunch to those who qualify if the school closes.

Many children across the country rely on their meals at school to receive the basic nourishment needed for healthy growth. Some schools have a drive-up door to which parents can pick up those meals, and other districts are delivering meals. On the down side, one school counselor reported that her counseling team was told at the end of one day that the school would close the next day. She said that she and her team were working frantically to reach out to students via emails and phone calls and trying to make plans to provide services virtually. Some counselors who worked in schools that closed abruptly created check-in sheets that they emailed out to all of their clients. These sheets asked questions in age-specific language about how students are feeling, how well they slept the night before, what meals they have eaten, and other general questions about students' well-being. One high school counselor whose clientele consists of seniors created a senior check-in sheet. This sheet included directions on how to make a virtual appointment with the counselor and how the counselor could best contact the student (email, text, cell phone, google classroom, Instagram). Other questions were relevant to the students' four-year-plans, what they plan to do after graduation, whether or not they have applied to any universities or colleges, and what assistance they might need at this time.

One high school counseling team reached out to their families through email and provided information on how their students could make an appointment for a virtual counseling session.

The team also developed a google classroom of optional activities to help students and parents thrive through distance learning. The intent was to help make a difference in the physical and emotional well-being of their students and families. They also invited their clients to suggest topics of interest so that the counselors could post relevant information in the google classroom. In another district, school counselors in high schools are utilizing google classroom to post updates regarding the district's plans during school closures and *go lunch* for their students who receive free lunch. They also posted *career of the day* links each day to all four grade levels, posted links to resources on college information, and linked resources on mental health information. They are also using both ASCA, ACA, and resources from their local professional organizations to assist students with current information. Checking emails and text messaging is very important as many students try to connect via social media.

Other school counselors reported that they are creating classroom guidance lessons relevant to the crisis and posting them on YouTube or on their districts' website for parents and students to view. Some counselors sent me lists of free videos and other lesson plans for use at home or at school. Many of the school counselors who responded to me had created video talks of themselves reaching out to students and their families and assuring them that the school counselor is still available to assist. Another counselor created an online book explaining the coronavirus to elementary students and shared this in an online listserv for anyone to use. One counselor educator referred the author to the many Facebook groups specifically for school counselors. If school counselors want to engage with others and find a host of ideas shared by many of these counselors for the challenges of a pandemic, they can search on Facebook for *school counselor groups*. There are many groups listed, some by states, others by secondary or elementary levels, and some that are for private or charter schools. Several of these sites are listed at the end of this chapter under Resources.

Counselor Impact

The Facebook groups mentioned help support school counselors by providing ideas, but they also provide the emotional support needed during a crisis. School counselors who live and work in remote areas or small school districts may feel particularly isolated and would find these groups very helpful. As with any type of crisis work, school counselors are only as good as their own self-care. When dealing with the possibility of becoming ill themselves, school counselors must adhere to the health and safety measures put out by the Centers for Disease Control and Prevention (CDC). Briefly, these include:

- **Wash your hands** often with soap and water for at least 20 seconds, especially after you have been in a public place, or after blowing your nose, coughing, or sneezing.
- If soap and water are not readily available, **use a hand sanitizer that contains at least 60% alcohol**. Cover all surfaces of your hands and rub them together until they feel dry.
- **Avoid touching your eyes, nose, and mouth** with unwashed hands.
- **Avoid close contact** with people who are sick
- Put **distance between yourself and other people** if COVID-19 is spreading in your community.
- **Clean AND disinfect frequently touched surfaces daily**. This includes tables, doorknobs, light switches, countertops, handles, desks, phones, keyboards, toilets, faucets, and sinks.
- **If surfaces are dirty, clean them:** Use detergent or soap and water prior to disinfection.

Finally, school counselors have an intrapersonal dichotomy to negotiate. How a school counselor can assist possibly infected students or their families and maintain his or her own health is quite difficult to decipher. Not all schools will cancel their sessions. Therefore, how might school counselors assist students or families who come to their office? What safety features might schools employ to help staff maintain safety and health? Without having knowledge of where students or parents traveled or with whom they have come into contact, school counselor's ability to practice might be compromised. These are all considerations that school counselors must navigate during a pandemic.

Mental Health Implications

School counselors are trained to pay attention to students who might exhibit signs of mental illness. When children, particularly adolescents, are isolated from their friends, they might become agitated, angry, resentful, and generally unpleasant to be around! However, the challenges of a pandemic might cause some students to become depressed or anxious. Many schools will close for a period of time, which will isolate students and possibly exacerbate symptoms. Setting up ways to communicate with students via social media could help counselors continue to monitor students who are at risk. School counselors will continue to make referrals to other mental health professionals in the community as indicated. Parents of students who have severe symptoms related to depression, anxiety, or other mental health disorders should be informed and provided with counseling options.

During a crisis, parents might be overwhelmed themselves and might need support in how to manage information they give to their children regarding the pandemic. As with any type of crisis, it is not healthy for children to tune in to television or social media constantly where they are inundated with negative talk about what is happening. This can be frightening to young children in particular and can cause unnecessary worry and fear. School counselors can coach parents to turn off the electronics and involve their children in games, outside play, reading, and activities that the school counselors provide. There are several resources provided for parents at the end of this chapter.

School counselors should take the time to contact outside mental health professionals and to find out if they are seeing new clients and whether they are conducting face-to-face sessions or online sessions. The Centers for Disease Control and Prevention (CDC), the Council for Accreditation of Counseling and Related Programs (CACREP), and various state governments lifted some HIPPA requirements, professional standards, and state regulations to make it easier for counselors to transition from face-to-face sessions to online sessions.

Ethical Considerations

No matter how school counselors determine ways to continue to provide services to their constituents, they must continue to adhere to the ASCA Code of Ethical Standards (ASCA, 2016). The following standards are relevant to school counselors as they navigate the challenges of a pandemic.

A.1. Supporting Student Development

Primarily, school counselors are charged with supporting student development. To summarize, this standard includes being respectful of students and families, providing brief interventions and making referrals as necessary, respecting the beliefs and values of their clients, and encouraging each student's maximum development. School counselors are concerned with every student's academic, career and social/emotional needs and is aware of the importance of the role of parents and guardians in students' development.

Additionally, maintaining appropriate boundaries and being aware that any sexual or romantic relationship with students is considered a breach of ethics and is prohibited regardless of a student's age and applies to both in-person and electronic interactions and relationships. It might be tempting or very easy to slip into a casual relationship with students, particularly if social media is being widely used during a crisis. The importance of maintaining professional boundaries cannot be emphasized enough. Students might think that it is fun to interact with school personnel via text messaging, iChat, and other venues. They may find it difficult to take these interactions seriously, particularly if the adults are not acting in a professional manner. Opportunities for cyberbullying and posting rumors or inaccurate information might increase. These are possibilities that school counselors must think about before embarking on new ways to communicate with students.

A.2. Confidentiality

Confidentiality is the hallmark of the counselor and client relationship. Moving counseling services to a virtual format might create challenges for information meant to be confidential. The highest standard of care is that virtual counseling is only conducted with counselor training or certification, with software that is encrypted and secure, and that the setting for both the counselor and the client is private. During this recent pandemic, some professional organizations, state legislatures, and other entities are making mental health services available to all those who need them by allowing counselors to use telephone and other non-secure means of talking to clients.

A.15. Virtual/Distance School Counseling

School counselors must adhere to the same ethical guidelines in a virtual/distance setting that school counselors use in face-to-face settings. It is important for counselors to recognize and acknowledge the unique challenges and limitations of virtual/distance school counseling. Counselors cannot be available every day all day; therefore, they must implement procedures for students to follow in both emergency and nonemergency situations when the school counselor is not available. Posting the school counselor's availability on the school website is one way to inform students and parents of the school counseling staff's schedules. Sending out an email to all families in the school counselor's caseload is another way to insure that clients understand how to access counseling services.

Additionally, counselors must reduce as much as possible the limits of confidentiality in virtual counseling sessions and make sure that students and parents recognize those limits. Since students are presumably at home during contact with school personnel, they must be informed about both the benefits and limitations of virtual counseling sessions. It is the responsibility of the school counselor to educate students on how to participate in the electronic school counseling relationship to minimize and prevent potential misunderstandings. School counselors could create a training module regarding virtual counseling to post on the school or district website, or they can introduce each session with information about confidentiality limitations and the virtual counselor/student relationship.

Multicultural Considerations

There are a number of critical issues to consider related to the pandemic and the diversity of our public and private schools. First, not all students will have access to the internet if their schools are closed. How will they engage in online learning, and how will they have access to the school counselor if this is the case? The school counselor should make sure that administrators take this possibility into consideration when creating a plan for a continuation of student learning if schools are closed. Language barriers are another consideration. Families whose first language is not English may feel particularly isolated if they do not understand what is being communicated from the school district. School counselors know their constituents and can predict their needs in a pandemic. They can then advocate for these needs so that information is provided in a way that all clientele understand the risks of COVID-19, how to stay safe and healthy, and how to access additional help if needed. There are excellent videos on the internet that rely mostly on cartoons and other pictures to provide examples of what to do to stay healthy during a pandemic. Lastly, it is important that school counselors mitigate the temptation of some to blame the pandemic on certain ethnic or age groups. Providing accurate information to families is one way to combat this unfortunate tendency.

Case Discussion Questions

1. What competencies might be needed to provide virtual services to students in the case of long-term school closings? Do you hold these competencies? If not, where can you receive training?
2. Clearly, school counselors must create a *bank* of online resources for students and families that will be helpful during a pandemic. Research the online resources and create your *bank*.
3. Create an email and a video presentation that introduces yourself to parents and provides information on what services you can continue to offer during a school closing.
4. Research the most reliable ways for you to receive accurate information during a pandemic. Create a list of these resources and include them in your *bank*.
5. Research the rules and regulations of virtual counseling sessions. Professional organizations have ethical codes specific to these, and state counseling boards also have requirements for virtual sessions. Find out what you would need to do to provide online counseling services.

Resources

For Counselors

For many resources for school counselors: www.schoolcounselor.org/school-counselors/professional-development/learn-more/coronavirus-resources
For all counselors: www.facebook.com/AmericanSchoolCounselorAssociation/
For elementary counselors: www.facebook.com/groups/590701787640166/
For middle school counselors: www.facebook.com/groups/176582632507419/
For high school counselors: www.facebook.com/groups/149658681898931/

For Parents

www.cdc.gov/coronavirus/2019-ncov/community/schools-childcare/talking-with-children.html
www.unicef.org/coronavirus/6-ways-parents-can-support-their-kids-through-coronavirus-covid-19
www.pbs.org/parents/thrive/how-to-talk-to-your-kids-about-coronavirus

References

American School Counselor Association. (2016). *Ethical standards for school counselors*. Alexandria, VA: American School Counselor Association.
Beck, J. (2011). *Cognitive behavioral therapy: Basics and beyond* (2nd ed.). New York, NY: Guilford Press.
Deutsches Primatenzentrum (DPZ), & German Primate Center. (2020, March 5). Preventing spread of SARS coronavirus-2 in humans: Infection researchers identify potential drug. *ScienceDaily*. Retrieved from www.sciencedaily.com/releases/2020/03/200305132039.htm
Scripps Research Institute. (2020, March 17). COVID-19 coronavirus epidemic has a natural origin. *ScienceDaily*. Retrieved from www.sciencedaily.com/releases/2020/03/200317175442.htm

Epilogue

Cheryl Sawyer

Every day, the media reports on unique challenges to our world, many of which come in the form of crisis. Whether crisis is personal, such as illness, rape, and divorce, or community based, such as a school shooting or natural disaster, crisis can present unique challenges that can affect the ability of a child to perform in school, an educator to guide a lesson, the expected performance of a school counselor, or even a community's ability to stabilize. Crisis is defined as "a perception or experiencing of an event or situation as an intolerable difficulty that exceeds the person's current resources and coping mechanisms" (James, 2008, p. 3). These phenomena often happen without warning and with unanticipated consequences rippling throughout the educational community.

While the burden of providing post-crisis counseling or therapy for the students, staff, or immediate community does not usually fall on the school counselor alone, the school counselor is often intricately involved in supporting the school and often the extended educational community through the initial critical intervention, often guiding those affected to responsive care that has longer-term effects. Effective, responsive counselors must be cognizant of the various types of crises as well as established theories of intervention and combine this knowledge with the realities surrounding each unique situation. For instance, Hurricane Katrina created a crisis for students who lived in New Orleans by forcing them to relocate to safer, drier areas of the country. Greater Houston area schools were impacted differently during this crisis when they received thousands of traumatized and displaced children into a very diverse and different Houston school system within only a few days.

Prepared counselors will collect and organize available resources and support personnel that they access with a moment's notice. Some counselors have an easily accessible *response* travel bag containing activities that they retrieve in the event of a death at a neighboring school. Others have pre-selected books on their shelves that they use when supporting a more individual crisis such as illness or divorce. Competent counselors analyze their own personal strengths and skills and plan strategies for acquiring additional personnel to support areas of need. Not every counselor needs to visit the victims of a bus wreck at the hospital, yet most know to whom they can reach out for assistance with this task. A counselor who wants to be able to respond effectively in the future has a documented plan for self-care that can be implemented at the end of a long, hard day of supporting others. Failure to address self-care in the aftermath of a crisis can lead directly to counselor burnout.

Empowering a student during a crisis is crucial to a successful and long-term outcome. Crisis, by its very definition, involves unexpected change. A counselor whose mission is to guide and support students through this change will focus on working with students to create a base structure that can flex with the change yet still find an element of control in a seemingly chaotic situation. Recognizing and recreating even small patterns can provide students with an element of familiarity and comfort as they integrate new realities into known schemas. For instance, a student who has experienced sudden relocation due to a devastating flood might establish personal control by recreating some semblance of a typical daily routine. A few minutes of quiet meditation followed by traditional morning cup of tea can be replicated in a variety of settings, whether in the student's home, a camper, a hotel room, or even a corner of the school counselor's office. Although a student's base, their home, has changed, continuing at least part of the student's familiar schema can create a sense of control and empowerment. Encouraging a student to establish a parallel routine for doing their homework can help the student find familiarity and control in a new living situation. Students who have learned to put on headphones, close their eyes, and listen to music can control their environment whether in the school cafeteria, the bus, the classroom, or an overcrowded shelter. The establishment of small replicable patterns can often provide the necessary structure so that students feel some level of empowerment during a time of unsettling change.

Students who experience symptoms of post-traumatic stress disorder (PTSD) are often more strongly impacted during a crisis. For many students, both known and unknown elements of any crisis can trigger the autonomic nervous system (ANS) and exacerbate both the PTSD and the crisis. Triggers have the potential to replay previous disruptive sequences and initiate powerful past emotions or physical sensations. The student's ANS has often lost the ability to differentiate between past and present; therefore, perceptions, thoughts, behaviors, and actions from the past can be replicated in the midst of the existing crisis (Rothschild, 2000; Schwartz, 2018). The student may experience unanticipated hopelessness, rage, depression, flashbacks, impulsivity, psychosis, or even symptoms of dissociation that, while triggered by the current crisis, are not actually connected to the immediate crisis. These students often need immediate attention and support in order to prevent a secondary crisis.

Counselor self-care is crucial to the well-being of the students, the counselor's friends and family, and the counselor. Self-care begins with acquiring and internalizing best practices, theory, and supervised experiences associated with crisis. A counselor with strong self-efficacy in addressing crisis enters the situation armed with confidence. Counselors who are capable during a crisis also have an ingrained understanding that adhering to a preestablished self-care plan is a crucial part of crisis response. This effective self-care plan will include strategies for maintaining the counselor during the crisis as well as after. Practical, personal elements cannot be cast aside. Although the counselor must be focused on the crisis at hand, a competent counselor knows the value of personal hydration, a few minutes for focused breathing, a healthy snack, and a competent, trustworthy friend who can be available for conversation after a day of vigilantly and effectively supporting students through crises.

You have the knowledge, skill, and compassion to help others heal from crises and tragedies. You use your energy to help them find hope in a chaotic world. They have shared their darkness with you during a critical period of their lives because you built a bridge to assure that they are not alone. However, their pain is not your pain. Do not hold onto it. Let their pain wash through you like water through a sieve. Only save the thoughts that you were able to help them. You were kind. You brought calm. You listened and you brought hope. Now, it is time for you to let it all go.

We all have our bad days
We're not strangers to the rain
There's demons hiding in the dark—
With eyes fired-up in pain.
But before you pull that trigger,
Or put hanging to the test
Consider who you're hurting,
And WHO cleans up the mess.
The horror of a suicide
The pain that we'll all feel

Will outlast other memories
Cause you gave us this ordeal.
So if you're screaming
Or you're scheming, Our answer's crystal clear
Do your friends a favor
Get some counseling this year.
Dr. Cheryl Sawyer

References

James, R. (2008). *Crisis intervention strategies* (6th ed.). Belmont, CA: Thomson.

Rothschild, B. (2000). *The body remembers: The psychophysiology of trauma and trauma treatment.* New York: W. W. Norton & Company.

Schwartz, J. (2018, January 26). New PTSD study shows recovery for Fort Hood soldiers in just two weeks. *TCA Regional News.* Retrieved from http://search.proquest.com/docview/1991433929/

Appendices

Appendix A

Critical Incident Template

The Critical Incident Template is an outline that will assist school counselors in knowing what components can be included in their critical incident and personal safety plan for students. This template is a reference tool to help school counselors devise procedures that will assess students in critical incidences.

1. **Risk Assessment Screening Tool**—This includes both qualitative measures such as questions and quantitative measures such as a screening tools or formal assessment.
2. **Level of Risk**—Assessing the level of risk as low, moderate, or severe and properly documenting should serve as a product of the assessment screening process.
3. **Step-by-Step Procedures for Student Stabilization**—If it is determined a student is in any way at-risk due to an indication of moderate to high level of risk, with an intent present, a plan, means or access to weapons, and/or the presence of hopelessness or depression, procedures to stabilize the student is the priority.
4. **Personal Safety Plan or Self-Care Agreement**—There are several components of a personal safety plan. As a school counselor, you may have other items for inclusion to consider. Creating a safety plan and including the students and their parents in the planning process guarantee that all parties understand the problem and agree to the interventions. A safety plan should include input from school administration, campus law enforcement, the school counselor, the social worker, the victim and perpetrator, and their parents. However, document the warning signs, coping strategies, people and social settings (i.e. parents should be included), professionals or agencies that can be contacted during a crisis, and interventions to create a safe environment. The end result should be a listing of who completes various tasks, by what date these tasks will be completed, and who will document the completion of tasks for the safety plan.
5. **Step-by-Step Procedures**—If it is determined that a critical incident occurred (i.e. suicide or natural disaster), then procedures for school counselors should be in place and must be followed. A team approach for addressing these procedures insures that no one person is burdened with the aftermath of a crisis. The steps to responding would include arranging for the personal safety of students and staff involved, notifications to all pertinent parties, putting in place interventions to take action on behalf of those people affected by the situation, and making appropriate referrals to those in need.
6. **Documentation Processes for Critical Incidences**—There are several forms of documentation necessary for school counselors to complete once any critical incident has taken place.

   No-Harm Contract—The no-harm contract is completed when students make a threat to harm themselves or others. It consists of a statement promising not to harm self or others and promising that if the students feels he or she wants to harm, then they must call the crisis hotline or contact a trusted adult.

Emergency Conference Forms (ECF)—The ECF is a form parents and/or guardians sign to indicate they were notified of the threat to self-harm.

Release of Information—This form is always necessary to complete when referrals are made and other professionals have agreed to provide service to the student in imminent danger. School counselors should establish an open line of communication of feedback from other mental health professionals.

Referrals—Referrals should be made to community professionals based on the needs of the student and the facts of the incident. Provide the name of 3–5 entities, the address, the telephone number, an email address, and website if applicable.

Appendix B
Campus Crisis Plan Template

The Campus Crisis Plan Template is an outline that will assist school counselors in knowing what components should be included in their campus crisis plan for students. This template is a reference tool to help school counselors devise procedures that will assist professionals in establishing a return to stability and safety.

Procedures

Checklist—Helps outline necessary steps or materials that need to be taken, completed.

Flow Chart—Demonstrates the hierarchy of contact and communication tree.

District Level Crisis Team—The name of the lead, the crisis team members, and their contact information are outlined in this portion of the plan.

Crisis Fact Sheet and Media Communication Form—There should be a sheet that allows the documentation of facts to be recorded. Then, using the media communication form, the fact sheet should be used to form the approved strand of communication.

Counseling Sign-In Sheet—The purpose of the sign-in sheet is to document which students, faculty, or staff were counseled; it is a tool to devise a plan for individuals to follow-up.

Narrative Debriefing for Teachers—This debriefing tool governs the information teachers can convey to students, usually providing language of comfort, safety, and security.

Presentation Debriefing for Teachers—This PowerPoint slide has talking points for teachers to use with students.

Group or Guidance Lesson Counseling Template—Group or guidance lessons are quite likely to be held in the event of a critical incident.

Sample Notification Letter to Parents—This is a generic notification letter that is designed with the parents in mind, providing the facts regarding the incident and describing how their children are safe to be in the school.

Sample Notification Letter to Crisis Team—This is a specific notification letter to the crisis team detailing the incident and/or what needs are present that the crisis team can assist with.

Sample Notification Letter for a Completed Suicide—This letter is one of condolence and empathy. It provides a general yet factual overview of the occurrence.

Sample Notification Letter to Teachers—This correspondence details the critical incident and extends support from the counseling office/department.

Index

active shooter lockdown practice 209; counseling for 210–213; counselor impact on 213; description of case 209–210; discussion questions 214–215; ethical considerations 213–214; mental health 213; multicultural considerations 214; resources for 215

Adler, Alfred 149

Adlerian theory 149

adolescents: alcohol use 69; consensual sexual relationship 178; cutting 102; drug use in 69–70; gender identity of 77; risky sexual behavior 27, 31; serious criminal charges of 95; sexuality 29; *see also* homeless students; intimacy between adult and minor student; sex on campus with multiple partners

adult behavior (inappropriate) 127; *see also* confidante to pregnant student; custody issues; gay and in relationship with adult male; incarcerated parent; intimacy between adult and minor student; sexual abuse by a parent; sexual advances from teacher; violence in the home

Advanced Law Enforcement Rapid Response Training (ALERRT) Center, Texas State University 216

adverse childhood experiences (ACE) 129; family violence 137; incarcerated parent 185; *see also* violence in the home

advocacy, school counselors for violence in home 138

age of consent 178

alcohol use *see* illegal substances (under influence of)

ALICE (alert, lockdown, inform, counter, and evaluate) training 209

American Academy of Child and Adolescent Psychiatry (AACAP) 54

American Counseling Association (ACA) 100, 225; advocacy competencies 81; School Counseling Interest Network for School Counselors 211

American Psychiatric Association (APA) 102

American School Counselor Association (ASCA) 12, 57, 138, 167, 225; *Code of Ethics* 91, 98; Ethical Standards for School Counselors 6, 99, 107, 115, 134–135, 142–144, 159, 228; *School Counselor Professional Standards and Competencies* 86

anxiety disorder 50

anxiety disorder not otherwise specified 209

ASCA SCENE 37

athletics, male athletes 40–41; *see also* coaching staff allowing student fights

attachment theory, Bowlby 165

attention deficit hyperactivity disorder (ADHD) 50, 133

autonomic nervous system (ANS) 98, 99, 133, 232

behavioral therapy 54

behavior disorders 50

borderline personality disorder (BPD) 107

Bowlby, John 165

bullying 37–38; exploring problem with student 55; potential trigger for mental illness 50–51

Campus Crisis Plan Template 239

Cass's model, homosexual identity 157–158, 161

Center for American Progress 33

Centers for Disease Control and Prevention (CDC) 12, 27, 34, 161; mental illness 49; pandemic 225, 227, 228; school-associated homicides 216; sexual abuse 178

child abuse 37–38; mandatory reporting of 137–138; *see also* violence in the home

child protective services (CPS) 89, 129, 130, 132–135, 139–142

Children's Bureau 129

child sexual abuse *see* sexual abuse by a parent

chronosystem 121

citizen-children 120

coaching staff allowing student fights: athleticism and male students 40–41; case discussion questions 45; counseling for 42–43; counselor impact on 43; description of case 41; ethical considerations 44–45; multicultural considerations 45; resources for 46; social media and television glorifying athletics 40

cognitive behavioral therapy (CBT): active shooter lockdown practice 211; incarcerated parent 186; intimacy between adult and minor student 179–180; pandemic 225–226; personal student situations 172; school shooting 218; serious mental health 54; terroristic threat victims 22; trauma victim counseling 5

Taylor & Francis eBooks

www.taylorfrancis.com

A single destination for eBooks from Taylor & Francis
with increased functionality and an improved user
experience to meet the needs of our customers.

90,000+ eBooks of award-winning academic content in
Humanities, Social Science, Science, Technology, Engineering,
and Medical written by a global network of editors and authors.

TAYLOR & FRANCIS EBOOKS OFFERS:

A streamlined
experience for
our library
customers

A single point
of discovery
for all of our
eBook content

Improved
search and
discovery of
content at both
book and
chapter level

REQUEST A FREE TRIAL
support@taylorfrancis.com

Routledge
Taylor & Francis Group

CRC Press
Taylor & Francis Group

Made in the USA
Coppell, TX
20 June 2023

18340921R00146